The CASEMENT Report

The Casement Report

Foreword

On the third of August 1916 at the Pentonville Prison in London, Roger Casement was hanged and executed. Following a salacious and highly publicized trial, Casement was arrested for treason by the British Government and High Court for his involvement in the Irish Nationalist movement and the 1916 Easter Rising rebellion. Having been a collaborator to the American-exiled Irish Republic Brotherhood in addition to being part of political deals with Germany of the Central Powers during World War I, Casement emerged as a main target and opponent of the Crown, Britain, and the British Empire during the early 20th century. His 'treacherous' acts involved support for Germany by waging an Irish insurrection against Britain so as to make them weaker in face of their enemy. If the Triple Entente, or Allies, are defeated in World War I (WWI), Casement had made a deal with the Germans for support and protection of Ireland's postcolonial borders and sovereignty. He also aligned himself to the "Hindu—German Conspiracy", a nationalist movement which sought Indian independence from the British Raj.

Casement's north Atlantic political strategies proved more inadequate with time as the success of the Allies in WWI drew closer. He was eventually discovered in hiding at Rathoneen in McKenna's Fort—now renamed in his honor—where he was arrested for treason and espionage against the British Crown. High treason was not leveled only because of his support for the Irish nationalist movement but also what was seen as a betrayal and divestment from his once-dutiful role to the British Foreign Office. Prior to his arrest, Casement was known in Britain as a critical public voice who advocated for universalism and global human rights in the 20th century. He attracted government and media attention for his fieldwork in the Congo which was later published as *The Casement Report*, the topic of this facsimile publication.

Considered one of the earliest written works which harbored anticolonial sentiments—prior to the *Heart of Darkness* by Joseph Conrad—Casement's report was critical of the resource exploitation in the Congo as engineered by the Belgian government under King Leopold II, and problematized the human abuses, racism, and monopolistic governance inherent to colonial governments. The report resulted in the establishment of the Congo Reform Association, of which Casement was a member, which lobbied to put an end to Leopold's control of the Congo Free State. Later Casement traveled to South America where he wrote further exposes on the working conditions of the indigenous people of Peru in the Putumayo District in the Amazon, where rubber was harvested by the Anglo-Peruvian Amazon Rubber Co. Unpaid labor, rape, mutilation, and starvation were some of the details reported by Casement about these distant colonial industries which the British public had no informative reporting about or awareness. For his efforts, he was knighted by the Crown.

The report was an exploration of imperialism's underbelly and a product of the growing awareness in the West about the cost of its industrial progress and Enlightened knowledge development. Its public appeal came at a time when the dethroning of the 'ancient regime' was under full-swing in the West, and his reports fueled these sentiments by presenting transparent conditions of the frontlines. Published at the turn of the 20th century, it paralleled other experiences of explorers, scientists, and missionaries who traveled to the colonies and came back to their homelands calling for global human rights, equal access, and social betterment after witnessing the atrocities of colonialism. The transition to fair-wage economies and post-abolition governments in the Americas also heeded to new social mobilization for global freedom, sovereignty, and diplomacy.

Even though the British Empire celebrated and embraced Casement's work, it was mostly to advance its own political interests and position as an anti-slavery and pro-abolitionism government. By utilizing Casement's sensitive and compassionate reporting, it would be able to depict its foreign policy and empire as philanthropic and genteel, especially when compared to brute European colonizers. Strategizing its offshore ambitions as more moral and superior to the rest, Britian did not anticipate that Casement himself would interrogate its self-aggrandizing narrative and rebel against them:

> *It is a mistake for an Irishman to mix himself up with the English. He is bound to do one of two things—either to go to the wall if he remains Irish or to become an Englishman himself. You see I very nearly did become one once. At the Boer War time, I had been away from Ireland for years, out of touch with everything native to my heart and mind, trying hard to do my duty, and every fresh act of duty made me appreciably nearer the ideal of the Englishman. I had accepted Imperialism. British rule was to be accepted at all costs, because it was the best for everyone under the sun, and those who opposed that extension ought rightly to be 'smashed.' I was on the high road to being a regular Imperialist jingo—although at heart underneath all, and unsuspected almost by myself, I had remained an Irishman. Well, the war, [i.e., the Boer War] gave me qualms at the end—the concentration camps bigger ones—and finally, when up in those lonely Congo forests where I found Leopold I found also myself, the incorrigible Irishman*
>
> –From "Where Casement Would Have Stood Today", Jack White's Address to the Roger Casement Sinn Feil Club in Dublin, 1936.

When Casement went to court, the public was divided and called on the High Court, especially during his appeal, for clemency given his important role in shaping the anticolonial discourse which was popular at the time. In order to undermine sympathy with the defendant, the British government circulated extracts from an alleged 'Black Diaries' in which Casement details homosexual encounters, as well as activities with minors. Although anticolonialism was common in the British public at the time, homosexual love wasn't and paved the way for his eventual execution.

Still contested and with no clarity to the validity of the diary's contents, Casement's biography and his contributions to the anticolonial as well as decolonial movements call for revisitation today in 2023. Being publicly celebrated as a human rights activist yet also occupying the role of an unsung hero and alleged subjugated homosexual, Casement's story reveals that amplifying the unknown and the underrepresented is necessary work, and will continue to be.

AHMAD MAKIA

ACCOUNTS AND PAPERS:

SIXTY-FIVE VOLUMES.

—(14.)—

COLONIES AND BRITISH POSSESSIONS—*continued.*

AFRICA—*continued.*

Session

2 *February* 1904 —— 15 *August* 1904.

VOL. LXII.

1904. 32

AFRICA. No. 4 (1904).

CORRESPONDENCE relating to the Recruitment of Labour in the British Central Africa Protectorate for Employment in the Transvaal.

[In continuation of "Africa No 2 (1903)."]

Presented to both Houses of Parliament by His Majesty's Command. March 1904.

LONDON:
PRINTED BY HARRISON AND SONS

AFRICA. No. 1 (1904).

CORRESPONDENCE

AND

REPORT FROM HIS MAJESTY'S CONSUL AT BOMA

RESPECTING THE

ADMINISTRATION

OF THE

INDEPENDENT STATE OF THE CONGO.

Presented to both Houses of Parliament by Command of His Majesty.
February 1904.

LONDON:
PRINTED FOR HIS MAJESTY'S STATIONERY OFFICE,
BY HARRISON AND SONS, ST. MARTIN'S LANE,
PRINTERS IN ORDINARY TO HIS MAJESTY.

And to be purchased, either directly or through any Bookseller, from
EYRE AND SPOTTISWOODE, EAST HARDING STREET, FLEET STREET, E.C.,
AND 32, ABINGDON STREET, WESTMINSTER, S.W.;
OR OLIVER AND BOYD, EDINBURGH;
OR E. PONSONBY, 116, GRAFTON STREET, DUBLIN.

[Cd. 1933.] *Price* 8½*d.*

TABLE OF CONTENTS.

Correspondence and Report from His Majesty's Consul at Boma respecting the Administration of the Independent State of the Congo.

No. 1.

The Earl of Cromer to the Marquess of Lansdowne.—(Received February 9.)

(Extract.) *On the Nile, near Kiro, January* 21, 1903

I HAVE just visited the Belgian stations of Kiro and Lado, as also the station of Gondokoro in the Uganda Protectorate.

Your Lordship may like to receive some remarks on the impressions I derived as regards the Belgian positions on the Upper Nile.

I should, in the first instance, observe that Commandant Hanolet, who is in charge of the district, was absent in the interior of the country; but Sir Reginald Wingate and myself were most courteously received by the officers in command at Kiro and Lado.

From the point of view of appearance, the two Belgian stations contrast favourably with any of the Soudanese stations on the Nile, and still more favourably with Gondokoro in the Uganda Protectorate. The principal dwelling-houses are of brick. They seem to be well built. The stations are kept scrupulously clean. The troops are well housed. Flourishing gardens have been created. I counted the graves of nine Europeans at Kiro, all of whom died of fever, but I am informed that the health of the place is now greatly improved.

I had heard so many and such contradictory accounts of the Belgian Administration that I was very desirous of ascertaining some concise and definite evidence on this subject. During a hurried visit, and with opportunities of observation confined to the banks of the river, I scarcely anticipated that I should be able to arrive at any independent opinion on the point at issue. I saw and heard, however, quite enough to gain an insight into the spirit which pervades the Administration.

It must be remembered that the 1,100 miles of country which I traversed between Khartoum and Gondokoro has, until recently, been the prey of slave-dealers, Egyptian Pashas, and dervishes. Under the circumstances, it might well have been expected that much time would be required to inspire confidence in the intentions of the new Government. It is, however, certain that, with the exception of a portion of the Nuer tribe, who live in a very remote region on the upper waters of the Sobat, confidence has been completely established in those districts which are under British rule. Except in the uninhabitable "Sudd" region, numerous villages are dotted along the banks of the river. The people, far from flying at the approach of white men as was formerly the case, run along the banks, making signs for the steamer to stop. It is clear that the Baris, Shilluks, and Dinkas place the utmost trust and confidence in the British officers with whom they are brought in contact. In spite of the difficulties of communicating with them through an interpreter—himself but slightly educated—it was impossible to mistake their manifest signs and expressions of security and content. They flock into the Settlements without fear; and if, as often happens, they will not work, it is merely because they are lazy and have few wants, not because they entertain doubt that they will be paid for working. These remarks apply equally to Gondokoro, although I was only able to see a few of the natives there. I had not time to visit the principal Bari village, which lies at some little distance from the river.

The contrast when once Congolese territory is entered is remarkable. From the frontier to Gondokoro is about 80 miles. The proper left, or western, bank of the river is Belgian. The opposite bank is either under the Soudanese or the Uganda Government. There are numerous islands, and as all these are under British rule—for the thalweg, which, under Treaty, is the Belgian frontier, skirts the western bank of the river—

I cannot say that I had an opportunity of seeing a full 80 miles of Belgian territory. At the same time, I saw a good deal, and I noticed that, whereas there were numerous villages and huts on the eastern bank and on the islands, on the Belgian side not a sign of a village existed. Indeed, I do not think that any one of our party saw a single human being in Belgian territory, except the Belgian officers and men and the wives and children of the latter. Moreover, not a single native was to be seen either at Kiro or Lado. I asked the Swedish officer at Kiro whether he saw much of the natives. He replied in the negative, adding that the nearest Bari village was situated at some distance in the interior. The Italian officer at Lado, in reply to the same question, stated that the nearest native village was seven hours distant.

The reason of all this is obvious enough. The Belgians are disliked. The people fly from them, and it is no wonder they should do so, for I am informed that the soldiers are allowed full liberty to plunder, and that payments are rarely made for supplies. The British officers wander, practically alone, over most parts of the country, either on tours of inspection or on shooting expeditions. I understand that no Belgian officer can move outside the settlements without a strong guard.

It appears to me that the facts which I have stated above afford amply sufficient evidence of the spirit which animates the Belgian Administration, if, indeed, Administration it can be called. The Government, so far as I could judge, is conducted almost exclusively on commercial principles, and, even judged by that standard, it would appear that those principles are somewhat short-sighted.

No. 2.

Sir C. Phipps to the Marquess of Lansdowne.—(Received September 21.)

My Lord, *Brussels, September* 19, 1803.

I HAVE the honour to transmit herewith copy of a note, together with its inclosures, which has been addressed by the Congo Government to the Representatives at Brussels of the Powers parties to the Act of Berlin to which your Lordship's Circular despatch of the 8th August respecting the affairs of the Independent State of the Congo had been communicated.*

M. de Cuvelier, in handing me these documents, stated that he had been instructed to follow the same procedure as that adopted by His Majesty's Government.

I have, &c.

(Signed) CONSTANTINE PHIPPS.

Inclosure in No. 2.

LE Gouvernement de l'État Indépendant du Congo, ayant eu connaissance de la dépêche du Foreign Office, datée du 8 Août dernier, remise aux Puissances Signataires de l'Acte de Berlin, constate qu'il est d'accord avec le Gouvernement de Sa Majesté sur deux points fondamentaux, à savoir, que les indigènes doivent être traités avec humanité et menés graduellement dans les voies de la civilisation, et que la liberté de commerce, dans le bassin conventionnel du Congo, doit être entière et complète.

Mais il nie que la manière dont est administré l'État entraînerait un régime systématique "de cruauté ou d'oppression" et que le principe de la liberté commerciale apporterait des modifications au droit de propriété tel qu'il est universellement compris, alors qu'il n'est pas un mot à cet effet dans l'Acte de Berlin. L'État du Congo note qu'il ne se trouve dans cet Acte aucune disposition qui consacrerait des restrictions quelconques à l'exercice du droit de propriété ou qui reconnaîtrait aux Puissances Signataires un droit d'intervention dans les affaires d'administration intérieure les unes des autres. Il tient à se montrer fidèle observateur de l'Acte de Berlin, de ce grand Acte International qui lie toutes les Puissances Signataires ou adhérentes, en ce que dit le sens grammatical si clair de son texte, que nul n'a pouvoir de diminuer ou d'amplifier.

La note Anglaise remarque que c'est en ces dernières années qu'a pris consistance la campagne menée en Angleterre contre l'État du Congo, sous le double prétexte de mauvais traitements des natifs et de l'existence de monopoles commerciaux.

* See Africa No. 14 (1903).

Il est à remarquer, en effet, que cette campagne date du jour où la prospérité de l'État s'affirma. L'État se trouvait fondé depuis des années et administré comme il l'est aujourd'hui, ses principes sur la domanialité des terres vacantes, l'organisation et le recrutement de sa force armée étaient connus et publics, sans que ces philanthropes et ces commerçants, de l'opinion desquels fait état le début de la note, s'en montrassent préoccupés. C'était l'époque où le Budget de l'État ne pouvait s'équilibrer que grâce aux subsides du Roi-Souverain et aux avances de la Belgique, et où le mouvement commercial du Congo n'attirait pas l'attention. On ne trouve le terme "the Congo atrocities" utilisé alors qu'à propos de "the alleged ill-treatment of African natives by English and other adventurers in the Congo Free State." * A partir de 1895, le commerce de l'État du Congo prend un essor marqué, et le chiffre des exportations monte progressivement de 10 millions en 1895 à 50 millions en 1902. C'est aussi à partir d'alors que le mouvement contre l'État du Congo se dessine. Au fur et à mesure que l'État affirmera davantage sa vitalité et ses progrès, la campagne ira s'accentuant, s'appuyant sur quelques cas particuliers et isolés pour invoquer des prétextes d'humanité et dissimuler le véritable objectif des convoitises qui, dans leur impatience, se sont cependant trahies sous la plume des pamphlétaires et par la voix de membres de la Chambre des Communes, mettant nettement en avant la disparition et le partage de l'État du Congo.

Il fallait, dans ce but, dresser contre l'État toute une liste de chefs d'accusation. Dans l'ordre humanitaire, on a repris, pour les rééditer à l'infini, les cas allégués de violences contre les indigènes. Car, dans cette multitude de "meetings," d'écrits, de discours, dirigés ces derniers temps contre l'État, ce sont toujours les mêmes faits affirmés et les mêmes témoignages produits. Dans l'ordre économique, on a accusé l'État de violation de l'Acte de Berlin, nonobstant les considérations juridiques des hommes de loi les plus autorisés qui justifient, à toute évidence de droit, son régime commercial et son système foncier. Dans l'ordre politique, on a imaginé cette hérésie en droit international d'un État, dont l'indépendance et la souveraineté sont entières, qui relèverait d'ingérences étrangères.

En ce qui concerne les actes de mauvais traitement à l'égard des natifs, nous attachons surtout de l'importance à ceux qui, d'après la note, ont été consignés dans les dépêches des Agents Consulaires de Sa Majesté. A la séance de la Chambre des Communes du 11 Mars, 1903, Lord Cranborne s'était déjà référé à ces documents officiels, et nous avons demandé à son Excellence Sir C. Phipps que le Gouvernement Britannique voulût bien nous donner connaissance des faits dont il s'agissait. Nous réitérons cette demande.

Le Gouvernement de l'État n'a jamais d'ailleurs nié que des crimes et délits se commissent au Congo, comme en tout autre pays ou toute autre Colonie. La note reconnaît elle-même que ces faits délictueux ont été déférés aux Tribunaux et que leurs auteurs ont été punis. La conclusion à en tirer est que l'État remplit sa mission ; la conclusion que l'on en déduit est que "many individual instances of cruelty have taken place in the Congo State" et que "the number of convictions falls considerably short of the number of actual offences committed." Cette déduction ne paraît pas nécessairement indiquée. Il semble plus logique de dire que les condamnations sévères prononcées seront d'un salutaire exemple et qu'on peut en espérer une diminution de la criminalité. Que si effectivement des actes délictueux, sur les territoires étendus de l'État, ont échappé à la vigilance de l'autorité judiciaire, cette circonstance ne serait pas spéciale à l'État du Congo.

La note Anglaise procède surtout par hypothèses et par suppositions : "It was alleged . . . . . It is reported . . . . . It is also reported . . . . . " et elle en arrive à dire que "His Majesty's Government do not know precisely to what extent these accusations may be true." C'est la constatation que, aux yeux du Gouvernement Britannique lui-même, les accusations dont il s'agit ne sont ni établies ni prouvées. Et, en effet, la violence, la passion et l'invraisemblance de nombre de ces accusations les rendent suspectes aux esprits impartiaux. Pour n'en donner qu'un exemple, on a fait grand état de cette allégation que, sur un train descendant de Léopoldville à Matadi, trois wagons étaient remplis d'esclaves, dont une douzaine étaient enchaînés, sous la garde de soldats. Des renseignements ont été demandés au Gouverneur-Général. Il répond : "Les individus représentés comme composant un convoi d'esclaves étaient, pour la plus grande majorité (125), des miliciens dirigés du district de Lualaba-Kassaï, du Lac Léopold II et des Bangalas, sur le camp du Bas-Congo. Vous trouverez annexés les états relatifs à ces individus. Quant aux hommes

* "Transactions of the Aborigines Protection Society, 1890–1896," p. 155.

enchaînés, ils constituaient un groupe d'individus condamnés par le Tribunal territorial de Basoko et qui venaient purger leur peine à la maison centrale de Boma. Ce sont les numéros 3642 à 3649 du registre d'écrou de la prison de Boma."

C'est ainsi encore qu'une "interview" toute récente, reproduisant les accusations coutumières de cruauté, est due à un ancien agent de l'Etat "déclaré impropre au service," et qui n'a pas vu accepter par l'État sa proposition d'écrire dans la presse des articles favorables à l'Administration.

La note ignore les réponses, démentis, ou rectifications qu'ont amenés, dans les différents temps où elles se sont produites, les attaques contre les Agents de l'État. Elle ignore les déclarations officielles qu'en Juin dernier, le Gouvernement de l'État fit publiquement à la suite des débats du 20 Mai à la Chambre des Communes, débats annexés à la note. Nous annexons ici le texte de ces déclarations, qui ont, par avance, rencontré les considérations de la dépêche du 8 Août.

Le seul grief nouveau qu'elle énonce—en vue sans doute d'expliquer ce fait non sans importance, que le Consul Anglais qui a résidé au Congo depuis 1901 ne paraît pas appuyer de son autorité personnelle les dénonciations de particuliers—c'est que cet Agent aurait été "principally occupied in the investigation of complaints preferred by British subjects." L'impression en résulterait que de telles plaintes auraient été exceptionnellement nombreuses. Sans aucun doute, le Consul, en diverses occasions, s'est mis en rapport avec l'Administration de Boma dans l'intérêt de ses ressortissants, mais il ne paraît pas que ces affaires, si l'on en juge par celles d'entre elles dont a eu à s'occuper la Légation d'Angleterre auprès du Gouvernement Central à Bruxelles, soient autres, par leur nombre ou leur importance, que celles de la vie administrative courante : des cas ont notamment visé le réglement de successions délaissées au Congo par des ressortissants Anglais ; quelques-uns ont eu pour objet la réparation d'erreurs de procédure judiciaire comme il s'en produit ailleurs, et il n'est pas avancé que ces réclamations n'ont pas reçu la suite qu'elles comportaient. Le même Consul, dont la nomination remonte à 1898, écrivait le 2 Juillet, 1901, au Governeur-Général :—

"I pray believe me when I express now, not only for myself, but for my fellow-countrymen in this part of Africa, our very sincere appreciation of your efforts on behalf of the general community—efforts to promote goodwill among all and to bring together the various elements of our local life."

Les prédécesseurs de Mr. R. Casement—car des Consuls Anglais avec juridiction sur le Congo ont été appointés par le Gouvernement de Sa Majesté depuis 1888—ne paraissent pas davantage avoir été absorbés par l'examen de plaintes multiples ; tout au moins une telle appréciation ne se trouve pas consignée dans le Rapport, le seul publié, de M. le Consul Pickersgill, qui, par le fait qu'il rend compte de son voyage à l'intérieur du Congo, jusqu'aux Stanley Falls, dément cette sorte d'impossibilité, pour les Agents Consulaires Anglais, d'apprécier *de visu* toute partie quelconque de leur juridiction.

Comme allégations contre le système d'administration de l'État, la note vise les impôts, la force publique et ce qu'on appelle le travail forcé.

Au fond, c'est la contribution de l'indigène du Congo aux charges publiques que l'on critique, comme s'il existait un seul pays ou une seule Colonie où l'habitant, sous une forme ou sous une autre, ne participe pas à ces charges. On ne conçoit pas un État sans ressources. Sur quel fondement légitime pourrait-on baser l'exemption de tout impôt pour les indigènes, alors qu'ils sont les premiers à bénéficier des avantages d'ordre matériel et moral introduits en Afrique ? A défaut de numéraire, il leur est demandé une contribution en travail. D'autres ont dit la nécessité, pour sauver l'Afrique de sa barbarie, d'amener le noir à la compréhension du travail, précisément par l'obligation de l'impôt :—

"It is a question (of native labour) which has engaged my most careful attention in connection with West Africa and other Colonies. To listen to the right honourable gentleman, you would almost think that it would be a good thing for the native to be idle. I think it is a good thing for him to be industrious ; and by every means in our power, we must teach him to work. . . . . No people ever have lived in the world's history who would not work. In the interests of the natives all over Africa, we have to teach them to work."

Ainsi s'exprimait Mr. Chamberlain à la Chambre des Communes, le 6 Août, 1901. Et récemment, il disait :—

"We are all of us taxed, and taxed heavily. Is that a system of forced labour ? . . . . . To say that because we put a tax on the native therefore he is reduced to a condition of servitude and of forced labour is, to my mind, absolutely ridiculous. . . . . It is perfectly fair to my mind that the native should contribute something towards the cost of administering the country." (House of Commons, the 9th March, 1903.)

"If that really is the last word of civilization, if we are to proceed on the assumption that the nearer the native or any human being comes to a pig the more desirable is his condition, of course I have nothing to say. . . . . I must continue to believe that, at all events, the progress of the native in civilization will not be secured until he has been convinced of the necessity and the dignity of labour. Therefore, I think that anything we reasonably can do to induce the native to labour is a desirable thing."

Et il défendait le principe d'une taxe sur le natif parce que "the existence of the tax is an inducement to him to work." (House of Commons, the 24th March, 1903.)

Aussi l'exemple de taxes sur les indigènes se retrouve-t-il presque partout en Afrique. Au Transvaal, chaque natif paie une taxe de capitation de *2l.*; dans l'Orange River Colony, le natif est soumis à une "poll tax;" dans la Southern Rhodesia, le Bechuanaland, le Basutoland, dans l'Uganda, au Natal, il est perçu une "hut tax;" au Cap, on trouve cette "hut tax" et une "labour tax;" dans l'Afrique Orientale Allemande, il est également perçu un impôt sur les huttes, payable en argent, en produits, ou en travail. Cette sorte d'impôt a été appliquée encore dans le Protectorat de Sierra-Leone, où elle a pu être payée "in kind by rice or palm-nuts," et la suggestion a été faite "that work on roads and useful works should be accepted in lieu of payment in money or produce."

On voit donc que le mode de paiement de l'impôt, en argent ou en nature, n'en altère pas la légitimité, lorsque son taux n'est pas excessif. Tel est le cas au Congo, où les prestations fournies par l'indigène ne représentent pas plus de quarante heures de travail par mois. Encore est-il que ce travail est rétribué et que l'impôt payé en nature fait, en quelque sorte, l'objet d'une ristourne à l'indigène.

Partout le paiement de l'impôt est obligatoire; son non-paiement entraîne des voies de contrainte. Les textes qui établissent les taxes sur les huttes frappent l'indigène récalcitrant de peines, telles que l'emprisonnement et le travail forcé. Au Congo non plus, l'impôt n'est pas facultatif. On a vu, ailleurs, les actes d'autorité qu'a parfois rendus nécessaires le refus des indigènes de se soumettre à la loi: telles les difficultés à Sierra-Leone, à propos desquelles un publiciste Anglais, parlant des agents de la force publique, affirme:—

"Between July 1894 and February 1896, no fewer than sixty-two convictions—admittedly representing a small proportion of offences actually committed—were recorded against them for flogging, plundering, and generally maltreating the natives."

D'autres exemples pourraient être rappelés de l'opposition que rencontre chez les populations indigènes l'établissement des règles gouvernementales. Il est fatal que la civilisation se heurte à leurs instincts de sauvagerie, à leurs coutumes et pratiques barbares; et il se conçoit qu'elles ne se plient pas sans impatience à un état social qui leur apparaît comme restrictif de leurs licences et de leurs excès et qu'elles cherchent même à s'y soustraire. C'est une chose commune en Afrique que l'exode d'indigènes, passant d'un territoire à l'autre, dans l'espoir de trouver de l'autre côté des frontières une autorité moins établie ou moins forte, et de s'exonérer de toute dépendance et de toute obligation. Il se pourrait, à coup sûr, que des indigènes de l'État se soient, sous l'empire de telles considérations, déplacés vers les territoires voisins, encore qu'une sorte d'émigration sur une large échelle, comme la présente la note Anglaise, n'ait jamais été signalée par les Commandants des provinces frontières. Il est, au contraire, constaté, dans la région du Haut-Nil, que des natifs qui s'étaient installés en territoire Britannique sont revenus sur la rive gauche à la suite de l'établissement d'impositions nouvellement édictées par l'autorité Anglaise. Si c'est, d'ailleurs, ces régions qui sont visées, les informations de la note semblent être en contradiction avec d'autres renseignements donnés, par exemple, par Sir Harry Johnston:—

"This much I can speak of with certainty and emphasis: that from the British frontier near Fort George to the limit of my journeys into the Mbuba country of the Congo Free State, up and down the Semliki, the natives appear to be prosperous and happy. . . . . The extent to which they were building their villages and cultivating their plantations within the precincts of Fort Mbeni showed that they had no fear of the Belgians."

Le Major H. H. Gibbons, qui s'est trouvé plusieurs mois sur le Haut-Nil, écrit:—

"Ayant eu l'occasion de connaître plusieurs officiers et de visiter leurs stations de l'État du Congo, je suis convaincu que la conduite de ces messieurs a été bien mal interprétée par la presse. J'ai cité comme preuve mon expérience personnelle, qui est en opposition avec une version récemment publiée par la presse Anglaise, qui les accuse de grandes cruautés."

La déclaration de Juin dernier, ci-jointe, a fait justice des critiques contre la force publique de l'État en signalant que son recrutement est réglé par la loi et qu'il n'atteint qu'un homme sur 10,000. Dire que "the method of obtaining men for military service is often but little different from that formerly employed to obtain slaves," c'est méconnaître les prescriptions minutieuses édictées pour, au contraire, éviter les abus. Les levées s'opèrent dans chaque district; les Commissaires de District règlent, de commun accord avec les Chefs indigènes, le mode de conscription. Les engagements volontaires et les multiples réengagements complètent aisément les effectifs qui atteignent à peine le chiffre modique de 15,000 hommes.

Ceux qui allèguent, comme le dit la note, que "the men composing the armed force of the State were in many cases recruited from the most warlike and savage tribes," ignorent que la force publique est recrutée dans toutes les provinces et parmi toute la population du territoire. Les intérêts de l'État protestent contre cette notion d'une armée que l'autorité elle-même formerait d'éléments indisciplinés et sauvages et des exemples—tels que les excès qui ont été mis à charge des auxiliaires irréguliers utilisés dans l'Uganda, ainsi que les révoltes qui se sont produites jadis au Congo, imposent, au contraire, une circonspection spéciale pour la composition de la force armée. Les cadres Européens, qui se composent d'officiers Belges, Italiens, Suédois, Norwégiens, et Danois, y maintiennent une sévère discipline, et l'on chercherait en vain à quelles réelles circonstances fait allusion l'assertion que les soldats "not infrequently terrorized over their own officers." Elle n'est pas plus fondée que cette autre assertion, "that compulsion is often exercised by irresponsible native soldiers uncontrolled by an European officer." Depuis longtemps, l'autorité était consciente des dangers que présentait l'existence de postes de soldats noirs, dont le Rapport de Sir D. Chalmers, sur l'insurrection à Sierra-Leone, a constaté les inévitables abus de pouvoirs. Au Congo, ils ont été graduellement supprimés.

Il apparaîtra, à ceux qui ne nient pas l'évidence, que des reproches articulés contre l'État, le plus injuste est d'avancer "that no attempt at any administration of the natives is made, and that the officers of the Government do not apparently concern themselves with such work."

On peut s'étonner de trouver semblable affirmation dans une dépêche d'un Gouvernement dont l'un des membres, Lord Cranborne, Sous-Secrétaire d'État pour les Affaires Étrangères, disait le 20 Mai dernier:—

"There was no doubt that the administration of the Congo Government had been marked by a very high degree of a certain kind of administrative development. There were railways, there were steamers upon the river, hospitals had been established, and all the machinery of elaborate judicial and police systems had been set up."

Un autre Membre de la Chambre des Communes reconnaissait—

"That the Congo State had done good work in excluding alcoholic liquors from the greater part of their domain, that they had established a certain number of hospitals, had diminished small-pox by means of vaccination, and had suppressed the Arab Slave Trade."

Si atténuées que soient ces appréciations, encore démentent-elles cette affirmation d'aujourd'hui que "the natives are left entirely to themselves, so far as any assistance in their government or in their affairs is concerned."

Telles ne semblent pas être les conclusions auxquelles, déjà en 1898, arrivait le Consul Anglais Pickersgill.

"Has the welfare of the African," se demande-t-il, "been duly cared for in the Congo State?" Il répond: "The State has restricted the liquor trade . . . . . . it is scarcely possible to over-estimate the service which is being rendered by the Congo Government to its subjects in this matter. . . . . . Intertribal wars have been suppressed over a wide area, and, the imposition of European authority being steadily pursued, the boundaries of peace are constantly extending. . . . . . The State must be congratulated upon the security it has created for all who live within the shelter of its flag and abide by its laws and regulations. . . . . . Credit is also due to the Congo Government in respect of the diminution of cannibalism. . . . . . The yoke of the notorious Arab Slave Traders has been broken, and traffic in human beings amongst the natives themselves has been diminished to a considerable degree."

Ce Rapport constatait aussi que les travaux des natifs étaient rémunérés et rendait hommage aux efforts de l'État pour instruire les jeunes indigènes et ouvrir des écoles.

Depuis 1898 l'amélioration de la condition générale de l'indigène a encore progressé. Le portage à dos d'homme, dont précisément Mr. Pickersgill signalait le côté pénible pour les indigènes, a disparu là où il était le plus actif, en raison de la mise en exploitation des voies ferrées. Ailleurs, l'automobile est utilisée comme moyen de transport. La "sentry"—le poste de soldats nègres qu'il critiquait non sans raison—n'existe plus. Le bétail est introduit dans tous les districts. Des Commissions d'Hygiène sont instituées. Les écoles et les ateliers se sont multipliés.

"L'indigène," dit le document ci-joint, "est mieux logé, vêtu, nourri; il remplace ses huttes par des habitations plus résistantes et mieux appropriées aux exigences de l'hygiène; grâce aux facilités de transport, il s'approvisionne des produits nécessaires à ses besoins nouveaux; des ateliers lui sont ouverts, où il apprend des métiers manuels—tels que, ceux de forgeron, charpentier, mécanicien, maçon; il étend ses plantations, et, à l'exemple des blancs, s'inspire des modes de culture rationnels; les soins médicaux lui sont assurés; il envoie ses enfants dans les colonies scolaires de l'État et aux écoles des missionnaires."

Il est juste de reconnaître, a-t-on dit à la Chambre des Communes, que la régénération matérielle et morale de l'Afrique Centrale ne peut être l'œuvre d'un jour. Les résultats obtenus jusqu'à présent sont considérables; nous chercherons à les consolider et à les accentuer, malgré les entraves que l'on s'efforce de mettre à l'action de l'État, action que l'intérêt bien entendu de la civilisation serait, au contraire, de favoriser.

La note Anglaise ne démontre pas que le système économique de l'État est opposé à l'Acte de Berlin. Elle ne rencontre pas les éléments de droit et de fait par lesquels l'État a justifié la conformité de ses lois foncières et de ses concessions avec les dispositions de cet Acte. Elle n'explique pas pourquoi ni en quoi la liberté de commerce, termes dont la Conférence de Berlin s'est servie dans leur sens usuel, grammatical et économique, ne serait plus entière au Congo parce qu'il s'y trouve des propriétaires.

La note confond l'exploitation de son bien par le propriétaire avec le commerce. L'indigène, qui récolte pour compte du propriétaire, ne devient pas propriétaire des produits récoltés et ne peut naturellement les céder à autrui, pas plus que l'ouvrier qui extrait les produits d'une mine ne peut en frustrer le propriétaire en en disposant lui-même. Ces règles sont de droit et sont mises en lumière dans de multiples documents: consultations juridiques et décisions judiciaires dont quelques-unes sont annexées. Le Gouvernement de Sa Majesté ne conteste pas que l'État a le droit de répartir les terres domaniales entre les occupants *bonâ fide* et que l'indigène ne peut plus prétendre aux produits du sol, mais seulement lorsque "land is reduced into individual occupation." La distinction est sans base juridique. Si l'État peut céder les terres, c'est que l'indigène n'en a pas la propriété, et à quel titre alors conserverait-il un droit aux produits d'un fonds dont la propriété est légitimement acquise par d'autres? Pourrait-on soutenir, par exemple, que la Compagnie du Chemin de Fer du Bas-Congo ou la Société du Sud-Cameroun ou l'Italian Colonial Trading Company sont tenues de tolérer le pillage par les indigènes des terres qu'elles ont reçues, parce qu'elles ne les occuperaient pas actuellement? En fait, d'ailleurs, au Congo, l'appropriation des terres exploitées en régie ou par les Compagnies Concessionnaires est chose réalisée. L'État et les Sociétés ont consacré à leur mise en valeur, notamment des forêts, des sommes considérables se chiffrant par millions de francs. Il n'y a donc pas de doute que dans tous les territoires du Congo, l'État exploite réellement et complètement ses propriétés, tout comme les Sociétés exploitent réellement et complètement leurs Concessions.

Cet état de choses existant et consolidé dans l'État Indépendant permettrait, en ce qui le concerne, de ne point insister plus longuement sur la théorie formulée par la note et qui envisage tour à tour les droits de l'État, ceux des occupants *bonâ fide*, ceux des indigènes.

Cependant, elle s'impose à l'attention des Puissances par les graves difficultés qu'elle ferait surgir si elle était implicitement acceptée.

La note contient les trois propositions suivantes:—

"The State has the right to partition the State lands among *bonâ fide* occupants."

"The natives will, as the land is so divided out amongst *bonâ fide* occupiers, lose their right of roaming over it and collecting the natural fruits which it produces."

"Until unoccupied land is reduced into individual occupation and so long as the produce can only be collected by the native, the native should be free to dispose of that produce as he pleases."

Il n'est pas une de ces propositions qui ne semble exclure les deux autres, et à vrai dire ces contradictions aboutissent à la négation du droit de Concession.

S'il a existé des occupants *bonâ fide*, ils sont devenus propriétaires : l'occupation, lorsqu'elle trouve à s'exercer, est dans toutes les législations un des modes d'acquisition de la propriété, et, au Congo, les titres en dérivant ont été légalement enregistrés. Si la terre n'a été valablement occupée par personne, elle est sans maître ou, plus exactement, elle a l'État pour maître : il peut en disposer au profit d'un tiers, et celui-ci trouve dans cet acte de disposition un titre complet et absolu. Dans l'un comme dans l'autre cas, il ne se conçoit pas que les fruits du sol puissent être réservés à d'autres qu'au propriétaire sous le prétexte qu'il n'est pas apte, en fait, à récolter les produits de son fonds.

Par une singulière contradiction, le système de la note dit qu'à la suite de l'attribution des terres par l'État, les indigènes "lose their right of collecting the natural fruits," et, d'autre part, qu'ils conservent le droit de disposer de ces produits "until unoccupied land is reduced into individual occupation." On ne comprend pas la notion d'un droit appartenant aux natifs qui existerait ou non de par le fait de tiers. Ou bien, par suite de l'attribution des terres, ils ont perdu leurs droits, et alors ils les ont perdus totalement et complètement ; ou bien, ils les ont conservés, et ils doivent les conserver, quoique "the land is reduced into individual occupation."

Que faut-il d'ailleurs entendre dans le système de la note par occupants "*bonâ fide*" et par "individual occupation ?" Qui sera juge du point de savoir si l'occupant a mis ses terres en état d'occupation individuelle, s'il était apte à en recueillir les produits ou si c'était encore l'indigène ? Ce serait, en tous cas, des points relevant essentiellement du droit interne.

La note, au surplus, est incomplète sur un autre point. Elle dit que là où l'exploitation ne se ferait pas encore par les ayants droit, la faculté d'exploiter devrait appartenir aux indigènes. Elle voudrait donc donner un droit aux indigènes au préjudice des Gouvernements ou des concessionnaires blancs, mais n'explique pas comment ni par qui le tort ainsi causé serait compensé ou indemnisé. Quoique le système ainsi préconisé ne puisse avoir d'application dans l'État du Congo, puisqu'il ne s'y trouve plus de terres inappropriées, cette remarque s'impose dans l'intérêt des blancs établis dans le bassin conventionnel. S'il est équitable de bien traiter les noirs, il est juste de ne pas spolier les blancs, qui, dans l'intérêt de tous, doivent rester la race dirigeante.

Économiquement parlant, il serait déplorable qu'en dépit des droits régulièrement acquis par les blancs, les terres domaniales se trouvassent livrées aux indigènes, fût-ce temporairement. Ce serait le retour à leur état d'abandon de jadis, alors que les natifs les laissaient inproductives, car les récoltes de caoutchouc, les plantations de café, de cacao, de tabac, &c., datent du jour où l'État en a pris lui-même l'initiative : le mouvement des exportations était insignifiant avant l'essor que lui ont donné les entreprises gouvernementales. Ce serait aussi l'inobservance certaine des mesures d'exploitation rationnelle, de plantation et de replantation auxquelles s'astreignent l'État et les Sociétés Concessionnaires pour assurer la conservation des richesses naturelles du pays.

Jamais au Congo, que nous sachions, les demandes d'achat des produits naturels n'ont été adressées aux légitimes propriétaires. Jusqu'ici l'on n'a cherché à y acheter que des produits provenant de recels, et l'État, comme c'était son devoir, a fait poursuivre ces tentatives délictueuses.

La politique de l'État n'a pas, comme on l'a dit, tué le commerce : elle l'a, au contraire, créé, et elle perpétue la matière commerciale ; c'est grâce à elle que, sur le marché commercial d'Anvers et bientôt au Congo même—on examine la possibilité d'y établir des dépôts de vente—peuvent être offertes annuellement à tous indistinctement, sans privilège ni monopole, 5,000 tonnes de caoutchouc récolté au Congo, alors qu'antérieurement, par exemple en 1887, l'exportation du caoutchouc se chiffrait à peine par 30 tonnes. C'est l'État qui, après avoir à ses frais créé la matière commerciale, en maintient soigneusement la source au moyen des plantations et replantations.

Il n'est pas à oublier que l'État du Congo a dû compter sur ses propres ressources. Ce fut une nécessité pour lui d'utiliser son domaine dans l'intérêt général. Toutes les recettes du domaine sont versées au Trésor, ainsi que le revenu des actions dont l'État est détenteur en raison de Concessions accordées. Ce n'est même qu'en tirant tout le parti utile de ses domaines et en engageant la plus grande partie de leurs revenus qu'il a pu contracter des emprunts et provoquer à des entreprises de chemins de fer par des garanties d'intérêt, réalisant ainsi l'un des moyens les plus désirés par la Conférence de Bruxelles pour faire pénétrer la civilisation au centre de l'Afrique. Aussi n'a-t-il pas hésité à gager sesdomaines dans ce but.

L'Acte de Berlin ne s'y oppose pas, car il n'a édicté aucune proscription des droits de propriété, comme on veut, après coup, le lui faire dire, tendant ainsi, consciemment ou non, à la ruine de tout le bassin conventionnel du Congo.

Il n'échappera pas non plus aux Puissances que les conclusions de la note Anglaise, en suggérant une référence à la Cour de La Haye, tendent à faire considérer comme cas d'arbitrage des questions de souveraineté et d'administration intérieure que la doctrine courante a toujours exclues des décisions d'arbitres. Pour ce qui concerne le cas actuel, il est à supposer que la suggestion d'une référence à la Cour de La Haye a une portée générale, s'il est vrai que, de l'avis des Chambres de Commerce Anglaises, "the principles and practice introduced into the administration of the affairs of the French Congo, the Congo Free State, and other areas in the conventional basin of the Congo being in direct opposition to the Articles of the Act of Berlin 1885." Le Gouvernement de l'État n'a cessé, pour sa part, de préconiser l'arbitrage pour les dissentiments d'ordre international qui en comportaient l'application: ainsi, il voudrait voir déférées à l'arbitrage les divergences de vues qui se sont produites au sujet du bail des territoires du Bahr-el-Ghazal.

Après un examen attentif de la note Anglaise, le Gouvernement de l'État du Congo reste convaincu qu'en raison du vague et du manque complet de preuves, ce dont elle fait implicitement l'aveu, il n'est pas une juridiction au monde, en en supposant une qui ait compétence pour être saisie, qui puisse, bien loin de prononcer une sorte de condamnation, prendre une autre décision que celle de ne pas donner suite à de simples suppositions.

Si l'État du Congo se voit attaqué, l'Angleterre peut se dire que, plus que nulle autre nation, elle s'est trouvée, elle aussi, en butte aux attaques et aux accusations de toute espèce, et longue serait la liste des campagnes poursuivies en divers temps et jusque dans récentes occasions contre son administration coloniale. Elle n'a certes pas échappé aux critiques que lui ont valu ses guerres multiples et sanglantes contre les populations indigènes ni aux reproches de violenter les natifs et de porter atteinte à leur liberté. Ne lui a-t-on pas fait grief de ces longues insurrections à Sierra-Leone—de cet état d'hostilité dans la Nigérie, où tout dernièrement, d'après les journaux Anglais, la répression militaire a, en une seule circonstance, coûté la vie à 700 indigènes, à la plupart de leurs Chefs et au Sultan—de cette lutte qui se poursuit au Somaliland au prix du sacrifice de nombreuses vies humaines, sans que cependant il ne soit exprimé à la Chambre des Communes d'autre regret que celui du chiffre élevé des dépenses ?

Alors que ces attaques adressées à l'Angleterre l'ont laissée indifférente, il y a lieu d'être surpris de la voir aujourd'hui attacher une toute autre importance à celles dirigées contre l'État du Congo.

On peut croire, cependant, que les préférences des indigènes de l'État du Congo demeurent acquises au Gouvernement d'une petite nation pacifique, dont les visées restent pacifiques comme a été pacifique sa création basée sur les Traités conclus avec les indigènes.

(Signé) CHR. DE CUVELIER.

Bruxelles, le 17 *Septembre,* 1903.

(Translation.)

THE Government of the Independent State of the Congo have examined the despatch from the Foreign Office, dated the 8th August last, which was communicated to the Signatory Powers of the Berlin Act, and declare themselves in agreement with His Majesty's Government on two fundamental points, viz., that natives ought to be treated with humanity and gradually led into the paths of civilization, and that freedom of commerce in the Conventional Basin of the Congo ought to be entire and complete.

They deny, however, that the manner in which the State is administered involves a systematic régime "of cruelty or oppression," and that the principle of commercial freedom would introduce modifications in the rights of property as universally understood, seeing that there is not a word to this effect in the Berlin Act. The Congo State observes that there is in that Act no provision which would sanction restrictions of any kind on the exercise of the rights of property, or give to one Signatory Power the right of intervention in the interior administration of another. It desires faithfully to observe the Berlin Act, that great International Act which binds all Signatory or adhering Powers, according to the clear grammatical sense of the text, which none has power either to take from or add to.

The English note observes that it is within the last few years that a definite shape has been assumed by the campaign conducted in England against the Congo State, on the twofold pretext of the ill-treatment of natives and the existence of commercial monopolies.

It is indeed worthy of remark that this campaign dates from the time when the prosperity of the State became assured. The State had been founded for years, and administered in the same way as it is now, its principles in regard to the State-ownership of vacant lands, and the manner in which its armed forces were organized and recruited, were known to the public, without any interest in the matter being shown by the philanthropists and traders to whose opinion the note begins by referring. This was the period during which the State Budget could only be balanced by means of the King-Sovereign's subsidies and Belgian loans, and when the commerce of the Congo did not attract attention. The term "Congo atrocities" was at that time only used in connexion with "the alleged ill-treatment of African natives by English and other adventurers in the Congo Free State."* After 1895 the trade of the Congo State developed remarkably, and the amount of its exports shows a progressive increase from 10 millions in 1895 to 50 millions in 1902. It is also about this time that the anti-Congo movement took shape. As the State gave increased proof of vitality and progress, the campaign became more active, reliance being placed on a few individual and isolated cases with a view to using the interests of humanity as a pretext and concealing the real object of a covetousness which, in its impatience, has betrayed itself in the writings of pamphleteers and in the speeches of Members of the House of Commons, in which the abolition and partition of the Congo State has been clearly put forward.

Such being the object in view, it became necessary to bring a whole series of charges against the State. So far as the humanitarian side of the question is concerned, the alleged cases of violence offered to natives have once more been brought forward and re-edited *ad infinitum*. For in all the meetings, writings, and speeches which have latterly been directed against the State, it is always the same facts which are brought up, and the same evidence which is produced. With regard to the economic side of the question, the State has been accused of having violated the Act of Berlin, notwithstanding the legal opinions of such lawyers as are most qualified to speak to the point, which afford ample legal justification both for its commercial and for its land system. With regard to the political side, a heresy in international law has been imagined, viz., that a State, the independence and sovereignty of which are absolute, should, at the same time, owe its position to the intervention of foreign Powers.

With regard to the cases of ill-treatment of natives, we attach special importance to those which, according to the note, have been reported in the despatches of His Majesty's Consular Agents. At the sitting of the House of Commons on the 11th March, 1903, Lord Cranborne referred to these official documents, and we have requested through his Excellency Sir C. Phipps that the British Government will make known to us the facts alluded to. We repeat the request.

The Government of the State have, however, never denied that crimes and offences are committed in the Congo, as in every other country or Colony. The note itself recognizes that these offences have been brought before the Tribunals, and that the criminals have been punished. The conclusion to be drawn from this is that the State fulfils its mission; the conclusion actually drawn is that "many individual instances of cruelty have taken place in the Congo State," and that "the number of convictions falls considerably short of the number of offences actually committed." This deduction does not appear necessarily to follow. It would seem more logical to say that the severe sentences inflicted will serve as a wholesome example, and that a decrease of crime may on that account be looked for. If some offences have indeed, in the extensive territories of the State, escaped the vigilance of the judicial authorities, this is a circumstance which is not peculiar to the Congo State.

The English note proceeds chiefly on hypotheses and suppositions: "It was alleged . . . . It is reported . . . . It is also reported . . . ." and it even says that "His Majesty's Government do not know precisely to what extent these accusations may be true." This is an acknowledgment that, in the eyes of the British Government themselves, the accusations in question are neither established nor proved. And, indeed, the violence, the passion, and the improbability of many of these accusations must raise doubt in an impartial mind as to their genuineness. To give but one

* "Transactions of the Aborigines Protection Society, 1890–1896," p. 155.

example:—a great deal has been made of the statement that, in a train coming down from Leopoldville to Matadi, three carriages were full of slaves, a dozen of whom were in chains and guarded by soldiers. The Governor-General was asked for a report on the case. He replied: "The individuals represented as composing a convoy of slaves were, the great majority of them (125), levies proceeding from the district of Lualaba-Kasai, Lake Leopold II, and the Bangalas to the camp in the Lower Congo. Annexed you will find lists of these persons. As regards the men in chains, they were certain individuals on whom sentence had been passed by the territorial Tribunal at Basoko, and who were on their way to undergo their sentence at the central prison at Boma. They are Nos. 3642 to 3649 on the prison register at Boma."

In the same way, quite a recent "interview," in which the usual accusations of cruelty were reproduced, is due to a person formerly in the employ of the State, who was "declared unfit for service," and who has failed to persuade the State to accept his proposal to write for the press articles favourable to the Administration.

The note ignores the replies, contradictions, and corrections which the attacks on the Agents of the State have occasioned at the various times when they have taken place. It ignores the official declarations publicly made by the Government of the State in June last, after the debate in the House of Commons on the 20th May, the report of which is annexed to the note. We also annex the text of these declarations which dealt, by anticipation, with the considerations set forth in the despatch of the 8th August.

The only fresh cause of complaint which the note brings forward—doubtless with the object of explaining the not unimportant fact that the English Consul, who has resided in the Congo since 1901, does not appear to support, by his personal authority, the accusations of private individuals—is that this Agent has been "principally occupied in the investigation of complaints preferred by British subjects." The impression which one would derive from this is that such complaints have been exceptionally numerous. No doubt the Consul has, on different occasions, communicated with the Administration at Boma in the interests of his countrymen, but the subjects of his representations, if one may judge by such of their number as the English Legation has had to bring to the notice of the Central Government at Brussels, do not appear, either in number or importance, to have been more than matters of every day administrative routine: some cases in particular concerned the regulation of the succession to property in the Congo left by deceased English subjects; the object in others was to repair errors of judicial procedure, such as occur elsewhere, and it is not even alleged that the proper action has not been taken upon these representations. The same Consul, who was appointed in 1898, wrote to the Governor-General on the 2nd July, 1901, as follows:—

"I pray believe me when I express now, not only for myself, but for my fellow-countrymen in this part of Africa, our very sincere appreciation of your efforts on behalf of the general community—efforts to promote goodwill among all and to bring together the various elements of our local life."

Nor do the predecessors of Mr. R. Casement—for English Consuls with jurisdiction in the Congo were appointed by His Majesty Government as long ago as 1888—appear to have been absorbed in the examination of innumerable complaints; at all events, that is not the view taken in the Report (the only one published) by Consul Pickersgill, who, by the mere fact of giving an account of his journey into the interior of the Congo as far as Stanley Falls, disproves the alleged impossibility for the English Consular Agents to form an opinion *de visu* in regard to every part of their district.

With regard to the charges against the administrative system of the State, the note deals with taxes, public armed forces, and what is termed forced labour.

It is, at bottom, the contributions made by the Congo natives to the public charges which are criticized, as if there existed a single country or Colony in which the inhabitants do not, under one form or another, bear a part in such charges. A State without resources is inconceivable. On what legitimate grounds could the exemption of natives from all taxes be based, seeing that they are the first to benefit by the material and moral advantages introduced into Africa? As they have no money, a contribution in the shape of labour is required from them. It has been said that, if Africa is ever to be redeemed from barbarism, it must be by getting the negro to understand the meaning of work by the obligation of paying taxes:—

"It is a question (of native labour) which has engaged my most careful attention in connection with West Africa and other Colonies. To listen to the right honourable gentleman, you would almost think that it would be a good thing for the native to be idle. I think it is a good thing for him to be industrious; and by every means in our power we must teach him to work. . . . . No people ever have lived in the world's history who would not work. In the interests of the natives all over Africa, we have to teach them to work."

Such was the language used by Mr. Chamberlain in the House of Commons on the 6th August, 1901; and still more recently he expressed himself as follows:—

"We are all of us taxed, and taxed heavily. Is that a system of forced labour? . . . . . To say that because we put a tax on the native therefore he is reduced to a condition of servitude and of forced labour is, to my mind, absolutely ridiculous. . . . . . It is perfectly fair to my mind that the native should contribute something towards the cost of administering the country." (House of Commons, the 9th March, 1903.)

"If that really is the last word of civilization, if we are to proceed on the assumption that the nearer the native or any human being comes to a pig the more desirable is his condition, of course I have nothing to say. . . . . I must continue to believe that, at all events, the progress of the native in civilization will not be secured until he has been convinced of the necessity and the dignity of labour. Therefore, I think that anything we reasonably can do to induce the native to labour is a desirable thing."

And he defended the principle of taxing the native on the ground that "the existence of the tax is an inducement to him to work." (House of Commons, the 24th March, 1903.)

Moreover, it is to be observed that in nearly every part of Africa the natives are taxed. In the Transvaal every native pays a "head tax" of 2*l.*; in the Orange River Colony he is subject to a "poll tax;" in Southern Rhodesia, Bechuanaland, Basutoland, Uganda, and Natal a "hut tax" is levied; in Cape Colony we find a "hut tax" and a "labour tax;" in German East Africa also a tax is levied on huts, payable either in money, in kind, or in labour. This species of tax has also been applied in the Sierra Leone Protectorate, where payment could be made "in kind by rice or palm nuts," and it has been suggested that work on roads and useful works should be accepted in lieu of payment in money or produce.

The legality of a tax is, therefore, not affected by the mode of its payment, whether in money or in kind, so long as the amount is not excessive. It is certainly not so in the Congo, where the work done by the native does not represent more than forty hours' work a-month. Such work, moreover, is paid for, and the tax in kind thus gives the native as it were some return for his labour.

Payment of taxes is obligatory everywhere; and non-payment involves measures of compulsion. The regulations under which the hut-tax is levied impose on the native, for non-payment, such penalties as imprisonment and forced labour. Nor in the Congo is payment of taxes optional. Repressive measures have occasionally been rendered necessary elsewhere by the refusal of natives to conform to the law, *e.g.*, the disturbances at Sierra Leone, in connexion with which an English publicist, speaking of the police force, states:—

"Between July 1894 and February 1896 no fewer than sixty-two convictions, admittedly representing a small proportion of offences actually committed, were recorded against them for flogging, plundering, and generally maltreating the natives."

Further instances might be recalled of the opposition encountered among native populations to the institution of governmental regulations. Civilization necessarily comes into collision with their savage instincts and barbarous customs and habits; and it can be understood that they submit but impatiently to, and even try to escape from, a state of society which seems to them to be restrictive of their licence and excesses. It frequently happens in Africa that an exodus of natives takes place from one territory to another, in the hope of finding beyond the frontier a Government less well established or less strong, and of thus freeing themselves from all obligations and restraints. Natives of the State may quite well, under the influence of considerations of this kind, have crossed into neighbouring territories, although no kind of emigration on a large scale, such as is referred to in the English note, has ever been reported by the Commandants of the frontier provinces. On the contrary, it is a fact that natives in the Upper Nile region who had settled in British territory have returned to the left bank in consequence of the imposition of new taxes by the English authorities. Besides, if it is these territories which are alluded to, the information contained in the note would seem to be in contradiction with other particulars furnished, for instance, by Sir Harry Johnston.

"This much I can speak of with certainty and emphasis, that from the British frontier near Fort George to the limit of my journeys into the Mbuba country of the Congo Free State, up and down the Semliki, the natives appear to be prosperous and happy. . . . The extent to which they were building their villages and cultivating their plantations within the precincts of Fort Mbeni showed that they had no fear of the Belgians."

Major H. H. Gibbons, who was for several months on the Upper Nile, writes :—

" Having had occasion to know many officers, and to visit their stations in the Congo State, I am convinced that their behaviour has been much misunderstood by the press. I have quoted as a proof my experience, which is at variance with an article recently published in the English press, in which they are accused of great cruelties."

The declaration of last June, of which a copy is inclosed, has disposed of the criticisms directed against the public forces of the State, by pointing out that recruitment for them is regulated by law, and that it is only one man in every 10,000 who is affected. To say that " the method of obtaining men for military service is often but little different from that formerly employed to obtain slaves " is to misunderstand the carefully drawn regulations which have, on the contrary, been issued to check abuses. Levies take place in each district ; the district Commissioners settle the mode of conscription in agreement with the native Chiefs. Voluntary enlistment, and numerous re-enlistments, easily fill up the ranks, which only reach, all told, the moderate total of 15,000 men.

Those who allege, as the note says, that " the men composing the armed force of the State were in many cases recruited from the most warlike and savage tribes " must be unaware that the public forces are recruited from every province, and from the whole population. It is inconceivable that the authorities of a State, with due regard to its interests, should form an army out of undisciplined and savage elements, and instances are to be found—such as the excesses said to have been perpetrated by irregular levies in Uganda, and the revolts which formerly occurred in the Congo—which, on the contrary, render it necessary that special care should be exercised in raising armed forces. The European establishment, consisting of Belgian, Italian, Swedish, Norwegian, and Danish officers, maintains strict discipline, and it would be vain to seek the actual facts alluded to in the assertion that the soldiers " not infrequently terrorized over their own officers." Such an assertion is as unfounded as the one " that compulsion is often exercised by irresponsible native soldiers, uncontrolled by an European officer." For a long time past the authorities have been alive to the danger arising from the existence of stations of negro soldiers, who inevitably abuse their authority, as recognized in the Report of Sir D. Chalmers on the insurrection in Sierra Leone. In the Congo such stations have been gradually abolished.

Those who do not refuse to accept patent facts will recognize that of the reproaches levied at the State, the most unjust is the statement " that no attempt at any administration of the natives is made, and that the officers of the Government do not apparently concern themselves with such work."

It is astonishing to come across such an assertion in a despatch from a Government, one of whose members, Lord Cranborne, Under-Secretary of State for Foreign Affairs, stated on the 20th May last :—

" There was no doubt that the administration of the Congo Government had been marked by a very high degree of a certain kind of administrative development. There were railways, there were steamers upon the river, hospitals had been established, and all the machinery of elaborate judicial and police systems had been set up."

Another member of the House of Commons acknowledged—

" That the Congo State had done good work in excluding alcoholic liquor from the greater part of their domain ; that they had established a certain number of hospitals, had diminished small-pox by means of vaccination, and had suppressed the Arab Slave Trade."

However limited these admissions, still they contradict the assertion now made that " the natives are left entirely to themselves, so far as any assistance in their government or in their affairs is concerned."

Such does not seem to have been the conclusion at which Mr. Pickersgill, the English Consul, had arrived as long ago as 1898.

" Has the welfare of the African," he asks, " been duly cared for in the Congo State ?" He answers : " The State has restricted the liquor trade . . . . . it is scarcely possible to over-estimate the service which is being rendered by the Congo Government to its subjects in this matter. . . . . Intertribal wars have been suppressed over a wide area, and, the imposition of European authority being steadily pursued, the boundaries of peace are constantly extending. . . . . The State must be congratulated upon the security it has created for all who live within the shelter of its flag and abide by its laws and regulations. . . . . Credit is also due to the Congo Government in respect of the diminution of cannibalism. . . . . The yoke of the notorious Arab slave-traders has been broken, and traffic in human beings amongst the natives themselves has been diminished to a considerable degree."

This Report also showed that the labour of the native was remunerated, and gave due credit to the State for its efforts to instruct the young natives, and to open schools.

Since 1898 the general condition of the native has been still further improved. The system of carriers ("le portage à dos d'homme"), the hardships of which, so far as the native was concerned, were specially pointed out by Mr. Pickersgill, has disappeared from those parts of the country where it was most practised, in consequence of the opening of railways. Elsewhere motor cars are used as means of transport. The "sentry," the station of negro soldiers which the Consul criticized, not without reason, no longer exists. Cattle have been introduced into every district. Sanitary Commissions have been instituted. Schools and workshops have multiplied.

"The native," says the inclosed document,* "is better housed, better clad, and better fed; he is replacing his huts by better built and healthier dwelling-places; thanks to existing transport facilities, he is able to obtain the produce necessary to satisfy his new wants; workshops have been opened for him, where he learns handicrafts, such as those of the blacksmith, carpenter, mechanic, and mason; he extends his plantations and, taking example by the white man, learns rational modes of agriculture; he is always able to obtain medical assistance; he sends his children to the State school-colonies and to the missionary schools."

As stated in the House of Commons, it is only right to recognize that the material and moral regeneration of Central Africa cannot be the work of a day. The results so far obtained have been considerable, and these we shall try to consolidate and develop, in spite of the way in which an effort is being made to hamper the action of the State, which in the real interests of civilization should rather be promoted.

The English note does not show that the economic system of the State is in opposition to the Berlin Act. It does not meet the points of law and fact by means of which the State has demonstrated the conformity of its system of land tenure and concessions with the provisions of that Act. It does not explain either how or why freedom of trade—a term used at the Conference of Berlin in its usual, grammatical, and economic sense—is incomplete in the Congo State because there are landowners there.

The note confuses the utilization of his property by the owner with trade. The native who collects on behalf of the owner does not become the owner of what is so collected, and naturally cannot dispose of it to a third party, any more than a miner can rob the proprietor of the produce of the mine and dispose of it himself. These rules are in accordance with the principles of justice and are explained in numerous documents, such as legal opinions and judicial decisions, some of which are annexed. His Majesty's Government do not deny that the State is justified in allotting domain lands to *bonâ fide* occupants, or that the native has no longer any right to the produce of the soil as soon as the "land is reduced into individual occupation." The distinction is without legal foundation. If the State can part with land, it is because the native is not the owner; by what title could he then retain a right to the produce of property which has been lawfully acquired by others? Could it be contended, for instance, that the Lower Congo Railway Company, or the South Cameroons Company, or the Italian Colonial Trading Company are, on the ground that they are not at present in occupation, bound to allow the native to plunder the territories allotted to them? As a matter of fact, moreover, in the Congo State the appropriation of lands worked on Government account or by the Concessionary Companies is an accomplished fact. The State and the Companies have devoted large sums, amounting to many millions of francs, to the development of the lands in question, and more especially to that of the forests. There can, therefore, be no doubt that throughout the territories of the Congo the State really and completely works its property, just as the Companies really and completely work their Concessions.

The state of affairs then which actually exists, and is established in the Independent State, is such that there is really no need, as far as the State itself is concerned, to dwell longer on the theory set forth in the note which deals in turn with the rights of the State, with those of *bonâ fide* occupiers, and those of the natives.

Still this theory calls for the attention of the Powers in view of the serious difficulties which would arise were it to be implicitly accepted.

The note lays down the three following propositions:—

"The State has the right to partition the State lands among *bonâ fide* occupants."

"The natives will, as the land is so divided out amongst *bonâ fide* occupiers, lose their right of roaming over it and collecting the natural fruits which it produces."

"Until unoccupied land is reduced into individual occupation, and so long as the produce can only be collected by the native, the native should be free to dispose of that produce as he pleases."

* See Annex No. 1.

There is no single one of these propositions but apparently excludes the other two, and, as a matter of fact, such contradictions amount to a denial of the right to grant Concessions.

If *bonâ fide* occupiers ever existed they have become proprietors ; occupation, where it can be exercised, is under all legislative codes, one of the methods by which property can be acquired, and in the Congo State titles of ownership deriving from it have been legally registered. If the land has never been legally occupied, it is without an owner, or, rather the State is the owner: the State can allot it to a third party, for whom such allotment is a complete and absolute title. In either case it is hard to see how the fruits of the soil can be reserved for any but the owner on the pretext that the latter is not able to collect the produce of his property.

By a curious contradiction it is observed in the note that, as a consequence of the allotment of lands by the State, the natives " lose their right of collecting the natural fruits," and, on the other hand, that they retain the right of disposing of these fruits " until unoccupied land is reduced into individual occupation." It is difficult to understand what is meant by a right which belongs to the natives or not according to the action of a third party. Either they lost their rights on the lands being allotted, and in that case they have lost them entirely and completely, or else they have retained them, and are entitled to retain them, although " the land is reduced into individual occupation."

Again, what are we to understand by the expressions " *bonâ fide* " occupiers and " individual occupation ? " Who is to determine whether the occupier has brought his lands into a state of individual occupation, whether he is able to collect their produce, or whether it is still for the native to do so ? In any case, such a question is essentially one to be settled by municipal law.

The note is, moreover, incomplete in another respect. It states that where the land has not yet been worked by those who have a right to it, the option of working should belong to the native. Rights would thus be given to the natives to the prejudice of the Government or of white concessionnaires, but the note does not explain how nor by whom the wrong thus caused would be repaired or made good. Though the system thus advocated cannot be applied in the Congo State, as there are no longer any unappropriated lands there, attention should be called to the statement in the interest of white men established in the conventional basin. If it is right to treat the negro well, it is none the less just not to despoil the white man, who, in the interest of all, must remain the dominant race.

From an economic point of view, it would be very regrettable if, in spite of the rights regularly acquired by white men, the domain lands were, even temporarily, handed over to the natives. Such a course would involve a return to their former condition of abandonment, when the natives left them unproductive, for the collection of rubber, the plantation of coffee, cocoa, tobacco, &c., date from the day when the State itself took the initiative: the export trade was insignificant before the impetus it received from Government enterprise. Such a course would furthermore certainly involve the neglect of rational methods of work, of planting and of replanting—measures which the State and the Concessionary Companies have assumed as an obligation with a view to securing the preservation of the natural riches of the country.

Never in the Congo, so far as we know, have requests to buy natural produce been addressed to the rightful owners. Up to now the only attempts made have been to buy the produce which has been stolen, and the State, as was its duty, has had those guilty of these unlawful attempts prosecuted.

It is not true, as has been asserted, that the policy of the State has killed trade ; it has, on the contrary, created the materials which trade deals in and keeps up the supply ; it is thanks to the State that, on the Antwerp market—and soon even in the Congo where the possibility of establishing trade depôts is being considered—5,000 tons of rubber collected in the Congo can be annually put on sale to all and sundry without privilege or monopoly, while formerly, in 1887, for instance, the rubber export amounted to hardly 30 tons. It is the State which, after having created, at its own expense, the material of trade, carefully preserves the source of it by means of planting and replanting.

It must not be forgotten either that the Congo State has been obliged to rely on its own resources. It was forced to utilize its domain in the public interest. All the receipts of the domain go into the Treasury, as also the dividends of the shares which the State holds in exchange for Concessions granted. It has only been by fully utilizing its domain lands, and pledging the greater part of their revenues, that it has been able to raise loans, and encourage the construction of railways by guarantees of interest, thus realizing one of the means most advocated by the Brussels Conference for promoting civilization in Central Africa. Nor has it hesitated to mortgage its domain lands with this object.

The Berlin Act is not opposed to such a course, for it never proscribed the rights of property as there is now an *ex post facto* attempt to make out, an attempt tending, consciously or not, to the ruin of the whole conventional basin of the Congo.

It will not escape the notice of the Powers that the English note, by suggesting a reference to the Court at The Hague, tends to bring into consideration as cases for arbitration questions of sovereignty and internal administration as questions for arbitration which, according to prevailing doctrines, are excluded from arbitral decisions. As far as the present case is concerned, it must be assumed that the suggestion of referring the matter to the Court at The Hague has a general meaning, if it is true that, in the opinion of the English Chambers of Commerce, "the principles and practice introduced into the administration of the affairs of the French Congo, the Congo Free State, and other areas in the conventional basin of the Congo being [*sic*] in direct opposition to the Articles of the Act of Berlin, 1885." The Government of the Congo State have never ceased advocating arbitration as a mode of settling questions which are of an international nature, and can thus be suitably treated, as, for instance, the divergencies of opinion which have arisen in connexion with the lease of the territories of the Bahr-el-Ghazal.

The Government of the Congo State, after careful examination of the English note, remain convinced that, in view of its vagueness, and the complete lack of evidence, which is implicitly admitted, there is no tribunal in the world, supposing there were one possessing competent jurisdiction, which could, far from pronouncing a condemnation, take any decision other than to refuse action on mere supposition.

If the Congo State is attacked, England may admit that she, more than any other nation, has been the object of attacks and accusations of every kind, and the list would be long of the campaigns which have at various times, and even quite recently, been directed against her colonial administration. She has certainly not escaped criticism in regard to her numerous and bloody wars against native populations, nor the reproach of oppressing natives and invading their liberty. Has she not been blamed in regard to the long insurrections in Sierra Leone; to the disturbed state of Nigeria, where quite recently, according to the English newspapers, military measures of repression cost, on one single occasion, the lives of 700 natives, of most of their Chiefs, and of the Sultan; and to the conflict in Somaliland, which is being carried on at the cost of many lives, without, however, exciting expressions of regret in the House of Commons, except on the score of the heavy expense?

Seeing that these attacks have left England indifferent, it is somewhat surprising to find her now attaching such importance to those made on the Congo State.

There is, however, reason to think that the natives of the Congo State prefer the Government of a small and pacific nation, whose aims remain as peaceful as its creation which was founded on Treaties concluded with the natives.

(Signed) CHR. DE CUVELIER.

Brussels, September 17, 1903.

Annexes.*

I. "Bulletin Officiel de l'État Indépendant du Congo," Juin 1903.

II. Judgments delivered by the Tribunals of French Congo.

III. Opinions of Messrs. Van Maldeghem and de Paepe, Van Berchem, Barboux, and Nys.

Translations of Extracts from Annex I.

Page 142.

In conformity with Articles II and XIII of the Berlin Act, it (the Congo State) has assured to all flags, without distinction of nationality, free access to all its interior waters and full and entire freedom of navigation. The railway, which has been constructed to obviate the innavigability of the lower river, is open to the traffic of all nations in conformity with Article XVI.

* Copies have been sent to the Library of each House of Parliament.

In conformity with Article III, there is no differential treatment either of ships or goods, and no tax is levied on foreigners which is not equally borne by nationals.

In conformity with Article IV, no transit due has been imposed.

In conformity with Article VI, freedom of conscience and the free exercise of worship are guaranteed to natives, to foreigners, and to the missions of all creeds.

In conformity with Article VII, the State has adhered to the Convention of the Universal Postal Union.

Availing itself of the power conferred by Article X, the Congo State has declared itself perpetually neutral, and in no circumstance has failed in the duties imposed by neutrality.

In conformity with Article XII, it has endeavoured, in case of any international difference, to have recourse to mediation and arbitration, and has never declined to accept such procedure.

In conformity with the Declaration of the 2nd July, 1890, the import and export duties levied do not exceed the limits fixed by the Agreements of the 8th April, 1892, and the 10th March, 1902, between the State, France and Portugal.

Article I of the Act of Berlin lays down that "the trade of all nations shall enjoy complete freedom in the Conventional basin of the Congo," and, by Article V, "no monopoly or favour of any kind in matters of trade" shall be granted there. These provisions, like the rest, have been respected by the Congo State in the letter and in the spirit.

Page 144.

Freedom of trade is complete in the Congo, and is restricted neither by monopoly nor privilege. Every one is free to sell or buy every sort of produce in which it is lawful to trade. The law protects this freedom by forbidding any interference with the freedom of business transactions; it punishes "any one who has employed violence or threats with a view to compel the natives, whether on the roads in the interior, or in the markets, to part with their goods to particular persons or at particular prices;"* it punishes "those who, by violence, abuse, or threats, shall have interfered with the freedom of trade, with a view either to stop trade caravans on the public roads or to obstruct the freedom of traffic whether by land or water."†

It is asserted that the principle of the freedom of trade is infringed by the appropriation by the State of vacant and ownerless lands within its boundaries. When by the Decree of the 1st July, 1885, the State declared that "no one has the right to occupy vacant lands without a title; vacant lands are to be considered as belonging to the State,"‡ it did so in reliance on a legal principle which is universally admitted, its action in this matter was not, as has been said, the first step in a deliberate policy of exclusiveness. That principle was inscribed in the Codes of all civilized countries; it has been sanctioned by all Colonial legislative systems.

Page 152.

If it were true that, by declaring all ownerless lands to be Government property, the Congo State had expropriated the natives, all these various legislative systems could be attacked on the same ground. It is generally admitted that the native has no real title to the ownership of the vast stretches of country which from time immemorial he has allowed to lie fallow, or to the forests which he has never turned to profit. But the law of the Congo State is careful to maintain the natives in the enjoyment of the lands they occupy and, as a matter of fact, not only are they not disturbed in this enjoyment, but they are actually extending the lands they cultivate and their plantations as their needs grow. The State has been at much pains to prevent the natives from being robbed.

"No one has the right to dispossess natives of the lands which they occupy (Ordinance of the 1st July, 1885, Article 2).

"The lands occupied by the native population under the authority of their Chiefs, shall continue to be governed by the local customs and usages (Decree of the 14th September, 1886, Article 2).

"All Acts or Agreements which would tend to drive the natives from the territories they occupy, or to deprive them directly or indirectly of their liberty or means of livelihood, are prohibited (Decree of the 14th September, 1886, Article 2).

* Penal Code, Art. 56 (Decree of the 26th May, 1888, Bulletin Officiel, 1897, p. 31).

† Penal Code, Art. 57 (idem, p. 31).

‡ Bulletin Officiel, 1885, p. 31.

"In cases where the lands which form the subject of application are occupied in part by natives, the Governor-General, or his Delegate, shall intervene in order, if possible, to effect an arrangement with them, securing to the applicant the lands so occupied, either by cession or by lease, but the State is not to be put to any expense in the matter (Decree of the 9th April, 1893, Article 5).

"When native villages are inclosed in lands which have either been disposed of or leased, the natives may, so long as the land has not been officially measured, take into cultivation, without the consent of either the owner or the lessor, the vacant lands surrounding their villages (Decree of the 9th April, 1893, Article 6).

"The members of the Land Commission shall examine with special care the question whether the lands applied for ought not to be reserved either for the public use or with a view to allow of the extension of cultivation by the natives (Decree of the 2nd February, 1898, Article 2)."

Page 156.

If it is inexact to say that the natives have been robbed of immemorial rights, it is equally so to assert that the policy of the State has aimed at the exclusion of private trading in order to assure greater advantages for its own commercial enterprises.

Such a statement can only be the result of a misapprehension of the various phases through which the Congo trade has passed since 1885. At that time private enterprise was centred in the Lower Congo only. The Government, far from wishing to close the Upper Congo, declared its access free to all. The Decree of the 30th April, 1887, led, on the contrary, to various commercial firms establishing themselves above Stanley Pool, owing to the facilities it afforded for settling on the domain lands.

Article 6 of that Decree provided:—

"Non-natives who desire to found commercial or agricultural establishments in the districts above Stanley Pool, or in others to be eventually designated by the Governor-General of the Congo, shall be at liberty to take possession with this view of an area, the maximum size of which shall be fixed by the Governor-General; provided that they fulfil such conditions as he shall lay down, they shall enjoy a preferential right to the eventual acquisition of property in such lands at a price which shall be fixed by him beforehand."

And Article 7 added:—

"The non-natives who, in the same regions, shall desire to occupy lands, of which the area shall exceed the maximum referred to in the preceding Article, may occupy them provisionally on such conditions as the Governor-General shall determine. He shall further decide whether the preferential right alluded to in the preceding Article shall be given to them in regard to this larger extent of land."*

With a view to assist commercial enterprise in the regions of the interior, the Government even exempted from export duty—the only customs duties which they could at that time levy—all native produce coming from the territories above Stanley Pool.

"From the 1st January, 1888," so ran Article 1 of the Ordinance of the 19th October, 1887, "and till further orders, native produce coming from the State territories on the left bank of Stanley Pool and above that lake shall be exempted from export duty."†

Later, by the Decree of the 17th October, 1889,‡ the Government announced that applications might be presented for concessions to work rubber and other vegetable produce in the State forests of the Upper Congo where such produce was not already worked by the native population.

By the Decree of the 9th July, 1890, the collection of ivory within the State domains was entirely given up to private persons throughout such parts of the Congo as were at that time visited by the steamers.

These Regulations were applicable to all foreign enterprise, without distinction of nationality; they show that there was no such policy of ostracism in regard to private enterprise such as is now attributed to the State.

It has not been the fault of the Government that nationals of all countries have not profited by this liberal system. They continued, however, to confine themselves, with few exceptions, to the Lower Congo. The Companies which decided to extend their operations in the central districts of the Congo found every facility for the establishment of agencies, and acquired the favourable position which they now enjoy.

* Bulletin Officiel, 1887, p. 72.

† Bulletin Officiel, 1888, p. 3.

‡ Bulletin Officiel, 1889, p. 218.

The State can hardly be blamed because, in face of the almost universal inaction on the part of private individuals, it endeavoured to turn its territories to account by working its domain lands, either on its own account or through others. It was, however, the only way to secure the funds necessary for the Budget, the charges in which steadily increased with the extension of the public service, and to give the country the benefit of an economic system by imposing upon the concessionary Companies the obligation to undertake works of public utility.

The Government, further, were careful not to abandon a policy of moderation in the matter. When by the Decree of the 30th October, 1892, they defined regions reserved for working by the domain (those, that is to say, in which it had been ascertained, after inquiry, that the natives had never engaged in the collection of rubber), they still left vast zones at the disposal of the public, and allowed to private persons the exclusive right to work the rubber on the Government properties there. As a matter of fact, the zones in question comprised more than a quarter of the vacant State lands, apart from the whole country below Stanley Pool. Nevertheless, the Companies persisted for some years more in not moving towards these regions; it has only been since 1897 that there have been any signs of general activity. It was then that the numerous factories which are still to be found there were started in the Kassai, Ikelemba, and Lulonga districts, and on the banks of the Congo. But it is to be noted that with one exception none but Belgian Companies decided to put their capital into those enterprises, and to take the consequent risks. Foreigners have held aloof, in spite of the fact that they were at perfect liberty to establish themselves in these regions; even the firms which had been long established in the Lower Congo, and especially the English houses, did not consider the moment favourable for establishing branches in the Upper Congo. The above remark is generally applicable, in so far that, also in the territories for which Concessions have been given, not one of the concessionary Companies has found any foreign interests previously existing; indeed, certain foreigners who were interested in one of the most important of them, the Anglo-Belgian India-Rubber and Exploration Company, which was founded by an English group, have parted with their interests.

The commercial field open to private persons in the Congo never has been and is not limited; trade is free, so far as it is legitimate, throughout the country, and in certain regions the State, far from organizing any excessive working of its domain lands, has even renounced the exercise of its rights of property. To give one instance only the Dutch Company, the value of whose exports was 730,000 fr. in 1887, exported in 1901 goods to the value of more than 3,000,000 fr.

Page 162.

The work of organization has since been going on over the whole country by the more and more effective occupation of the territory; posts and stations have been multiplied, and now number 215; the work of the administrative, judicial, and sanitary authorities has expanded; transport facilities have been introduced; two lines of railways have been laid in the Lower Congo, and there are others either being constructed or proposed in the Upper Congo; seventy-nine steamers and boats have been put on the river and its affluents; 1,500 kilom. of telegraph and telephone lines have been laid; carriage roads have been built, on which the use of automobiles will put an end to the system of carriers ("portage à dos d'homme"); vaccine institutes have been established with a view to putting a stop, through the increased use of lymph, to the ravages of small-pox; water-works have been built in important centres, such as Boma and Matadi; hospitals for blacks and whites have been founded at different posts, as also Red Cross stations and a bacteriological institute; importation of spirituous liquors and trade in them has been prohibited almost everywhere, while the importation of alcoholic drinks made with absinthe, as also trade in them, have been forbidden everywhere; the trade in improved fire-arms and ammunition for them has been absolutely forbidden; cattle have been introduced at all the stations, and model farms have been established; Sanitary Commissions have been instituted whose duty it is to watch over the requirements of the elements of public health.

This general development is necessarily accompanied by an improvement of the conditions in which the native lives, wherever he comes into contact with the European element. Materially, he is better housed, better clad, and better fed; he is replacing his huts by better built and healthier dwelling-places; thanks to existing transport facilities, he is able to obtain the produce necessary to satisfy his new wants; workshops have been opened for him, where he learns handicrafts, such as those of the blacksmith, carpenter, mechanic, and mason; he extends his plantations, and, taking example by the white man, learns rational modes of agriculture; he is always able to obtain medical assistance; he sends his children to the State school-colonies and to the missionary schools. Steps have been taken to safeguard the individual liberty of the blacks, and especially to prevent labour contracts between blacks and non-natives degenerating into disguised slavery. It is on this point that the Decree of the 8th November, 1888, enters into the most minute details concerning the length of the engagement, the form of the contract, and the payment of wages. Recent legislation in French Congo, which has very properly been praised by the English organs, has been dictated by the like solicitude for the natives.

The native is free to seek by work the remuneration which contributes to the increase of his well-being. One of the objects, indeed, of the general policy of the State is to aim at the regeneration of the race by impressing them with the high idea of the necessity of work. It is intelligible that Governments, conscious of their moral responsibility, should not advocate the right of the inferior races to be idle, which would entail the continuance of a social system opposed to civilization. The Congo State aims at carrying out its educational mission by requiring the native to contribute, by means of a tax in kind, for which, however, payment is made to him, to the development of the State forests; the amount of such payments was, in the Budget for 1903, nearly 3,000,000 fr. The legality of such a system of developing the State property rests not only on the universal principle which attributes to the State the possession of ownerless lands, but also on the cession which the local Chiefs have made to the State, by peaceful methods and Treaties, of such political and land rights as they may have possessed; and on the fact that it is the State itself which has revealed to the natives the existence of those natural riches of which they were ignorant by showing them how to work; it is the State, too, which has bound itself, equally with private persons, to plant and replant, and thus to insure the preservation and perpetuity of those natural riches which the carelessness of some and the lust of gain of others could not have failed to destroy.

Page 165.

The system which the State has followed, while forwarding the economical development of the country, has at the same time caused a considerable commercial movement, inasmuch as the exports now amount to a value of 50,000,000, and 5,000 tons of rubber from the Congo forests are sold every year at Antwerp to the highest bidder.

Whatever may have been said this prosperity has not been attained to the detriment of the native. It has been asserted that the native populations must of necessity be badly treated because they are subjected on the one hand to military service, and on the other to the payment of certain taxes.

Military service is no more slavery in the Congo than anywhere else where the system of conscription is in force. The manner in which the public forces are recruited and organized has formed the subject of the most minute legislative provisions, with a view to the avoidance of abuses. As a matter of fact military service is not a heavy burden to the population, from whom it only takes one man in 10,000. To show the errors which have been believed in regard to the public forces it is necessary once more to point out that they are composed entirely of regular troops, and there are no "irregular levies" composed of undisciplined and barbarous elements. Care has been taken gradually to get rid of posts of black soldiers, and at the present moment every military post is commanded by a white officer. The increase in the number of officials has allowed of giving European officers to all detachments of these forces.

In regard to contributions in kind which are levied on the native by the authorities, such taxes are as legitimate as any other. They do not impose on the native burdens of a different or heavier kind than the forms of impost enforced in the neighbouring Colonies, such as the hut tax. The native thus bears his share of the public burden as a return for the protection afforded him by the State, and this share is a light one since on an average it means for the native no more than forty hours of work a-month.

It is unfortunately true that acts of violence have been committed against the natives in the Congo, as everywhere else in Africa: the Congo State has never sought either to deny or to conceal them. The detractors of the State show themselves to be prejudiced when they quote these acts as the necessary consequence of a bad system of administration, or when they assert that they are tolerated by the higher authorities.

Whenever any European official has been guilty of such acts he has been punished by the Courts, and a certain number of Europeans are at this moment in the prisons of the State expiating their offences against the penal laws which protect the life and person of the native. If the enormous extent of the Congo State is taken into account, such cases are the exception, as is obvious from the fact that recent publications attacking the Congo State have been obliged, in support of their indictment, to take up incidents nearly ten years old, and even to have recourse, amongst others, to the testimony of a commercial agent actually condemned for his excesses against the blacks. It is worthy of remark that the Catholic missionaries have never called attention to this general system of cruelty which is imputed to the State, and if judicial statistics demonstrate the stern measures that have been taken by the Criminal Courts, it does not follow that there is more crime in the Congo than in other Central African Colonies.

No. 3.

Mr. Casement to the Marquess of Lansdowne.—(Received December 12.)

My Lord, *London, December* 11, 1903.

I HAVE the honour to submit my Report on my recent journey on the Upper Congo.

I left Matadi on the 5th June, and arriving at Léopoldville on the 6th, remained in the neighbourhood of Stanley Pool until the 2nd July, when I set out for the Upper Congo. My return to Léopoldville was on the 15th September, so that the period spent in the Upper River was one of only two and a-half months, during which time I visited several points on the Congo River itself, up to the junction of the Lulongo River, ascended that river and its principal feeder, the Lopori, as far as Bongandanga, and went round Lake Mantumba.

Although my visit was of such brief duration, and the points touched at nowhere lay far off the beaten tracks of communication, the region visited was one of the most central in the Congo State, and the district in which most of my time was spent, that of the Equator, is probably one of the most productive. Moreover, I was enabled, by visiting this district, to contrast its present day state with the condition in which I had known it some sixteen years ago. Then (in 1887) I had visited most of the places I now revisited, and I was thus able to institute a comparison between a state of affairs I had myself seen when the natives lived their own savage lives in anarchic and disorderly communities, uncontrolled by Europeans, and that created by more than a decade of very energetic European intervention. That very much of this intervention has been called for no one who formerly knew the Upper Congo could doubt, and there are to-day widespread proofs of the great energy displayed by Belgian officials in introducing their methods of rule over one of the most savage regions of Africa.

Admirably built and admirably kept stations greet the traveller at many points; a fleet of river steamers, numbering, I believe, forty-eight, the property of the Congo Government, navigate the main river and its principal affluents at fixed intervals. Regular means of communication are thus afforded to some of the most inaccessible parts of Central Africa.

A railway, excellently constructed in view of the difficulties to be encountered, now connects the ocean ports with Stanley Pool, over a tract of difficult country, which formerly offered to the weary traveller on foot many obstacles to be overcome and many days of great bodily fatigue. To-day the railway works most efficiently, and I noticed many improvements, both in the permanent way and in the general management, since the date of my last visit to Stanley Pool in January 1901. The cataract region, through which the railway passes, is a generally unproductive and even sterile tract of some 220 miles in breadth. This region is, I believe, the home, or birthplace, of the sleeping sickness—a terrible disease, which is, all too rapidly, eating its way into the heart of Africa, and has even traversed the entire continent to well-nigh the shores of the Indian Ocean. The population of the Lower Congo has been gradually reduced by the unchecked ravages of this, as yet, undiagnosed and incurable disease, and as one cause of the seemingly wholesale diminution of human life which I everywhere observed in the regions revisited, a prominent place must be assigned to this malady. The natives certainly attribute their alarming death-rate to this as one of the inducing causes, although they attribute, and I think principally, their rapid decrease in numbers to other causes as well. Perhaps the most striking change observed during my journey into the interior was the great reduction observable everywhere in native life. Communities I had formerly known as large and flourishing centres of population are to-day entirely gone, or now exist in such diminished numbers as to be no longer recognizable. The southern shores of Stanley Pool had formerly a population of fully 5,000 Batekes, distributed through the three towns of Ngaliema's (Léopoldville), Kinchasa, and Ndolo, lying within a few miles of each other. These people, some twelve years ago, decided to abandon their homes, and in one night the great majority of them crossed over into the French territory on the north shores of Stanley Pool. Where formerly had stretched these populous native African villages, I saw to-day only a few scattered European houses, belonging either to Government officials or local traders. In Léopoldville to-day there are not, I should estimate, 100 of the original natives or their descendants now residing. At Kinchasa a few more more may be found dwelling around one of the European trading depôts, while at Ndolo none remain, and there is nothing there but a station of the Congo Railway Company and a Government post. These Bateke people were not, perhaps, particularly desirable subjects for an energetic Administration, which desired, above all things, progress and speedy results. They were themselves interlopers from the northern shores of the Congo River, and derived a very profitable existence as trading middlemen, exploiting the less sophisticated population among whom they had established themselves. Their loss to the southern shores of Stanley Pool is none the less to be deplored, I think, for they formed, at any rate, a connecting link between an incoming European commercial element and the background of would-be native suppliers.

Léopoldville is sometimes spoken of as a Congo town, but it cannot rightly be so termed. Apart from the Government station, which, in most respects, is very well planned, there is nothing at all resembling a town—barrack would be the correct term. The Government station of Léopoldville numbers, I was informed by its Chief, some 130 Europeans, and probably 3,000 native Government workmen, who all dwell in well ordered lines of either very well-built European houses, or, for the native staff, mud-built huts. Broad paths, which may be termed streets, connect the various parts of this Government Settlement, and an elementary effort at lighting by electricity has already evolved three lights in front of the house of the Commissaire-Général. Outside the Government staff, the general community, or public of Léopoldville, numbers less than one dozen Europeans, and possibly not more than 200 native dependents of their households or trading stores. This general public consists of two missionary establishments, numbering in all 4 Europeans; a railway station with, I think, 1 European; 4 trading establishments—1 Portuguese, 1 Belgian, 1 English, and 1 German—numbering 7 Europeans, with, perhaps, 80 or 100 native dependents; 2 British West African petty traders, and a couple of Loango tailor boys, who make clothes for the general community. This, I think, comprises almost all those not immediately dependent upon the Government.

These shops and traders do scarcely any business in native produce, of which there may be said to be none in the district, but rely upon a cash trade in Congolese currency, carried on with the large staff of Government employés, both European and native. Were this cash dealing to cease, the four European shops would be forced to put up their shutters. During the period of my stay at Léopoldville it did actually cease, and, for reasons which were not known publicly, the large native staff of Congo Government workmen, instead of receiving a part of their monthly wages in cash to spend locally—as also those being paid off on the expiry of their contracts—were remunerated by the Government in barter goods, which were issued from a Government store. This method of payment did not satisfy either the native Government employés or the local traders, and I heard many complaints on this score. The traders complained, some of them to myself, that as they had no other form of trading open to them, save this with the Government staff against cash, for the Government to itself now pay these men in goods was to end, at a blow, all trade dealings in the district. The native workmen complained, too, that they were paid in cloth which often they did not want in their own homes, and in order to have the wherewithal to purchase what they wanted, a practice at once arose amongst these men to sell for cash, at a loss to themselves, the cloth they had been forced to receive in payment from the Government store. The workmen lost on this transaction, and so did the traders. Pieces of cloth which were charged by the Government at 10 fr. each in paying off the workmen, these men would readily part with for 7 fr., and even for 6 fr. in cash. I myself, one day in June, bought for 7 fr. a-piece, from two just-discharged Government workmen, two pieces of cloth which had been charged against them at 10 fr. each. These men wished to buy salt at one of the local stores, and to obtain the means of doing so, they readily sacrificed 3 fr. in each 10 fr. of their pay. The traders, too, complained that by this extensive sale of cotton goods at reduced rates by the Government employés, their own sales of cloth at current prices were rendered well-nigh impossible throughout the district.

The 3,000 Government workpeople at Léopoldville are drawn from nearly every part of the Congo State. Some, those from the cataract district especially, go voluntarily seeking employment, but many—and I believe a vast majority—are men, or lads, brought from districts of the Upper Congo, and who serve the authorities not primarily at their own seeking. On the 16th June last, five Government workpeople brought me their contracts of engagement with a request that I might tell them how long a period they still had to serve. They were all Upper Congo men, and had already nearly completed the full term of their engagement. The contracts, in each case, appeared as having been signed and drawn up at Boma on behalf of the Governor-General of the Congo State, and were, in each case, for a term of seven years. The men informed me that they had never been to Boma, and that the whole of their period of service had been spent either at Léopoldville or on the Upper Congo. In three of these cases I observed that an alteration had been made in the period of service, in the following terms:—

"Je réduis de sept à cinq ans le terme de service du . . . . ."

This entry was signed by the acting State Inspector of the district. It seemingly had not been observed, for it was struck out by his successor, and, as a matter of fact, the full period of seven years was, in each case, within a few months of completion.

On the whole the Government workmen at Léopoldville struck me as being well cared for, and they were certainly none of them idle. The chief difficulty in dealing with so large a staff arises from the want of a sufficiency of food supply in the surrounding country. The staple food of the entire Upper Congo is a preparation of the root of the cassava plant, steeped and boiled, and made up into loaves or puddings of varying weight. The natives of the districts around Léopoldville are forced to provide a fixed quantity each week of this form of food, which is levied by requisitions on all the surrounding villages. The European Government staff is also mainly dependent upon food supplies obtained from the natives of the neighbourhood in a similar manner. This, however necessary, is not a welcome task to the native suppliers who complain that their numbers are yearly decreasing, while the demands made upon them remain fixed, or tend even to increase.

The Government station at Léopoldville and its extensive staff, exist almost solely in connection with the running of Government steamers upon the Upper Congo.

A hospital for Europeans and an establishment designed as a native hospital are in charge of a European doctor. Another doctor also resides in the Government station whose bacteriological studies are unremitting and worthy of much praise. The native hospital—not, I am given to understand, through the fault of the local medical staff—is, however, an unseemly place. When I visited the three mud huts which serve this purpose, all of them dilapidated, and two with the thatched roofs almost gone, I found seventeen sleeping sickness patients, male and female, lying about in the utmost dirt. Most of them were lying on the bare ground—several out on the pathway in front of the houses, and one, a woman, had fallen into the fire just prior to my arrival (while in the final, insensible stage of the disease), and had burned herself very badly. She had since been well bandaged, but was still lying out on the ground with her head almost in the fire, and while I sought to speak to her, in turning, she upset a pot of scalding water over her shoulder. All of the seventeen persons I saw were near their end, and on my second visit, two days later, the 19th June, I found one of them lying dead out in the open.

In somewhat striking contrast to the neglected state of these people, I found, within a couple of hundred yards of them, the Government workshop for repairing and fitting the steamers. Here all was brightness, care, order, and activity, and it was impossible not to admire and commend the industry which had created and maintained in constant working order this useful establishment. In conjunction with a local missionary, some effort was made during my stay at Léopoldville, to obtain an amelioration of the condition of the sleeping-sickness people in the native hospital, but it was stated, in answer to my friend's representations, that nothing could be done in the way of building a proper hospital until plans now under consideration had been matured elsewhere. The structures I had visited, which the local medical staff greatly deplored, had endured for several years as the only form of hospital accommodation provided for the numerous native staff of the district.

The Government stores at Léopoldville are large and well built, and contain not only the goods the Government itself sends up river in its fleet of steamers, but also the goods of the various Concession Companies. As a rule, the produce brought down river by the Government steamers is transhipped direct into the railway trucks which run alongside the wharf, and is carried thence by train to Matadi for shipment to Europe. The various Companies carrying on operations on the Upper Congo, and who hold Concessions from the Congo Government, are bound, I was told, by Conventions to abstain from carrying, save within the limits of their Concessions, either goods or passengers. This interdiction extends to their own merchandise and to their own agents. Should they carry, by reason of imperative need, outside these limits any of their own goods or their own people, they are bound to pay to the Congo Government either the freight or passage money according to the Government tariff, just as though the goods or passengers had been conveyed on one of the Government vessels. The tariff upon goods and passengers carried along the interior waterways is a fairly high one, not perhaps excessive under the circumstances, but still one that, by reason of this virtual monopoly, can produce a yearly revenue which must go far towards maintaining the Government flotilla. By the estimates for 1902, published in the "Bulletin Officiel" of January this year, the transport service is credited with a production of 3,100,000 fr. of public revenue for 1902, while the expenditure for the same year is put at 2,023,376 fr. That this restriction of public conveyance to Government vessels alone is not altogether a public gain my own experience demonstrated. I had wished to leave Stanley Pool for the Upper Congo at an early date after my arrival in Léopoldville, but as the Government vessels were mostly crowded, I could not proceed with any comfort by one of these. The steam-ship "Flandre," one of the largest of these vessels, which left Léopoldville for Stanley Falls on the 22nd June, and by which I had, at first, intended to proceed, quitted port with more than twenty European passengers over her complement, all of whom, I was informed, would have to sleep on deck. I accordingly was forced to seek other means of travelling, and through the kindness of the Director of one of the large commercial Companies (the "Société Anonyme Belge du Haut-Congo") I found excellent accommodation, as a guest, on one of his steamers. Although thus an invited guest and not paying any passage money, special permission had to be sought from the Congo Government before this act of courtesy could be shown me, and I saw the telegram from the local authority, authorizing my conveyance to Chumbiri.

This commercial Company has three other steamers, but the interdiction referred to applies to the entire flotilla of trading vessels of Congolese nationality on the Upper River. Despite the fact that these vessels are not allowed to earn freight or passage, they are all, for their tonnage, heavily taxed, while the Government vessels, which earn considerable sums on transport of general goods and passengers, pay no taxes. The four vessels of the Société Anonyme Belge du Haut-Congo referred to, of which the largest is only, I believe, one of 30 tons, pay annually, I was informed, the following taxes:—

	Fr.
For permission to cut firewood	17,870
Licence for each steamer, according to her tonnage	400 to 600
The master of each vessel must be licensed, for which a tax of 20 fr. per annum is levied.	

Himself and each European member of the crew must then pay 30 fr. per annum as "imposition personnelle," whilst each native member of the crew costs his employers 3 fr. per head for engagement licence annually, and 10 fr. per head per annum as "imposition personnelle."

The "President Urban," the largest steamer of the Company referred to, under these various heads pays, I was informed, a sum of not less than 11,000 fr. in taxes per annum. Should she carry any of the agents of the Company owning her, or any of its goods, save within the restricted area of its Concession, her owners must pay to the Congo Government both passage money and freight on these, just as though they had been sent by one of the Government vessels.

No firewood may be cut by the public within half-an-hour's steaming distance of any of the Government wooding posts, which are naturally chosen at the best wooding sites available along the various waterways, so that the 10,000 fr. wood-cutting licence which the "President Urban" pays entitles her only to cut up for fuel such suitable timber as her crew may be able to find in the less accessible spots.

At F * I spent four days. I had visited this place in August 1887 when the line of villages comprising the settlement contained from 4,000 to 5,000 people. Most of these villages to-day are entirely deserted, the forest having grown over the abandoned sites, and the entire community at the present date cannot number more than 500 souls. There is no Government station at F *, but the Government telegraph line which connects Léopoldville with Coquilhatville, the headquarters of the Equator district, runs through the once townlands of the F * villages close to the river bank. The people of the riverside towns, and from 20 miles inland, have to keep the line clear of undergrowth, and in many places the telegraph road serves as a useful public path between neighbouring villages. Some of the natives of the neighbourhood complained that for this compulsory utilitarian service they had received no remuneration of any kind; and those at a distance that they found it hard to feed themselves when far from their homes they were engaged on this task. Inquiry in the neighbourhood established that no payment for this work had seemingly been made for fully a year.

Men are also required to work at the neighbouring wood-cutting post for the Government steamers, which is in charge of a native Headman or Kapita, who is under the surveillance of a European "Chef de Poste" at Bolobo, the nearest Government station, which lies about 40 miles up-stream. These wood-cutters, although required compulsorily to serve and sometimes irregularly detained, are adequately paid for their services.

The F * villages have to supply kwanga (the prepared cassava root already referred to) for the neighbouring wood-cutting post, and the quantity required of them is, they asserted, in excess of their means of supply and out of proportion to the value received in exchange. The supply required of them was fixed, I found, at 380 kwanga (or boiled cassava puddings) every six days, each pudding weighing from 4½ lb. to 6 lb., or a total of from 1,700 lb. to 1 ton weight of carefully prepared food-stuffs per week. For this a payment of one brass rod per kwanga is made, giving a sum of 19 fr. in all for the several villages whose task it is to keep the wood post victualled. These villages by careful computation I reckoned contained 240 persons all told—men, women, and children. In addition to preparing and carrying this food a considerable distance to the Government post, these people have to take their share in keeping the telegraph line clear and in supplying Government workmen. One elderly man was arrested at the period of my visit to serve as a soldier and was taken to Bolobo, 40 miles away, but was subsequently released upon representations made by a missionary who knew him. The number of wood-cutters at the local post is about thirty I was informed, so that the amount of food levied is beyond their requirements, and the excess is said to be sold by them at a profit to the crews of passing steamers. At one of the smallest of these F * villages, where there are not more than ten persons all told, and only three of these women able to prepare and cook the food, 40 kwanga (180 lb. to 270 lb. weight of food) had to be supplied every week at a payment of 40 rods (2 fr.). These people said: "How can we possibly plant and weed our gardens, seek and prepare and boil the cassava, make it into portable shape, and then carry it nearly a day's journey to the post? Moreover, if the kwanga we make are a little small or not well-cooked, or if we complain that the rods given us in settlement are too short, as they sometimes are, then we are beaten by the wood-cutters, and sometimes we are detained several days to cut firewood as a punishment."

Statements of this kind might be tediously multiplied.

The local mission station at F * requires much smaller kwanga than the Government size, getting from 1½ lb. to 2 lb. weight of food at the same price—viz., 1 rod. The kwanga made up for general consumption, as sold in local markets, weigh only about 1 lb. each. The Government requires, delivered free, even at considerable distances, from four and a-half to six times the weight of prepared food to that sold publicly for ½*d*.

In most parts of the Upper Congo the recognized currency consists of lengths of brass wire; these lengths varying according to the district. At one period the recognized length of a brass rod was 18 inches, but to-day the average length of a rod cannot be more than 8 or 9 inches. The nominal value of one of these rods is ½*d*., twenty of them being reckoned to the franc; but the intrinsic value, or actual cost of a rod to any importer of the brass wire direct from Europe, would come to less than a ¼*d*., I should say. Such as it is, clumsy and dirty, this is the principal form of currency known on the Upper Congo where, saving some parts of the French Congo I visited, European money is still quite unknown.

The reasons for the decrease of population at F * given me, both by the natives and by others, point to sleeping sickness as probably one of the principal factors. There has also been emigration to the opposite side of the river, to the French shore, but this course has never, I gather, been popular. The people have not easily accommodated themselves to the altered condition of life brought about by European Government in their midst. Where formerly they were accustomed to take long voyages down to Stanley Pool to sell slaves, ivory, dried fish, or other local products against such European merchandise as the Bateke middlemen around the Pool had to offer in exchange, they find themselves to-day debarred from all such form of activity.

The open selling of slaves and the canoe convoys, which once navigated the Upper Congo, have everywhere disappeared. No act of the Congo State Government has perhaps produced more laudable results than the vigorous suppression of this wide-spread evil. In the 160 miles' journey from Léopoldville to F * I did not see one large native canoe in mid-stream, and only a few small canoes creeping along the shore near to native villages. While the suppression of an open form of slave dealing has been an undoubted gain, much that was not reprehensible in native life has disappeared along with it. The trade in ivory has to-day entirely passed from the hands of the natives of the Upper Congo, and neither fish nor any other outcome of local industry now changes hands on an extensive scale or at any distance from home.

So far as I could observe in the limited time at my disposal, the people of F * now rarely leave their homes save when required by the local Government official at Bolobo to serve as soldiers, or woodcutters at one of the Government posts, or to convey the weekly supplies of food required of them to the nearest Government station. These demands for food-stuffs comprise fowls and goats for consumption by the European members of the Government staff at Léopoldville, or for passengers on the Government steamers. They emanate from the Chief of the post at Bolobo who, I understand, is required in so far as he can, to keep up this supply. In order to obtain this provision he is forced to exercise continuous pressure on the local population, and within recent times that pressure has not always taken the form of mere requisition. Armed expeditions have been necessary and a more forcible method of levying supplies adopted than the law either contemplated or justifies. Very specific statements as to the harm one of these recent expeditions worked in the country around F * were made to me during my stay there. The officer in command of the G * district, at the head of a band of soldiers passed through a portion of the district wherein the natives, unaccustomed to the duties expected of them, had been backward in sending in both goats and fowls.

The result of this expedition, which took place towards the end of 1900, was that in fourteen small villages traversed seventeen persons disappeared. Sixteen of these whose names were given to me were killed by the soldiers, and their bodies recovered by their friends, and one was reported as missing. Of those killed eleven were men, three women, and one a boy child of 5 years. Ten persons were tied up and taken away as prisoners, but were released on payment of sixteen goats by their friends, except one, a child, who died at Bolobo. In addition 48 goats were taken away and 225 fowls; several houses were burned, and a quantity of their owners' property either pillaged or destroyed. Representations on behalf of the injured villages were made to the Inspecteur d'État at Léopoldville, who greatly deplored the excesses of his subordinate, and sent to hold an inquiry and to pay compensation to the relatives of those killed and for the live-stock or goods destroyed or taken away. The local estimate of the damage done amounted to 71,730 brass rods (3,586 fr.), which included 20,500 brass rods (1,025 fr.), assessed as compensation for the seventeen people. Three of these were Chiefs, and the amount asked for would have worked out at about 1,000 brass rods (50 fr.) per head, not probably an extravagant estimate for human life, seeing that the goats were valued at 400 rods each (20 fr.). A total sum, I was told, of 18,000 brass rods (950 fr.) was actually paid to the injured villages by the Government Commissioner, who came from Stanley Pool; and this sum, it was said, was levied as a fine for his misconduct on the official responsible for the raid. I could not learn what other form of punishment, if any, was inflicted on this officer. He remained as the Government Representative for some time afterwards, was then transferred to another post in the immediate neighbourhood, and finally went home at the expiration of his period of service.

At Bolobo, where I spent ten days waiting for a steamer to continue my journey, a somewhat similar state of affairs prevails to that existing at F *. Bolobo used to be one of the most important native Settlements along the south bank of the Upper Congo, and the population in the early days of civilized rule numbered fully 40,000 people, chiefly of the Bobangi tribe. To-day the population is believed to be not more than 7,000 or 8,000 souls. The Bolobo men were famous in former days for their voyages to Stanley Pool and their keen trading ability. All of their large canoes have to-day disappeared, and while some of them still hunt hippopotami—which are still numerous in the adjacent waters—I did not observe anything like industry among them.

Indeed, it would be hard to say how the people now live or how they occupy their own time. They did not complain so much of the weekly enforced food supplies required of them, which would, indeed, seem to be an unavoidable necessity of the situation, as to the unexpected calls frequently made upon them. Neither rubber nor ivory is obtained in this neighbourhood. The food supply and a certain amount of local labour is all that is enforced. As woodcutters, station hands in the Government post, canoe paddlers, workers on the telegraph route or in some other public capacity, they are liable to frequent requisition.

The labour required did not seem to be excessive, but it would seem to be irregularly called for, unequally distributed, and only poorly remunerated, or sometimes not remunerated at all.

Complaints as to the manner of exacting service are much more frequent than complaints as to the fact of service being required. If the local official has to go on a sudden journey men are summoned on the instant to paddle his canoe, and a refusal entails imprisonment or a beating. If the Government plantation or the kitchen garden require weeding, a soldier will be sent to call in the women from some of the neighbouring towns. To the official this is a necessary public duty which he cannot but impose, but to the women suddenly forced to leave their household tasks and to tramp off, hoe in hand, baby on back, with possibly a hungry and angry husband at home, the task is not a welcome one.

One of the weightier tasks imposed upon the neighbourhood during my stay at Bolobo was the construction of a wooden pier at the Government beach whereat Government vessels might come alongside.

I visited this incompleted structure several times, and estimated that from 1,500 to 2,000 trees and saplings had already been used in its partial construction. All of these were cut down and carried in by the men of some of the neighbouring towns, and for this compulsory service no remuneration had, up to that date, I was on all sides informed, been made to any one of them. They were ordered, they said, to do it as a public duty. The timber needed had to be sought at a considerable distance, most of the trees had been carried some miles, and the task was not altogether an agreeable one. The chief complaint I heard directed against this work, however, was that the pier was being so badly put up that when finished it would be quite useless, and all their work would thus be thrown away. My own opinion of the structure was that this criticism was well founded, and that the first annual rise of the river would sweep most of the ill-laid timbers away.

The Bolobo people do not object so much to the regular food tax, just because this is regular, and they can prepare and regularly meet it, as to the sudden and unexpected labour tasks, such as canoe journeys, or this more onerous pier building. They could, I perceived, trace no connection between this hastily-conceived exaction on their time and labour and a system of general contribution in the public interest, which, to be readily admitted, should be clearly defined. Were a regular annual tax levied in money, or some medium of barter exchange serving as a legal currency, the people would in time be brought to see that a payment of this kind evenly distributed and enforced was, indeed, a public duty they were bound to acquit themselves of, and one their Government was justified in strictly enforcing; but they do not assign any such value to the unsystematic calls upon them which prevail to-day. To be hastily summoned from their usual home avocations, or even from their possibly habitual idleness, to perform one or other of the tasks indicated above, and to get neither food nor pay for their exertions, as is often the case, seems to these unprogressive people not a public service they are called upon to perform in the public interest, but a purely personal burden laid upon their bodies and their time by the local agent of an organization which, to them, would seem to exist chiefly for its own profit.

The weight of the kwanga required at Bolobo seemed to be less than that enforced at F*, and I found that this variance existed throughout the Upper Congo.

At Bolobo the kwanga loaves supplied to the Government post weighed each a little over 3 lb. That made for ordinary sale in the public market just over 1 lb.: one of each that I weighed myself gave 3 lb. 2 oz. to the Government loaf, and 13 oz. to that made for general consumption. The price paid in each case was the same—viz., one brass rod.

At the village of H*, some 4 or 5 miles from the Government post, which I visited, I found the village to number some forty adult males with their families. This village has to supply weekly to the Government post 400 of these loaves (say 1,250 lb. weight of food) for which a payment of 20 fr. (400 rods) is made. The people of H* told me that when short of cassava from their own fields for the preparation of this supply, they bought the root in the local market and had to pay for it in the raw state just twice what they received for the prepared and cooked product they delivered at the post. I had no means of verifying this statement, but I was assured by many persons that it was strictly true. In addition to supplying this food weekly, H* is liable to the usual calls for canoe paddlers, day labourers at the Government station (male and female), timber gatherers for the pier, and woodcutters at the local wood-post of the Government steamers.

There was a good deal of sickness in this town, and in that beyond it at the date of my visit. Sleeping sickness and, still more, small-pox. Both diseases have done much to reduce the population. Emigration to the French shore, once active, would seem now to have ceased. Efforts are made locally, to improve the physical and sanitary condition of the people, and improvements due to these efforts are becoming apparent, but I was given to understand that progress is very slow.

The insufficiency of food generally observable in this part of the Congo would seem to account for much sickness, and probably for the mental depression of the natives I so often observed, itself a frequent cause of disease. The Chief of the Government post at G* during a part of my stay there told me that he thought the district was quite exhausted, and that it must be ever increasingly difficult to obtain food from it for the public requirements of the local administration.

Some 40miles above Bolobo a large " camp d'instruction," with from 600 to 800 native recruits and a staff of several European officers is established at a place called Yumbi. I had, to my regret, no opportunity of visiting this camp, although I met one of its officers who very kindly invited me there, promising a hearty welcome. He informed me that native food supplies were fairly plentiful in the neighbourhood of this camp, and that the principal rations of the soldiers consisted of hippopotamus meat, the Congo in that neighbourhood affording a seemingly inexhaustible supply of these creatures.

In front of the house of one of the natives in a village, I saw some seventy hippopotamus skulls. The animals, I was told, had all been killed by one man. Many are speared, and some are shot by the native hunters with cap-guns. A somewhat considerable trade in these weapons appears to have been done until recently by the Government Agents in the district, and I found several of the Bolobo young men with guns of this description which they had bought at different times from the local official, generally paying for them with ivory tusks. The sale of these arms by Representatives of the Congo Government would seem to have ceased somewhat more than a year ago, since which date the holders of the guns have been exposed to some trouble in order to obtain licences. Dealing in or holding guns of this description would seem to be regulated by clearly drawn up Regulations, which, however, do not seem to have been observed until last year. A tax of 20 fr. is now levied on the issue of a licence to bear arms, which the law renders obligatory on every gun holder, but this tax is also collected in an irregular manner.

I learned while at Bolobo that a large influx from the I* district (which comprises the "Domaine de la Couronne") had lately taken place into the country behind G*. The nearest Settlement of these emigrants was said to be about 20 to 25 miles from G*, and I determined to visit this place. I spent three days on this journey, visited two large villages in the interior belonging to the K* tribe, wherein I found that fully half the population now consisted of refugees belonging to the L* tribe who had formerly dwelt near I*. I saw and questioned several groups of these people, whom I found to be industrious blacksmiths and brass-workers. These people consisted of old and young men, women, and children. They had fled from their country and sought an asylum with their friends the K* during the last four years. The distance they had travelled in their flight they put at about six or seven days' march—which I should estimate at from 120 to 150 miles of walking. They went on to declare, when asked why they had fled, that they had endured such ill-treatment at the hands of the Government officials and the Government soldiers in their own country that life had become intolerable, that nothing had remained for them at home but to be killed for failure to bring in a certain amount of rubber or to die from starvation or exposure in their attempts to satisfy the demands made upon them. The statements made to me by these people were of such a nature that I could not believe them to be true. The fact remained, however, that they had certainly abandoned their homes and all that they possessed, had travelled a long distance, and now preferred a species of mild servitude among the K * to remaining in their own country. I took careful note of the statements made to me by these people, which will be found in the transcript attached (Inclosure 1).* I subsequently found when at M * some days later, other L *, who confirmed the truth of the statements made to me at N *.

On reaching Bolobo in September I obtained information amply confirming the statements made to me. My own further inquiries at M * are embodied in the accompanying document (Inclosure 1).†

Leaving Bolobo on the 23rd July, I passed on up river in a small steam-launch I had been fortunate enough to secure for my private use. We touched at several points on the French shore, and on the 25th July reached Lukolela, where I spent two days. This district had, when I visited it in 1887, numbered fully 5,000 people; to-day the population is given, after a careful enumeration, at less than 600. The reasons given me for their decline in numbers were similar to those furnished elsewhere, viz., sleeping-sickness, general ill-health, insufficiency of food, and the methods employed to obtain labour from them by local officials and the exactions levied on them. The Lukolela district furnishes a small supply of rubber, which is required by the Local Government posts to be brought in at fixed periods as a general contribution. Food—"kwanga" and fish—are also required of the riverside dwellers. The towns I visited were very ill-kept and tumble-down, and bore no comparison, either in the class of dwelling-houses now adopted or in the extent of cultivated ground around them, to the condition in which these people formerly dwelt.

Several reasons for the increase of sickness and the great falling-off in the population of the district were stated by the local missionary, who has resided for many years at Lukolela, in two letters which he recently addressed to the Governor-General of the Congo State. A copy of these letters was handed to me by the writer—the Rev. John Whitehead—on my calling in at Lukolela on my way down river on the 12th September. I had no opportunity of verifying, by personal observation, the statements made by Mr. Whitehead in his letter, for my stay at Lukolela was only one of a few hours. I have, however, no right to doubt Mr Whitehead's veracity, and he declared himself prepared to accept full responsibility for the statements his letter contained. A copy of these letters is appended (Inclosure 2).‡

The Government post at Lukolela I did not visit, but viewed from the river it presents a charming aspect; well-built houses, surrounded by plantations of coffee-trees, extend for some distance along the shore.

From Lukolela I proceeded to O *, which I purposed visiting. O *, with its two adjoining villages, when I had last seen them in the autumn of 1887, had presented a scene of the greatest animation. The population of the three towns then numbered some 4,000 to 5,000 people—O * alone, it was estimated, containing at least 3,000. Scores of men had put off in canoes to greet us with invitations that we should spend the night in their village. On steaming into O *, I found that this village had entirely disappeared, and that its place was occupied by a large "camp d'instruction," where some 800 native recruits, brought from various parts of the Congo State, are drilled into soldierhood by a Commandant and a staff of seven or eight European officers and non-commissioned officers.

There is also a large plantation of coffee-trees, a telegraph office, and a trading store, but I could see no indications of native life beyond those dependent on these establishments. The once villages and their fields had been converted into a very well-laid-out and admirably-maintained military station. From the Commandant and his officers a cordial welcome was received. The camp as a military centre is excellently chosen, the situation of Irebu commanding not only the Lake Mantumba waterway, but one of the chief navigable channels of the Congo; and it is, moreover, situated opposite the estuary of the great Ubangi River, which is probably the most

* See p. 60. † See p. 60. ‡ See p. 64.

important Congo affluent. The Commandant informed me that a very large supply of native food, amply sufficient for the soldiers under his command, was supplied weekly by the natives of the surrounding district.

It is difficult to exactly estimate the number of soldiers enrolled and maintained by the Congo Government. There are, I think, four separate "camps d'instruction" upon the Upper Congo, each of which should have an effective of 700 men. The effective strengths of the companies of Manyuema, Lake Léopold II, Lualaba-Kasai, Aruwimi, and Ruzizi-Kivu were fixed respectively by Circular of the Governor-General, dated the 25th June, 1902, at 750, 475, 850, 450, and 875 men. There are many other companies of the "Force Publique" in the Congo State, and I think it might safely be estimated that the number of men with the colours does not amount to less than 18,000. By a Circular addressed to the local authorities, dated the 26th May last, the Governor-General stated that it was necessary to add 200 men to each of the camps in the Upper Congo. In the same Circular a proposed increase of the general strength of the army was indicated in the following terms:—

"Notre programme militaire est très vaste et sa réalisation exige une attention soutenue et de grands efforts, mais sans son exécution intégrale notre situation demeurera précaire.

"S'il le fallait, mais je ne pense pas même que ce soit nécessaire, le Gouvernement se montrerait disposé à augmenter dans une certaine mesure le contingent pour 1903."

The same Circular added that:—

"Certains districts en effet ne remplacent pas les miliciens décédés, désertés en cours de route et ceux réformés à leur arrivée au camp.

"De plus, pendant la période d'instruction dans les camps un grand nombre de déchets se produisent aussi parmi ces recrues, les transports de miliciens laissant encore a désirer."

The Commandant informed me that some of the natives who had fled into the French territory opposite ten years ago, when the Irebu tribes had deserted their homes, were now gradually returning to Congo State territory. I found, subsequently, that this was the case, the people alleging that since the rubber tax had been dropped in the Mantumba district they preferred returning to their home lands to remaining on the strange sites in French territory, to which they had fled when that tax was at work.

From Irebu I proceeded some 25 miles to Ikoko, once a large village on the north shore of Lake Mantumba. I remained in Lake Mantumba seventeen days visiting, during that time, the Government post at Bikoro on the east shore of the lake, and many native towns scattered around the lake side. I also ascended by boat one of the rivers falling into the lake, and visited three native villages in the forest situated along this waterway. Lake Mantumba is a fine sheet of water about 25 or 30 miles long and some 12 or 15 miles broad at the broadest part, surrounded by a dense forest. The inhabitants of the district are of the Ntomba tribe, and are still rude savages, using very fine bows and arrows and ill-made spears as their weapons. There are also in the forest country many families or clans of a dwarf race called Batwas, who are of a much more savage and untameable disposition than the Ntombas, who form the bulk of the population. Both Batwas and Ntombas are still cannibals, and cannibalism, although repressed and not so openly indulged in as formerly, is still prevalent in the district. The Mantumba people were, in the days before the establishment of Congo State rule, among the most active fishermen and traders of the Upper Congo. In fleets of canoes they used to issue out upon the main waters of the Congo and travel very great distances, fighting their way if necessary, in search of purchasers of their fish or slaves, or to procure these latter. All this has ceased and, save for small canoes used in catching fish, I saw neither on the lake itself nor at the many villages I touched along its shores, any canoes comparable to those so frequently seen in the past. A man I visited told me that a fine canoe he bought for 2,000 brass rods (100 fr.), in which to send the weekly imposition of fish to the local State post, had been kept by the official there, had been used to transport Government soldiers in, and was now attached to a Government wood-cutting post, which he named, out on the main river. He had received nothing for the loss of this canoe, and when I urged him to lay the matter before the local official responsible, who had doubtless retained the canoe in ignorance, he pulled up his loin cloth and, pointing to where he had been flogged with a chicotte, said: "If I complained I should only get more of these." Although afraid to complain locally, he declared he would be perfectly willing to accompany me if I would take him before one of the Congo Judges or, above all, down to Boma. I assured him that a statement such as that he had made to me would meet with attention at Boma, and that if he could prove its truth he would get satisfaction for the loss of the canoe.

Statements of a similar character, often supported by many witnesses, were made to me more than once during my journey around the lake, some of them pointing to far greater derelictions of duty. The same man told me, on the same occasion, that one of the Government officials of the district (the same man, indeed, who had retained the canoe) had recently given him three wives. The official, he declared, had been "making war" on a town in the forest I was then in, for failing to bring in its fixed food supply, and as a result of the punitive measures undertaken the town had been destroyed and many prisoners taken. As a result, several women so taken were homeless, and were distributed. "Wives were being given away that day," said my informant, "he gave me three, but another man got four." The man went on to say that one of these "wives" had since escaped, aided, as he complained, by one of his own townsmen, who was a slave from her own native town.

The population of the lake-side towns would seem to have diminished within the last ten years by 60 or 70 per cent. It was in 1893 that the effort to levy an india-rubber imposition in this district was begun, and for some four or five years this imposition could only be collected at the cost of continual fighting. Finding the task of collecting india-rubber a well nigh impossible one, the authorities abandoned it in this district, and the remaining inhabitants now deliver a weekly supply of food-stuffs for the up-keep of the military camp at Irebu, or the big coffee plantation at Bikoro. Several villages I visited supply also to the latter station a fortnightly tax of gum-copal, which the surrounding forests yield abundantly. Gum-copal is also exposed and washed up on the shores of the lake. The quantity of this commodity supplied by each village on which it is assessed is put at 10 bags per fortnight. Each bag is officially said to contain 25 kilog., so that the imposition would amount to a quarter of a ton weight per fortnight. I found, when trying to lift some of these bags I saw being packed at a native village I was in, that they must weigh considerably more than 25 kilog., so that I concluded that each sack represents that quantity net of gum-copal. There is a considerable loss in cleaning, chipping, and washing crude gum as collected. The quantity brought by each village would thus work out at 6½ tons per annum. When I visited the Government station at P *, the chief of that post showed me ten sacks of gum which he said had been just brought in by a very small village in the neighbourhood. For this quarter of a ton of gum-copal he said he had paid the village one piece of blue drill—a rough cotton cloth which is valued locally, after adding the cost of transport, at 11½ fr. a-piece. By the Congo Government "Bulletin Officiel" of this year (No. 4, April 1903) I found that 339½ tons of gum-copal were exported in 1902, all from the Upper Congo, and that this was valued at 475,490 fr. The value per ton would, therefore, work out at about 56*l.* The fortnightly yield of each village would therefore seem to be worth a maximum of 14*l.* (probably less), for which a maximum payment of 11½ fr. is made. At one village I visited I found the majority of the inhabitants getting ready the gum-copal and the supply of fish which they had to take to P * on the morrow. They were putting it into canoes to paddle across the lake—some 20 miles—and they left with their loads in the night from alongside my steamer. These people told me that they frequently received, instead of cloth, 150 brass rods (7½ fr.) for the quarter of a ton of gum-copal they took fortnightly.

The value of the annual payment in gum-copal made by each town would seem to be about 360*l.*, while at an average of 9 fr. as the remuneration each receives fortnightly, they would appear to receive some 10*l.* in annual return.

In the village of Montaka, at the south end of the lake, where I spent two days, the people seemed, during my stay, to be chiefly engrossed in the task of chipping and preparing the gum-copal for shipment to Bikoro, and in getting ready their weekly yield of fish for the same post. I saw the filling with gum of the ten basket-sacks taking place under the eyes of the Chief—who himself contributed—and a State sentry who was posted there. Each household in the town was represented at this final task, and every adult householder of Montaka shared in the general contribution. Assuming the population of Montaka at from 600 to 800—and it cannot now be more although a town of 4,000 souls ten years ago—fully 150 householders are thus directly affected by the collection and delivery, each fortnight, of this "impôt en nature," and are affected for the great majority of the days throughout the year.

Since for the 6½ tons of gum-copal which the 150 householders of Montaka contribute annually, they are seen to receive not more than a total payment of 10*l.* in the year—viz., 26 fortnightly payments of, on an average, say 9 fr. 50 c., giving 247 fr. annually—it follows that the remuneration each adult householder of Montaka receives for his entire year's work is the one hundred and fiftieth part of that total—or just 1*s.* 4*d.* This is just the value of an adult fowl in Montaka. I bought ten fowls, or chickens rather, the morning of my going away, and for the only reasonably sized one among them I gave 30 rods (1 fr. 50 c.), the others, small fledglings, ranging from 15 to 20 rods each (75 cents. to 1 fr.).

The 6½ tons of gum-copal supplied annually by these 150 householders being valued at about 364*l.*, it follows that each householder had contributed something like 2*l.* 8*s.* per annum in kind.

The labour involved may or may not be unduly excessive—but it is continuous throughout the year—each man must stay in his town and be prepared each week and fortnight to have his contribution ready under fear of summary punishment.

The natives engaged as workmen on my steamer were paid each a sum of 20 rods (1 fr.) per week for food rations only, and 100 rods (5 fr.) per month wages. One of these native workmen thus earned more in one week of my service—which was that of any other private establishment employing ordinary labour—than the Montaka householder got in an entire year for his compulsory public service rendered to the Government.

At other villages which I visited, I found the tax to consist of baskets, which the inhabitants had to make and deliver weekly as well as, always, a certain amount of food-stuffs—either kwanga or fish. These baskets are used at Bikoro in packing up the gum-copal for conveyance down the river and to Europe—the river transport being effected by Government steamers. The basket-makers and other workers complained that they were sometimes remunerated for their labour with reels of sewing cotton and shirt buttons (of which they had no use) when supplies of cloth or brass wire ran short at Bikoro. As these natives go almost entirely naked, I could believe that neither thread or shirt buttons were of much service to them. They also averred that they were frequently flogged for delay or inability to complete the tale of these baskets, or the weekly supply of food. Several men, including a Chief of one town, showed broad weals across their buttocks, which were evidently recent. One, a lad of 15 or so, removing his cloth, showed several scars across his thighs, which he and others around him said had formed part of a weekly payment for a recent shortage in their supply of food. That these statements were not all untrue was confirmed by my visit to P *, when the "domaine privé" store was shown to me. It had very little in it, and I learned that the barter stock of goods had not been replenished for some time. There appeared to be from 200 to 300 pieces of coarse cotton cloth, and nothing else, and as the cloth was visibly old, I estimated the value of the entire stock at possibly 15*l.* It certainly would not have fetched more if put up to auction in any part of the Upper Congo.

The instructions regulating the remuneration of the native contributors and the mode of exploitation of the "forêts domaniales" were issued in the "Bulletin Officiel" of 1896, under authority of Decrees dated the 30th October and the 5th December, 1892.

These general instructions require that:—

"L'exploitation se fait par les agents de l'Intendance, sous la direction du Commissaire de District.

"Tout ce qui se rapporte à l'exploitation du domaine privé doit être séparé nettement des autres services gouvernementaux.

"Les agents préposés à l'exploitation du domaine privé consacrent tous leurs soins au développement de la récolte du caoutchouc et des autres produits de la forêt.

"Quel que soit le mode d'exploitation adopté à cet effet, ils sont tenus d'accorder aux indigènes une rémunération qui ne sera en aucun cas inférieure au montant du prix de la main-d'œuvre nécessaire à la récolte du produit; cette rémunération est fixée par le Commissaire de District, qui soumet son tarif à l'approbation du Gouverneur-Général.

"L'Inspecteur d'État en mission vérifie si ce tarif est en rapport avec le prix de la main-d'œuvre; il veille à sa stricte application, et il examine si les conditions générales d'exploitation ne donnent lieu à aucune plainte justifiée.

"Il fait comprendre aux agents chargés du service que, par le fait de rétribuer équitablement l'indigène, ils emploient le seul moyen efficace d'assurer la bonne administration du domaine et de faire naître chez lui le goût et l'habitude du travail."

Both from the condition of the Domaine Privé Store I inspected at P*, and the obvious poverty and universal discontent of the native contributors, whose towns I visited during the seventeen days spent in Lake Mantumba, it was clear that these instructions had long since ceased to be operative. The responsibility for the non-application of such necessary regulations could not be attributed to the local officials, who, obviously, if left without the means of adequate remuneration could not themselves make good the oversights or omissions of their superiors. That these omissions form part of a systematic breach of instructions conceived in the interest of the native I do not assert, but it was most apparent that neither in Lake Mantumba nor the other portions of the Domaine Privé which I visited was any adequate provision made for inculcating the natives with any just appreciation of the value of work.

The station at Bikoro has been established as a Government plantation for about ten years. It stands on the actual site of the former native town of Bikoro, an important Settlement in 1893, now reduced to a handful of ill-kept, untidy huts, inhabited by only a remnant of its former expropriated population.

Another small village, Bomenga, stands on the other side of the Government houses; the plantation enveloping both villages, and occupying their old cassava fields and gardens, which are now planted with coffee trees. Further inland these give place to cocoa and india-rubber trees (*fantumia elastica*), and also to the indigenous Landolphia creeper, which is being extensively cultivated. The entire plantation covers 800 hectares. There are 70 kilom. of well-cleared pathway through it, one of these roads measuring 11 kilom. in almost a straight line; 400 workmen are employed, consisting in small part of local natives, but chiefly of men brought from a distance. One numerous group I saw I was informed were "prisoners" from the Ruki district. There are 140,000 coffee trees and 170,000 cocoa trees actually in the ground, the latter a later planting than the coffee. Last year the yield was: coffee 112 tons, and cocoa 7 tons, all of which, after cleaning and preparing at the Government depôt at Kinchasa, was shipped to Europe on the Government account. India-rubber planting was not begun until November 1901. There are now 248 hectares already under cultivation, having 700,000 young Landolphia creepers, and elsewhere on the plantation, on portions mainly given up to coffee growing, there are 50,000 *fantumia elastica* and 50,000 *manihot glaziovii* trees. The station buildings are composed entirely of native materials, and are erected entirely by local native labour. The Chief of the Post has very ably directed the work of this plantation, which engrosses all his time, and until quite recently he had no assistant. A subordinate official is now placed under his orders. When he took over the district he told me there were sixty-eight native soldiers attached to the post, which number he has now been able to reduce to nineteen. In the days when the india-rubber tax prevailed in Lake Mantumba there were several hundreds of soldiers required in that region. No rubber is now worked in the neighbourhood I am informed.

Despite the 70 kilom. of roadway through the plantation, much of which has to be frequently—indeed daily—traversed, the two Europeans have no means of locomotion provided them, and must make their daily inspection to various points of this large plantation on foot.

In addition to the control of this flourishing establishment, the Chief of the Post is the Executive Chief of the entire district, but it is evident that but little time or energy could be left to the most energetic official for duties outside the immediate scope of his work as a coffee and india-rubber grower, in addition to those "engrossing cares" the general instructions cited above impose upon the agents who exploit the State domain.

I have dwelt upon the condition of P* and the towns I visited around Lake Mantumba in my notes taken at the time, and these are appended hereto (Inclosure 3).* A careful investigation of the conditions of native life around the lake confirmed the truth of the statements made to me—that the great decrease in population, the dirty and ill-kept towns, and the complete absence of goats, sheep, or fowls—once very plentiful in this country—were to be attributed above all else to the continued effort made during many years to compel the natives to work india-rubber. Large bodies of native troops had formerly been quartered in the district, and the punitive measures undertaken to this end had endured for a considerable period.

* See p. 70.

During the course of these operations there had been much loss of life, accompanied, I fear, by a somewhat general mutilation of the dead, as proof that the soldiers had done their duty. Each village I visited around the lake, save that of Q * and one other, had been abandoned by its inhabitants. To some of these villages the people have only just returned; to others they are only now returning. In one I found the bare and burnt poles of what had been dwellings left standing, and at another—that of R *—the people had fled at the approach of my steamer, and despite the loud cries of my native guides on board, nothing could induce them to return, and it was impossible to hold any intercourse with them. At the three succeeding villages I visited beyond R *, in traversing the lake towards the south, the inhabitants all fled at the approach of the steamer, and it was only when they found whose the vessel was that they could be induced to return.

At one of these villages, S *, after confidence had been restored and the fugitives had been induced to come in from the surrounding forest, where they had hidden themselves, I saw women coming back carrying their babies, their household utensils, and even the food they had hastily snatched up, up to a late hour of the evening. Meeting some of these returning women in one of the fields I asked them why they had run away at my approach, and they said, smiling, "We thought you were Bula Matadi" (*i.e.*, "men of the Government"). Fear of this kind was formerly unknown on the Upper Congo; and in much more out-of-the-way places visited many years ago the people flocked from all sides to greet a white stranger. But to-day the apparition of a white man's steamer evidently gave the signal for instant flight.

The chief of the P * post told me that a similar alarm reigned almost everywhere in the country behind his station, and that when he went on the most peaceful missions only a few miles from his house the villages were generally emptied of all human beings when he entered them, and it was impossible in the majority of cases to get into touch with the people in their own homes. It was not so in all cases, he said, and he instanced certain villages where he could go certain of a friendly reception, but with the majority, he said, he had found it quite impossible to ever find them "at home." He gave, as an explanation, when I asked for the reason of this fear of the white man, that as these people were great savages, and knew themselves how many crimes they had committed, they doubtless feared that the white man of the Government was coming to punish their misconduct. He added that they had undoubtedly had an "awful past" at the hands of some of the officials who had preceded him in the local administration, and that it would take time for confidence to be restored. Men, he said, still came to him whose hands had been cut off by the Government soldiers during those evil days, and he said there were still many victims of this species of mutilation in the surrounding country. Two cases of the kind came to my actual notice while I was in the lake. One, a young man, both of whose hands had been beaten off with the butt ends of rifles against a tree, the other a young lad of 11 or 12 years of age, whose right hand was cut off at the wrist. This boy described the circumstances of his mutilation, and, in answer to my inquiry, said that although wounded at the time he was perfectly sensible of the severing of his wrist, but lay still fearing that if he moved he would be killed. In both these cases the Government soldiers had been accompanied by white officers whose names were given to me. Of six natives (one a girl, three little boys, one youth, and one old woman) who had been mutilated in this way during the rubber régime, all except one were dead at the date of my visit. The old woman had died at the beginning of this year, and her niece described to me how the act of mutilation in her case had been accomplished. The day I left Lake Mantumba five men whose hands had been cut off came to the village of T * across the lake to see me, but hearing that I had already gone away they returned to their homes. A messenger came in to tell me, and I sent to T * to find them, but they had then dispersed. Three of them subsequently returned, but too late for me to see them. These were some of those, I presume, to whom the official had referred, for they came from the country in the vicinity of P * station. Statements of this character, made both by the two mutilated persons I saw and by others who had witnessed this form of mutilation in the past, are appended (Inclosure 4).*

The taxes levied on the people of the district being returnable each week or fortnight, it follows that they cannot leave their homes. At some of the villages I visited near the end of Lake Mantumba the fish supplies have to be delivered weekly to the military camp at Irebu, or when the water is high in the lake

* See p. 76.

and fish harder to catch, every ten days. The distance from Irebu of one of these towns could not have been less than 45 miles. To go and come between their homes and the camp involved to the people of this town 90 miles of canoe paddling, and with the lake stormy and its waters rough—as is often the case—the double journey would take at least four days. This consumption of time must be added to that spent in the catching of the fish, and as the punishment for any falling off in quantity or delay in delivery is not a light one, the Chief responsible for the tax stoutly opposes any one quitting the town. Some proof of this incidentally arose during my stay, and threatened to delay my journey. Being short-handed I sought, when at Ikoko, to engage six or seven young men of the town as woodcutters to travel on board the steamer. I proposed to engage them for two or three months, and offered good wages, much more than by any local service they could hope to earn. More men offered than I needed, and I selected six. The State Chief of the village hearing of this at once came to me to protest against any of his people leaving the town, and said that he would have all the youths I had engaged tied up and sent over to the Government official at Bikoro. There were at the time three soldiers armed with Albini rifles quartered at Ikoko, and the Chief sent for them to arrest my would-be crew. The Chief's argument, too, was perfectly logical. He said, "I am responsible each week for 600 rations of fish which must be delivered at Bikoro. If it fails I am held responsible and will be punished. I have been flogged more than once for a failure in the fish supply, and will not run any risks. If these men go I shall be short-handed, therefore they must stay to help in getting the weekly tax." I was forced to admit the justice of this argument, and we finally arrived at a compromise. I promised the Chief that, in addition to paying wages to the men I took, a sum representing the value to him of their labour should be left at Ikoko, so that he might hire extra hands to get the full quantity of fish required of him. S I admitted that he had been forced to flog men from villages which failed in their weekly supplies, but that he had for some months discontinued this course. He said that now he put defaulters into prison instead. If a village which was held to supply, say, 200 rations of fish each week brought only 180 rations, he accepted no excuse, but put two men in "block." If thirty rations were wanting he detained three of the men, and so on—a man for each ten rations. These people would remain prisoners, and would have to work at Bikoro, or possibly would be sent to Coquilhatville, the administrative head-quarters of the Equator district, until the full imposition came in.

I subsequently found when in the neighbourhood of Coquilhatville that summary arrest and imprisonment of this kind for failure to complete the tale of local imposition is of constant occurrence. The men thus arrested are kept often in the "chain gang" along with other prisoners, and are put to the usual class of penitential work. They are not brought before or tried by any Court or sentenced to any fixed term of imprisonment, but are merely detained until some sort of satisfaction is obtained, and while under detention are kept at hard work.

Indeed, I could not find that a failure to meet the weekly tax is punishable by law and no law was cited to me as a warrant for this summary imprisonment, but if such a law exists it is to be presumed that it does not treat the weekly taxpayers' failure as a grave criminal offence. The men taken are frequently not those in fault; the requisitioning authority cannot discriminate. He is forced to insure compliance with the demands imposed on each village, and the first men to hand from the offending community of necessity have to pay in the chain-gang the general failure and possibly the individual fault of others. Men taken in this way are sometimes not seen again in their own homes. They are either taken to distant Government stations as workmen, or are drafted as soldiers into the Force Publique. The names of many men thus taken from the Mantumba district were given to me, and in some cases their relatives had heard of their death in distant parts of the country. This practice was, I believe, more general in the past, but that it still exists to-day, and on an extensive scale, I had several instances of observing in widely separated districts. The officials effecting these arrests do not seem to have any other course open to them, unless it be a resort to military punitive measures or to individual corporal punishment; while the natives assert that, as the taxes are unequally distributed, and their own numbers constantly decreasing, the strain upon them each week often becomes unbearable, and some of their number will shirk the constantly recurring unwelcome task. Should this shirking become general instead of being confined to individuals, punitive measures are undertaken against the refractory community. Where these do not end in fighting, loss of life and destruction of native property, they entail very heavy fines which are levied on the defaulting village. An expedition of the minor kind occurred some five months before my presence in Lake Mantumba. The village in fault was that of R *, the one where when I sought to visit it no people would remain to face me. This village was said to have been some three weeks in arrears with the fish it was required to supply to the camp at Irebu. An armed force occupied it, commanded by an officer, and captured ten men and eight canoes. These canoes and the prisoners were conveyed by water to Irebu, the main force marching back by land.

My informant, who dwelt in a village near R *, which I was then visiting, said he saw the prisoners being taken back to Irebu under guard of six black soldiers, tied up with native rope so tightly that they were calling aloud with pain. The force halted the night in his town. These people were detained at Irebu for ten days until the people of R * had brought in a supply of fish and had paid a fine. Upon their release two of these men died, one close to Irebu and the other within sight of the village I was in, and two more, my informant added, died soon after their return to R *. A man, who saw them, said the prisoners were ill and bore the marks on wrists and legs of the thongs used in tying them. Of the canoes captured only the old ones were returned to R *, the better ones being confiscated.

The native relating this incident added that he thought it stupid of the white men to take both men and canoes away from a small place like R * as a punishment for a shortage in its fish supply. "The men were wanted to catch fish and so were the canoes," he said, "and to take both away only made it harder for the people of R* to perform their task." I went to R* in the hope of being able to verify the truth of this and other statements made to me as to the hardships recently inflicted on its people by reason of their disobedience, but owing to their timidity, to whatever cause this might have been due, it was impossible for me to get into touch with any of them. That a very close watch is kept on the people of the district and their movements is undoubted. In the past they escaped in large numbers to the French territory, but many were prevented by force from doing this, and numbers were shot in the attempt.

To-day the Congolese authorities discourage intercourse of this kind, not by the same severe measures as formerly, but probably none the less effectively. By a letter dated the 2nd July, 1902, the present Commandant of the camp of Irebu wrote as follows to the Rev. E. V. Sjoblom, a Swedish Missionary (since dead), who was then in charge of the Mission at Ikoko:

"Je vous serais bien obligé de ne pas permettre à vos jeunes gens de se rendre sur la rive Française et vendre aux indigènes Français qui ont fui notre rive, des vivres, produits du travail de nos indigènes, que eux-mêmes n'ont pas fui et ne se sont pas soustraits au travail que nous leur avons imposé."

From Lake Mantumba I proceeded to the immediate neighbourhood of Coquilhatville, where five days were spent, chiefly at native communities which stretch for some distance along the east bank of the Congo. These villages formerly extended for 15 miles, and were then filled with a numerous population. To-day they are broken up into isolated settlements, each much reduced in numbers, and with (in most cases) the houses badly constructed. There were no goats or sheep to be seen, whereas formerly these were very plentiful, and food for the crew was only obtained with difficulty. In the village of V *, which I twice visited, the usual tax of food-stuff, with firing for the steamers, had to be supplied to Coquilhatville, which is distant only some 6 miles. A Government sentry was quartered here, who, along with one of the Chiefs of the town, spoke fully of the condition of the people. The sentry himself came from the Upper Bussira River, some hundreds of miles distant. This was, he said, his third period of service with the Force Publique. As his reason for remaining so long in this service he asserted that, as his own village and country were subjected to much trouble in connection with the rubber tax, he could not live in his own home, and preferred, he said, laughing, "to be with the hunters rather than with the hunted." Both a Chief V* and this sentry represented the food taxes levied on this village as difficult for the people to collect, and only inadequately remunerated. There would appear in all these statements a contradiction in terms. The contributions required of the natives are continually spoken of as a "tax," and are as continually referred to as being "paid for" or "remunerated." It is obvious that taxes are neither bought nor sold, but the contradiction is only one of terms. The fact is that the weekly or fortnightly contributions everywhere required of the native communities I visited are levied as taxes, or "prestations annuelles," by authority of a Royal Decree of the Sovereign of the Congo State. The Decrees authorizing the levy of these taxes are dated the 6th October, 1891 (Article 4), that of the 5th December,

1892, and (for the district of Manyeuma) that of the 28th November, 1893. There is a further Decree, dated the 30th April, 1897, requiring the establishment and up-keep by native Chiefs of coffee and cocoa plantations. I nowhere saw or heard of such plantations existing as institutions maintained by the natives themselves. There are plantations of both existing, but these are the property of either the Government itself or of some European agency acting with its sanction and partly in its interests, on lands declared as public lands. With regard to the two first Decrees establishing a system of taxation, provision was made for the investiture of a native Chief recognized by the local Government authority, who should give to this Chief a copy of the *procès-verbal*, as registered in the public archives, and a medal or other symbol of office. With this investiture a list was ordered to be drawn up, indicating the name of the village, its exact situation, the names of the Headmen, the number of its houses, and the actual number of the population—men, women, and children. The Decree then goes on to provide for the manner in which the "prestations annuelles" imposed on each village were to be assessed. A list of the products to be furnished by each village—such as maize, sorghum, palm oil, ground-nuts, &c., corvées of workmen or soldiers—was to be drawn up by the Commissaire of the district. It was provided that this list should also indicate the lands which were to be cleared and cultivated under the direction of the Chiefs, the nature of such cultivation put in hand, and "all other works of public utility which might be prescribed in the interest of public health, the exploitation or improvement of the soil, or otherwise." These lists had first of all to be submitted for his approval to the Governor-General. I could not find that, save in respect of the strict enforcement of the contributions, this law was generally or rigorously observed. In many villages where I asked for it no copy of any *procès-verbal* could be produced, and in several cases no act of investiture of the local Chief seemed to have ever taken place. Plantations, such as those outlined in the Decree which made provision for them, nowhere exist in any part of the country I traversed. The enumeration of the houses and people had in some instances been made, I was informed, but it was many years ago; and as the population had since greatly declined, this enumeration could not to-day always serve as an accurate basis on which to reckon the extent of the existing contribution.

At the village of A*, which I visited twice during my stay in the neighbourhood, A furnished me with particulars as to his own public obligations. His portion of A* had formerly been extensive, and at the date when an enumeration was made contained many people. To-day it has only six adult householders, including himself, inhabiting now eleven huts in all, with their wives and children—a total population of twenty-seven persons. My attention was first drawn to him and his village by my meeting with a young boy—a lad of 7 years old, I should judge—whom I found in the village of U* as the recently acquired property of B. B told me he had bought the boy, C, from A for 1,000 rods (50 fr.). A, he said, having to meet a fine imposed by the Commissaire-Général for shortage in some of the weeks' supplies, and being 1,000 rods short of the amount required, had pawned his nephew C to him for that sum. This had taken place on the , and my interview with B and the boy took place on the . The next day I walked to A*, which lies within a few miles of Coquilhatville, and saw A and his town and people. There were then exactly eight men in the town, including himself; but as two have since been detained as prisoners at Coquilhatville for deficiencies in the weekly supplies, there were, when I last saw A* in September, only six adult males there. The weekly imposition levied on A's part of A* was—

Kwanga	150 rations (about 700 lbs. weight of food).
Fish	95 rations.
Palm thatching mats	900
Firewood, for steamer fuel	2 canoe loads.

Also each week one large fresh fish or, in lieu thereof, two fowls for the European table at Coquilhatville. In addition, the men had to help in hunting game in the woods for the European station staff.

The payments made each week for these supplies (when they were completely delivered) were:—

	Fr.	c.
Kwanga, 150 rods	7	50
Fish, 95 rods	4	75
Palm mats, 180 rods	9	0
2 canoe loads firewood, 1 rod	0	5
	21	30

Payments for firewood were made by a paper receipt to be redeemed annually, but A told me he had refused to accept the annual payment of 50 rods (2 fr. 50 c.) for 104 canoe loads of wood delivered during the twelve months. To obtain these supplies A had frequently to purchase both fish and palm mats. The fish, as a rule, cost from 10 to 20 rods per ration, and the market price of thatching mats is 1 rod each; while the kwanga, which the Government paid 1 rod for, fetched just 5 rods each in the open market. The value of A's weekly contribution was, according to current prices, as follows :—

	Rods.	Value.
		Fr. c.
150 rations, kwanga, each 5 rods	750	37 50
95 ,, fish, each 10 rods	950	47 50
900 palm mats, each 1 rod..	900	45 0
2 canoe loads firewood, each 20 rods	40	2 0
Total	..	132 0

Thus, taking no account of the fresh fish or fowls, A's small township of eight households lost 110 fr. 70 c. per week. At the year's end, while they had contributed 6,864 fr. worth of food and material to the local Government station, they had received as recompense 1,107 fr. 60 c. A, personally, had a larger share of the tax to meet than any of the others, and I found that the value of his personal contribution reached 80*l.* 3*s.* 4*d.* per annum by local prices, while he received in settlement 9*l.* 15*s.* in Government payments. He therefore contributed on his household of two wives, his mother, and dependents, inhabiting three grass and cane huts, an amount equal to 70*l.* 8*s.* 4*d.* per annum net.

These figures, I found on inquiry, were confirmed as correct by those who were acquainted with the local conditions. A stated that his elder brother, D, was in reality Chief of the township, but that some eight months previously D had been arrested for a deficiency in the fish and kwanga supplies. The Commissaire had then imposed a fine of 5,000 rods (250 fr.) on the town, which A, with the assistance of a neighbouring Chief named C, had paid. D was not thereupon at once released, and soon afterwards escaped from the prison at Coquilhatville, and remained in hiding in the forest. Soldiers came from the Government station and tied up eight women in the town. A and all the men ran away upon their coming, but he himself returned in the morning. The Commissaire-Général visited A*, and told A that as D had run away he (A) was now the recognized Chief of the town. He was then ordered to find his fugitive brother, whose whereabouts he did not know, and a town in the neighbourhood name E, suspected of harbouring him, was fined 5,000 rods, Since that date, although D had returned to A* to reside, A had been held against his will, as responsible Chief of the town. He was a young man of about 23 or 24 years of age I should say. He had repeatedly, he stated, begged to be relieved of the honour thrust upon him, but in vain. His brother, D, had recently been put again in prison at Coquilhatville in connection with the loss of two cap-guns furnished him when Chief in order to procure game for the local white men's table. The present impositions laid on A* were, A asserted, much more than it was possible for him to meet. He had repeatedly appealed to the Commissaire-Général and other officers at Coquilhatville, including the law officer, begging them to visit his town and see for themselves—as I might see—that he was speaking the truth. But, so far, no one would listen to him, and he had been always rebuffed. On the last occasion of his making this appeal, only three days before I saw him, he had been threatened with prompt imprisonment if he failed in his supplies, and he said he now saw no course before him but flight or imprisonment. He could not run away, he said, and leave his mother and dependents; besides, he would be surely found, and, in any case, whatever town harboured him would be fined as E had been.

On a certain Sunday, when he had gone in with the usual weekly supplies, which are returnable on Sundays, he had been short of eight rations of fish and ten rations of kwanga and 330 palm mats, representing a value of 84 rods (4 fr. 20 c.), as estimated on the scale of Government payments. On the same date the other and larger portion of A* town was also short of its tale of supplies, and a fine of 5,000 brass rods (250 fr.) was imposed upon the collective village. A's share of this fine was fixed by the natives among themselves at 2,000 rods, of which 1,000 rods were to be his own personal contribution. Having himself now no money and no other means of obtaining it, he had pledged—with the consent of the father—his little nephew, D's son, whom I had seen with B. In making inquiry, A's story received much confirmation. He was, at any rate, known as a man of very good character, and everything pointed to his statement being true. On my return down river, I again saw A, who came after nightfall to see me, in the hope that I might perhaps be able to help him. He said that, since I had left a month previously, two of the boys of his town had been detained at Coquilhatville as prisoners when taking the rations on two successive weeks, owing to a deficiency on each occasion of 18 rods in value (90 cents.), and that these two boys—whose names he gave me—were still in prison. He had been that very day, he said, to beg that they might be released, but had failed, and there were now only five adult males in his village, including himself.

While in Coquilhatville on this mission, he declared that he had seen eleven men brought in from villages in the neighbourhood, who were put in prison before him—all of them on account of a shortage in the officially fixed scale of supplies required from their districts. I offered to take him away with me in order to lay his case before the judicial authorities elsewhere, but he refused to leave his mother. That A's statements were not so untrustworthy as on the face they might seem to be, was proved a few days later by a comparison of his case with that of another village I visited. This was a town named W *, lying some three miles inland in a swampy forest situated near the mouth of the X * River. On quitting Coquilhatville, I proceeded to the mouth of this river, which enters the Congo some forty-five miles above that station, and I remained two days in that neighbourhood. Learning that the people of the immediate neighbourhood had recently been heavily fined for failure in their food supplies, which have to be delivered weekly at that station, and that these fines had fallen with especial severity on W *, I decided to visit that town.

It was on the 21st August that I visited W *, where I found that the statements made to me were borne out by my personal observation. The town consisted of a long single street of native huts lying in the midst of a clearing in the forest. In traversing it from end to end I estimated the number of its people at about 600 all told.

At the upper end of the town a number of men and women assembled, and some came forward, when they made a lengthy statement to the following effect. From this upper end of the town wherein I was 100 rations of kwanga had to be supplied weekly, and thirty fowls at a longer interval. These latter were for the use of Coquilhatville, while the kwanga was very largely for the use of the wood-cutters at the nearest Government wood-cutting post on the main river. The usual prices for these articles, viz., for the kwanga, 1 rod each, and for the fowls 20 rods were paid. The people also had to take each week 10 fathoms of firewood to the local wood-post, for which they often got no payment, and their women were required twice a week to work at the Government coffee plantation which extends around the wood-post.

I saw some bundles of firewood being got ready for carriage to this place. They were large and very heavy, weighing, I should say, from 70 to 80 lb. each. Some months earlier, at the beginning of the year, owing, as they said, to their failure to send in the fowls to Coquilhatville, an armed expedition of some thirty soldiers, commanded by a European officer, had come thence and occupied their town. At first they had fled into the forest, but were persuaded to come in. On returning, many of them—the principal men—were at once tied up to trees. The officer informed them that as they had failed in their duty they must be punished. He required first that twenty-five men should be furnished as workmen for Government service. These men were taken away to serve the Government as labourers, and those addressing me did not know where these men now were. They gave eighteen names of men so taken, and said that the remaining seven came from the lower end of the town through which I had passed on entering, where the relatives themselves could give me particulars if I wished. The twenty-five men had not since been seen in W *, nor had any one there cognizance of their whereabouts. The officer had then imposed as further punishment a fine of 55,000 brass rods (2,750 fr.)—110*l.* This sum they had been forced to pay, and as they had no other means of raising so large a sum they had, many of them, been compelled to sell their children and their wives. I saw no live-stock of any kind in W * save a very few fowls—possibly under a dozen—and it seemed, indeed, not unlikely that, as these people asserted, they had great difficulty in always getting their supplies ready. A father and mother stepped out and said that they had been forced to sell their son, a little boy called F, for 1,000 rods to meet their share of the fine. A widow came and declared that she had been forced, in order to meet her share of the fine, to sell her daughter G, a little girl whom I judged from her description to be about 10 years of age. She had been sold to a man in Y *, who was named, for 1,000 rods, which had then gone to make up the fine.

A man named H stated that while the town was occupied by the soldiers, a woman who belonged to his household, named I, had been shot dead by one of the soldiers. Her husband, a man named K, stepped forward and confirmed the statement. They both declared that the woman had quitted her husband's house to obey a call of Nature, and that one of the soldiers, thinking she was going to run away, had shot her through the head. The soldier was put under arrest by the officer, and they said they saw him taken away a prisoner when the force was withdrawn from their town, but they knew nothing more than this. They did not know if he had been tried or punished. No one of them had ever been summoned to appear, no question had been addressed to them, and neither had the husband nor the head of I's household received any compensation for her death. Another woman named L, the wife of a man named M, had been taken away by the native sergeant who was with the soldiers. He had admired her, and so took her back with him to Coquilhatville. Her husband heard she had died there of small-pox, but he did not know anything certain of her circumstances after she had been taken away from W *. A man named N said he had sold his wife O to a man in Y * for 900 rods to meet his share of the fine.

It was impossible for me to verify these statements, or to do much beyond noting down, as carefully as possible, the various declarations made. I found, however, on returning to Y *, that the statements made with regard to the little boy F and the girl G were true. These children were both in the neighbourhood, and owing to my intervention F was restored to his parents. The girl G, I was told, had again changed hands, and was promised in sale to a town on the north bank of the Congo, named Iberi, whose people are said to be still open cannibals. Through the hands of the local missionary this transfer was prevented, and I paid the 1,000 rods to her original purchaser, and left G to be restored to her mother from the Mission. I saw her there on the 9th September, after she had been recovered through this missionary's efforts, while about to be sent to her parent.

With regard to the quantity of food supplies levied upon W *, I did not obtain the total amount required of the entire community, but only that which the upper end of the town furnished. The day of my visit happened to be just that when the kwanga, due at the local wood-post, was being prepared for delivery on the morrow. I saw many of the people getting their shares ready. Each share of kwanga, for which a payment of 1 rod is made by the Government, consisted of five rolls of this food tied together. One of these bundles of five rolls I sought to buy, offering the man carrying it 10 rods—or ten times what he was about to receive for it from the local Government post. He refused my offer, saying that, although he would like the 10 rods, he dare not be a bundle of his ration short. One of these bundles was weighed and found to weigh over 15 lb. This may have been an extraordinarily large bundle, although I saw many others which appeared to be of the same size. I think it would be safe to assume that the average of each ration of kwanga required from this town was not less than 12 lb. weight of cooked and carefully prepared food—a not ungenerous offering for ½*d*. By this computation the portion of W * I visited sends in weekly 1,200 lb. weight of food at a remuneration of some 5 fr. Cooked bread-stuffs supplied at 9 or 10 fr. per ton represent, it must be admitted, a phenomenally cheap loaf. At the same time with this kwanga, being prepared for the Government use, I saw others being made up for general public consumption. I bought some of these, which were going to the local market, at their current market value, viz., 1 rod each. On weighing them I found they gave an average of 1 lb. each. The weight of food-stuffs required by the Government from this town would seem to have exceeded in weight twelve times that made up for public consumption.

Whilst I was in Y * a fresh fine of 20,000 rods (1,000 fr.) was in course of collection among the various households along the river bank. This fine had been quite recently imposed by direction of —— for a further failure on the part of the Y * towns in the supply of food-stuffs from that neighbourhood. I saw at several houses piles of brass rods being collected to meet it, and in front of one of these houses I counted 2,700 rods which had been brought together by the various dependents of that family; 6,000 rods of this further fine was, I was told, to be paid by W *, which had not then recovered from its previous much larger contribution. The W * men begged me to intervene, if I could at all help them to escape this further imposition. One of them—a strong, indeed a splendid-looking man—broke down and wept, saying that their lives were useless to them, and that they knew of no means of escape from the troubles which were gathering around them. I could only assure these people that their obvious course to obtain relief was by appeal to their own constituted authorities, and that if their circumstances were clearly understood by those responsible for these fines, I trusted and believed some satisfaction would be forthcoming.

These fines, it should be borne in mind, are illegally imposed: they are not "fines of Court"; are not pronounced after any judicial hearing, or for any proved offence against the law, but are quite arbitrarily levied according to the whim or ill-will of the executive officers of the district, and their collection, as well as their imposition, involves continuous breaches of the Congolese laws. They do not, moreover, figure in the account of public revenues in the Congo "Budgets;" they are not paid into the public purse of the country, but are spent on the needs of the station or military camp of the officer imposing them, just as seems good to this official.

I can nowhere learn upon what legal basis, if any, the punishments inflicted upon native communities or individuals for failure to comply with the various forms of "prestations" rest.

These punishments are well-nigh universal and take many shapes, from punitive expeditions carried out on a large scale to such simpler forms of fine and imprisonment as that lately inflicted on U *.

I cannot find in the Penal Code of the Congo Statute Book that a failure to meet or a non-compliance with any form of prestation or *impôt* is anywhere defined as a crime; and so far as I can see no legal sanction could be cited for any one of the punishments so often inflicted upon native communities for this failure.

By a Royal Decree of the 11th August, 1886, provision was made for the punishments to be inflicted for infractions of the law not punishable by special penalties.

Since no special penalty in law would seem to have been provided for cases of failure or refusal to comply with the demands of the tax-gatherer, it would seem to be in the terms of this Decree that the necessary legal sanctions could alone lie.

But this Decree provides for all otherwise unspecified offences far other punishments, and far other modes of inflicting them than so many of those which came to my notice during my brief journey.

Article 1 of this Decree provides that:—

"Les contraventions aux décrets, ordonnances, arrêtes, règlements d'administration intérieure et de police, à l'égard desquelles la loi ne détermine pas de peines particulières, seront punies d'un à sept jours de servitude pénale et d'une amende n'excédant pas 200 fr., ou d'une de ces peines seulement."

Article 2 requires that:—

"Ces peines seront appliquées par les Tribunaux de l'État conformément aux lois en vigueur."

It would be manifestly impossible to say that either in form or mode of procedure this law had been applied to the failure of the community at W * to meet the demands made upon them.

Neither the summary arrest and taking away from their homes of the men whose names were given to me nor the imposition of the very heavy fine of brass rods find any warrant in this page of the Congo Statute Book.

If a legal warrant exists for the action of the authorities in this case—as in the numerous other cases brought to my notice—that action would still call for much adverse comment.

The amount of the fine levied on W * was not only out of all proportion to the gravity of the offence committed, but was of so crushing a character as to preclude the possibility of its being acquitted by any reasonable or legitimate means that community disposed of.

Among the earliest enactments of civilized administrations, recognition has invariably been given to the pronouncement that no fine or imposition, or exaction, shall exceed the powers of the person on whom it is imposed to meet it.

But if, as I venture to presume, no Congolese law or judicial pronouncement exists, or could exist, for the levying, in this manner, of these fines, very explicit Regulations for the treatment of the natives on general lines and their right to judicial protection do exist.

In the "texte coordonné des diverses instructions relatives aux rapports des Agents de l'État avec les indigènes," which are to be found in the "Bulletin Officiel" of 1896 (p. 255), these Regulations are published at length and would seem, textually, to leave little room for criticism.

Were their application enforced it is abundantly clear that a situation such as that I found in existence at W * could not arise, and much of the general unhappiness and distress of the natives I witnessed on all sides would disappear along with the fines and much also of the "prestations," within the first month of the translation into action of these Regulations.

One paragraph only need here be cited to emphasize the bearing and import of these remarks:—

"Les agents doivent se souvenir que les peines disciplinaires prévues par le règlement de discipline militaire ne sont applicables qu'aux recrutés militaires, uniquement pour des infractions contre la discipline, et dans les conditions spécialement prévues par le dit règlement.

"Elles ne sont applicables, sous aucune prétexte, aux serviteurs de l'État non militaire ni aux indigènes, que ceux-ci soient ou non en rébellion vis-à-vis de l'Etat.

"Ceux d'entre eux qui sont prévenus de delits ou crimes doivent être déférés aux Tribunaux compétents et jugés conformément aux lois."

At neither W * nor Y * is any rubber worked. With my arrival in the Lulongo River, I was entering one of the most productive rubber districts of the Congo State, where the industry is said to be in a very flourishing condition. The Lulongo is formed by two great feeders—the Lopori and Maringa Rivers—which, after each a course of some 350 miles through a rich, forested country, well peopled by a tribe named Mongos, unite at Bassankusu, some 120 miles above where the Lulongo enters the Congo. The basins of these two rivers form the Concession known as the A.B.I.R., which has numerous stations, and a staff of fifty-eight Europeans engaged in exploiting the india-rubber industry, with head-quarters at Bassankusu. Two steamers belonging to the A.B.I.R. Company navigate the waterways of the Concession, taking up European goods and bringing down to Bassankusu the india-rubber, which is there transhipped on board a Government steamer which plies for this purpose between Coquilhatville and Bassankusu, a distance of probably 160 miles. The transport of all goods and agents of the A. B. I. R. Company, immediately these quit the Concession, is carried on exclusively by the steamers of the Congo Government, the freight and passage-money obtained being reckoned as part of the public revenue. I have no actual figures giving the annual output of india-rubber from the A.B.I.R. Concession, but it is unquestionably large, and may, in the case of a prosperous year, reach from 600 to 800 tons. The quality of the A.B.I.R. rubber is excellent, and it commands generally a high price on the European market, so that the value of its annual yield may probably be estimated at not less than 150,000*l*. The merchandise used by the Company consists of the usual class of Central African barter goods—cotton cloths of different quality, Sheffield cutlery, matchets, beads, and salt. The latter is keenly sought by the natives of all the interior of Africa. There is also a considerable import by the A.B.I.R. Company, I believe, of cap-guns, which are chiefly used in arming the sentinels—termed "forest guards"—who, in considerable numbers, are quartered on the native villages throughout the Concession to see that the picked men of each town bring in, with regularity, the fixed quantity of pure rubber required of them every fortnight. I have no means of ascertaining the number of this class of armed men employed by the A.B.I.R. Company, but I saw many of them when up the Lopori River, and the gun of one of these sentries—himself an Ngombe savage—had branded on the stock "Depôt 2210." In addition to its numerous forest guards, armed with cap-guns, which, at close quarters, can be a very effective weapon, the A. B. I. R. Company has a fairly strong armament of rifles. These are limited to twenty-five rifles for the use of each factory. The two steamers, I believe, have also a similar armament.

The Secteur of Bongandanga, which was the only district of the A.B.I.R. Concession I visited, has three "factories," so that the number of rifles permitted in that one district would be seventy-five. I do not know if any limits or what limits are imposed on the number of cartridges which are permitted for the defence of these factories. One of the largest Congo Concession Companies had, when I was on the Upper River, addressed a request to its Directors in Europe for a further supply of ball-cartridge. The Directors had met this demand by asking what had become of the 72,000 cartridges shipped some three years ago, to which a reply was sent to the effect that these had all been used in the production of india-rubber. I did not see this correspondence, and cannot vouch for the truth of the statement; but the officer who informed me that it had passed before his own eyes was one of the highest standing in the interior.

When at Stanley Pool in June I had seen in one of the Government stores at Léopoldville a number of cases of rifles marked A. B. I. R. awaiting transport up river in one of the Government vessels; and upon my return to that neighbourhood, I was told by a local functionary that 200 rifles had, in July, been so shipped for the needs of the Lomami Company.

The right of the various Concession Companies operating within the Congo State to employ armed men—whether these bear rifles or cap-guns—is regulated by Government enactments, which confer on these commercial Societies what are termed officially "rights of police" ("droits de police"). A Circular of the Governor-General dealing with this question, dated the 20th October, 1900, points out the limits within which this right may be exercised. Prior to the issue of this Circular (copy of which is attached—Inclosure 5),* the various Concession Companies would appear to have engaged in military operations on a somewhat extensive scale, and to have made war upon the natives on their own account. The Regulations this Circular provides, to insure the licensing of all arms, rifles, and cap-guns, do not seem to be strictly observed, for in several cases the sentries or forest guards I encountered on my journey up the Lulongo had no licence (Modèle C) of the kind required by the Circular; and in two cases I found them provided with arms of precision. That the extensive use of armed men in the pay of the so-called Trading Societies, or in the service of the Government, as a means to enforce the compliance with demands for india-rubber, had been very general up to a recent date, is not denied by any one I met on the Upper Congo.

In a conversation with a gentleman of experience on this question, our remarks turned upon the condition of the natives. He produced a disused diary, and in it, I found and copied the following entry:—

M. P. called on us to get out of the rain, and in conversation with M. Q. in presence of myself and R., said: 'The only way to get rubber is to fight for it. The natives are paid 35 centimes per kilog., it is claimed, but that includes a large profit on the cloth; the amount of rubber is controlled by the number of guns, and not the number of bales of cloth. The S. A. B. on the Bussira, with 150 guns, get only 10 tons (rubber) a-month; we, the State, at Momboyo, with 130 guns, get 13 tons per month.' 'So you count by guns?' I asked him. 'Partout,' M. P. said, 'Each time the corporal goes out to get rubber cartridges are given to him. He must bring back all not used; and for every one used, he must bring back a right hand.' M. P. told me that sometimes they shot a cartridge at an animal in hunting; they then cut off a hand from a living man. As to the extent to which this is carried on, he informed me that in six months they, the State, on the Momboyo River, had used 6,000 cartridges, which means that 6,000 people are killed or mutilated. It means more than 6,000, for the people have told me repeatedly that the soldiers kill children with the butt of their guns."

In conversation upon this entry, I was told that the M. P. referred to was an officer in the Government service, who, at the date in question, had come down from the Momboyo River (a tributary of the great Ruki River, and forming a part, I believe, of the "Domaine de la Couronne") invalided, on his way home. He had come down in very bad health. He stated then that he was going home, not to return to the Congo, but he died, only a little way further down the river, very soon afterwards.

The same gentleman stated that he had reported this conversation orally at Boma, as instancing the methods of exaction then in force. It is probable that the issue of the circular quoted was not unconnected with these remarks.

The region drained by the Lulongo being of great fertility has, in the past, maintained a large population. In the days prior to the establishment of civilized rule in the interior of Africa, this river offered a constant source of supply to the slave

* See p

markets of the Upper Congo. The towns around the lower Lulongo River raided the interior tribes, whose prolific humanity provided not only servitors, but human meat for those stronger than themselves. Cannibalism had gone hand in hand with slave raiding, and it was no uncommon spectacle to see gangs of human beings being conveyed for exposure and sale in the local markets. I had in the past, when travelling on the Lulongo River, more than once viewed such a scene. On one occasion a woman was killed in the village I was passing through, and her head and other portions of her were brought and offered for sale to some of the crew of the steamer I was on. Sights of this description are to-day impossible in any part of the country I traversed, and the full credit for their suppression must be given to the authorities of the Congo Government. It is, perhaps, to be regretted that in its efforts to suppress such barbarous practices the Congo Government should have had to rely upon, often, very savage agencies wherewith to combat savagery. The troops employed in punitive measures were—and often are—themselves savages, only removed by outward garb from those they are sent to punish. Moreover, the measures employed to obtain recruits for the public service were themselves often but little removed from the malpractices that service was designed to suppress. The following copy of an order for Government workmen drawn up by a former Commissaire of the Equator District, and having reference to the Maringa affluent of the Lulongo River indicates that the Congo Government itself did not hesitate some years ago to purchase slaves (required as soldiers or workmen), who could only be obtained for sale by the most deplorable means :—

"Le Chef Ngulu de Wangata est envoyé dans la Maringa, pour m'y acheter des esclaves. Prière à MM. les agents de l'A.B.I.R. de bien vouloir me signaler les méfaits que celui-ci pourrait commettre en route.

"Le Capitaine-Commandant,
(Signé) "SARRAZZYN."

"*Colquilhatville, le* 1er *Mai*, 1896."

This document was shown to me during the course of my journey. The officer who issued this direction was, I was informed, for a considerable period chief executive authority of the district; and I heard him frequently spoken of by the natives who referred to him by the sobriquet he had earned in the district, "Widjima," or "Darkness."

The course of the Lulongo River below Bassakanusu to its junction with the Congo lies outside the limits of the A.B.I.R. Concession, and the region is, I believe, regarded as one of the free-trading districts wherein no exclusive right to the products of the soil is recognized. The only trading-house in this district is one termed the La Lulanga, which has three depôts, or factories, along the river bank, the principal of which is at Mampoko. This Company has a small steamer in which its native produce is collected, but the general transport of all its goods, as in the case of the Concession Societies, is performed by Government craft. The La Lulanga does not, I understand, enjoy the rights of police as defined by the Governor-General's Circular of the 20th October, 1900, but it employs a considerable number of armed men equally termed "forest guards." These men are quartered throughout the lower course of the Lulongo River, and I found that, as with the A.B.I.R., the sole duty they performed was to compel by force the collection of india-rubber or the supplies which each factory needed. As the district in which the La Lulanga Society carries on these operations is one that had already been subjected to still more comprehensive handling by two of the large Concession Companies, who only abandoned it when, as one of their agents informed me, it was nearly exhausted, the stock of rubber vines in it to-day is drawing to an end, and it is only with great difficulty that the natives are able to produce the quantity sufficient to satisfy their local masters. In the course of my dealings with the natives I found that several of the sentries of this Company had quite recently committed gross offences which, until my arrival, appeared to have gone undetected—certainly unpunished. Murder and mutilation were charged against several of them by name by the natives of certain townships close to the head-quarters of this Company, who sought me in the hope that I might help them. These people in several cases said that they had not complained elsewhere because they had felt that it was useless. As long as the rubber tax imposed upon them endured in its present compulsory form with the sanction of the authorities, they said it was idle to draw attention to acts which were but incidental to its collection.

The La Lulanga Company, not any more than the A.B.I.R., would seem to have a legal right to levy taxes, but the fact remains that from the natives who supply these two trading Companies with all that they export as well as with their local supplies of food and material, the Congo Government itself requires no contribution to the public revenue. These people, therefore, must be either legally exempted from supporting the Government of their country, or else a portion of the contributions they make to the A.B.I.R. and Lulanga Companies must be claimed by that Government in lieu of the taxes it is justified in imposing on these districts.

In the case of the A.B.I.R. Society, it is said that a portion of the profits are paid into the public revenues of the Congo Government (who hold certain shares in the undertaking), and that these figure annually in the Budget as "produit de portefeuille." In making this explanation to me, an agent of one of the Upper Congo trading Companies said the term should more correctly be "produit de porte-fusil," and to judge from the large numbers of armed men I saw employed, the correction was not inapposite.

The Concession Companies, I believe, account for the armed men in their service on the ground that their factories and agents must be protected against the possible violence of the rude forest dwellers with whom they deal; but this legitimate need for safeguarding European establishments does not suffice to account for the presence, far from those establishments, of large numbers of armed men quartered throughout the native villages, and who exercise upon their surroundings an influence far from protective. The explanation offered me of this state of things was that, as the "impositions" laid upon the natives were regulated by law, and were calculated on the scale of public labour the Government had a right to require of the people, the collection of these "impositions" had to be strictly enforced. When I pointed out that the profit of this system was not reaped by the Government, but by a commercial Company, and figured in the public returns of that Company's affairs, as well as in the official Government statistics, as the outcome of commercial dealings with the natives, I was informed that the "impositions" were in reality trade, "for, as you observe, we pay the natives for the produce they bring in." "But," I observed, "you told me just now that these products did not belong to the natives, but to you, the Concessionnaire, who owned the soil; how, then, do you buy from them what is already yours?" "We do not buy the india-rubber. What we pay to the native is a remuneration for his labour in collecting our produce on our land, and bringing it to us."

Since it was thus to the labour of the native alone that the profits of the Company were attributed, I inquired whether he was not protected by contract with his employer; but I was here referred back to the statement that the native performed these services as a public duty required of him by his Government. He was not a contracted labourer at all, but a free man, dwelling in his own home, and was simply acquitting himself of an "imposition" laid upon him by the Government, "of which we are but the collectors by right of our Concession." "Your Concession, then, implies," I said, "that you have been conceded not only a certain area of land, but also the people dwelling on that land?" This, however, was not accepted either, and I was assured that the people were absolutely free, and owed no service to any one but to the Government of the country. But there was no explanation offered to me that was not at once contradicted by the next. One said it was a tax, an obligatory burden laid upon the people, such as all Governments have the undoubted right of imposing; but this failed to explain how, if a tax, it came to be collected by the agents of a trading firm, and figured as the outcome of their trade dealings with the people, still less, how, if it were a tax, it could be justly imposed every week or fortnight in the year, instead of once, or at most, twice a year.

Another asserted that it was clearly legitimate commerce with the natives because these were well paid and very happy. He could not then explain the presence of so many armed men in their midst, or the reason for tying up men, women, and children, and of maintaining in each trading establishment a local prison, termed a "maison des otages," wherein recalcitrant native traders endured long periods of confinement

A third admitted that there was no law on the Congo Statute Book constituting his trading establishment a Government taxing station, and that since the product of his dealings with the natives figured in his Company's balance-sheets as trade, and paid customs duty to the Government on export, and a dividend to the shareholders, and as he himself drew a commission of 2 per cent. on his turnover, it must be trade; but this exponent could not explain how, if these operations were purely commercial, they rested on a privilege denied to others, for since, as he asserted, the products of his district could neither be worked nor bought by any one but himself, it was clear they were not merchandise, which, to be merchandise, must be marketable. The summing up of the situation by the majority of those with whom I sought to discuss it was that, in fact, it was forced labour conceived in the true interest of the native, who, if not controlled in this way, would spend his days in idleness, unprofitable to himself and the general community. The collection of the products of the soil by the more benevolent methods adopted by the Trading Companies was, in any case, preferable to those the Congo Government would itself employ to compel obedience to this law, and therefore if I saw women and children seized as hostages and kept in detention until rubber or other things were brought in, it was better that this should be done by the cap-gun of the "forest guard" than by the Albini armed soldiers of the Government who, if once impelled into a district, would overturn the entire country side.

No more satisfactory explanation than this outline was anywhere offered me of what I saw in the A.B.I.R. and Lulanga districts. It is true alternatives of excuse with differing interpretations of what I saw were offered me in several quarters, but these were so obviously untrue, that they could not be admitted as having any real relation to the things which came before me.

At a village I touched at up the Lulonga River, a small collection of dwellings named Z *, the people complained that there was no rubber left in their district, and yet that the La Lulanga Company required of them each fortnight a fixed quantity they could not supply. Three forest guards of that Company were quartered, it was said, in this village, one of whom I found on duty, the two others, he informed me, having gone to Mampoko to convoy the fortnight's rubber. No live-stock of any kind could be seen or purchased in this town, which had only a few years ago been a large and populous community, filled with people and well stocked with sheep, goats, ducks, and fowls. Although I walked through most of it, I could only count ten men with their families. There were said to be others in the part of the town I did not visit, but the entire community I saw were living in wretched houses and in most visible distress. Three months previously (in May, I believe), they said a Government force, commanded by a white man, had occupied their town owing to their failure to send in to the Mampoko head-quarters of the La Lulanga Company a regular supply of india-rubber, and two men, whose names were given, had been killed by the soldiers at that time.

As Z * lies upon the main stream of the Lulongo River, and is often touched at by passing steamers, I chose for the next inspection a town lying somewhat off this beaten track, where my coming would be quite unexpected. Steaming up a small tributary of the Lulongo, I arrived, unpreceded by any rumour of my coming, at the village of A **. In an open shed I found two sentries of the La Lulanga Company guarding fifteen native women, five of whom had infants at the breast, and three of whom were about to become mothers. The chief of these sentries, a man called S— who was bearing a double-barrelled shot-gun, for which he had a belt of cartridges—at once volunteered an explanation of the reason for these women's detention. Four of them, he said, were hostages who were being held to insure the peaceful settlement of a dispute between two neighbouring towns, which had already cost the life of a man. His employer, the agent of the La Lulanga Company at B ** near by, he said, had ordered these women to be seized and kept until the Chief of the offending town to which they belonged should come in to talk over the palaver. The sentry pointed out that this was evidently a much better way to settle such troubles between native towns than to leave them to be fought out among the people themselves.

The remaining eleven women, whom he indicated, he said he had caught and was detaining as prisoners to compel their husbands to bring in the right amount of india-rubber required of them on next market day. When I asked if it was a woman's work to collect india-rubber, he said, "No; that, of course, it was man's work." "Then why do you catch the women and not the men?" I asked. "Don't you see," was the answer, "if I caught and kept the men, who would work the rubber? But if I catch their wives, the husbands are anxious to have them home again, and so the rubber is brought in quickly and quite up to the mark." When I asked what would become of these women if their husbands failed to bring in the right quantity of rubber on the next market day, he said at once that then they would be kept there until their husbands had redeemed them. Their food, he explained, he made the Chief of A ** provide, and he himself saw it given to them daily. They came from more than one village of the neighbourhood, he said, mostly from the Ngombi or inland country, where he often had to catch women to insure the rubber being brought in in sufficient quantity. It was an institution, he explained, that served well and saved much trouble. When his master came each fortnight to A ** to take away the rubber so collected, if it was found to be sufficient, the women were released and allowed to return with their husbands, but if not sufficient they would undergo continued detention. The sentry's statements were clear and explicit, as were equally those of several of the villagers with whom I spoke. The sentry further explained, in answer to my inquiry, that he caught women in this way by direction of his employers. That it was a custom generally adopted and found to work well; that the people were very lazy, and that this was much the simplest way of making them do what was required of them. When asked if he had any use for his shot-gun, he answered that it had been given him by the white man "to frighten people and make them bring in rubber," but that he had never otherwise used it. I found that the two sentries at A ** were complete masters of the town. Everything I needed in the way of food or firewood they at once ordered the men of the town to bring me. One of them, gun over shoulder, marched a procession of men—the Chief of the village at their head—down to the water side, each carrying a bundle of firewood for my steamer. A few chickens which were brought were only purchased through their intermediary, the native owner in each case handing the fowl over to the sentry, who then brought it on board, bargained for it, and took the price agreed upon. When, in the evening, the Chief of the village was invited to come and talk to me, he came in evident fear of the sentries seeing him or overhearing his remarks, and the leader, S, finding him talking to me, peremptorily broke into the conversation and himself answered each question put to the Chief. When I asked this latter if he and his townsmen did not catch fish in the C ** River, in which we learned there was much, the sentry, intervening, said it was not the business of these people to catch fish—"they have no time for that, they have got to get the rubber I tell them to."

At nightfall the fifteen women in the shed were tied together, either neck to neck or ankle to ankle, to secure them for the night, and in this posture I saw them twice during the evening. They were then trying to huddle around a fire. In the morning the leading sentry, before leaving the village, ordered his companion in my hearing to "keep close guard on the prisoners." I subsequently discovered that this sentry, learning that I was not, as he had at first thought, a missionary, had gone or sent to inform his employer at C ** that a strange white man was in the town.

An explanation of what I had witnessed at A ** was later preferred by the representative of this Company for my information, but was in such direct conflict with what I had myself observed that it could not be accepted either as explaining the detention of the women I had seen tied neck to neck, or as a refutation of the statements of the sentry, made to me at a time when he had no thought that his avowals had any bearing on his employer's interests.

From A ** I proceeded to Bongandanga, a station of the A.B.I.R. Company which lies some 120 or 130 miles up the Lopori, a tributary of the Lulongo, and only halted for very brief periods *en route*. I arrived at Bongandanga on the 29th August when what was locally termed the rubber market was in full swing. The natives of the surrounding country are, on these market days, which are held at intervals of a fortnight, marched in under a number of armed guards, each native carrying his fortnight's supply of india-rubber for delivery to the agent of the Company. During my stay at Bongandanga I had frequent occasion to meet the two agents of this Society, who received me with every kindness and hospitality.

The A.B.I.R. station was well built and well cared for, and gave evidence of unremitting industry on the part of those in charge of it. There were two good houses for the European staff and a number of large well-built bamboo stores for the storing and drying of india-rubber. All the houses were constructed of native materials, indeed, with the exception of a small stock of barter goods in one of the stores and the European provisions required for the white men, everything I saw came from the surrounding district, provided in one form or another by its native inhabitants. This applies to practically every European establishment in the interior of the country, the only differences being as to the manner in which the help of the natives may be sought and recompensed. Building material of all kinds from very heavy timber to roofing mats and native string to tie these on with are provided by the natives; but their services in supplying these indispensable adjuncts to civilized existence do not appear to be everywhere equally remunerated. At Bongandanga I saw thirty-three large tree trunks, each of which could not have weighed less than ½ a ton, some of them nearer 1 ton, which, I was told, had been felled and carried in by the natives for his use in building a new house. He explained that as the natives came in from different districts fortnightly, and then had only to carry very small baskets of india-rubber, this additional burden was imposed upon them, but that this was one reserved for unwilling workers of india-rubber. It was, in fact, one of the punishments for backward 'récolteurs."

At Bongandanga the men of the district named E **, distant about 20 miles, had been brought in with the rubber from that district. They marched in in a long file, guarded by sentries of the A.B.I.R. Company, and when I visited the factory grounds to observe the progress of the "market," I was informed by the local agent that there were 242 men actually present. As each man was required, I was told, to bring in 3 kilog. nett of rubber, the quantity actually brought in on that occasion should have yielded about three-quarters of a ton of pure rubber. The rubber brought by each man, after being weighed and found correct, was taken off to be cut up in a large store, and then placed out on drying shelves in other stores. As considerable loss of weight arises in the drying to obtain 3 kilog. nett a dead weight of crude rubber considerably in excess of that quantity must be brought in. There were everywhere sentries in the A.B.I.R. grounds, guarding and controlling the natives, many of whom carried their knives and spears. The sentries were often armed with rifles, some of them with several cartridges slipped between the fingers of the hands ready for instant use; others had cap-guns, with a species of paper cartridge locally manufactured for charging this form of muzzle-loader. The native vendors of the rubber were guarded in detachments or herds, many of them behind a barricade which stretched in front of a house I was told was the factory prison, termed locally, I found, the "maison des otages." The rubber as brought up by each man under guard, was weighed by one of the two agents of the A.B.I.R. present, who sat upon the verandah of his house. If the rubber were found to be of the right weight its vendor would be led off with it to the cutting up store or to one of the drying stores. In the former were fully 80 or 100 natives who had already passed muster, squatting on raised cane platforms, busily cutting up into the required sizes the rubber which had been passed and accepted. At the corners of these platforms stood, or equally squatted, sentries of the A.B.I.R. with their rifles ready.

In another store where rubber was being dried seven natives came in while I was inspecting it carrying baskets which were filled with the cut-up rubber, which they then at once began sorting and spreading on high platforms. These seven men were guarded by four sentries armed with rifles.

Somewhat differing explanations were offered me of the reasons for the constant guarding of the natives I observed during the course of the "market." This was first said to be a necessary precaution to insure tranquillity and order within the trading factory during the presence there of so many raw and sturdy savages. But when I drew attention to the close guard kept upon the natives in the drying and cutting sheds, I was told that these were "prisoners." If the rubber brought by its native vendor were found on the weighing machine to be seriously under the required weight, the defaulting individual was detained to be dealt with in the "maison des otages." One such case occurred while I was on the ground. The defaulter was directed to be taken away, and was dragged off by some of the sentries, who forced him on to the ground to remain until the market was over. While being held by these men he struggled to escape, and one of them struck him in the mouth whence blood issued, and he then remained passive. I did not learn how this individual subsequently purged his offence, but when on a later occasion I visited the inclosure in front of the prison I counted fifteen men and youths who were being guarded while they worked at mat-making for the use of the station buildings. These men, I was then told, were some of the defaulters of the previous market day, who were being kept as compulsory workmen to make good the deficiency in their rubber.

Payments made to the rubber-bringers, depending on the quantity brought, consisted of knives, matchets, strings of beads, and sometimes a little salt. I saw many men who got a wooden handled knife of Sheffield cutlery, good and strong—others got a matchet. The largest of these knives with a 9-inch blade, and the smaller with a 5-inch, cost in Europe, I find, 2*s.* 10*d.*, and 1*s.* 5*d.* per dozen respectively, less $2\frac{1}{2}$ per cent. cash discount. The men who got the knife of the larger kind, or a matchet, had brought in, I understood, a full basket of pure rubber, which may have represented a European valuation of some 27 fr. To the original cost of one of these knives, say $2\frac{3}{4}$*d.*, should be added fully 100 per cent. to cover transport charges, so that their local cost would be about 6*d.* Among the natives themselves these knives pass at 25 rods (1·25 fr.) and 15 rods (75 centimes) each. From two of these rubber workers I later purchased two of these knives, giving twenty-five teaspoonfuls of salt for the larger, and six teaspoonfuls with an empty bottle for the smaller. From a third member of their party, whose payment had consisted of a string of thirty-nine blue and white glass beads (locally valued at 5 rods), I bought his fortnight's salary for five teaspoonfuls of salt. This youth, indeed, confessed that his basket of rubber had not been so well filled as those of the others.

I went to the homes of these men some miles away and found out their circumstances. To get the rubber they had first to go fully a two days' journey from their homes, leaving their wives, and being absent for from five to six days. They were seen to the forest limits under guard, and if not back by the sixth day trouble was likely to ensue. To get the rubber in the forests—which generally speaking are very swampy—involves much fatigue and often fruitless searching for a well-flowing vine. As the area of supply diminishes, moreover, the demand for rubber constantly increases. Some little time back I learned the Bongandanga district supplied 7 tons of rubber a-month, a quantity which it was hoped would shortly be increased to 10 tons. The quantity of rubber brought by the three men in question would have represented, probably, for the three of them certainly not less than 7 kilog. of pure rubber. That would be a very safe estimate, and at an average of 7 fr. per kilog. they might be said to have brought in 2*l.* worth of rubber. In return for this labour, or imposition, they had received goods which cost certainly under 1*s.*, and whose local valuation came to 45 rods (1*s.* 10*d.*). As this process repeats itself twenty-six times a-year, it will be seen that they would have yielded 52*l.* in kind at the end of the year to the local factory, and would have received in return some 24*s.* or 25*s.* worth of goods, which had a market value on the spot of 2*l.* 7*s.* 8*d.* In addition to these formal payments they were liable at times to be dealt with in another manner, for should their work, which might have been just as hard, have proved less profitable in its yield of rubber, the local prison would have seen them. The people everywhere assured me that they were not happy under this system, and it was apparent to a callous eye that in this they spoke the strict truth.

In September I visited a native village called D * *, situated some miles from the A.B.I.R. factory at Bongandanga. I went there to see one of the natives, who, with his wife and little children, had come to visit me. My going to his town was solely a friendly visit to this man's household, since I was told that he was an excellent character, and one who set a good example to his countrymen. On the way, at some 4 or 5 miles only from the A.B.I.R. factory, I passed through a part of D * * (which is a very long town) where were several sentries of the A.B.I.R. Society. One of these had a 6-chamber revolver loaded with six 4·50 Ely cartridges—doubtless given, like the shot-gun at A * *, for intimidation rather than for actual use. Another sentry present had only his cap-gun. He said there were in this one village six sentries of the A.B.I.R., but that the other four had just gone into Bongandanga guarding some prisoners. These were, it was explained to me, some of the natives of the country side who had not brought in what was thought to be a sufficiency of india-rubber. A little further on I met two more sentries of the A.B.I.R. in this town. Coming home from D * * by another road I found two other sentries apparently acting as judges and settling a "palaver" among the natives, this being one of the commonest uses to which these men put their authority in their own interest, levying blackmail and interfering in the domestic concerns of the natives by compelling payment for their "judicial" decisions.

The following day my host at D * * came in to say that the sentries were making trouble with him on account of my visit of the previous day, declaring that they would inform the agent of the A.B.I.R. that he and others had told me lies about their treatment by that Company, and that they would all be put in the prison gang and sent away out of their country. That evening C E spoke to me of my visit to D * * of the previous day, assuring me that the natives were all liars and rogues. The fact that I had personally gone to see a native community, theoretically as free as I was myself, and that I had spoken at first hand to some of these natives themselves, caused, I could not but perceive, considerable annoyance.

That the fears of my native host were not entirely groundless I subsequently learned by letter from Bongandanga, wherein I was informed that two of his wives and one of the children I had seen had fled in the middle of the night for refuge to the Mission evangelist—the sentries quartered at D * * having arrested my friend at midnight, and that he had been brought in a prisoner to the A.B.I.R. factory.

As to the condition of the men who paid by detention in the "maison des otages" their shortcomings in respect of rubber, I was assured by the local agent that they were not badly treated and that "they got their food." On the other hand, I was assured in many quarters that flogging with the chicotte—or hippopotamus-hide whip—was one of the measures used in dealing with refractory natives in that institution. I was told that men have frequently been seen coming away from the factory, after the rubber markets, who had been flogged, and that on two occasions this year, the last of them in March, two natives had been so severely flogged that they were being carried away by their friends.

The A.B.I.R. Society effectually controls the movements of the natives both by water as well as by land. Since almost every village in the Concession is under control, its male inhabitants are entered in books, and according to age and strength have to furnish rubber or, in the villages close to the factory, food-stuffs, such as antelope meat or wild pig (which the elders are required to hunt), as also the customary kwanga bread, or bananas. and fowls and ducks. An agent showed me some of these village lists, during the purchasing of the rubber, of the 242 E ** men, explaining that the impositions against the individuals named are fixed by the Government, and are calculated on the bodily service each man owes it, but from which he is exempted in the Concession in order to work rubber and assist the progressive development of the A.B.I.R. Company's territory. He added that it was not the few guns he disposed of at F ** which compelled obedience to this law, but the power of the Congo State "Force Publique," which, if a village absolutely refuses obedience, would be sent to punish the district to compel respect to these civilized rights. He added that, as the punishment inflicted in these cases was terribly severe, it was better that the milder measures and the other expedients he was forced to resort to should not be interfered with. These measures, he said, involved frequent imprisonment of individuals in his local "house of hostages." A truly recalcitrant man, he said, who proved enduringly obstinate in his failure to bring in his allotted share of rubber, would in the end be brought to reason by these means. He would find, I was assured, as a result of his perversity that the whole of his time must be spent either in the prison or else in being marched under guard between it and his native town. Terms of fifteen days, from "market" day to "market" day, were the usual period of detention, and generally proved sufficient—during which time the prisoners worked around the factory—but longer periods were not at all unknown. My informant added that an excellent project for dealing with obstinate opponents to the rubber industry had recently been mooted, but had not been carried into practice. This was to transport to the Upper Lopori, or the Upper Maringa, far from their homes and tribes, such men as could not be reclaimed by milder methods. In these distant regions they would have no chance of running away, but would be kept under constant guard and at constant work. This proposal had, however, been disapproved of by the local authorities. In one town I visited, the Chief and some thirty people gave me the names of several men of the town who had, about eighteen months previously, been transported in this manner to G **, an A.B.I.R. post, some 340 miles by water from Bongandanga. Three, whose names were stated, had already died, only two had returned, the others being still detained.

Deaths even in the local prison are not, however, unknown. I heard of several. The late Chief of H **, a town I visited with the agent of the A.B.I.R. station had died some months before as the result, it was said, of imprisonment. He had been arrested because another man of the town had not brought in antelope meat when required. After one and a-half months' imprisonment the Chief was released. He was then so weak that he could not walk the 2 miles home to H **, but collapsed on the way and died early the following morning. This was on the 14th June last.

On the September a man named T came to see me. He had been very badly wounded in the thigh, and walked with difficulty. He stated that a sentry of the A.B.I.R., a man named U, had shot him, as I saw; and at the same time had killed V, a friend. The sentries had come to arrest the Chief of H ** on account of meat, which was short for the white man—not the present white man, but another—and his people had gathered around the Chief to protect him. An inquiry I gathered had been held by a Law Officer into this and other outrages committed the previous year, and as a result the sentry U had been removed from the district. T went on to say to me that this sentry was now back in the country at large, and a free man. When I asked him if he himself had not been compensated for the injuries entailing partial disablement he had received, he said: "Four months ago I was arrested for not having got meat, and was kept one and a-half months in prison on that account. U, who killed V, and shot me here in the thigh, is a free man, as all men know; but I, who am wounded, have to hunt meat."

This statement I found on fuller inquiry in other quarters was confirmed; and it became apparent that while the murderer was at large, one of those he had seriously injured, and almost incapacitated, was still required to hunt game, and paid for his failure by imprisonment. On further inquiry, I gathered that this occasion was the only one locally known when a qualified Law Officer had ever visited the Lopori, although charges from that region involving very grave accusations had, on several occasions, been preferred. There being no Magistrate resident in the whole of the A.B.I.R. Concession, inquiries, unless conducted by the agents of the A.B.I.R. themselves, have to be investigated at Coquilhatville—distant fully 270 miles from Bongandanga, and over 400 miles from some parts of the Concession.

It is true an officer of the Congo Executive is deputed to exercise a qualified surveillance within this Concession; but he is not a qualified Magistrate or legally empowered to act as such.

The occupant of this post is a military officer of inferior rank, who is quartered, with a force of soldiers, near to Basankusu, the chief station of the A.B.I.R. Company.

This officer, when he enters the A.B.I.R. territory, is accompanied by soldiers, and his actions would appear to be generally confined to measures of a punitive kind, the necessity for such measures being that which almost everywhere applies—namely, a refusal of or falling off in the supplies of india-rubber.

At the date of my visit to the Lopori he was engaged in a journey, not unconnected with fighting, to the Maringa River. His independence is not complete, nor is his disassociation from the A.B.I.R. Company's agencies as marked as, in view of the circumstances attending the collection of rubber, it should be.

His journeys up the two great rivers, the Maringa and Lopori, which drain the A.B.I.R. territory, are made on the steamers of that Company, and he is, to all intents, a guest of the Company's agents.

The supervision of this officer extends also over the course of the Lulongo river, outside the A.B.I.R. Concession, and he it was who had occupied the town of Z* on an occasion some months before my visit, when two native men had been killed.

The Commissaire-Général of the Equator District has also, at recent periods, visited the A.B.I.R. Concession, but this officer, although the Chief of the Executive and the President of the Territoral Court of the entire district, came as a visitor to the A.B.I.R. stations and as guest on the steamer of that Company.

No steamer belonging to the Congo Government regularly ascends either the Lopori or Maringa rivers, and the conveyance of mails from the A.B.I.R. territory depends, for steamer transport, on the two vessels of that Company.

On the 15th June last, the Director of this Company by letter informed the Missions of Bongandanga and Baringa that he had given orders to the steamers of the Company to refuse the carriage of any letters or correspondence coming from or intended for either of those Mission stations, which are the only European establishments, not belonging to the A.B.I.R. Company, existing within the limits of the Concession.

Resulting from this order the missionaries at these two isolated posts are now compelled, save when, some three times a year, the Mission steamer visits them, to dispatch all their correspondence by canoes to their agent at Ikau, lying just outside the Concession.

This involves the engagement of paddlers and a canoe journey of 120 to 130 miles from each of these Missions down to Ikau.

But as the A.B.I.R. Company claims a right to interrogate all canoes passing up or down stream, this mode of transport leaves some elements of insecurity, apart from the delay and inconvenience otherwise entailed.

At the date of my visit to the Concession, the Mission at Baringa, situated 120 miles up the Maringa river, had despatched a canoe manned by native dependents with mails intended for the outer world—the nearest post office being at Coquilhatville, some 260 miles distant.

When seeking to pass the A.B.I.R. station at Waka, situated half-way down the Maringa river, this canoe was required by the European agent there to land and to deliver to him its correspondence.

The native canoe men reported that this agent had opened the packet and questioned them, and that the letters intrusted to them for delivery to the Mission representative at Tkau were not restored to them without delay and much inconvenience.

It might not be too much to expect that, in return for the very extensive privileges it enjoys of exploitation of public lands and a large native population, the A.B.I.R. Company should be required, in the entire absence of the public flotilla, to lischarge the not onerous task of conveying the public mails by its steamers which so frequently navigate the waterways of the Concession in the collection of india-rubber.

Were a qualified Magistrate appointed to reside within the limits of this Concession—as within the other Upper Congo Concessions, some of them territories as large as a European State, and still containing a numerous native population—the public service could not but be the gainer.

As it is to-day, no Court is open to the appeals of these people that lies at all within their reach, and no European agency, save isolated Mission stations, has any direct influence upon them except that immediately interested in their profitable exploitation.

It is only right to say that the present agent of the A.B.I.R. Society I met at Bongandanga seemed to me to try, in very difficult and embarrassing circumstances, to minimize as far as possible, and within the limits of his duties, the evils of the system I there observed at work.

The requisitions of food-stuffs laid on the villages adjoining the factories were said to be less onerous than those affecting the rubber towns. They rested, I was informed, on the same legal basis as that authorizing rubber working, and a failure to meet them involved the same desultory modes of arrest and imprisonment. During my stay at Bongandanga several instances of arrest in failures of this kind came to my notice.

On a Sunday in August, I saw six of the local sentries going back with cap-guns and ammunition pouches to E**, after the previous day's market, and later in the day, when in the factory grounds, two armed sentries came up to the agent as we walked, guarding sixteen natives, five men tied neck by neck, with five untied women and six young children. This somewhat embarrassing situation, it was explained to me, was due to the persistent failure of the people of the village these persons came from to supply its proper quota of food. These people, I was told, had just been captured "on the river" by one of the sentries placed there to watch the waterway. They had been proceeding in their canoes to some native fishing grounds, and were espied and brought in. I asked if the children also were held responsible for food supplies, and they, along with an elderly woman, were released, and told to run over to the Mission, and go to school there. This they did not do, but doubtless returned to their homes in the recalcitrant village. The remaining five men and four women were led off to the "maison des otages" under guard of the sentry.

An agent explained that he was forced to catch women in preference to the men as then supplies were brought in quicker; but he did not explain how the children deprived of their parents obtained their own food supplies.

He deplored this hard necessity, but he said the vital needs of his own station, as well as of the local missionaries, who, being guests of the A.B.I.R. Society, had to be provided for, sternly imposed it upon him if the peopled failed to keep up their proper supplies.

While we thus talked an armed sentry came along guarding four natives—men—who were carrying bunches of bananas, a part of another food imposition. This sentry explained to his master that the village he had just visited had failed to give antelope meat, alleging the very heavy rain of the previous night as an excuse for not hunting.

The agent apologized to me for his inability to give me meat during my stay, pointing out the obvious necessity he now was under of catching some persons without delay. He should certainly, he said, have to send out and catch women that very night.

On leaving the A.B.I.R. grounds, still accompanied by this gentleman, another batch of men carrying food supplies were marched in by three armed guards, and were conducted towards the "maison des otages," which two other sentries apparently guarded.

At 8 P.M. that evening, just after the Sunday service, a number of women were taken through the Mission grounds past the church by the A.B.I.R. sentries, and in the morning I was told that three such seizures had been effected during the night. On the 2nd September I met, when walking in the A.B.I.R. grounds with the subordinate agent of the factory, a file of fifteen women, under the guard of three unarmed sentries, who were being brought in from the adjoining villages, and were led past me. These women, who were evidently wives and mothers, it was explained in answer to my inquiry, had been seized in order to compel their husbands to bring in antelope or other meat which was overdue, and some of which it was very kindly promised should be sent on board my steamer when leaving. As a matter of fact, half an antelope was so sent on board by the good offices of this gentleman.

As I was leaving Bongandanga, on the 3rd September, several elderly Headmen of the neighbouring villages were putting off in their canoes to the opposite forest, to get meat wherewith to redeem their wives, whom I had seen arrested the previous day. I learned later that the husband of one of these women brought in, two days afterwards, to the Mission-station, his infant daughter, who, being deprived of her mother, had fallen seriously ill, and whom he could not feed. At the request of the missionary this woman was released on the 5th September. I took occasion to say to the agent of the A.B.I.R. Company, before leaving, that the practice of imprisoning women for impositions said to be due by their husbands was to my mind unquestionably illegal, and that I should not fail to draw the attention of the Governor-General of the Congo State to what I had seen. The excuse offered, both on this occasion as on others when I had ventured to allude to the condition of the natives around Bongandanga, was that the station compared most favourably with all others within the A.B.I.R. Concession, which were run, I was assured, on much sterner lines than those which caused me pain at Bongandanga. I later made official communication to the local Government at Boma on these points, in so far as the system I had seen at work affected the English missionaries within the A.B.I.R. Concession, and in that letter I sought to show that neither the local agent nor his subordinate were responsible for a state of affairs which greatly wounded the feelings of my countrymen at Bongandanga, and which had filled me with a pained surprise. My attention, it was true, had been drawn to the systematic imprisonment of women in parts of the Upper Congo some two years previously, in a case wherein a British coloured subject—a native of Lagos—along with three Europeans, all of them in the service of the Compagnie Anversoise du Commerce au Congo—a Concession Company—had been charged with various acts of cruelty and oppression which had caused much loss of life to the natives in the Mongala region. These men had been arrested by the authorities in the summer of 1900, and had been sentenced to long terms of imprisonment, against which they had made appeal. The facts charged against the British coloured subject (who sought my help) were, among others, that he had illegally arrested women and kept them in illegal detention at his trading station, and it was alleged that many of these women had died of starvation while thus confined. This man himself, when I had visited him in Boma gaol in March 1901, said that more than 100 women and children had died of starvation at his hands, but that the responsibility for both their arrest and his own lack of food to give them was due to his superiors' orders and neglect. The Court of Appeal at Boma gave final Judgment in the case on the 13th February, 1901; and in connection with the Lagos man's degree of guilt, a copy of this Judgment, in so far as it affected him, at my request had been communicated to me by the Governor-General. From this Judgment I learned that the case against the accused had been clearly proved. Among other extenuating circumstances, which secured, however, a marked reduction of the first sentence imposed on the coloured man, the Court of Appeal cited the following:—

"That it is just to take into account that, by the correspondence produced in the case, the chiefs of the Concession Company have, if not by formal orders, at least by their example and their tolerance, induced their agents to take no account whatever of the rights, property, and lives of the natives; to use the arms and the soldiers which should have served for their defence and the maintenance of order to force the natives to furnish them with produce and to work for the Company, as also to pursue as rebels and outlaws those who sought to escape from the requisitions imposed upon them. . . . . . . That, above all, the fact that the arrest of women and their detention, to compel the villages to furnish both produce and workmen, was tolerated and admitted even by certain of the administrative authorities of the region."

I had gathered at the time of this finding of the Boma High Court that steps had then been taken to make it everywhere effective and to insure obedience to the law in this respect, and that a recurrence of the illegalities brought to light in the Mongala region had been rendered impossible in any part of the Congo State. From what I saw during the few days spent in the A.B.I.R. Concession, and again outside its limits in the Lower Lulongo, it seemed to be clear that the action taken by the authorities nearly three years ago could not have produced the results undoubtedly then desired.

On my leaving Bongandanga on the 3rd September I returned down the Lopori and Lolongo Rivers, arriving at J**. The following day, about 9 at night, some natives of the neighbourhood came to see me, bringing with them a lad of about 16 years of age whose right hand was missing. His name was X and his relatives said they came from K**, a village on the opposite side of the river some few miles away. As it was late at night there was some difficulty in obtaining a translation of their statements, but I gathered that X's hand had been cut off in K** by a sentry of the La Lulanga Company, who was, or had been, quartered there. They said that this sentry, at the time that he had mutilated X, had also shot dead one of the chief men of the town. X, in addition to this mutilation, had been shot in the shoulder blade, and, as a consequence, was deformed. On being shot it was said he had fallen down insensible, and the sentry had then cut off his hand, alleging that he would take it to the Director of the Company at Mampoko. When I asked if this had been done the natives replied that they believed that the hand had only been carried part of the way to Mampoko and then thrown away. They did not think the white man had seen it. They went on to say that they had not hitherto made any complaint of this. They declared they had seen no good object in complaining of a case of this kind since they did not hope any good would result to them. They then went on to say that a younger boy than X, at the beginning of this year (as near as they could fix the date at either the end of January or the beginning of February), had been mutilated in a similar way by a sentry of the same trading Company, who was still quartered in their town, and that when they had wished to bring this latter victim with them the sentry had threatened to kill him and that the boy was now in hiding. They begged that I would myself go back with them to their village and ascertain that they were speaking the truth. I thought it my duty to listen to this appeal, and decided to return with them on the morrow to their town. In the morning, when about to start for K **, many people from the surrounding country came in to see me. They brought with them three individuals who had been shockingly wounded by gun fire, two men and a very small boy, not more than 6 years of age, and a fourth—a boy child of 6 or 7—whose right hand was cut off at the wrist. One of the men, who had been shot through the arm, declared that he was Y of L **, a village situated some miles away. He declared that he had been shot as I saw under the following circumstances: the soldiers had entered his town, he alleged, to enforce the due fulfilment of the rubber tax due by the community. These men had tied him him up and said that unless he paid 1,000 brass rods to them they would shoot him. Having no rods to give them they had shot him through the arm and had left him. The soldiers implicated he said were four whose names were given me. They were, he believed, all employés of the La Lulanga Company and had come from Mampoko. At the time when he, Y, was shot through the arm the Chief of his town came up and begged the soldiers not to hurt him, but one of them, a man called Z, shot the Chief dead. No white man was with these sentries, or soldiers, at the time. Two of them, Y said, he believed had been sent or taken to Coquilhatville. Two of them—whom he named—he said were still at Mampoko. The people of L ** had sent to tell the white man at Mampoko of what his soldiers had done. He did not know what punishment, if any, the soldiers had received, for no inquiry had since been made in L **, nor had any persons in that town been required to testify against their aggressors. This man was accompanied by four other men of his town. These four men all corroborated Y's statement.

These people were at once followed by two men of M **, situated, they said, close to K **, and only a few miles distant. They brought with them a full-grown man named A A, whose arm was shattered and greatly swollen through the discharge of a gun, and a small boy named B B, whose left arm was broken in two places from two separate gun shots—the wrist being shattered and the hand wobbling about loose and quite useless. The two men made the following statement: That their town, like all the others in the neighbourhood, was required to furnish a certain quantity of india-rubber fortnightly to the head-quarters of the La Lulanga Company at Mampoko; that at the time these outrages were committed, which they put at less than a year previously, a man named C C was a sentry of that Company quartered in their village; that they two now before me had taken the usual fortnight's rubber to Mampoko. On returning to M ** they found that C C, the sentry, had shot dead two men of the town named D D and E E, and had tied up this man A A and the boy B B, now before me, to two trees. The sentry said that this was to punish the two men for having taken the rubber to Mampoko without having first shown it to him and paid him a commission on it. The two men asserted that they had at once returned to Mampoko, and had begged the Director of the Company to return with them to M ** and see what his servants had done. But, they alleged, he had refused to comply with their request. On getting back to their town they then found that the man A A and the child B B were still tied to the trees, and had been shot in the arms as I now saw. On pleading with the sentry to release these two wounded individuals, he had required a payment of 2,000 brass rods (100 fr.). One of the two men stayed to collect this money, and another returned to Mampoko to again inform the Director of what had been done. The two men declared that nothing was done to the sentry C C, but that the white man said that if the people behaved badly again he was to punish them. The sentry C C, they declared, remained some time longer in M **, and they do not now know where he is.

These people were immediately followed by a number of natives who came before me bringing a small boy of not more than 7 years of age, whose right hand was gone at the wrist. This child, whose name was F F, they had brought from the village of N **. They stated that some years ago (they could not even approximately fix the date save by indicating that F F was only just able to run) N ** had been attacked by several sentries of the La Lulanga Company. This was owing to their failure in supplying a sufficiency of india-rubber. They did not know whether these sentries had been sent by any European, but they knew all their names, and the Chief of them was one called G G. G G had shot dead the Chief of their town, and the people had run into the forest. The sentries pursued them, and G G had knocked down the child F F with the butt of his gun and had then cut off his hand. They declared that the hand of the dead man and of this boy F F had then been carried away by the sentries. The sentries who did this belonged to the La Lulanga Company's factory at O **. The man who appeared with F F went on to say that they had never complained about it, save to the white man who had then been that Company's agent at O **. They had not thought of complaining to the Commissaire of the district. Not only was he far away, but they were afraid they would not be believed, and they thought the white men only wished for rubber, and that no good could come of pleading with them.

At the same time a number of men followed, with the request that I would listen to them. W declared that their town P **, which had formerly been on the north bank of the X ** River (where I had myself seen it), had now been transferred by force to the south bank, close to the factory at Q **. He said that this act of compulsory transference was the direct act of the Commissaire-Général of the . . . . . district. The Commissaire had visited P ** on his steamer, and had ordered the people of that town to work daily at Q ** for the La Lulanga factory. W had replied that it was too far for the women of P ** to go daily to Q ** as was required; but the Commissaire, in reply, had taken fifty women and carried them away with him. The women were taken to Q **. Two men were taken at the same time. To get these women back, W went on to say, he and his people had to pay a fine of 10,000 brass rods (500 fr.). They had paid this money to the Commissaire-Général himself. They had then been ordered by the Commissaire to abandon their town, since it lay too far from the factory, and build a fresh town close to Q **, so that they might be at hand for the white man's needs. This they had been forced to do—many of them were taken across by force. It was about two years ago W thought that this deportation had been effected, and they now came to beg that I would use my influence with the local authorities to permit their return to their abandoned home. Where they were now situated close to Q ** they were most unhappy, and they only desired to be allowed to return to the former site of P **. They have to take daily to Q ** the following :—

10 baskets gum-copal.
1,000 long canes (termed "ngodji"), which grow in the swamps, and are used in thatching and roofing.
500 bamboos for building.

Each week they are required to deliver at the factory—

200 rations of kwanga.
120 rations of fish.

In addition, fifty women are required each morning to go to the factory and work there all day. They complained that the remuneration given for these services was most inadequate, and that they were continually beaten. When I asked the Chief W why he had not gone to D F to complain if the sentries beat him or his people, opening his mouth he pointed to one of the teeth which was just dropping out, and said: "That is what I got from the D F four days ago when I went to tell him what I now say to you." He added that he was frequently beaten, along with others of his people, by the white man.

One of the men with him, who gave his name as H H, said that two weeks ago the white man at Q** had ordered him to serve as one of the porters of his hammock on a journey he proposed taking inland. H H was then just completing the building of a new house, and excused himself on this ground, but offered to fetch a friend as a substitute. The Director of the Company had, in answer to this excuse, burnt down his house, alleging that he was insolent. He had had a box of cloth and some ducks in the house—in fact, all his goods, and they were destroyed in the fire. The white man then caused him to be tied up, and took him with him inland, and loosed him when he had to carry the hammock.

Other people were waiting, desirous of speaking with me, but so much time was taken in noting the statements already made that I had to leave, if I hoped to reach K** at a reasonable hour. I proceeded in a canoe across the Lulongo and up a tributary to a landing-place which seemed to be about . . . . miles from I**. Here, leaving the canoes, we walked for a couple of miles through a flooded forest to reach the village. I found here a sentry of the La Lulanga Company and a considerable number of natives. After some little delay a boy of about 15 years of age appeared, whose left arm was wrapped up in a dirty rag. Removing this, I found the left hand had been hacked off by the wrist, and that a shot hole appeared in the fleshy part of the forearm. The boy, who gave his name as I I, in answer to my inquiry, said that a sentry of the La Lulanga Company now in the town had cut off his hand. I proceeded to look for this man, who at first could not be found, the natives to a considerable number gathering behind me as I walked through the town. After some delay the sentry appeared, carrying a cap-gun. The boy, whom I placed before him, then accused him to his face of having mutilated him. The men of the town, who were questioned in succession, corroborated the boy's statement. The sentry, who gave his name as K K, could make no answer to the charge. He met it by vaguely saying some other sentry of the Company had mutilated I I; his predecessor, he said, had cut off several hands, and probably this was one of the victims. The natives around said that there were two other sentries at present in the town, who were not so bad as K K, but that he was a villain. As the evidence against him was perfectly clear, man after man standing out and declaring he had seen the act committed, I informed him and the people present that I should appeal to the local authorities for his immediate arrest and trial. In the course of my interrogatory several other charges transpired against him. These were of a minor nature, consisting of the usual characteristic acts of blackmailing, only too commonly reported on all sides. One man said that K K had tied up his wife and only released her on payment of 1,000 rods. Another man said that K K had robbed him of two ducks and a dog. These minor offences K K equally demurred to, and again said that I I had been mutilated by some other sentry, naming several. I took the boy back with me and later brought him to Coquilhatville, where he formally charged K K with the crime, alleging to the Commandant, who took his statement, through a special Government interpreter, in my presence, that it had been done "on account of rubber." I have since been informed that, acting on my request, the authorities at Coquilhatville had arrested K K, who presumably will be tried in due course. A copy of my notes taken in K**, where I I charged K K before me, is appended (Inclosure 6).*

It was obviously impossible that I should visit all the villages of the natives who came to beg me to do so at J** or elsewhere during my journey, or to verify on the spot, as in the case of the boy, the statements they made. In that one case the truth of the charges preferred was amply demonstrated, and their significance was not diminished by the fact that, whereas this act of mutilation had been committed within a few miles of Q**, the head-quarters of a European civilizing agency, and the guilty man was still in their midst, armed with the gun with which he had first shot his victim (for which he could produce no licence when I asked for it, saying it was his employers'), no one of the natives of the terrorized town had

* See p. 78.

attempted to report the occurrence. They had in the interval visited Mampoko each fortnight with the india-rubber from their district. There was also in their midst another mutilated boy X, whose hand had been cut off either by this or another sentry. The main waterway of the Lulongo River lay at their doors, and on it well nigh every fortnight a Government steamer had passed up and down stream on its way to bring the india-rubber of the A.B.I.R. Company to Coquilhatville. They possessed, too, some canoes; and, if all other agencies of relief were closed, the territorial tribunal at Coquilhatville lay open to them, and the journey to it down stream from their village could have been accomplished in some twelve hours. It was no greater journey, indeed, than many of the towns I had elsewhere visited were forced to undertake each week or fortnight to deliver supplies to their local tax collectors. The fact that no effort had been made by these people to secure relief from their unhappy situation impelled me to believe that a very real fear of reporting such occurrences actually existed among them. That everything asserted by such a people, under such circumstances, is strictly true I should in no wise assert. That discrepancies must be found in much alleged by such rude savages, to one whose sympathies they sought to awaken, must equally be admitted. But the broad fact remained that their previous silence said more than their present speech. In spite of contradictions, and even seeming misstatements, it was clear that these men were stating either what they had actually seen with their eyes or firmly believed in their hearts. No one viewing their unhappy surroundings or hearing their appeals, no one at all cognizant of African native life or character, could doubt that they were speaking, in the main, truly; and the unhappy conviction was forced upon me that in the many forest towns behind the screen of trees, which I could not visit, these people were entitled to expect that a civilized administration should be represented among them by other agents than the savages euphemistically termed "forest guards."

The number of these "forest guards" employed in the service of the various Concession Companies on the Congo must be very considerable; but it is not only the Concession Companies which employ "forest guards," for I found many of these men in the service of the La Lulanga Company, which is neither a Concession Company nor endowed with any "rights of police," so far as I am aware. In the A.B.I.R. Concession there must be at least twenty stations directed by one or more European agents.

Each one of these "factories" has, with the permission of the Government, an armament of twenty-five rifles. According to this estimate of the A.B.I.R. factories, and adding the armament of the two steamers that Company possesses, it will be found that this one Concession Company employs 550 rifles, with a supply of cartridges not, I believe, as yet legally fixed. These rifles are supposed by law not to be taken from the limits of the factories, whereas the "sentries" or "forest guards" are quartered in well-nigh every rubber-producing village of the entire Concession.

These men are each armed with a cap-gun, and the amount of ammunition they may individually expend would seem to have no legal limits. These cap-guns can be very effective weapons. On the Lower Lulongo I bought the skin of a fine leopard from a native hunter who had shot the animal the previous day. He produced a cap-gun and his ammunition for my inspection, and I learned from all the men around him that he alone had killed the beast with his own gun. This gun, he informed me, he had purchased some years ago from a former Commissaire of the Government at Coquilhatville, whose name he gave me.

It would be, I think, a moderate computation to put the number of cap-guns issued by the A.B.I.R. Company to its "sentries" as being in the proportion of six to one to the number of rifles allowed to each factory. These figures could be easily verified, but whatever the proportion may be of cap-guns to rifles, it is clear that the A.B.I.R. Society alone controls a force of some 500 rifles and a very large stock of cap-guns.

The other Concession Companies on the Congo have similar privileges, so that it might not be an excessive estimate to say that these Companies and the subsidiary ones (not enjoying rights of police) between them, direct an armed force of not less than 10,000 men.

Their "rights of police," by the Circular of Governor-General Wahis of October 1900, were seemingly limited to the right to "requisition" the Government forces in their neighbourhood to maintain order within the limits of the Concession. That Circular, while it touched upon the arming of "Kapitas" with cap-guns, did not clearly define the jurisdiction of these men as a police force or their use of that weapon, but it is evident that the Government has been cognizant of, and is responsible for, the employment of these armed men. By a Royal Decree, dated the 10th March, 1892, very clear enactments were promulgated dealing with the use of all fire-arms other than flint-locks. By the terms of this Decree all fire-arms and their munitions, other than flint-lock guns, were required, immediately upon importation, to be deposited in a depôt or private store placed under the control of the Government. Each weapon imported had to be registered upon its entry into the depôt and marked under the supervision of the Administration, and could not be withdrawn thence save on the presentation of a permit to carry arms. These permits to carry arms were liable each to a tax of 20 fr., and could be withdrawn in case of abuse. By an Ordinance of the Governor-General of the Congo State, dated the 16th June, 1892, various Regulations making locally effective the foregoing Decree were published. It is clear that the responsibility for the extensive employment of men armed with cap-guns by the various commercial Companies on the Upper Congo rests with the governing authority, which either by law permitted it or did not make effective its own laws.

The six natives brought before me at I ** had all of them been wounded by gun-fire, and the guns in question could only have come into the hands of their assailants through the permission or the neglect of the authorities. Two of these injured individuals were children—one of them certainly not more than 7 years of age—and the other a child (a boy of about the same age), whose arm was shattered by gun-fire at close quarters. Whatever truth there might be in the direct assertions of these people and their relatives, who attested that the attacks upon them had been made by sentries of the La Lulanga Company, it was clear that they had all been attacked by men using guns, which a law already eleven years old had clearly prohibited from being issued, save in special cases, and "to persons who could offer sufficient guarantee that the arms and the munitions which should be delivered to them would not be given, ceded, or sold to third parties"—and, moreover, under a licence which could at any time be withdrawn.

Three of these injured individuals, subsequent to the initial attack upon them, had had their hands cut off—in each case, as it was alleged to me, by a sentry of the La Lulanga Company. In the one case I could alone personally investigate—that of the boy I I—I found this accusation proved on the spot, without seemingly a shadow of doubt existing as to the guilt of the accused sentry. These six wounded and mutilated individuals came from villages in the immediate vicinity of I **, and both from their lips and from those of others who came to me from a greater distance it was clear that these were not the only cases in that neighbourhood. One man, coming from a village 20 miles away, begged me to return with him to his home, where, he asserted, eight of his fellow-villagers had recently been killed by sentries placed there in connection with the fortnightly yield of india-rubber. But my stay at I ** was necessarily a brief one. I had not time to do more than visit the one village of R ** and in that village I had only time to investigate the charge brought by I I. The country is, moreover, largely swampy forest, and the difficulties of getting through it are very great. A regularly equipped expedition would have been needed, and the means of anything like an exhaustive inquiry were not at my disposal. But it seemed painfully clear to me that the facts brought to my knowledge in a three days' stay at I ** would amply justify the most exhaustive inquiry being made into the employment of armed men in that region, and the use to which they put the weapons intrusted to them—ostensibly as the authorized dependants of commercial undertakings. From what I had observed in the A.B.I.R. Concession it is equally clear to me that no inquiry could be held to have been exhaustive which did not embrace the territories of that Company also.

The system of quartering Government soldiers in the villages, once universal, has to-day been widely abandoned; but the abuses once prevalent under this head spring to life in this system of "forest guards," who, over a wide area, represent the only form of local gendarmerie known. But that the practice of employing Government native soldiers in isolated posts has not disappeared is admitted by the highest authorities.

A Circular on this subject, animadverting on the disregard of the reiterated instructions issued, which had forbidden the employment of black troops unaccompanied by a European officer, was dispatched by the Governor-General as recently as the 7th September, 1903, during the period I was actually on the Upper Congo. In this Circular the Commandants and officers of the Force Publique are required to rigorously observe the oft-repeated instructions on this head, and it is pointed out that, in spite of the most imperative orders forbidding the employment of black soldiers by themselves on the public service—"on continue en maints endroits à pratiquer ce déplorable usage." Copy of this Circular is appended (Inclosure 7).*

From my observation of the districts I travelled on in the Upper Congo, it would seem well-nigh impossible for European officers to be always with the soldiers who may be sent on minor expeditions. The number of officers is limited; they have much to do in drilling their troops, and in camp and station life, while the territory to be exploited is vast. The ramifications of the system of taxation, outlined in the foregoing sketch of it, show it to be of a wide-spread character, and since a more or less constant pressure has to be exercised to keep the taxpayers up to the mark, and over a very wide field, a certain amount of dependance upon the uncontrolled actions of native soldiers (who are the only regular police in the country) must be permitted those responsible for the collection of the tax. The most important article of native taxation in the Upper Congo is unquestionably rubber, and to illustrate the importance attaching by their superiors to the collection and augmentation of this tax, the Circular of Governor-General Wahis, addressed to the Commissionaires de District and Chefs de Zône on the 29th March, 1901, was issued. A copy of that Circular is attached (Inclosure 8).†

The instructions this Circular conveys would be excellent if coming from the head of a trading house to his subordinates, but addressed, as they are, by a Governor-General to the principal officers of his administration, they reveal a somewhat limited conception of public duty. Instead of their energies being directed to the government of their districts, the officers therein addressed could not but feel themselves bound to consider the profitable exploitation of india-rubber as one of the principal functions of Government. Taken into account the interpretation these officials must put upon the positive injunctions of their chief, there can be little doubt that they would look upon the profitable production of india-rubber as among the most important of their duties. The praiseworthy official would be he whose district yielded the best and biggest supply of that commodity; and, succeeding in this, the means whereby he brought about the enhanced value of that yield would not, it may be believed, be too closely scrutinized.

When it is remembered that the reprimanded officials are the embodiment of all power in their districts, and that the agents they are authorized to employ are an admittedly savage soldiery, the source whence spring the unhappiness and unrest of the native communities I passed through on the Upper Congo need not be sought far beyond the policy dictating this Circular.

I decided, owing to pressure of other duties, to return from Coquilhatville to Stanley Pool. The last incident of my stay in the Upper Congo occurred on the night prior to my departure. Late that night a man came with some natives of the S ** district, represented as his friends, who were fleeing from their homes, and whom he begged me to carry with me to the French territory at Lukolela. These were L L of T ** and seven others. L L stated that, owing to his inability to meet the impositions of the Commissaire of the S ** district, he had, with his family, abandoned his home, and was seeking to reach Lukolela. He had already come 80 miles down stream by canoe, but was now hiding with friends in one of the towns near Coquilhatville. Part of the imposition laid upon his town consisted of two goats, which had to be supplied each month for the white man's table at S **. As all the goats in his neighbourhood had long since disappeared in meeting these demands, he could now only satisfy this imposition by buying in inland districts such goats as were for sale. For these he had to pay 3,000 rods each (150 fr.), and as the Government remuneration amounted to only 100 rods (5 fr.) per goat, he had no further means of maintaining the supply. Having appealed in vain for the remission of this burden, no other course was left him but to fly. I told this man I regretted I could not help him, that his proper course was to appeal for relief to the authorities of the district; and this failing, to seek the higher authorities at Boma. This, he said, was clearly impossible for him to do. On the last occasion when he had sought the officials at S **, he had been told that if his next tax were not forthcoming he should go into the "chain gang." He added that a neighbouring Chief who had failed in this respect had just died in the prison gang, and that such would be his fate if he were caught. He added that, if I disbelieved him, there were those who could vouch for his character and the truth of his statement; and I told him and his friend that I should inquire in that quarter, but that it was impossible for me to assist a fugitive. I added, however, that there was no law on the Congo Statute Book

* See p. 80. † See p. 81.

which forbade him or any other man from travelling freely to any part of the country, and his right to navigate in his canoe the Upper Congo was as good as mine in my steamer or any one else's. He and his people left me at midnight, saying that unless they could get away with me they did not think it possible they could succeed in gaining Lukolela. A person at T * *, to whom I referred this statement, informed me that L L's statement was true. He said: What L L told you, *re* price of goats, was perfectly true. At U * * they are 3,000, and here they are 2,500 to 3,000 rods. Ducks are from 200 to 300 rods. Fowls are from 60 to 100 rods. *Re* "dying in the chains," he had every reason to fear this, for recently two Chiefs died in the chain, viz., the Chief of a little town above U * *; his crime: because he did not move his houses a few hundred yards to join them to . . . . . as quickly as the Commissaire thought he should do. Second, the Chief of T * *; crime: because he did not go up every fortnight with the tax. These two men were chained together and made to carry heavy loads of bricks and water, and were frequently beaten by the soldiers in charge of them. There are witnesses to prove this.

Leaving the township of Coquilhatville on the 11th September, I reached Stanley Pool on the 15th September.

I have, &c.
(Signed) R. CASEMENT.

Inclosure 1 in No. 3.

(See p. 29.)

Notes on Refugee Tribes encountered in July 1903.

HEARING of the L * refugees from I *, I decided to visit the nearest Settlement of these fugitives, some 20 miles away, to see them for myself.

At N * found large town of K *, and scattered through it many small settlements of L * refugees. The town of N * consists approximately of seventy-one K * houses, and seventy-three occupied by L *. These latter seemed industrious, simple folk, many weaving palm fibre into mats or native cloth; others had smithies, working brass wire into bracelets, chains, and anklets; some iron-workers making knives. Sitting down in one of these blacksmith's sheds, the five men at work ceased and came over to talk to us. I counted ten women, six grown-up men, and eight lads and women in this one shed of L *. I then asked them to tell me why they had left their homes. Three of the men sat down in front of me, and told a tale which I cannot think can be true, but it seemed to come straight from their hearts. I repeatedly asked certain parts to be gone over again while I wrote in my note-book. The fact of my writing down and asking for names, &c., seemed to impress them, and they spoke with what certainly impressed me as being great sincerity.

I asked, first, why they had left their homes, and had come to live in a strange far-off country among the K *, where they owned nothing, and were little better than servitors. All, when this question was put, women as well, shouted out, "On account of the rubber tax levied by the Government posts."

I asked particularly the names of the places whence they had come. They answered they were from V * *. Other L * refugees here at N * were W * *, others again were X * *, but all had fled from their homes for the same reason—it was the "rubber tax."

I asked then how this tax was imposed. One of them, who had been hammering out an iron neck collar on my arrival, spoke first. He said:—

"I am N N. These other two beside me are O O and P P, all of us Y **. From our country each village had to take twenty loads of rubber. These loads were big: they were as big as this . . . ." (Producing an empty basket which came nearly up to the handle of my walking-stick.) "That was the first size. We had to fill that up, but as rubber got scarcer the white man reduced the amount. We had to take these loads in four times a-month."

Q. "How much pay did you get for this?"

A. (Entire audience.) "We got no pay! We got nothing!"

And then N N, whom I asked, again said:—

"Our village got cloth and a little salt, but not the people who did the work. Our Chiefs eat up the cloth; the workers got nothing. The pay was a fathom of cloth and a little salt for every big basket full, but it was given to the Chief, never to the men. It used to take ten days to get the twenty baskets of rubber—we were always in the forest and then when we were late we were killed. We had to go further and further into the forest to find the rubber vines, to go without food, and our women had to give up cultivating the fields and gardens. Then we starved. Wild beasts—the leopards—killed some of us when we were working away in the forest, and others got lost or died from exposure and starvation, and we begged the white man to leave us alone, saying we could get no more rubber, but the white men and their soldiers said: 'Go! You are only beasts yourselves, you are nyama (meat).' We tried, always going further into the forest, and when we failed and our rubber was short, the soldiers came to our towns and killed us. Many were shot, some had their ears cut off; others were tied up with ropes around their necks and bodies and taken away. The white men sometimes at the posts did not know of the bad things the soldiers did to us, but it was the white men who sent the soldiers to punish us for not bringing in enough rubber."

Here P P took up the tale from N N:—

"We said to the white men, 'We are not enough people now to do what you want us. Our country has not many people in it and we are dying fast. We are killed by the work you make us do, by the stoppage of our plantations, and the breaking up of our homes.' The white man looked at us and said: 'There are lots of people in Mputu'" (Europe, the white man's country). "'If there are lots of people in the white man's country there must be many people in the black man's country.' The white man who said this was the chief white man at F F *, his name was A B, he was a very bad man. Other white men of Bula Matadi who had been bad and wicked were B C, C D, and D E." "These had killed us often, and killed us by their own hands as well as by their soldiers. Some white men were good. These were E F, F G, G H, H I, I K, K L."

These ones told them to stay in their homes and did not hunt and chase them as the others had done, but after what they had suffered they did not trust more any one's word, and they had fled from their country and were now going to stay here, far from their homes, in this country where there was no rubber.

Q. "How long is it since you left your homes, since the big trouble you speak of?"

A. "It lasted for three full seasons, and it is now four seasons since we fled and came into the K* country."

Q. "How many days is it from N * to your own country?"

A. "Six days of quick marching. We fled because we could not endure the things done to us. Our Chiefs were hanged, and we were killed and starved and worked beyond endurance to get rubber."

Q. "How do you know it was the white men themselves who ordered these cruel things to be done to you? These things must have been done without the white man's knowledge by the black soldiers."

A. (P P): "The white men told their soldiers: 'You kill only women; you cannot kill men. You must prove that you kill men.' So then the soldiers when they killed us" (here he stopped and hesitated, and then pointing to the private parts of my bulldog—it was lying asleep at my feet), he said: "then they cut off those things and took them to the white men, who said: 'It is true, you have killed men.'"

Q. "You mean to tell me that any white man ordered your bodies to be mutilated like that, and those parts of you carried to him?"

P P, O O, and all (shouting): "Yes! many white men. D E did it."

Q. "You say this is true? Were many of you so treated after being shot?"

All (shouting out): "Nkoto! Nkoto!" (Very many! Very many!)

There was no doubt that these people were not inventing. Their vehemence, their flashing eyes, their excitement, was not simulated. Doubtless they exaggerated the numbers, but they were clearly telling what they knew and loathed. I was told that they often became so furious at the recollection of what had been done to them that they lost control over themselves. One of the men before me was getting into this state now.

I asked whether L* tribes were still running from their country, or whether they now stayed at home and worked voluntarily.

N N answered: "They cannot run away now—not easily; there are sentries in the country there between the Lake and this; besides, there are few people left."

P P said: "We heard that letters came to the white men to say that the people were to be well treated. We heard that these letters had been sent by the big white men in 'Mputu' (Europe); but our white men tore up these letters, laughing, saying: 'We are the "basango" and "banyanga" (fathers and mothers, *i.e.*, elders). Those who write to us are only "bana" (children).' Since we left our homes the white men have asked us to go home again. We have heard that they want us to go back, but we will not go. We are not warriors, and do not want to fight. We only want to live in peace with our wives and children, and so we stay here among the K *, who are kind to us, and will not return to our homes."

Q. "Would you not like to go back to your homes? Would you not, in your hearts, all wish to return?"

A. (By many.) "We loved our country, but we will not trust ourselves to go back."

P P: "Go, you white men, with the steamer to I *, and see what we have told you is true. Perhaps if other white men, who do not hate us, go there, Bula Matadi may stop from hating us, and we may be able to go home again."

I asked to be pointed out any refugees from other tribes, if there were such, and they brought forward a lad who was a X * *, and a man of the Z * *. These two, answering me, said there were many with them from their tribes who had fled from their country.

Went on about fifteen minutes to another L * group of houses in the midst of the K * town. Found here mostly W * *, an old Chief sitting in the open village Council-house with a Z * * man and two lads. An old woman soon came and joined, and another man. The woman began talking with much earnestness. She said the Government had worked them so hard they had had no time to tend their fields and gardens, and they had starved to death. Her children had died; her sons had been killed. The two men, as she spoke, muttered murmurs of assent.

The old Chief said: "We used to hunt elephants long ago, there were plenty in our forests, and we got much meat; but Bula Matadi killed the elephant hunters because they could not get rubber, and so we starved. We were sent out to get rubber, and when we came back with little rubber we were shot."

Q. "Who shot you?"

A. "The white men . . . . . sent their soldiers out to kill us."

Q. "How do you know it was the white man who sent the soldiers? It might be only these savage soldiers themselves."

A. "No, no. Sometimes we brought rubber into the white man's stations. We took rubber to D E's station, E E *, and to F F * and to . . . .'s station. When it was not enough rubber the white man would put some of us in lines, one behind the other, and would shoot through all our bodies. Sometimes he would shoot us like that with his own hand; sometimes his soldiers would do it."

Q. "You mean to say you were killed in the Government posts themselves by the Government white men themselves, or under their eyes?"

A. (Emphatically.) "We were killed in the stations of the white men themselves. We were killed by the white man himself. We were shot before his eyes."

The names D E, B C, and L M, were names I heard repeatedly uttered.

The Z * * man said he, too, had fled; now he lived at peace with the K *.

The abnormal refugee population in this one K * town must equal the actual K * population itself. On every hand one finds these refugees. They seem, too, to pass busier lives than their K * hosts, for during all the hot hours of the afternoon, wherever I walked through the town—and I went all through N * until the sun set—I found L * weavers, or iron and brass workers, at work.

Slept at M M's house. Many people coming to talk to us after dark.

Left N * about 8 to return to the Congo bank. On the way back left the main path and struck into one of the side towns, a village called A A *. This lies only some 4 or 5 miles from the river. Found here thirty-two L * houses with forty-three K *, so that the influx of fugitives here is almost equal to the original population. Saw many L *. All were frightened, and they and the K * were evidently so ill at ease that I did not care to pause. Spoke to one or two men only as we walked through the town. The L * drew away from us, but on looking back saw many heads popped out of doors of the houses we had passed.

Got back to steamer about noon.

Heard that L * came sometimes to M * from I *. I am now 100 miles (about) up-river from N *. Went into one of the M * country farm towns called B B *. Found on entering plantation two huts with five men and one woman, who I at once recognized by their head-dress as L *, like those at N *. The chief speaker, a young man named . . . . . . who lives at B B *. He seems about 22 or 23, and speaks with an air of frankness. He says: "The L * here and others who come to M *, come from a place C C *. It is connected with the lake by a stream. His own town in the district of C C * is D D *. C C * is a big district and had many people. They now bring the Government india-rubber, kwanga, and fowls, and work on broad paths connecting each village. His own village has to take 300 baskets of india-rubber. They get one piece of cotton cloth, called locally sanza, and no more." (Note.—This cannot be true. He is doubtless exaggerating.) Four other men with him were wearing the rough palm-fibre cloth of the country looms, and they pointed to this as proof that they got no cloth for their labours. K K continuing said: "We were then killed for not bringing in enough rubber."

Q. "You say you were killed for not bringing in rubber. Were you ever mutilated as proof that the soldiers had killed you?"

A. "When we were killed the white man was there himself. No proof was needed. Men and women were put in a line with a palm tree and were shot."

Here he took three of the four men sitting down and put them one in line behind the other, and said: "The white men used to put us like that and shoot all with one cartridge. That was often done, and worse things."

Q. "But how, if you now have to work so hard, are you yourselves able to come here to M * to see your friends?"

A. "We came away without the sentries or soldiers knowing, but when we get home we may have trouble."

Q. "Do you know the L * who are now at N *?" (Here I gave the names of N N, O O, and P P.)

A. "Yes; many L* fled to that country. N N we know ran away on account of the things done to them by the Government white men. The K* and L * have always been friends. That is why the L * fled to them for refuge."

Q. "Are there sentries or soldiers in your villages now?"

A. "In the chief villages there are always four soldiers with rifles. When natives go out into the forest to collect rubber they would leave one of their number behind to stay and protect the women. Sometimes the soldiers finding him thus refused to believe what he said, and killed him for shirking his work. This often happens."

Asked how far it was from M * to their country they say three days' journey, and then about two days more on to I * by water, or three if by land. They begged us to go to their country, they said: "We will show you the road, we will take you there, and you will see how things are, and that our country has been spoiled, and we are speaking the truth."

Left them here and returned to the river bank.

The foregoing entries made at the time in my note-book seemed to me, if not false, greatly exaggerated, although the statements were made with every air of conviction and sincerity. I did not again meet with any more L * refugees, for on my return to G * I stayed only a few hours. A few days afterwards, while I was at Stanley Pool, I received further evidence in a letter of which the following is an extract:—

* * * * * * *

"I was sorry not to see you as you passed down, and so missed the opportunity of conveying to you personally a lot of evidence as to the terrible maladministration practised in the past in the district. I saw the official at the post of E E *. He is the successor of the infamous wretch D E, of whom you heard so much yourself from the refugees at N *. This D E was in this district in . . ., . . ., and . . ., and he it was that depopulated the country. His successor, M N, is very vehement in his denunciations of him, and declares that he will leave nothing undone that he can do to bring him to justice. He is now stationed at G G *, near our station at H H *. Of M N I have nothing to say but praise. In a very difficult position he has done wonderfully. The people are beginning to show themselves and gathering about the many posts under his charge. M N told me that when he took over the station at E E * from D E he visited the prison, and almost fainted, so horrible was the condition of the place and the poor wretches in it. He told me of many things he had heard of from the soldiers. Of D E shooting with his own hand man after man who had come with an insufficient quantity of rubber. Of his putting several one behind the other and shooting them all with one cartridge. Those who accompanied me, also heard from the soldiers many frightful stories and abundant confirmation of what was told us at N * about the taking to D E of the organs of the men slain by the sentries of the various posts. I saw a letter from the present officer at F F * to M N, in which he upbraids him for not using more vigorous means, telling him to talk less and shoot more, and reprimanding him for not killing more than one in a district under his care where there was a little trouble. M N is due in Belgium in about three months, and says he will land one day and begin denouncing his predecessor the next. I received many favours from him, and should be sorry to injure him in any way . . . . . He has already accepted a position in one of the Companies, being unable to continue longer in the service of the State. I have never seen in all the different parts of the State which I have visited a neater station, or a district more under control than that over which this M N presides. He is the M N the people of N * told us of, who they said was kind.

"If I can give you any more information, or if there are any questions you would like to put to me, I shall be glad to serve you, and through you these persecuted people."

From a separate communication, I extract the following paragraphs:—

". . . . . I heard of some half-dozen L * who were anxious to visit their old home, and would be willing to go with me; so, after procuring some necessary articles in the shape of provisions and barter, I started from our post at N *. It was the end of the dry season, and many of the water-courses were quite dry, and during some days we even found the lack of water somewhat trying. The first two days' travelling was through alternating forest and grass plain, our guides, as far as possible, avoiding the villages. . . . . . Getting fresh guides from a little village, we got into a region almost entirely forested, and later descended into a gloomy valley still dripping from the rain. According to our guides we should soon be through this, but it was not until the afternoon of the second day after entering that we once more emerged from the gloom. Several times we lost the track, and I had little inclination to blame the guides, for several times the undergrowth and a species of thorn palm were trodden down in all directions by the elephants. It would seem to be a favourite hunting ground of theirs, and once we got very close to a large herd who went off at a furious pace, smashing down the small trees, trumpeting, and making altogether a most terrifying noise. The second night in this forest we came across, when looking for the track, a little village of runaways from the rubber district. When assured of our friendliness they took us in and gave us what shelter they could. During the night another tornado swept the country and blew down a rotten tree, some branches of which fell in amongst my tent and the little huts in which some of the boys were sleeping. It was another most narrow escape.

"Early the next day we were conducted by one of the men of this village to the right road, and very soon found ourselves travelling along a track which had evidently been, at only a recent date, opened up by a number of natives. 'What was it?' 'Oh! it is the road along which we used to carry rubber to the white men.' 'But why used to?' 'Oh, all the people have either run away, or have been killed or died of starvation, and so there is no one to get rubber any longer.'

"That day we made a very long march, being nearly nine and a-half hours walking, and passing through several other large depopulated districts. On all sides were signs of a very recent large population, but all was as quiet as death, and buffaloes roamed at will amongst the still growing manioc and bananas. It was a sad day, and when, as the sun was setting, we came upon a large State post we were plunged into still greater grief. True, there was a comfortable house at our service, and houses for all the party; but we had not been long there before we found that we had reached the centre of what was once a very thickly populated region, known as C C *, from which many refugees in the neighbourhood of G * had come. It was here a white man, known by the name of D E, lived. . . . . He came to the district, and, after seven months of diabolical work, left it a waste. Some of the stories current about him are not fit to record here, but the native evidence is so consistent and so universal that it is difficult to disbelieve that murder and rapine on a large scale were carried on here. His successor, a man of a different nature, and much liked by the people, after more than two and a-half years has succeeded in winning back to the side of the State post a few natives, and there I saw them in their wretched little huts, hardly able to call their lives their own in the presence of the new white man (myself), whose coming among them had set them all a-wondering. From this there was no fear of losing the track. For many miles it was a broad road, from 6 to 10 feet in width, and wherever there was a possibility of water settling logs were laid down. Some of these viaducts were miles in length, and must have entailed immense labour; whilst rejoicing in the great facility with which we could continue our journey, we could not help picturing the many cruel scenes which, in all probability, were a constant accompaniment to the laying of these huge logs. I wish to emphasize as much as possible the desolation and emptiness of the country we passed through. That it was only very recently a well-populated country, and, as things go out here, rather more densely than usual, was very evident. After a few hours we came to a State rubber post. In nearly every instance these posts are most imposing, some of them giving rise to the supposition that several white men were residing in them. But in only one did we find a white man—the successor of D E. At one place I saw lying about in the grass surrounding the post, which is built on the site of several very large towns, human bones, skulls, and, in some places, complete skeletons. On inquiring the reason for this unusual sight: 'Oh!' said my informant, 'When the bambote (soldiers) were sent to make us cut rubber there were so many killed we got tired of burying, and sometimes when we wanted to bury we were not allowed to.'

"'But why did they kill you so?'

"'Oh! sometimes we were ordered to go, and the sentry would find us preparing food to eat while in the forest, and he would shoot two or three to hurry us along. Sometimes we would try and do a little work on our plantations, so that when the harvest time came we should have something to eat, and the sentry would shoot some of us to teach us that our business was not to plant but to get rubber. Sometimes we were driven off to live for a fortnight in the forest without any food and without anything to make a fire with, and many died of cold and hunger. Sometimes the quantity brought was not sufficient, and then several would be killed to frighten us to bring more. Some tried to run away, and died of hunger and privation in the forest in trying to avoid the State posts.'

"'But,' said I, 'if the sentries killed you like that, what was the use? You could not bring more rubber when there were fewer people.'

"'Oh! as to that, we do not understand it. These are the facts.'

"And looking around on the scene of desolation, on the untended farms and neglected palms, one could not but believe that in the main the story was true. From State sentries came confirmation and particulars even more horrifying, and the evidence of a white man as to the state of the country—the unspeakable condition of the prisons at the State posts—all combined to convince me over and over again that, during the last seven years, this 'domaine privé' of King Leopold has been a veritable 'hell on earth.'

"The present régime seems to be more tolerable. A small payment is made for the rubber now brought in. A little salt—say a pennyworth—for 2 kilogrammes of rubber, worth in Europe from 6 to 8 fr. The collection is still compulsory, but, compared with what has gone before, the natives consider themselves fairly treated. There is a coming together of families and communities and the re-establishment of villages; but oh! in what sadly diminished numbers, and with what terrible gaps in the families . . . . . Near a large State post we saw the only large and apparently normal village we came across in all the three weeks we spent in the district. One was able to form here some estimate of what the population was before the advent of the white man and the search for rubber . . . ."

It will be observed that the devastated region whence had come the refugees I saw at N *, comprises a part of the "Domaine de la Couronne."

Inclosure 2 in No. 3.

(See p. 29.)

(A.)

The Rev. J. Whitehead to Governor-General of Congo State.

Dear Sir, *Baptist Missionary Society, Lukolela, July 28, 1903.*

I HAVE the honour to acknowledge the receipt of the Circular and the List of Questions respecting the sleep sickness sent through the Rev. J. L. Forfeitt.

I hasten to do my best in reply, for the matter is of paramount importance, and I trust that if I may seem to trespass beyond my limits in stating my opinions in reference to this awful sickness and matters kindred thereto, my zeal may be interpreted as arising from excessive sorrow and sympathy for a disappearing people. I believe I shall be discharging my duty to the State and His Majesty King Leopold II, whose desire for the facts in the interests of humanity have long been published, if I endeavour to express myself as clearly as I can regarding the necessities of the natives of Lukolela.

The population in the villages of Lukolela in January 1891 must have been not less than 6,000 people, but when I counted the whole population in Lukolela at the end of December 1896 I found it to be only 719, and I estimated from the decrease, as far as we could count up the number of known deaths during the year, that at the same rate of decrease in ten years the people would be reduced to about 400, but judge of my heartache when on counting them all again on Friday and Saturday last to find only a population of 352 people, and the death-rate rapidly increasing. I note also a decrease very appallingly apparent in the inland districts during the same number of years; three districts are well-nigh swept out (these are near to the river), and others are clearly diminished; so that if something is not soon done to give the people heart and remove their fear and trembling (conditions which generate fruitfully morbid conditions and proneness to attacks of disease), doubtless the whole place will be very soon denuded of its population. The pressure under which they live at present is crushing them; the food which they sadly need themselves very often must, under penalty, be carried to the State post, also grass, cane string, baskets for the "caoutchouc" (the last three items do not appear to be paid for); the "caoutchouc" must be brought in from the inland districts; their Chiefs are being weakened in their prestige and physique through imprisonment, which is often cruel, and thus weakened in their authority over their own people, they are put into chains for the shortage of manioc bread and "caoutchouc."

In the riverine part of Lukolela we have done our very best as non-official members of the State to cope with disease in every way possible to us; but so far the officials of the State have never attempted even the feeblest effort to assist the natives of Lukolela to recover themselves or guard themselves in any way from disease. In times of small-pox, when no time can be lost in the interests of the community, I have, perhaps, gone sometimes beyond my rights as a private citizen in dealing with it. But there has always been the greatest difficulty in getting food for them (the patients) and nurses for them, even when the people were not compelled to take their food supply to the State post, but when food supplies and labour are compressed into one channel all voluntary philanthropy is paralyzed. It is quite in vain for us to teach these poor people the need of plenty of good food, for we appear to them as those who mock; they point to the food which must be taken to the post. A weekly tax of 900 brass rods' worth of manioc bread from 160 women, half of whom are not capable of much hard and continuous work, does not leave much margin for them to listen to teaching concerning personal attention in matters of food. At present they are compelled to supply a number of workmen, and some of these are retained after their terms are completed against their will; the villages need the presence of their men, there are at present but eighty-two in the villages of Lukolela, and I can see the shadow of death over nearly twenty of them.*

The inland people and their Chiefs tremble when they must go down to the river, so much has been done latterly to shake their confidence, and this fear is not strengthening them physically, but undermining their constitutions, such as they are. They hate the compulsory "caoutchouc" business, and they naturally do their best to get away from it. If something is not quickly done to give these timid and disheartened people contentment and their home life assured to them, sickness will speedily remove many, and those who remain will look upon the white man, of whatever nation or position, as their natural enemy (it is not far from that now). Some have already sworn to die, be killed, or anything else rather than be forced to bring in "caoutchouc," which spells imprisonment and subsequent death to them; what they hear as having been done they quite understand can be done to them, so they conclude they may as well die first as last. The State has fought with them twice already, if not more; but it is useless, they will not submit. A cave of Adullam is a thing not always easily reckoned with.

May I be permitted to seize the present opportunity of respectfully pleading on behalf of this people that their rights be respected, and that the attention as of a father to his children be sympathetically shown them? May I also be permitted to place before you a few suggestions which have been impelled into my mind face to face with this dying people of what is their need while medical inquiry goes forward, please God, to master this terrible scourge? I suggest the following as immediately needful for the riverine people:—

1. That the present small population of Lukolela be requested to vacate the present site of their dwellings, and form a community on the somewhat higher ground at present used for gardens, the soil of which has been impoverished by years of manioc growing. This is known by the name Ntomba; and that they be requested to clear the undergrowth on the beach, the sites of their present dwellings, and plant bananas, &c.

2. That no one known to have sleep-sickness be permitted to dwell on the new site; but all be removed to a site lower down the river; and that it shall be the duty of the people to supply their sick with the necessary food and caretakers. The islands are unsuitable, being uninhabitable for a large part of the year.

3. That they be compelled to bury their dead at a considerable distance from the dwellings, and to bury them in graves at least a fathom deep, and not as at present in shallow graves in close proximity to the houses.

4. That they be encouraged to build higher houses with more apertures for the ingress of sunshine and air in the daytime, and with floors considerably raised above the outside ground.

5. That a strong endeavour be made to get them to provide better latrine arrangements.

6. That they be encouraged to give up eating and drinking together from the same dish or vessel in common.

7. That the men be encouraged to follow their old practices of hunting, fishing, blacksmithing, &c., and with the women care for their gardens and homes, and that they be given every protection in these duties and in the holding of their property against the State soldiers and workmen and everybody else that wants to interfere with their rights.

8. All the foregoing they will not be able to do unless the present compulsory method of acquiring their labour and their food by the State is exchanged for a voluntary one.

9. That the Chiefs or present chief representatives of the deceased Chiefs among whom the

*** *September* 12. Mr. Whitehead informed me when I passed Lukolela this day, nine of these twenty have died since he wrote the above.—R. C.**

land was divided before the State came into existence (I believe about three will be found at Lukolela itself) be recognized as the executive of these matters, and that they be requested to devote their levies (restored as of old) made on the produce, &c., of their lands to the betterment of their towns and district, by making roads through their lands, &c.

10. To appoint sentries to carry out either the above or any other beneficent rules in any of the villages would be to endeavour to mend the present deplorable condition with an evil a hundred-fold worse.

All the above suggestions adjusted to suit the locality are equally applicable to the inland districts.

In answering the list of questions I would say:—

1. Sleep-sickness is sadly only too well known at Lukolela. It is prevalent in the whole of the riverine and inland districts. In the inland districts I am not yet able to say whether it is more prevalent than in the riverine one; that can only be ascertained by a more prolonged residence there than as yet I have had opportunity to make. In the riverine district I estimate that quite half of the deaths are from sleep-sickness. The cases do not occur in batches like cases of small-pox and measles do; there are too many in a given place unaffected at one time. It will, however, gradually sweep away whole families. The common notion among the natives is that the sickness came from down-river; and it was prevalent, though not to such an extent as now, as far back as the oldest people I have met can remember. Before our Mission was founded here a suspected case would be thrown into the river; but inland I do not think there is any evidence to show that they did otherwise than to-day—nurse their sick perfectly, heedless of the contagion in respect of them (the nurses) or their friends, and, as they do on the beach, bury their dead close to their houses, and in some cases live on the top of the graves.

2. From my own observation (since January 1891) the sickness is endemic; in the riverine villages the death-rate slowly increased until 1894, when the people quite lost heart and felt their homes were no longer secure to them, and then hunger, improper food, fear, and homelessness appeared to increase the death-rate from sleep-sickness and other causes most appallingly, and the rate has still further increased, especially during the last two years. The fewer the population becomes the proportionate rate of death increases most fearfully.

3. The district of Lukolela may be described as follows: The beach line is wooded, broken by one or two creeks, one of which winds for a considerable distance inland to a district which can be reached overland by a journey of at least three days at the shortest. There is more or less of low-lying land connected with the creeks. The 6 miles below the Mission station is lower than the 8 miles above. The highest point of our land is about 19 metres above high-water level, and possibly there is a further rise of 3 metres or so further up stream. The ground which I suggest the people be removed to may be on an average about 12 to 15 metres above high-water level. This ridge of river bank shelves down into low-wooded land and grass plains which are flooded at high water, though for the most part dry at the lowest ebb; then behind these rise small plateaus separated by low valleys of wooded and grassy land. From the pools and streams of this low ground the people get most of their fish; even when the river is at medium height a journey between the various plateaus where the villages and farms are found requires about half the time to be spent in wading, sometimes breast deep.

4. A large proportion of the population is comprised of slaves, mostly from the tributaries of the Equator district, some from the Mobsi, Likuba, and Likwala peoples on the north bank, some from Ngombe below Irebu, some from as far as the district of Lake Léopold II and other places. All the tribes represented seem equally affected, and neither slave nor freeman seems to have preferential treatment.

5. To an ordinary observer the men, women, and children appear to be affected alike. It is not easy to always differentiate the sickness from other maladies, for often it may be that the malady gives rise to various complications; these complications are extremely intractable if sleep-sickness be present. When a man in the prime of life has his prestige and spirit broken through fear and punishment he loses interest in his home, refuses to take food and drink; a sleep-sickness patient will do the same. With the women in all cases we have known there is also present amenorrhœa; sometimes treatment for this has restored the patient in this respect for a time, but there has in all cases we have known of this sort been a relapse; so whether the patient died of one or the other would be difficult to say.

6. The well-fed do not seem to fall before the scourge so rapidly as the ill-fed. The progress of the disease seems to us considerably slower as a rule with those who take care of their food and habits, but it attacks even the most scrupulously attentive to these matters.

There is a very bad practice amongst them: they will go sometimes days without eating, although they may have manioc and plantain, and other foods from the soil at hand, simply because they have no fish or flesh to eat with them; sometimes they pinch themselves in food to retain their brass rods for the purchase of some coveted article. The natives to-day are not so careful in the preparation of food, and it is more hastily performed; the manioc is eaten as nearly the raw state as they dare use it. The bitter manioc is mostly grown, as the yield from it is greater than from any other kind. Plantains are largely eaten roasted, and boiled, and beaten into a pudding. Palm-nuts, too, they are very fond of, and the oil forms a good part of the cooked foods. They use, especially in the absence of fish or flesh, the leaves of the manioc, which are bruised and boiled; in nearly every case, however, head- and stomach-ache follow, which pass off in a few days if bowels be active. Well-peppered food they enjoy, and rotten fish and flesh they do not, as a rule, despise. Their dried fish, of which a large quantity is eaten, is not by any means always free from maggots. Elephant meat seems to give them diarrhœa; dog-headed bats similarly; hippo meat generally produces slight constipation. I am afraid a dood deal of disease is passed from person to person in the preparation of food. There is a great deal of eating together and drinking together from one and the same vessel; they dip their hands in the mess prepared as they sit round the pot, and I cannot say that they are too careful of the condition of their hands at the time. Clothing is usually scant except for decoration; hence the colder the whether the less the clothing, the brighter and warmer the more they carry. Washing is not a very frequent exercise among the natives. They like, as a rule, teeth kept clean, washing them every day and after every meal. They like to smear their bodies with oil and camwood. The hair is left undressed or dressed as the case may be for weeks at a time without further cleansing. Sleeping is mostly done on raised constructions of sticks, varying from half a-foot from the ground to about 3 feet or so. I am afraid that not much in the way of covering is used while sleeping, a blanket being mostly worn during the day as an article of fine clothing. Many, especially those in temporary residence, sleep on the ground floor with only a mat intervening. Jiggers, bugs, mosquitcs, and vermin abound in their houses on the beach, but jiggers are not so plentiful, and mosquitos very rare inland. The inland people take great care of their water sources, but on the beach the river water is largely used, and this is of a dark brown colour; some is taken from the creeks, but it is very impure, abounding with decayed vegetation and clay, and some from springs, such as they are, and these are only surface drainings over the clayey subsoil. The sweepings or their huts and refuse from their food is not thrown far away, sometimes even being quite close up against one of the walls of the hut. In the daytime they relieve themselves in the nearest sheltered spot without further discrimination, and these places, in the present uncleared character of their surroundings, are very close at hand; in the night time they are not so particular, but will even relieve themselves in the open, and on the paths trod by every one. The common belief is that the disease is communicated by means of the secretions, and yet, strange to say, the natives take scarcely any precautions.

7. All the cases we have known have been fatal. We have thought sometimes we have done good with iodide of potassium and cod-liver oil, but if it did any good at all it was only very temporary. We judge from our observations that from the first symptoms which appear to be mental ones, the best cared for cases last for from one to three years. Others in which food is soon refused and neglect is suffered may speedily terminate in a few months, or even weeks, from the first certain indications. The first symptoms seem to be mental, the balance of thought fails at intervals, then come the physical signs of pain in the lower part of the back; often thought here to be piles, and they seek the usual remedies for this; later the pain extends to the whole back and then to the head, especially at the back of the neck, and drowsiness steals over the patient at inconvenient times, often the eyes become staring, the face assumes a haggard appearance, and anæmia casts its pallor over the whole body; intelligence rapidly diminishes, and often the patient dies foaming at the mouth; if burial does not take place quickly maggots soon make their appearance in the body. When the natives begin to stuff their remedies up their patient's nostrils to take away the "confusion of eyes" (a phrase which they use to describe a person going out of his senses) the patient will very likely become violently deranged, and then he has to be forcibly restrained in stocks or otherwise.

Isolation is undoubtedly the first thing to do, but when to begin the isolation is a difficulty, and when that is settled to maintain the isolation is still a greater one. The patients could not be left to die, they would need food, attending to (for they become so helpless latterly) and burying, and almost all who undertook that work would be sure eventually to succomb. To get a person here, however, to look after somebody else's relative is a well nigh impossibility by moral suasion.

I should have noted above that the experiment of better houses, such as the youths and workmen have built in the little village adjoining the Mission station (wattle and daub, with good high roofs), have given no benefit whatever. Very few of them will be able to remain for more than one or two years; the occupants are showing signs that are ominous; we shall need to burn them down at the decease of the occupants.

Apologizing for trespassing on your attention at so great a length, I beg you to accept, &c.

(Signed) JOHN WHITEHEAD

(B.)

The Rev. J. Whitehead to Governor-General of Congo State.

Baptist Missionary Society, Lukolela, Haut Congo,
September 7, 1903.

Dear Sir,

I HAVE recently paid a visit, along with my wife, to the inland district of Lukolela, and I have had related to me such accounts, and have myself seen such evidence of what seems to me both illegal and cruel occurrences, that my blood had been made to boil with indignation and abhorrence. I take upon myself the humanitarian duty, which is truly the call of God, to supplement my letter to you on the subject of sleep-sickness and the general decline of these peoples, and confirm some of my statements by the presentation of facts of which I have the knowledge. It may be that in some of my statements I may be trusting to bruised reeds, but, as far as possible, I am persuaded of the truth of what I present to your consideration.

On the 16th August, 1902, I called the attention of the Commissaire-General at Léopoldville to a murder which had been committed by a soldier by shooting two men while still in the chain.

They had been sent, in addition, to a youth who was walking unchained to draw water from a pool some 2 kilom. distant from the lower post of Lukolela by a telegraph clerk named M. Gadot (M. de Becker being the Chef de Poste resident at the upper station). The unchained youth was flogged by the soldier by a chicotte taken from a house on the way, and the youth fled, and the soldier shot the two men left. My letter was taken down river by a steamer which passed here in course of a week. Nothing was done by the men in charge of the posts here until, by letter of the 15th September, 1902, I was requested by the Chef de Post to send up my witnesses. Those witnesses could have been had the same day of the deed if the officers had done their duty. I went up with such witnesses as I was able to get together, and their evidence was taken. Nothing more was heard of the matter until the 24th April of this year, when I received a note from the State Agent here asking for certain people attached to our station, whose names he gave. He did not mention the reason of their being required at Léopoldville, but I guessed the reason. I was only able to send one of them, one other having returned to his home, and another being near to death. The man resident in the village, who was one of the witnesses I took up previously, was sent for to the State post and detained, and not allowed to return to make any provision of his journey to the pool. My apprentice and this man went down to the pool to bear witness concerning that murder; on the way the captain of the steamer ordered them off to carry and cut firewood; they demurred, naturally, but for peace sake did a little. In a storm of rain the shelter of the large steamer was denied them, and they spent the night sitting on the beach—the two of them beneath one frail umbrella. When they arrived at the pool, no one seemed to know why they had come; they were sent from pillar to post, then there seems to have been discovered some reason or other to interrogate them. The soldier concerned was with his fellows just the same as though there was no trial, and had, indeed, been no wrong done. But for the friendly offices of a sister Mission these two witnesses would have fared very badly during the six weeks they were detained at Léopoldville; they were practically shelterless and unfed; even as it was, they were hungry enough. At length they returned by our Mission steamer. It seems that the only sufferers in the matter were myself, in the loss of my apprentice for six weeks, and his loss of six weeks' wages, together with his considerable discomfort and the loss of the man from the village—not much, perhaps, in the eyes of the officials of the State, but much to them; then all their suffering is easily traceable to myself, for if I had not drawn the Commissaire's attention to the murder no witnesses would have been necessary, for who would have mentioned it? Considering the way in which this matter was dealt with, and the witnesses I produced were treated, I hesitate to bring other matters to light. The treatment these witnesses received only strengthens the distrust of the State, which, in this place, everywhere abounds. I therefore appeal for just treatment of witnesses and those who bring wrong-doing to light.

On the 6th March, 1903, I reported to the State Agent here (M. Lecomte) that I had seen at Mibenga a Chief, named Mopali, of Ngelo, who had been carried from the Lukolela post, where he had been imprisoned, so as to induce his village to bring more rubber. His head was wounded as with an iron instrument of some kind, his lips were swollen as if from a severe blow, and his legs were damaged as with blows from sticks. He and his bearer asserted that these wounds were given him while he was chained and made to carry firewood. M. Lecomte replied that the man had been seen by him before he left, and he was then all right and asked for my witnesses. I replied that the man himself and bearer were my informants. He said he wished to trace the doers of the deed. Nothing more was heard of the matter, so later I acquainted the Directeur-Général at Léopoldville by letter, dated the 10th July, of the facts. Meanwhile, up to the present, I have heard of nothing being done in the matter, only a repetition of a similar case.

I was at the village of Mopali on the 18th August, and I inquired for the poor fellow; some said he was dead, but most said that he had been carried by his wife, at his own request, away out of the way, so that he should not be found. He was afraid of the State chaining him again. From them I heard he had been even worse maltreated than at first I knew; they told me that his feet had been cut so that he despaired of walking again, and those who had seen him last said he got along by dragging himself along on his buttocks. I asked them pointedly whether they heard from Mopali where he got his wounds; was it not after he left the white man's presence? With one voice the little crowd I asked replied, "No; he received those wounds while in the chain." I gathered also that at first they were forced to take five baskets of rubber, and to make them take ten they had chained up Mopali, and that two more baskets had been recently added.

I learnt also that the youth who had run away from the soldier on the occasion of the murder of the two chained prisoners was dead. I asked how it was he was imprisoned at the post; they explained that he was taken to free his master from the chain, which had been put round his neck, to get more rubber from his village, and both youth and master were since dead. They recounted these things to me, and asked me if they were just. A case-hardened Jesuit would find it difficult to say yes. I could only blush with shame and say they were unjust.

On the 17th August, at Mibenga, the Chief, Lisanginya, made a statement to me in the presence of others, to the following effect: They had taken the usual tax of eight baskets of rubber, and he was sent for (I think it was the 8th June when he passed on his way through our station), and the white man (M. Lecomte, M. Gadot also being present) said the baskets were too few, and that they must bring other three; meanwhile, they put the chain round his neck, the soldiers beat him with sticks, he had to cut firewood, to carry heavy junks, and to haul logs in common with others. Three mornings he was compelled to carry the receptacle from the white man's latrine and empty it in the river. On the third day (sickening to relate) he was made to drink therefrom by a soldier named Lisasi. A youth named Masuka was in the chain at the same place and time, and saw the thing done. When the three extra baskets were produced he was set at liberty. He was ill for several days after his return. I referred to this in my letter of the 28th July, but it was too horrible a thing to write the additional item until I had heard the thing from the man's own lips. I blush again and again as I hear the fame of the State wherever I go, that when they chain a man now at the post they may make the chained unfortunate drink the white man's defecations.

In the evening of the 21st August, on returning to Mibenga, from a more inland town Bokoko, Mrs. Whitehead and myself saw Mpombo of Bobanga, village of Mbongi, some distance inland. He was in a horrible state. He stated that he had taken ten baskets of rubber to the post, and they wanted one more, so they chained him up to get it. He stated that he had been roughly treated by Mazamba, who had charge of him. In his utter weakness, he had stayed at Libonga (which was a village on the way), to get stronger, for about thirteen days. What must have been his condition when he arrived there I cannot imagine; he was so bad when I saw him at Mibenga. His left wrist appeared to be broken (broken by a log of wood, too heavy for him, slipping from his shoulder), one finger of the right hand was severely bruised, and had developed a large sore (this had been done he said with a stick with which he had been beaten), his back was badly bruised, the left shoulder was much bruised, and had been evidently slit with a knife, the left knee was bruised and feet swollen from being badly beaten, and altogether he was in a very disordered condition.

Later, I met Mabungikindo, a Chief from Bokoko, a large town inland, who was also returning from the chain in which he had been detained to get three more baskets of rubber. Their tax of rubber I understand had been doubled this year, and this was to get three more on the top of that. Poor fellow! How thin his thick-set frame had become! He was wearing his State Chief's medal. He took it in his hand and asked me to look at it. I cringed with shame. He asked me if we did that sort of thing in our country. I replied we did not. And this he said is how the State treats us: gives us this, and chains up the wearer and beats him. Is that good? Do you wonder, Sir, that the natives hate the State, and that its fame is almost impossible of cleansing in this part? Again and again I had the painful fortune to meet men coming back from imprisonment on account of rubber. The State through its Agents at Lukolela is driving these undisciplined people to desperation and rebellion. There is a rumour set abroad from the State post that the soldiers are coming from Yumbi to fight the inland people because of some words which have been brought back from Bolebe and Bonginda. If we are going to have another war, it will be one which has been engendered by this sort of treatment.

Allow me to trespass on your patience with another story of injustice which can scarcely be equalled by any of these barbarians. At Mibenga the Chiefs on the 14th August had great difficulty in getting their young men to carry down the tax of 500 mitakos' worth of manioc bread. This was owing to the fact that a youth named Litambala had run away from the post. The carriers usually returned the following day, but it was not till the morning of Sunday, the 16th, that they arrived, and it was found that one of them, named Mpia, had been chained up for Litambala. To deal thus with what is called a market is in the native eyes (and not unjustly so) pure treachery. Why had been Litambala detained? I will explain. Sometime ago a youth named Yamboisele was living on the river side, although a native of Mibenga; he fell ill of small-pox, and I nursed him through it—it was very bad. And it was only with diligent and careful nursing that he was saved from imminent death. After his recovery he did odd jobs about the station, and, unfortunately, began to be dishonest. When he was found out he was dismissed. I presumed he would return to his own home, but he engaged himself at the State. After some time he ran away, and although he had engaged himself without his people's knowledge his Chief, Lisanginya, was sent for, and they chained him up as a hostage for a replace for Yamboisele; after a brief space, the same day, on a promise of sending someone, he was released, and he sent a youth named Bondumbu. Presently Yamboisele turned up at Mibenga, and they took him to the post and asked for the release of Bomdumbu. They refused to release Bondumbu, and retained also Yamboisele. Presently Yamboisele (report says) was sent with 2,000 mitakos and 10 demijohns for water to the lower post, some distance down river, and he made off with the lot to the French side. When the carriers came down from Mibenga on the Saturday (this was the 16th May) they chained up Moboma, and he was beaten by the soldiers; I myself saw the weals from the strokes. The rest of the youths pleaded that he should not be tied up, as he did not belong to the same Chief, so they released him and chained up Manzinda. Next week they released him and chained up Mola, who had come down also as a carrier.

After two weeks the white man (the natives say it was M. Gado) sent Mango (a native of the village of Lukolela, not then in the employ of the State) to tie up a man to come and work in place of Mola. Lisanginya, the Chief, was away at time, but the man tied up Litambala and took him to the State, and Mola was set at liberty. Litambala continued a little time, till at length he was given some work to do, which he thought he was not strong enough for, and so ran away. Then in the week following the chaining of Mpia, so much trouble seemed likely to ensue in getting carriers for the manioc bread, and much recrimination of one another in the village, that Mombai, an able-bodied and diligent man, went to the post and gave himself up to free Mpia. But Yamboisele has not been heard of.

I have had several cases brought to my knowledge lately of the mode of slavery adopted at the post. Briefly, it is as follows: a man for some reason (sometimes his own and sometimes not) commences work at the post; he completes his term, and he is told he cannot have his pay unless he engages himself another term or brings another in his place. I know those who have left the earnings in the hands of the Chef de Poste rather than begin again. Such compulsion is contrary to civilized law, and is rightly termed slavery, and is utterly illegal. I quote one case in point—a recent one. On the 26th August I noticed a lad, Ngodele, at Mibenga; I noticed he was a lad from the State post, and I inquired why he was not at his work. The information was given that his term was finished, and the white man had sent him to say that when they sent another in his place he would give him his pay. I learnt that Ngondele had been compelled to go by his Chief, because the Chef de Poste had demanded some one to fill the place of another named Mokwala, who had died at the post.

I appeal to you, Sir, that these things may cease from being perpetrated on your subjects, and this defaming of the name of the State.

Accept, &c.
(Signed) JOHN WHITEHEAD.

Inclosure 3 in No. 3.

(See p. 33.)

Statement in regard to the Condition of the Natives in Lake Mantumba region during the period of the Rubber Wars which began in 1893.

THE disturbance consequent on the attempt to levy a rubber tax in this district, a tax which has since been discontinued, appears to have endured up to 1900.

The population during the continuance of these wars diminished, I estimate, by some 60 per cent., and the remnant of the inhabitants are only now, in many cases, returning to their destroyed or abandoned villages.

During the period 1893–1901 the Congo State commenced the system of compelling the natives to collect rubber, and insisted that the inhabitants of the district should not go out of it to sell their produce to traders.

The population of the country then was not large, but there were numerous villages with an active people—very many children, healthy looking and playful. They had good huts, large plantations of plaintains and manioc, and they were evidently rich, for their women were nearly all ornamented with brass anklets, bracelets, and neck rings, and other ornaments.

The following is a list of towns or villages—giving their approximate population in the year 1893 and at the present time. These figures are very carefully estimated:—

	1893.	1903.	Remarks.
Botunu	500	80	
Bosende	600	...	
Ngombe	500	40	These are not in the old village, but near it.
Irebo	3,000	60	Now a State camp with hundreds of soldiers and women.
Bokaka	500	30	
Lobwaka	200	30	
Boboko	300	35	
Mwenge	150	30	
Boongo	250	50	
Ituta	300	60	
Ikenze	320	20	
Ngero	2,500	300	In several small clusters of huts.
Mwebe	700	75	
Ikoko	2,500	800	Including fishing camps.

This list can be extended to double this number of villages, and in every case there has been a great decrease in the population. This has been, to a very great extent, caused by the extreme measures resorted to by officers of the State, and the freedom enjoyed by the soldiers to do just as they pleased. There are more people in the district near the villages mentioned, but they are hidden away in the bush like hunted animals, with only a few branches thrown together for shelter, for they have no trust that the present quiet state of things will continue, and they have no heart to build houses or make good gardens. In all the villages mentioned there are very few good huts, and when the natives are urged to make better houses for the sake of their health, the reply is, that there is no advantage to them in building good houses or making extensive gardens, as these would only give the State a greater hold upon them and lead to more exorbitant demands. The decrease has several causes:—

1. O * was deserted because of demands made for rubber by M. N O and several others were similar cases. The natives went to the French territory.

2. "War," in which children and women were killed as well as men. Women and children were killed not in all cases by stray bullets, but were taken as prisoners and killed. Sad to say, these horrible cases were not always the acts of some black soldier. Proof was laid against one officer who shot one woman and one man, while they were before him as prisoners with their hands tied, and no attempt was made by the accused to deny the truth of the statement. To those killed in the so-called "war" must be added large numbers of those

who died while kept as prisoners of war. Others were carried to far distant camps and have never returned. Many of the young were sent to Missions, and the death-rate was enormous. Here is one example: Ten children were sent from a State steamer to a Mission, and in spite of comfortable surroundings there were only three alive at the end of a month. The others had died of dysentery and bowel troubles contracted during the voyage. Two more struggled on for about fifteen months, but never recovered strength, and at last died. In less than two years only one of the ten was alive.

3. Another cause of the decrease is that the natives are weakened in body through insufficient and irregular food supply. They cannot resist disease as of old. In spite of assurances that the old state of things will not come again, the native refuses to build good houses, make large gardens, and make the best of the new surroundings—he is without ambition because without hope, and when sickness comes he does not seem to care.

4. Again a lower percentage of births lessen the population. Weakened bodies is one cause of this. Another reason is that women refuse to bear children, and take means to save themselves from motherhood. They give as the reason that if "war" should come a woman "big with child," or with a baby to carry, cannot well run away and hide from the soldiers. Confidence will, no doubt, be restored, but it grows but slowly.

There are two points in connection with the "war" (so-called):—

(1.) The cause.
(2.) The manner in which it was conducted.

(1.) The natives never had obeyed any other man than their own Chiefs. When Leopold II became their King they were not aware of the fact, nor had they any hand in the making of the new arrangement. Demands were made on them, and they did not understand why they should obey the stranger. Some of the demands were not excessive, but others were simply impossible. From the G H * people and the O * group of towns large demands of rubber were made. There was not much within their reach, and it was a dangerous thing to be a stranger in a strange part of the forests. The O * people offered to pay a monthly tribute of goats, fowls, &c., but M. N O would have rubber, so they left. The G H * had to bear the scourge of war frequently and many were killed. Now they supply what they probably would have supplied without the loss of one person, kwanga and fresh meats, and roofing materials and mats. Rubber was demanded from some others and war resulted. These are now providing the State with fish and fowls.

Another fertile source of war lay in the actions of the native soldiers. Generally speaking their statements against other natives were received as truth that needed no support. Take the following as an example: One morning it was reported that State soldiers had shot several people near the channel leading from H K * to the Congo. Several canoes full of manioc had been also seized, and the friends of the dead and owners of two of the canoes asked that they might have the canoes and food, and that they might take the bodies and bury them. But this was refused. It was alleged the people were shot in the act of deserting from the State into French territory. The Chief who was shot was actually returning from having gone with a message from M. O P to a village, and was killed east of the camp and of his home, while "France" lay to the west. The soldiers said that the people had been challenged to stop and that they refused, and that they had been shot as they paddled away. But really they had landed when called by the soldiers; they had been tied hand and foot, and then shot. One woman had struggled when shot, and had broken the vines with which her feet were tied, and she, though wounded, tried to escape. A second bullet made her fall, but yet she rose and ran a few steps, when a third bullet laid her low. Their hands had all been taken off—*i.e.*, the right hand of each—for evidence of the faithfulness of the soldiers. M. O P shot two of the soldiers, but the leader of the party was not shot, though the whole matter was carried through by him, and he it was that gave M. O P the false report.

A Chief complained that certain soldiers had taken his wives and had stolen all of his belongings that they cared to have. He made no complaint against the "tax" that the soldiers had gone there to secure, but told of the cruelty and oppression of the soldiers carried on for their own gain. The white officer kicked him off the verandah and said that he told many lies. The Chief turned round with fury written on his face, stood silently looking at the white man, and then stalked off; two days later there was a report that all the soldiers with their wives and followers had been killed in that Chief's town. A little later the white officer who refused to set matters right, along with another Belgian officer, were killed with a number of their soldiers in an expedition for the purpose of punishing the Chief and his people for killing the first lot of soldiers.

After the rubber demand was withdrawn, in some places labour was demanded. A very large proportion of the women from this village had to go to P * every week and work there two days. They returned here on the third day. Nearly every week there were complaints made that someone's wife had been kept by a soldier, and when it was suggested that the husband should himself go and report the matter to the white man, they would reply: "We dare not." Their fear was not so much of the white man but of the black soldiers.

(2.) The manner in which this war was conducted was very objectionable to any one with European ideas. The natives attacked P * and O *, but that was only after numerous expeditions had been made against them, and the whole population roused against the "white man." In 99 per cent. of the "wars" in this district the cause was simply failure on the part of the people to supply produce, labour, or men, as demanded by the State. There was the long struggle with L L L in his long resistance to State authority; but he at first was known as a quiet man who tried to please the State, and he only started on his career as a fighting man after he had been out to help M. N O. After the departure of M. N O to Colquilhatville, he went back and made demands and fought the people as he had done with M. N O as his Chief.

When this matter was reported to M. N O, he was angry, and called the Chief a "brigand," and said that he would be punished. For numerous offences he was put "on the chain," and some time after his release the fight occurred (in which fight the two white men were killed) and he joined with others in an ineffectual attempt to drive out the white man.

In most of the fights then the natives were merely trying to defend themselves and their homes from attacks made on them by black soldiers sent to "punish them for some failure to do their duty to the State;" and if the cause for war was weak, the way in which it was carried on was often revolting. It was stated that these soldiers were often sent out to make war on a village without a white officer accompanying them, so that there was nothing to keep them from awful excesses.

It is averred that canoes have been seen returning from distant expeditions with no white man in charge, and with human hands dangling from a stick in the bow of the canoe—or in small baskets—being carried to the white man as proofs of their courage and devotion to duty. If one in fifty of native reports are true, there has been great lack on the part of some white men. They, too, are accused of forgetting the subjects and conditions of war.

Statements made to me by certain natives are appended.

Many similar statements were made to me during the time I spent at Lake Mantumba, some of those made by native men being unfit for repetition.

Q Q's Statement.

I was born at K K *. After my father died my mother and I went to L L *. When we returned to K K * soon after that P Q came to fight with us because of rubber. KK * did not want to take rubber to the white man. We and our mothers ran away very far into the bush. The Bula Matadi soldiers were very strong and they fought hard, one soldier was killed, and they killed one K K * man. Then the white man said let us go home, and they went home, and then we, too, came out of the bush. This was the first fight. After that another fighting took place. I, my mother, grandmother, and my sister, we ran away into the bush. The soldiers came and fought us, and left the town and followed us into the bush. When the soldiers came into the bush near us they were calling my mother by name, and I was going to answer, but my mother put her hand to my mouth to stop me. Then they went to another side, and then we left that place and went to another. When they called my mother, if she had not stopped me from answering, we would all have been killed then. A great number of our people were killed by the soldiers. The friends who were left buried the dead bodies, and there was very much weeping. After that there was not any fighting for some time. Then the soldiers came again to fight with us, and we ran into the bush, but they really came to fight with M M *. They killed a lot of M M * people, and then one soldier came out to K K *, and the K K * people killed him with a spear. And when the other soldiers heard that their friend was killed they came in a large number and followed us into the bush. Then the soldiers fired a gun, and some people were killed. After that they saw a little bit of my mother's head, and the soldiers ran quickly towards the place where we were and caught my grandmother, my mother, my sister, and another little one, younger than us. Several of the soldiers argued about my mother, because each wanted her for a wife, so they finally decided to kill her. They killed her with a gun—they shot her through the stomach—and she fell, and when I saw that I cried very much, because they killed my mother and grandmother, and I was left alone. My mother was near to the time of her confinement at that time. And they killed my grandmother too, and I saw it all done. They took hold of my sister and asked where her older sister was, and she said: "She has just run away." They said, "Call her." She called me, but I was too frightened and would not answer, and I ran and went away and came out at another place, and I could not speak much because my throat was very sore. I saw a little bit kwanga lying on the ground and I picked it up to eat. At that place there used to be a lot of people, but when I got there there were none. My sister was taken to P *, and I was at this place alone. One day I saw a man coming from the back country. He was going to kill me, but afterwards he took me to a place where there were people, and there I saw my step-father . . . . He asked to buy me from this man, but the man would not let him. He said, "She is my slave now; I found her." One day the men went out fishing, and when I looked I saw the soldiers coming, so I ran away, but a string caught my foot and I fell, and a soldier named N N N caught me. He handed me over to another soldier, and as we went we saw some Q * people fishing, and the soldiers took a lot of fish from them and a Q * woman, and we went to P *, and they took me to the white man.

* * * * * * * *

(Signed) Q Q.

Signed by Q Q before me,
(Signed) ROGER CASEMENT,
His Britannic Majesty's Consul.

R R's Statement.

I, R R, came from N N*. N N* and R* fought, and they killed several R* people, and one R* man O O O took a man and sent him to L L L to go and tell the white man to come and fight with Nkoho. The white man who fought with N N* first was named Q R.* He fought with us in the morning; then I ran away with my mother. Then the men came to call us back to our town. When we were returning to our town, as we were nearing, we asked how many people were killed, and they told us three were killed. Q R had burned down all the houses, so we were scattered to other places again; only some of the men were left to build again. After a while we returned to our town and began to plant our gardens. I have finished the first part of the story.

We stayed a long time at our town, then the white man who fought with N N* first went and told R S that the N N* people were very strong, so R S made up his mind to come and fight us. When he came to O* we heard the news; it was high-water season. We got into our canoes to run away, but the men stayed behind to wait for the soldiers. When the white man came he did not try to fight them during the day, but went to the back and waited for night to come. When the soldiers came at night the people ràn away, so they did not kill anybody, only a sick man whom they found in a house, whom they (the soldiers) killed and disfigured his body very much. They hunted out all the native money they could get, and in the morning they went away. After they went away we came back to the town, but we found it was all destroyed. We remained in our town a long time; the white man did not come back to fight with us. After a while we heard that R S was coming to fight us. R S sent some Q* men to tell the N N* people to send people to go and work for him, and also to send goats. The N N* people would not do it, so he went to fight our town. When we were told by the men that the soldiers were coming, we began to run away. My mother told me to wait for her until she got some things ready to take with us, but I told her we must go now, as the soldiers were coming. I ran away and left my mother, and went with two old people who were running away, but we were caught, and the old people were killed, and the soldiers made me carry the baskets with the things these dead people had and the hands they cut off. I went on with the soldiers. Then we came to another town, and they asked me the way and the name of the place, and I said "I do not know;" but they said, "If you do not tell us we will kill you," so I told them the name of the town. Then we went into the bush to look for people, and we heard children crying, and a soldier went quickly over to the place and killed a mother and four children, and then we left off looking for the people in the bush, and they asked me again to show them the way out, and if I did not they would kill me, so I showed them the way. They took me to R S, and he told me to go and stay with the soldier who caught me. They tied up six people, but I cannot tell how many people were killed, because there were too many for me to count. They got my little sister and killed her, and threw her into a house and set fire to the house. When finished with that we went to O O*, and stayed there four days, and then we went to P P*, and because the people there ran away, they killed the P P* Chief. We stayed there several days; then we came to P*, and from there we came on to Q Q*, and there they put the prisoners in chains, but they did not put me in chains, and then he (R S) went to fight with L L*, and killed a lot of people and six people tied up. When he came back from L L* we started and came on to Q*.

* * * * * * *

My father was killed in the same fight as I was captured. My mother was killed by a sentry stationed at N N* after I left.

(Signed) R R.

Signed by R R, before me,
(Signed) ROGER CASEMENT,
His Britannic Majesty's Consul.

S S's Statement.

S S came from the far back R R*. One day the soldiers went to her town to fight; she did not know that the soldiers had come to fight them until she saw the people from the other side of the town running towards their end, then they, too, began to run away. Her father, mother, three brothers, and sister were with her. About four men were killed at this scare. It was at this fight that one of the station girls P P P was taken prisoner. After several days, during which time they were staying at other villages, they went back to their own town. They were only a few days in their own town when they heard that the soldiers who had been at the other towns were coming their way too, so the men gathered up all their bows and arrows and went out to the next town to wait for the soldiers to fight them. Some of the men stayed behind with all the women and children. After that S S and her mother went out to their garden to work; while there S S told her mother that she had dreamed that Bula Matadi was coming to fight with them, but her mother told her she was trying to tell stories. After that S S went back to the house, and left her mother in the garden. After she had been a little while in the house with her little brother and sister she heard the firing of guns. When she heard that she took up her little sister and a big basket with a lot of native money* in it, but she could not manage both, so she left the basket behind and ran away with the youngest child; the little boy ran away by himself. The oldest boys had gone away to wait for the soldiers at the other town. As she went past she heard her mother calling to her, but she told her to run away in another direction, and she would go on with the little sister. She found her little sister rather heavy for her, so she could not run very fast, and a great number of people went past her, and she was left alone with the little one. Then she left the main road and went to hide in the bush. When night came on she tried to find the road again and follow the people who had passed her, but she could not find them, so she had to sleep in the bush alone. She wandered about in the bush for six days, then she came upon a town named S S* At this town she found that the soldiers were fighting there too. Before entering the town she dug up some sweet manioc to eat, because she was very, very hungry. She went about looking for a fire to roast her sweet manioc, but she could not find any. Then she heard a noise as of people talking, so she hid her little sister in a deserted house, and went to see those people she had heard talking, thinking they might be those from her own town, but when she got to the house where the noise was coming from she saw one of the soldier's boys sitting at the door of the house, and then also she could not quite understand their language, so she knew that they were not her people, so she took fright and ran away in another direction from where she had put her sister. After she had reached the outside of the town she stood still, and remembered that she would be scolded by her father and mother for leaving her sister, so she went back at night. She came upon a house where the white man was sleeping; she saw the sentry on a deck chair outside in front of the house, apparently asleep, because he did not see her slip past him. Then she came to the house where her sister was, and took her, and she started to run away again. They slept in a deserted house at the very end of the town. Early in the morning the white man sent out the soldiers to go and look for people all over the town and in the houses. S S was standing outside in front of the house, trying to make her sister walk some, as she was very tired, but the little sister could not run away through weakness. While they were both standing outside the soldiers came upon them and took them both. One of the soldiers said: "We might keep them both, the little one is not bad-looking;" but the others said "No, we are not going to carry her all the way; we must kill the youngest girl." So they put a knife through the child's stomach, and left the body lying there where they had killed it. They took S S to the next town, where the white man had told them to go and fight. They did not go back to the house where the white man was, but went straight on to the next town. The white man's name was C D.† The soldiers gave S S something to eat on the way. When they came to this next town they found that all the people had run away.

In the morning the soldiers wanted S S to go and look for manioc for them, but she was afraid to go out as they looked to her as if they wanted to kill her. The soldiers thrashed her very much, and began to drag her outside, but the corporal (N N N) came and took her by the hand and said, "We must not kill her; we must take her to the white man." Then they went back to the town where C D was, and they showed him S S. C D handed her over to the care of a soldier. At this town she found that they had caught three people, and among them was a very old woman, and the cannibal soldiers asked C D to give them the old woman to eat, and C D told them to take her. Those soldiers took the woman and cut her throat, and then divided her and ate her. S S saw all this done. In the morning the soldier who was looking after her was sent on some duty by C D, and before the soldier went out he had told S S to get some manioc leaves not far from the house and to cook them. After he left she went to do as he had told her, and those cannibal soldiers went to C D and said that S S was trying to run away, so they wanted to kill her; but he told them to tie her, so the soldiers tied her to a tree, and she had to stand in the sun nearly all day. When the soldier who had charge of her came back he found her tied up. C D called to him to ask about S S, so he explained to C D what he had told S S to do, so he was allowed to untie her. They stayed several days at this place, then B D asked S S if she knew all the towns round about, and she said yes, then he told her to show them the way, so that they could go and catch people. They came to a town and found only one woman, who was dying of sickness, and the soldiers killed her with a knife. At several towns they found no people, but at last they came to a town where several people had run to as they did not know where else to go, because the soldiers were fighting everywhere. At this town they killed a lot of people—men, women, and children—and took some as prisoners. They cut the hands off those they had killed, and brought them to C D; they spread out the hands in a row for C D to see. After that they left to return to Bikoro. They took a lot of prisoners with them. The hands which they had cut off they just left lying, because the white man had seen them, so they did not need to take them to P*. Some of the soldiers were sent to P* with the prisoners, but C D himself and the other soldiers went to T T* where there was another white man. The prisoners were sent to S T. S S was about two weeks at P*, and then she ran away into the bush at P* for three days, and when she was found she was brought back to S T, and he asked her why she had run away. She said because the soldiers had thrashed her.

* * * * * * *

S S's mother was killed by soldiers, and her father died of starvation, or rather, he refused to eat because he was bereaved of his wife and all his children.

(Signed) S S.

Signed by S S before me,
(Signed) Roger Casement,
His Britannic Majesty's Consul.

---

* Brass rods.

† The name of a Military Officer in Command of the troops at that date.

T T's Statement.

States she belonged to the village of R*, where she lived with her grandmother. R* was attacked by the State soldiers long ago. It was in S T's time. She does not know if he was with the soldiers, but she heard the bugle blow when they were going away. It was in the afternoon when they came, they began catching and tying the people, and killed lots of them. A lot of people—she thinks perhaps fifty—ran away, and she was in the crowd with them, but the soldiers came after them and killed them all but herself. She was small, and she slid into the bush. The people killed were many, and women—there were not many children. The children had scattered when the soldiers came, but she stayed with the big people, thinking she might be safe.

When they were all killed she waited in the grass for two nights. She was very frightened, and her throat was sore with thirst, and she looked about and at last she found some water in a pot. She stayed on in the grass a third night, and buffaloes came near her and she was very frightened—and they went away. When the morning came she thought she would be better to move, and went away and got up a tree. She was three days without food, and was very hungry. In the tree she was near her grandmother's house, and she looked around and, seeing no soldiers, she crept to her grandmother's house and got some food and got up the tree again. The soldiers had gone away hunting for buffaloes, and it was then she was able to get down from the tree. The soldiers came back, and they came towards the trees and bushes calling out: "Now we see you; come down, come down!" This they used to do, so that people, thinking they were really discovered, should give themselves up; but she thought she would stay on, and so she stayed up the tree. Soon afterwards the soldiers went, but she was still afraid to come down. Presently she heard her grandmother calling out to know if she was alive, and when she heard her grandmother's voice she knew the soldiers were gone, and she answered, but her voice was very small—and she came down and her grandmother took her home.

That was the first time. Soon afterwards she and her grandmother went away to another town called U U*, near V V*, and they were there some days together, when one night the soldiers came. The white man sent the soldiers there because the U U* people had not taken to the State what they were told to take. Neither her own people nor the U U* people knew there was any trouble with the Government, so they were surprised. She was asleep. Her grandmother—her mother's mother—tried to awaken her, but she did not know. She felt the shaking, but she did not mind because she was sleepy.

The soldiers came quickly into the house—her grandmother rushed out just before. When she heard the noise of the soldiers around the house, and looked and saw her grandmother not there, she ran out and called for her grandmother; and as she ran her brass anklets made a noise, and some one ran after and caught her by the leg, and she fell and the soldiers took her.

There were not many soldiers, only some boys with one soldier (*Note.*—She means a corporal and some untrained men.—R. C.), and they had caught only one woman and herself. In the morning they began robbing the houses, and took everything they could find and take.

They were taken to a canoe, and went to V V*. The soldier who caught her was the sentry at V V*. At V V* she was kept about a week with the sentry, and when the V V* people took their weekly rations over to P* she was sent over. The other woman who was taken to V V* was ransomed by her friends. They came after them to V V*, and the sentry let her go for 750 rods. She saw the money paid. Her friends came to ransom her too, but the sentry refused, saying the white man wanted her because she was young—the other was an old woman and could not work.

*　　*　　*　　*　　*　　*　　*

(Signed)　　T T.

Signed by T T before me.
(Signed)　　ROGER CASEMENT,
His Britannic Majesty's Consul.

U U's Statement.

When we began to run away from the fight, we ran away many times. They did not catch me because I was with mother and father. Afterwards mother died; four days passed, father died also. I and an older sister were left with two younger children, and then the fighting came where I had run to. Then my elder sister called me: "U U, come here." I went. She said: "Let us run away, because we have not any one to take care of us." When we were running away we saw a lot of W W* people coming towards us. We told them to run away, war was coming. They said: "Is it true?" We said: "It is true; they are coming." The W W* people said: "We will not run away; we did not see the soldiers." Only a little while they saw the soldiers, and they were killed. We stayed in a town named X X*. A male relative called me: "U U, let us go;" but I did not want to. The soldiers came there; I ran away by myself: when I ran away I hid in the bush. While I was running I met with an old man who was running from a soldier. He (the soldier) fired a gun. I was not hit, but the old man died. Afterwards they caught me and two men. The soldiers asked: "Have you a father and mother?" I answered, "No." They said to me, "If you do not tell us we will kill you." I said:

"Father and mother are dead." After that my oldest sister was caught, too, in the bush, and they left my little brother and sister alone in the bush to die, because heavy rain came on, and they had not had anything to eat for days and days. At night they tied my hands and feet for fear that I should run away. In the morning they caught three people—two had children; they killed the children. Afterwards I was standing outside, and a soldier asked me, "Where are you going?" I said, "I am going home." He said, "Come on." He took his gun; he put me in the house; he wanted to kill me. Then another soldier came and took me. We heard a big noise; they told us that the fighting was over, but it was not so. When we were going on the way they killed ten children because they were very, very small; they killed them in the water. Then they killed a lot of people, and they cut off their hands and put them into baskets and took them to the white man. He counted out the hands—200 in all; they left the hands lying. The white man's name was "C D." After that C D sent us prisoners with soldiers to P * to S T. S T told me to weed grass. When I was working outside a soldier came and said: "Come here;" and when I went he wanted to cut my hand off, and so I went to the white man to tell him, and he thrashed the soldier.

On our way, when we were coming to P *, the soldiers saw a little child, and when they went to kill it the child laughed so the soldier took the butt of the gun and struck the child with it, and then cut off its head. One day they killed my half-sister and cut off her head, hands, and feet because she had on rings. Her name was Q Q Q. Then they caught another sister, and they sold her to the W W * people, and now she is a slave there. When we came to P * the white man said to send word to the friends of the prisoners to come with goats to buy off some of their relatives. A lot were bought off, but I had no one to come and buy me off because father was dead. The white man said to me, "You shall go to . . . . ." The white man (S T) gave me a small boy to care for, but I thought he would be killed, so I helped to get him away. S T asked me to bring the boy to him, but I said: "He has run away." He said he would kill me, but . . . . .

* * * * * * *

(Signed) U U.

Signed by U U before me.
(Signed) ROGER CASEMENT,
His Britannic Majesty's Consul.

Inclosure 4 in No. 3.

(See p. 34.)

*Notes in the Case of V V, a Native of L L * in the Mantumba District, both of whose hands have been hacked or beaten off, and with reference to other similar cases of Mutilation in that District.*

I FOUND this man in the . . . . . station at Q * on , and learned that he had been kept by the missionaries for some years, since the day when a party of native teachers had found him in his own town, situated in the forest some miles away from Q *. In answer to my inquiry as to how he came to lose his hands, V V's statement was as follows:—

"State soldiers came from P *, and attacked the R R * towns, which they burned, killing people. They then attacked a town called A B * and burned it, killing people there also. From that they went on to L L *. The L L * people fled into the forest, leaving some few of their number behind with food to offer to the soldiers—among whom was V V. The soldiers came to L L *, under the command of a European officer, whose native name was T U. The soldiers took prisoner all the men left in the town, and tied them up. Their hands were tied very tight with native rope, and they were tied up outside in the open; and as it was raining very hard, and they were in the rain all the time and all the night, their hands swelled, because the thongs contracted. His (V V's) hands had swollen terribly in the morning, and the thongs had cut into the bone. The soldiers, when they came to L L *, had only one native a prisoner with them; he was killed during the night. At L L * itself eight people, including himself (V V) were taken prisoners; all were men; two were killed during the night. Six only were taken down in the morning to Y Y *. The white man ordered four of the prisoners to be released; the fifth was a Chief, named R R R. This Chief had come back to L L * in the night to try secretly to get some fire to take back into the forest, where the fugitives were hiding. His wife had become sick during the heavy rain in the forest, and the Chief wanted the fire for her; but the soldiers caught him, and he was taken along with the rest. This Chief was taken to P*, but he believes that on the way, at Z Z *, he tried to escape, and was killed. V V's hands were so swollen that they were quite useless. The soldiers seeing this, and that the thongs had cut into the bone, beat his hands against a tree with their rifles, and he was released. He does not know why they beat his hands. The white man, T U, was not far off, and could see what they were doing. T U was drinking palm-wine while the soldiers beat his hands with their rifle-butts against the tree. His hands subsequently fell off (or sloughed away). When the soldiers left him by the waterside, he got back to L L *, and when his own people returned from the forest they found him there. Afterwards some boys—one of whom was a relation—came to L L *, and they found him without his hands.

There was some doubt in the translation of V V's statement whether his hands had been cut with a knife; but later inquiry established that they fell off through the tightness of the native rope and the beating of them by the soldiers with their rifle-butts.

On the 14th August, I again visited the State camp at Irebu, where, in the course of conversation with the officer in command, I made passing but intentional reference to the fact that I had seen V V. and had heard his story from himself. I added that from the boy's statement it would seem that the loss of his hands was directly attributable to an officer who was apparently close at hand and in command of the soldiers at the time. I added that I had heard of other cases in the neighbourhood. The Commandant at once informed me that such things were impossible, but that in this specific case of V V he should cause inquiry to be instantly made.

On my return from the Lulongo River I found that this remark in passing conversation had borne instant fruit, although previous appeals on behalf of the boy had proved unsuccessful. The Commissaire-Général of the Equator District had, learning of it, at once proceeded to Lake Mantumba, and a judicial investigation as to how V V lost his hands had been immediately instituted. The boy was taken to Bikoro, and I have since been informed that provision has been made for him and a weekly allowance.

When at the village of B C *, I had found there a boy of not more than 12 years of age with the right hand gone. This child, in answer to my inquiries, said that the hand had been cut off by the Government soldiers some years before. He could not say how long before, but judging from the height he indicated he could not then have been more than 7 years of age if now 12. His statement was fully confirmed by S S S and his relatives, who stood around him while I questioned him. The soldiers had come to B C * from Coquilhatville by land through the forest. They were led by an officer whose name was given as "U V." His father and mother were killed beside him. He saw them killed, and a bullet hit him and he fell. He here showed me a deep cicatrized scar at the back of the head, just at the nape of the neck, and said it was there the bullet had struck him. He fell down, presumably insensible, but came to his senses while his hand was being hacked off at the wrist. I asked him how it was he could possibly lie silent and give no sign. He answered that he felt the cutting, but was afraid to move, knowing that he would be killed if he showed any sign of life.

I made some provision for this boy.

The names of six other persons mutilated in a similar way were given to me. The last of these, an old woman, had died only a few months previously, and her niece stated that her aunt had often told her how she came to lose her hand. The town had been attacked by Government troops and all had fled, pursued into the forest. This old woman (whose name was V W) had fled with her son, when he fell shot dead, and she herself fell down beside him—she supposed she fainted. She then felt her hand being cut off, but had made no sign. When all was quiet and the soldiers had gone, she found her son's dead body beside her with one hand cut off and her own also taken away.

Of acts of persistent mutilation by Government soldiers of this nature I had many statements made to me, some of them specifically, others in a general way. Of the fact of this mutilation and the causes inducing it there can be no shadow of doubt. It was not a native custom prior to the coming of the white man; it was not the outcome of the primitive instincts of savages in their fights between village and village; it was the deliberate act of the soldiers of a European Administration, and these men themselves never made any concealment that in committing these acts they were but obeying the positive orders of their superiors. I obtained several specific instances of this practice of mutilation having been carried out in the town of Q * itself, when the Government soldiers had come across from P* to raid it or compel its inhabitants to work.

Inclosure 5 in No. 3.

(See p. 43.)

Circular dated October 20, 1900.

LE Gouvernement a délégué à des Sociétés Commerciales opérant dans certaines parties du territoire non soumise à l'action immédiate de son autorité une partie de ses pouvoirs en matière de police générale.

Ces Sociétés sont dites avoir "le droit de police." Des interprétations erronées ont été données à cette appellation.

On a voulu y voir l'attribution aux Directeurs de ces Sociétés et même à des agents subalternes, du droit de diriger des opérations militaires offensives, "de faire la guerre" aux populations indigènes; d'autres, sans même s'inquiéter d'examiner quelles pouvaient être les limites de ce droit de police, se sont servis de moyens que cette délégation avait mis entre leurs mains, pour commettre les abus les plus graves.

C'est-à-dire que "le droit de police" qui leur donnait le moyen de se protéger eux-mêmes et l'obligation de protéger les individus contre l'abus de la force, allait complètement à l'encontre de l'un de ces buts principaux.

En présence de cette situation, j'ai décidé que "le droit de police," terme dont je conserve provisoirement l'emploi, ne laisserait que le pouvoir de réquisitionner, à l'effet de maintenir ou de rétablir l'ordre, la force armée qui se trouvera soit dans la Concession, soit en dehors, mais même dans ce cas il doit être bien entendu que les officiers de l'État conserveront, au cours des événements le Commandant [? commandement] des soldats et seront seuls juges, sous leur responsabilité, des opérations militaires qu'il importerait d'entreprendre.

Les armes perfectionnées que les Sociétés posséderaient dans leurs diverses factoreries ou établissements et qui doivent faire l'objet comme les armes d'autres Sociétés n'ayant pas le droit de police, d'un permis modèle B, ne peuvent en aucun cas sortir des établissements pour lesquels elles ont été délivrées.

Quant aux fusils à piston ils ne peuvent être mis en dehors des factoreries qu'entre les mains des Capitas et à condition que ceux-ci aient un permis suivant modèle C.

Les fusils à piston ne sortiront ainsi des factoreries qu'isolément. Ne pouvant être remis en dehors des établissements commerciaux dans les mains de groupes plus ou moins importants ils ne constitueront ainsi jamais une force offensive.

Je donne à nouveau les ordres les plus formels pour que tous les fonctionnaires de l'État concourent à faire réprimer les infractions à ces strictes défenses.

Le Gouverneur-Général,
(Signé) WAHIS.

Boma, le 20 Octobre, 1900.

(Translation.)

THE Government have delegated to commercial Companies operating in certain parts of the territory not subject to the immediate exercise of Government authority a part of their powers in matters of general police.

These Companies are described as having "the right of police." Erroneous interpretations have been given to this expression.

It has been held by some as giving to the Directors of these Companies, and even to inferior officers, the right to undertake offensive military operations, to "make war" on the native population; others, without even troubling to ascertain what the limits of this right of police might be, have used the means afforded by this delegation of power to commit the gravest abuses.

That is to say, "the right of police," which gave them the means of protecting themselves, and imposed upon them the obligation of protecting individuals against abuse of force, was used in a manner absolutely opposed to one of these principal objects.

In view of these circumstances, I have decided that "the right of police," an expression the use of which I retain provisionally, shall imply no more than the power of requisitioning, with a view to maintaining or restoring order, the armed force existing either within or without the Concession; but even in this case it must be well understood that the officers of the State will retain command of the soldiers during the proceedings, and will be the sole judges, on their own responsibility, of the military operations which it may be desirable to undertake.

Improved weapons which the Companies possess in their various factories or establishments and for which, as for the arms of other Companies not having the right of police, a permit, form (B), must be taken out, may not in any case be removed from the establishments for which they were issued.

With regard to cap-guns, they may not be removed from the factories except into the hands of the Capitas, and on the condition that the latter are in possession of a permit, form (C).

Cap-guns will thus only be removed from the factories one by one. As they cannot be issued from the commercial establishments into the hands of more or less numerous groups, they will thus never constitute a means of offence.

I again give the most formal orders that all the State officials co-operate to repress violations of these strict prohibitions.

The Governor-General,
(Signed) WAHIS.

Boma, October 20, 1890.

Inclosure 6 in No. 3.

(See p. 56.)

*Note of Information taken in the Charge of Cutting off the boy I I's hand, preferred to Mr. Casement by the People of E *.*

AT village of E * in the C D * country, on left bank of E D *, tributary of the X * River.

Y Y, with many of the townsmen and a few women and children, also present.

A lad, about 14 or 15 years of age, I I by name, whose left hand had been cut off, the stump wrapped up in a rag, the wound being yet scarcely healed, appears, and, in answer to Consul's question, charges a sentry named K K (placed in the town by the local agent of the La Lulanga Society to see that the people work rubber) with having done it. This sentry is called, and after some delay appears with a cap-gun.

The following inquiry into the circumstances surrounding the loss of I I's hand then takes place:—

The Consul, through W W, speaking in E F *, and X X repeating his utterances both in F G * to the sentry and in the local dialect to the others, asks I I, in the presence of the accused:

"Who cut off your hand?"

I I: "The sentry there."

The sentry denies the charge (interrupting), and stating that his name is T T T and not K K. Consul requests him to keep silence—that he can speak later.

Y Y is called and questioned by Consul through the interpreters. After being exhorted to speak the truth without fear or favour, he states:

"The sentry before us cut off I I's hand."

Consul: "Did you yourself witness the act?"

Answer: "Yes."

Several of the Headmen of the town called upon by the Consul to testify.

To the first of these, who gave his name as Z Z, Consul asked, pointing to I I's mutilated wrist-bone: "Who cut off this boy's hand?"

Z Z (pointing to the sentry): "That man did it."

The second, who gave his name as A A A, asked by Consul: "Who cut off this boy's hand?"

Answers: "K K."

The third, giving his name as B B B, asked by Consul: "Who cut off this boy's hand?"

Answers: "This man here, the sentry."

Z Z (re-questioned): "Did you yourself see this sentry cut off this boy's hand?"

Answer: "Yes, I saw it."

A A A (re-questioned): "Did you yourself see this sentry cut off this boy's hand?"

Answers: "I should think so. Did I not get this wound here" (pointing to a cut by the tendon Achilles on the left heel) "the same day, when running away in fright? My own knife wounded me. I let it fall when I ran away."

Consul questions I I: "How long ago was it your hand was cut off?"

Answer: "He is not sure."

Two fellow-villagers—young men, named C C C and D D D—step out and state that they remember. The act occurred when the clay was being dug over at C D, when the slip-place for the steamers was begun.

E E E, of E *, another section of the village of R * *, questioned by Consul: "Did you see this lad's hand cut off?"

Answer: "Yes. I did not actually see it being cut off. I came up and saw the severed hand and the blood lying on the ground. The people had run away in all directions."

Consul asked interpreters to ask if there were others who had seen the crime and charged K K with it.

Nearly all those present, about forty persons, nearly all men, shouted out with one voice that it was K K who did it.

Consul: "They are all sure it was K K here?"

Universal response: "Yes; he did it."

Consul asked the accused K K: "Did you cut off this boy's hand?"

This question was put in the plainest language, and repeated six times, with the request that a plain answer—"yes" or "no"—should be given.

The accused failed to answer the question, beginning to talk of other things not relevant to the question, such as that his name was T T and not K K and that the people of R * * had done bad things to him.

He was told to confine himself to the question put to him, that he could talk of other things later, but that now it was his place to answer the questions put, just as simply and plainly as the others had answered. He had heard those answers and the charge they levied against him, and he should answer the Consul's questions in just the same way.

The accused continued to speak of irrevelant subjects, and refused or failed to give any answer to the question put to him.

After repeated attempts to obtain answer to the question: "Did you or did you not cut off this boy I I's hand?"

Consul states: "You are charged with this crime. You refuse to answer the questions I put to you plainly and straightforwardly as your accusers have done. You have heard their accusation. Your refusal to reply as you should reply—viz., yes or no—to a direct and simple question leaves me convinced that you cannot deny the charge. You have heard what has been charged against you by all these people. Since you decline to answer as they did, you may tell your story your own way. I shall listen to it."

Accused began to speak, but before his remarks could be translated to me through X X first, to whom he spoke direct, and then through W W, a young man stepped out of the crowd and interrupted.

There was noise and then the man spoke:—

He stated he was F F F of R * *. He had shot two antelopes, and he had brought two of their legs to this sentry as a gift. The sentry refused to accept them, and tied his wife up. The sentry said they were not a sufficient present for him, and he kept F F F's wife tied up until he, F F F, paid him 1,000 brass rods for her release

Here a young man giving his name as G G G stepped into the ring and accused the sentry of having robbed him openly of two ducks and a dog. They were taken from him for no reason save that the sentry wanted them and took them by force.

Consul again turned to the sentry and invited him to tell his story, and to give his answer to the charge against him in his own way. Consul enjoined silence on all, and not to interrupt the sentry.

K K stated that he did not take G G G's ducks. The father of G G G gave him a duck. (All laughed.) It is true that F F F killed two antelopes and gave him the two legs as a gift but he did not tie up his wife or require money for her release.

Consul: "That is all right. That finishes the ducks and the antelopes' legs; but now I want to hear about I I's hand. Tell me what you know about I I's hand being cut off."

K K again evaded the question.

Consul: "Tell him this. He is put here by his master in this town, is he not? This is his town. Now, does he say he does not know what goes on here where he lives?"

The sentry states: "It is true that this is his town, but he knows nothing about I I's hand being cut off. Perhaps it was the first sentry here before he came, who was a very bad man and cut people's hands off. That sentry has gone away—it was he who cut hands off, not himself. He does not know anything of it."

Consul: "What was the name then of this bad sentry, your predecessor, who cut people's hands off? You know it?"

The sentry gives no direct answer, and the question is repeated. He then gives a statement about several sentries, naming three, as predecessors of himself here at R * *.

Here a man named H H H jumped up, interrupting, and asserted that those three sentries did not reside at R * *, but had been stationed in his own town—his, H H H's, town.

Consul (to the sentry): "How long have you been in this town?"

Answer: "Five months."

Consul: "You are quite sure?"

Answer: "Five months."

Consul: "Do you, then, know this boy I I? Have you seen him before?"

Answer: "I do not know him at all."

Here the entire auditory roared with laughter, and expressions of admiration at the sentry's lying powers were given vent to.

The sentry, continuing, stated that possibly I I comes from H H H's town. Anyhow, he (the sentry) does not know I I; he does not know him at all.

Here F F F stepped out and said he was full brother of I I; they had lived here always. Their father was U U U, now dead; their mother is also dead.

Consul (to the sentry): "Then it is finished. You know nothing of this matter."

The sentry: "It is finished. I have told you all. I know nothing of it."

Here a man giving his name as I I I, of K K *, the neighbouring section of R * *, came forward with his wife.

He stated that the other sentries in their town were not so bad, but that this man was a villain.

The sentry had tied up his wife—the woman he brought forward—and had made him pay 500 rods before she was released. He had paid the money.

Here Consul asked I I how his hand had been cut off. He and C C C and D D D stated that he had first been shot in the arm, and then when he fell down the sentry had cut his hand off.

Consul: "Did you feel it being cut off?"

Answer: "Yes, I felt it."

This terminated the inquiry. The Consul informed Y Y and the people present that he should report what he had seen and heard to the Congo Government, and that he should beg them to investigate the charge against the sentry, who deserved severe punishment for his illegal and cruel acts. The things that the sentry was charged with doing were quite illegal, and if the Government of his country knew of such things being done, the perpetrators of such crimes would, in all cases, be punished.

(Signed) ROGER CASEMENT,
His Britannic Majesty's Consul.

Inclosure 7 in No. 3.

(See p. 59.)

Circular of September 7, 1903, forbidding Soldiers armed with Rifles from going out on Service without Europeans over them.

ÉTAT INDÉPENDANT DU CONGO.

Boma, le 7 Septembre, 1903.

LA lecture de rapports sur des opérations et reconnaissances militaires démontre que les prescriptions formelles—et si souvent répétées—du Gouvernement concernant l'instruction d'envoyer des soldats armés sous la conduite de gradés noirs ne sont pas observées rigoureusement.

Je constate même avec regret de la part de certains fonctionnaires et agents cette mauvaise volonté à se conformer à ces instructions, qui sont pourtant dictées par le souci des intérêts supérieurs de l'État.

Les opérations militaires doivent être conduites d'après les règlements sur le service en campagne que nos officiers et sous-officiers doivent appliquer fréquemment au cours des exercices journaliers et d'après les nombreuses prescriptions sur la matière. Et à cet effet le personnel supérieur, avant de se prononcer sur les opérations à conduire aura, au préalable, à examiner si les moyens dont disposent leurs sous-ordres sont suffisants.

J'ai l'honneur d'inviter les Chefs territoriaux à rappeler à leur personnel les instructions qui précèdent et à l'informer de ce que toute contravention à la défense d'envoyer des soldats armés sous la conduite de gradés noirs sera sévèrement réprimée et de nature même à provoquer la révocation de l'agent en faute.

Les soldats doivent être l'objet d'une surveillance constante afin qu'il leur soit impossible de se livrer à des cruantés auxquelles pourraient les pousser leurs instincts primitifs.

Les instructions défendent aussi d'employer les soldats au service des courriers et des transports.

Malgré cela on continue en maints endroits à pratiquer ce déplorable usage.

Il importe que les soldats ne soient plus constamment distraits de leur garnison et de leur métier militaire et qu'ils restent, en tout temps, sous le contrôle de leurs chefs; l'instruction et l'éducation militaires des hommes de la force publique ne peuvent qu'y gagner.

Je prie, en conséquence, le personnel intéressé de faire cesser immédiatement l'état de choses signalé ci-dessus : le service des courriers doit être assuré par des travailleurs ou des hommes spécialement désignés à cet effet.

Si l'autorité juge nécessaire, dans certains cas, de faire escorter soit un courrier soit un convoi de marchandises, il faut qne la patrouille soit organisée réglementairement et commandée par un Européen.

Ce n'est qu'à titre tout à fait exceptionnel et si c'est absolument nécessaire que cette patrouille pourra être commandée à défaut d'Européen par un gradé de choix et de confiance.

Mais dans ce cas, que l'autorité aura à justifier, les hommes commandés par un gradé noir devront être munis du fusil à piston d'armement qui coustitue une bonne arme défensive.

Le Vice-Gouverneur-Général,
(Signé) F. FUCHS.

(Translation.)

INDEPENDENT STATE OF THE CONGO.

Boma, September 7, 1903.

THE perusal of reports on military operations and reconnaissances shows that the formal orders of the Government, so frequently repeated, respecting the instruction to send armed soldiers under the command of black non-commissioned officers, are not rigorously observed.

I even note with regret this disinclination, on the part of certain officials and agents, to conform to these instructions, which are, however, dictated by care for the higher interests of the State.

Military operations must be conducted in accordance with the regulations respecting service in the field, of which our officers and non-commissioned officers must make frequent application at daily drill, and in accordance with the numerous instructions in the matter. And to this end the superior staff, before deciding on the operations to be undertaken, must ascertain beforehand whether the means at the disposal of those below them are sufficient.

I have the honour to invite the territorial Chiefs to remind their staff of the preceding instructions, and to inform them that any breach of the rule forbidding the dispatch of armed soldiers under the command of black non-commissioned officers will be severely put down, and may lead to the dismissal of the agent in fault.

The soldiers must be the object of constant supervision, so that it may be impossible for them to commit cruelties to which their primitive instincts might prompt them.

The instructions also forbid the employment of the soldiers on post or transport work.

Nevertheless, this deplorable custom continues to obtain in many places.

It is important that the soldiers should not in future be constantly withdrawn from their garrison and from their military duties, and that they should remain at all times under the control of their Chiefs. This cannot fail to improve the instruction and military education of the men of the public force. I therefore request the staff whom it concerns to put an end at once to the above-mentioned condition of affairs; the postal service must be assured by workmen or by men specially chosen for that purpose.

If the authorities deem it necessary in certain cases to have the post or a convoy of merchandise escorted, the patrol must be organized according to the regulations, and must be commanded by a European.

It is only in most exceptional cases, and if it is absolutely necessary, that this patrol can, failing European, be commanded by a specially-selected and trustworthy non-commissioned officer.

But in such cases, which will have to be justified by the authorities, the men commanded by a black non-commissioned officer must be provided with a regulation cap-gun, which constitutes a good defensive weapon.

The Vice-Governor-General,
(Signed) F. FUCHS.

Inclosure 8 in No. 3.

(See p. 59.)

Circular of Governor-General Wahis, addressed to the Commissioners of District and Chiefs of Zones.

LA qualité du caoutchouc exporté du Congo est sensiblement inférieure à ce qu'elle était il y a quelque temps. Cette différence a plusieurs causes, mais la principale résulte de l'adjonction au latex qui devrait être récolté, d'autres latex de valeur très inférieure ou même des matières poussiéreuses quelconques.

Cette cause de perte peut et doit disparaître. Les Commissaires de District et Chefs de Zone qui ont tous de l'expérience, connaissent les moyens de fraude que les indigènes cherchent souvent à employer.

Ils ont à prendre des mesures pour empêcher d'une façon complète ces tromperies. Il n'est pas douteux que là ou la population se soumet à l'impôt il ne sera pas impossible de l'amener à fournir un produit pur, mais il faut pour atteindre ce but une surveillance constante; dès que l'indigène constatera qu'elle se relâche, il essaiera de diminuer son travail en prenant du latex de mauvaise qualité, quand il obtient celui-ci facilement, ou en ajoutant au produit des matières étrangères.

Chaque fois que ces fraudes sont constatées elles doivent être réprimées. Les Commissaires de District et Chefs de Zone ont à examiner fréquemment les produits, afin de faire à temps des observations à leurs Chefs de Poste, et à ne plus laisser perdurer des situations qui causent le plus grand préjudice.

A cette cause de la diminution de la valeur du caoutchouc, il faut ajouter celle provenant de l'emballage défectueux du produit, qui par suite voyage souvent pendant plusieurs mois dans les plus mauvaises conditions. L'on peut dire qu'à cause de cette négligence une notable partie des efforts qui ont été faits pour obtenir une production en rapport avec la richesse du pays, doivent être considérés comme perdus, puisque la valeur du caoutchouc peut diminuer de moitié par suite de ce manque de soin.

J'ajouterai que la valeur du caoutchouc, même pur de tout mélange, a diminué depuis quelque temps sur tous les marchés; il faut donc que les Chefs Territoriaux fassent non seulement disparaître les deux causes de pertes qu'ils peuvent éliminer, mais encore qu'ils compensent la troisième en faisant des efforts continus pour augmenter la production dans la mesure prescrite par les instructions.

Mon attention sera d'une façon constante, fixée sur les prescriptions que je donne ici.

Le Gouverneur-Général,
(Signé) WAHIS.

Boma, le 29 *Mars*, 1901.

(Translation.)

THE quality of the rubber exported from the Congo is sensibly inferior to what it was some time ago. This difference arises from several causes, but principally from the addition, to the latex which is fit to be gathered, of other kinds of latex of very inferior value, or even of any dust-like matter.

This cause of loss can and must be removed. The Commissioners of districts and Chiefs of zones, who all have experience, know the fraudulent means which the natives often try to employ.

They must take measures completely to prevent these frauds. It cannot be doubted that in those parts where the population submits to the tax it will not be impossible to lead the natives to furnish pure produce; but in order to effect this, constant supervision is necessary, for as soon as the native notices that the supervision is becoming lax he will try to lessen his work by taking latex of a bad quality, if he obtains it easily, or by adding foreign matter.

Whenever these frauds are discovered they must be put down. The Commissioners of districts and Chiefs of zones must examine the produce at frequent intervals, in order to report in time to their Heads of stations, and not to permit a condition of affairs which is most prejudicial.

To this cause of the decline in the value of rubber must be added that arising from defective packing of the produce, which thus often travels during several months under the worst conditions. Much of the effort which has been taken to obtain produce in keeping with the richness of the country may be said to be lost through this neglect, for the value of the rubber may be diminished by half through this want of care.

I may add that the value of rubber, even when free from all admixture, has gone down in every market for some time past; territorial Chiefs must, therefore, not only remove the two causes of loss which they can eliminate, but they must also try to neutralize the third by making unceasing efforts to increase production to the extent laid down in the instructions.

The orders which I have here given will have my constant attention.

The Governor-General,
(Signed) WAHIS.

Boma, March 29, 1901.

No. 4.

The Marquess of Lansdowne to Sir C. Phipps.

Sir, *Foreign Office, February* 11, 1904.

WITH reference to Sir C. Phipps' despatch of the 19th September, 1903, I transmit to you herewith a Memorandum which has been prepared in reply to the note respecting the condition of affairs in the Congo addressed by the Government of the Independent State on the 17th September last, to the Powers parties to the Act of Berlin.

I request you to communicate this Memorandum to M. de Cuvelier, and in doing so to call special attention to the inclosed Report by Mr. Casement, His Majesty's Consul at Boma, upon his recent visit to certain districts of the Upper Congo.

I am, &c.
(Signed) LANSDOWNE.

Inclosure in No. 4.

Memorandum

HIS Majesty's Government have not until now offered any observations upon the note from M. de Cuvelier of the 17th September last, because they desired, before doing so, to learn the result of the inquiries instituted by Mr. Casement, His Majesty's Consul at Boma, during the visit which he has recently paid to certain districts of the Upper Congo.

Mr. Casement returned to this country at the beginning of last month, and has since furnished the report of which a copy is annexed to this Memorandum for communication to the Congo Government. The report will also be communicated to the Powers parties to the Berlin Act, to whom the despatch of the 8th August last was addressed, and it will be laid before Parliament.

The descriptions given in the report of the manner in which the administration is carried on and the methods by which the revenue is collected in the districts visited by Mr. Casement constitute a grave indictment, and need no comment beyond the statement that, in the opinion of His Majesty's Government, they show that the allegations to which reference is made in the despatch were not without foundation, and that there is ample ground for the belief that there are, at any rate, extensive regions in which the pledges given under the Berlin Act have not been fulfilled.

M. de Cuvelier's note dwells at considerable length upon the necessity of the natives contributing by some form of taxation to the requirements of the State, and upon the advantage of their being induced to work. The history of the development of the British Colonies and Protectorates in Africa shows that His Majesty's Government have always admitted this necessity. Defects of administration of the character referred to in M. de Cuvelier's note are, no doubt, always liable to occur in dealing with uncivilized races inhabiting vast areas and differing in manners, in customs and in all the attributes which are necessary for the construction of a social system. But whenever difficulties have arisen, most notably in the case of the Sierra Leone insurrection of which M. de Cuvelier makes special mention,* prompt and searching inquiry has been publicly made, redress of grievances has been granted where due, and every endeavour has been made to establish such considerate treatment of the natives as is compatible with the just requirements of the State.

The reference to the disturbed state of Nigeria appears to relate to the campaign undertaken early last year against Kano and Sokoto. The campaign was not a measure of "military repression" in the sense of being the suppression of a native rising. It was necessitated by the hostile action of powerful Mahommedan Chiefs within the Protectorate, over whom authority had not been previously asserted, who refused to maintain friendly relations with the Administration, hospitably entertained the murderer of a British officer and declared that the only relations between themselves and the Government were those of war. By the mention of the loss of 700 lives reference is no doubt made to the action at Burmi on the 27th July last, when about that number of the enemy were killed, including the ex-Sultan of Sokoto and most of the Chiefs who had joined him, while on the British side Major Marsh, the Commanding Officer, and ten men were killed, and three officers and sixty-nine men were wounded. This decisive and successful action completely broke up the party of the irreconcilables as well as a remnant of the Mahdi's following.

The military operations which are now in progress in Somaliland have been forced upon His Majesty's Government, as is generally known, by the assumption of power on the part of a fanatical Mullah, and by the cruelties which he practised upon tribes within the British Protectorate.

* The 62 convictions mentioned occurred between July 1894 and March 1898, not February 1896, as stated in the quotation from an "English publicist."

In both these cases, measures of military repression have been necessary to save the territories in question from falling once more under the complete control of uncivilized or fanatical Rulers, and of thus relapsing into barbarism. The Congo Government and other Powers possessing Colonies in Africa have had to meet similar contingencies, and no blame is attached to them, nor, so far as His Majesty's Government are aware, has ever been attached to them, for adopting measures to protect the cause of civilization.

After dealing with the treatment of natives, M. de Cuvelier's note proceeds to explain the views of the Congo Government with regard to the system of trade now existing in the State. The opinion of His Majesty's Government has been set forth; they hold that the matter is one which could properly be the subject of a reference to the Tribunal at The Hague, but they are still awaiting an answer on this point from the Powers to whom the despatch of the 8th August was addressed.

Memoranda will be forwarded separately giving examples of injuries suffered by British subjects which have been the cause of complaint. These Memoranda have been prepared in order to confirm the statement, upon which M. de Cuvelier throws doubt, that the time of His Majesty's Consul had been principally occupied in the investigation of such cases.

Foreign Office, February 11, 1904.

No. 5.

The Marquess of Lansdowne to His Majesty's Representatives at Paris, Berlin, Vienna, St. Petersburgh, Rome, Madrid, Constantinople, Brussels, The Hague, Copenhagen, Stockholm, and Lisbon.

Sir, *Foreign Office, February* 12, 1904.

I TRANSMIT to you, for communication to the Government to which you are accredited, a collection of papers, as marked in the margin,* which relate to the present condition of affairs in the Independent State of the Congo.

In handing these documents to the Minister for Foreign Affairs I request that you will call special attention to the Report by Mr. Casement, His Majesty's Consul at Boma, upon his recent visit to certain districts of the Upper Congo, and that you will at the same time inquire when an answer may be expected to my despatch of the 8th August last.

I am, &c.
(Signed) LANSDOWNE.

---

* Nos. 1, 2, 3, and 4.

AFRICA. No. 1 (1904).

CORRESPONDENCE and Report from His Majesty's Consul at Boma respecting the Administration of the Independent State of the Congo.

Presented to both Houses of Parliament by Command of His Majesty. February 1904.

LONDON:
PRINTED BY HARRISON AND SONS.

AFRICA. No. 7 (1904).

FURTHER CORRESPONDENCE

RESPECTING THE

ADMINISTRATION

OF THE

INDEPENDENT STATE OF THE CONGO.

[In continuation of "Africa No. 1 (1904)".]

Presented to both Houses of Parliament by Command of His Majesty.
June 1904.

LONDON:
PRINTED FOR HIS MAJESTY'S STATIONERY OFFICE,
BY HARRISON AND SONS, ST. MARTIN'S LANE,
PRINTERS IN ORDINARY TO HIS MAJESTY.

And to be purchased, either directly or through any Bookseller, from
EYRE & SPOTTISWOODE, EAST HARDING STREET, FLEET STREET, E.C.,
AND 32, ABINGDON STREET, WESTMINSTER, S.W.
OR OLIVER & BOYD, EDINBURGH;
OR E. PONSONBY, 116, GRAFTON STREET, DUBLIN.

[Cd. 2097.] *Price 7d.*

TABLE OF CONTENTS.

Further Correspondence respecting the Administration of the Independent State of the Congo.

[In continuation of "Africa No. 1 (1904)".]

No. 1.

Sir C. Phipps to the Marquess of Lansdowne.—(Received March 14).

My Lord, *Brussels, March* 13, 1904.

I HAVE the honour to inclose the rejoinder on the part of the Congo Government to the Report of His Majesty's Consul at Boma on the condition of the Congo.

In handing these "Notes" to me this afternoon M. de Cuvelier was instructed to call my attention to the passage where his Government expresses a desire to be placed in possession of the full Report, including names, dates, and places referred to. The "Notes" will be communicated to-morrow to the Representatives of the other Powers.

I have, &c.
(Signed) CONSTANTINE PHIPPS.

Inclosure in No. 1.

Notes on the Report of Mr. Casement, Consul of His Britannic Majesty, of the 11th December, 1903.

A LA séance de la Chambre des Communes du 11 Mars, 1903, Lord Cranborne avait dit:—

> "We have no reason to think that slavery is recognized by the authorities of the Congo Free State, but reports of acts of cruelty and oppression have reached us. Such reports have been received from our Consular officers."

Le Gouvernement de l'État du Congo demanda, par lettre du 14 Mars, 1903, à son Excellence Sir C. Phipps, de bien vouloir lui communiquer les faits qui avaient été l'objet de rapports de la part des Consuls Britanniques.

Cette demande ne reçut pas de suite.

La dépêche de Lord Lansdowne du 8 Août, 1903, portait:—

> "Representations to this effect (alleged cases of ill-treatment of natives and existence of trade monopolies) are to be found . . . . in despatches from His Majesty's Consuls."

L'impression était ainsi créée qu'à cette date le Gouvernement de Sa Majesté se trouvait en possession de renseignements Consulaires concluants: la nécessité d'un voyage de M. le Consul Casement dans le Haut-Congo n'en a pas moins paru évidente. La réflexion s'ensuit que les conclusions de la note du 8 Août étaient au moins prématurées; il s'en déduit également que, contrairement à l'appréciation de cette note, il a été loisible au Consul Britannique d'entreprendre dans les régions intérieures tel voyage qui lui convenait. Il est à noter en tout cas que le "White Paper" (Africa, No. 1, 1904), qui vient d'être présenté au Parlement, ne contient pas, nonobstant le désir qu'en a réitéré l'État du Congo, ces rapports Consulaires antérieurs, qui, cependant, offraient d'autant plus d'intérêt qu'ils dataient d'un temps où la campagne présente n'était pas née.

Le Rapport actuel signale qu'en certains points visités par le Consul, la population se trouve en décroissance. M. Casement n'indique pas les bases de ses recensements comparatifs en 1887 et en 1903. Il est à se demander comment pour cette dernière année le Consul a pu établir ses chiffres au cours de visites rapides et hâtives. Sur quels éléments certains s'appuye-t-il, par exemple, pour dire que la population des localités riveraines du Lac Mantumba *semble* avoir diminué dans les dix dernières années de 60 à 70 pour cent ? En un point désigné F*, il déclare que l'ensemble des villages ne compte pas aujourd'hui plus ne 500 âmes ; quelques lignes plus loin, ces mêmes villages ne comportent plus que 240 habitants en tout. Ce ne sont là que des détails, mais ils caractérisent immédiatement le défaut de précision de certaines appréciations du Consul. Au reste, il n'est malheureusement que trop exact que la diminution de la population a été constatée ; elle est due à d'autres causes qu'à un régime excessif ou oppressif exercé par l'Administration sur les populations indigènes. C'est en premier lieu la maladie du sommeil, qui décime partout les populations en Afrique équatoriale. Le Rapport remarque lui-même que : "a prominent place must be assigned to this malady,"[1] et que cette maladie est "probably one of the principal factors," de la diminution de la population.[2] Il suffit de lire la lettre du Révérend John Whitehead (Annexe II du Rapport), citée par le Consul, pour se rendre compte des ravages de la maladie, à laquelle ce missionnaire attribue la moitié des décès dans la région riveraine du district. Dans une interview récente, Mgr. Van Ronslé, Vicaire Apostolique du Congo Belge, avec l'autorité qui s'attache à une grande expérience des choses d'Afrique et à des séjours prolongés en de multiples résidences au Congo, a montré l'évolution du fléau, le dépérissement fatal des populations qui en sont frappées, quelles que soient d'ailleurs les conditions de leur état social, citant entre autres les pertes effrayantes de vies dues à ce mal dans l'Uganda. Que si l'on ajoute à cette cause fondamentale de la dépopulation au Congo, les épidémies de petite vérole, l'impossibilité actuelle pour les tribus de maintenir leur chiffre par des achats d'esclaves, la facilité de déplacement des indigènes, il s'explique que le Consul et les missionnaires aient relevé la diminution du nombre d'habitants de certaines agglomérations, sans que nécessairement ce soit le résultat d'un système d'oppression. L'Annexe No. I reproduit les déclarations sur ce point de Mgr. Van Ronslé. Ce qu'il dit des conséquences, sur le chiffre numérique de la population, de la suppression de l'esclavage, se trouve reproduit ailleurs :—

"The people (slave) are for the most part originally prisoners of war. Since the Decree of Emancipation they have simply returned to their own distant homes, knowing their owners have no power to recapture them. This is one reason why some think the population is decreasing, and another is the vast exodus up and down river."[3]—"So long as the Slave Trade flourished, the Bobangi flourished, but with its abolition they are tending to disappear, for their towns were replenished by slaves.[4]

Le Consul cite des cas, dont du reste les raisons lui sont inconnues, d'exode d'indigènes du Congo sur la rive Française. On ne voit pas à quel titre il en ferait grief à l'État, si l'on en juge d'après les motifs qui ont déterminé certains d'entre eux, à preuve les exemples de ces émigrations, donnés et expliqués par un missionnaire Anglais, le Révérend Père W. H. Bentley. L'un est relatif à la station de Lukolela :—

"The main difficulty has been the shifting of the population. It appears that the population, when the station was founded in 1865, was between 5,000 and 6,000 in the riverine Colonies. About two years later, the Chief, Mpuki, did not agree with his neighbours or they with him. When the tension became acute, Mpuki crossed over with his people to the opposite (French) side of the river. This exodus took away a large number of people. In 1890 or 1891, a Chief from one of the lower towns was compelled by the majority of his people to leave the State side, and several went with him. About 1893, the rest of the people at the lower towns either went across to the same place as the deposed Chief, or took up their residence inland. Towards the end of 1894, a soldier who had been sent to cut firewood for the State steamers on an island off the towns, left his work to make an evil request in one of the towns. He shot the man who refused him. The rascal of a soldier was properly dealt with by the State officer in charge ; but this outrage combined, with other smaller difficulties, to produce a panic, and nearly all the people left for the French side, or hid away inland. So the fine township has broken up."[5]

L'autre cas a trait à la station de Bolobo :—

"It is rare indeed for Bolobo, with its 30,000 or 40,000 people, divided into some dozen clans, to be at peace for any length of time together. The loss of life from these petty wars, the number

[1] Rapport, p. 21.
[2] Idem, p. 26.
[3] M. Boudot, missionnaire de la Congo Batolo Mission. "Regions Beyond," Décembre 1901, p. 337.
[4] W. H. Bentley, "Pioneering on the Congo," II, p. 229.
[5] Idem, p. 243.

of those killed for witchcraft, and of those who are buried alive with the dead, involve, even within our narrow limits here at Bolobo, an almost daily drain upon the vitality of the country, and an incalculable amount of sorrow and suffering. . . . . The Government was not indifferent to these murderous ways. . . . . In 1890 the District Commissioner called the people together, and warned them against the burying of slaves alive in the graves of free people, and the reckless killing of slaves which then obtained. The natives did not like the rising power of the State. . . . . Our own settlement among them was not unattended with difficulty. . . . . There was a feeling against white men generally, and especially so against the State. The people became insolent and haughty. . . . . Just at this time . . . . as a force of soldiers steamed past the Moye towns, the steamers were fired upon. The soldiers landed, and burnt and looted the towns. The natives ran away into the grass, and great numbers crossed to the French side of the river. They awoke to the fact that Bula Matadi, the State, was not the helpless thing they had so long thought. This happened early in 1891."[1]

Ces exemples donnent, comme on le voit, à l'émigration des indigènes, des causes n'ayant aucun rapport avec—

The methods employed to obtain labour from them by local officials and the exactions levied on them.[2]

Le Rapport s'étend longuement sur l'existence des impôts indigènes. Il constate que les indigènes sont astreints à des prestations de travail de diverses sortes, ici sous forme de fournitures de " chikwangues " ou de vivres frais pour les postes Gouvernementaux, là sous forme de participation à des travaux d'utilité publique, tels que la construction d'une jetée à Bololo, ou l'entretien de la ligne télégraphique à F——— ; ailleurs sous la forme de la récolte des produits domaniaux. Nous maintenons la légitimité de ces impôts sur les populations natives, d'accord en cela avec le Gouvernement de Sa Majesté, qui, dans le Mémorandum du 11 Février, 1904, déclare que l'industrie et le développement des Colonies et Protectorats Britanniques en Afrique montrent que le Gouvernement de Sa Majesté a toujours admis la nécessité de faire contribuer les natifs aux charges publiques et de les amener au travail. Nous sommes d'accord également avec le Gouvernement de Sa Majesté que si en cette matière des abus se commettent, comme, il est vrai, il s'en est produit en toutes Colonies, ces abus appellent des réformes, et qu'il est du devoir de l'autorité supérieure d'y mettre fin et de concilier, dans une juste mesure, les nécessités Gouvernementales avec les intérêts bien entendus des indigènes.

Mais l'État du Congo entend à cet égard se mouvoir librement dans l'exercice de sa souveraineté—comme, par exemple, le Gouvernement Britannique explique dans son dernier Mémorandum l'avoir fait à Sierra-Leone—en dehors de toute pression extérieure ou de toute ingérence étrangère, qui seraient attentatoires à ses droits essentiels.

Le Rapport du Consul vise manifestement à créer l'impression que la perception de l'impôt, au Congo, est violente, inhumaine et couelle, et nous voulons, avant tout, rencontrer l'accusation si souvent dirigée contre l'État, que cette perception donnerait lieu à d'odieux actes de mutilation. A cet égard, la lecture superficielle du Rapport est de nature à impressionner, par l'accumulation complaisante, non pas de faits nets, précis, vérifiés, mais de déclarations et d'affirmations des indigènes.

Une remarque préliminaire s'impose sur les conditions dans lesquelles le voyage du Consul s'est effectué.

Qu'il l'ait voulu ou non, M. le Consul Britannique a apparu aux populations comme le redresseur des griefs, réels ou imaginaires, des indigènes, et sa présence à La Lulonga, coïncidant avec la campagne menée contre l'État du Congo, en une région où s'exerce depuis longtemps l'influence des missionnaires Protestants, devait fatalement avoir pour les indigènes une signification qui ne leur à pas échappé. C'est en dehors des agents de l'État, en dehors de toute action ou de tout concours de l'autorité régulière que le Consul a fait ses investigations ; c'est assisté par des missionnaires Protestants Anglais qu'il a procédé ; c'est sur un vapeur d'une Mission Protestante qu'il a fait son inspection ; c'est dans les Missions Protestantes qu'il a généralement reçu l'hospitalité ; dans ces conditions, il a dû inévitablement être considéré par l'indigène comme l'antagoniste de l'autorité établie.

Nous n'en voulons d'autre preuve que le fait caractéristique d'indigènes, pendant le séjour du Consul à Bonginda, s'attroupant à la rive, au passage en pirogue d'agents de la Société " La Lulonga " et s'écriant :—

" Votre violence est finie, elle s'en va ; les Anglais seuls restent ; mourez vous autres ! "

[1] W. H. Bentley, " Pioneering on the Congo," II, pp. 234–236. [2] Rapport, p. 29.

Et cet aveu significatif d'un missionnaire Protestant qui, à propos de ce fait, explique :—

"The Consul was here at the time, and the people were much excited, and evidently thought themselves on top. . . . . The people have got this idea (that the rubber work was finished) into their heads of themselves, consequent, I suppose, upon the Consul's visit."

Dans ces circonstances, en raison de l'état d'esprit qu'elles révèlent chez les indigènes, en raison de leur caractère impressionnable et de leur désir naturel de se soustraire à la charge de l'impôt, il n'était pas douteux que les conclusions auxquelles arriverait le Consul ne seraient pas autres que celles de son Rapport.

Il suffira, pour mettre ce point en évidence et pour caractériser le manque de valeur de ses investigations, de s'arrêter à un seul cas, celui sur lequel s'est porté tout l'effort de Mr. Casement, nous voulons parler de l'affaire Epondo. C'est celle de l'enfant II dont le Rapport parle aux pages 56, 58, et 78.

Il est indispensable d'entrer un peu longuement dans les détails de cette affaire, qui sont significatifs.

Le Consul se trouvait, à la date du 4 Septembre, 1903, à la Mission de la "Congo Bololo Mission," à Bonginda, de retour d'un voyage dans la Rivière Lopori, au cours duquel il n'avait constaté aucun de ces actes de mutilation qu'il est d'usage de mettre à la charge des agents au Congo.

A Bonginda, des indigènes d'un village voisin (Bossunguma) viennent le trouver et lui signalent entre autres qu'une "sentinelle" de la Compagnie "La Lulonga," nommée Kelengo, avait, à Bossunguma, coupé la main d'un indigène du nom d'Epondo, dont les blessures étaient à peine guéries. Le Consul se transporte à Bossunguma ; il est accompagné des deux Révérends W. D. Armstrong et D. J. Danielson et se fait présenter l'indigène estropié, lequel, "en réponse à la question du Consul, accuse de ce méfait une sentinelle nommée Kelengo (placée dans cet endroit par l'agent local de la Société 'La Lulonga' pour vérifier si les indigènes récoltaient du caoutchouc)." Ce sont les termes du Consul : il s'agissait en effet d'établir un rapport de cause à effet entre la récolte du caoutchouc et ce cas prétendu de cruauté.

Le Consul procède à l'interrogatoire du Chef et de quelques indigènes du village. Ils répondent en accusant Kelengo ; la plupart déclarent avoir été témoins oculaires du fait. Le Consul fait demander par ses interprètes s'il se trouve là d'autres témoins qui ont vu le crime et en accusent Kelengo : "presque tous les individus présents, au nombre environ de quarante, s'écrient d'une seule voix que c'est Kelengo le coupable."

Il faut lire toute cette enquête telle qu'elle a été libellée par le Consul lui-même, en des sortes de procès-verbaux des 7, 8, et 9 Septembre (Annexe 2), pour se rendre compte de l'acharnement avec lequel les indigènes accablent Kelengo, et des dénégations de l'accusé se heurtant à l'unanimité de tous ceux qui le chargent. De partout surgissent les dénonciateurs et de la foule surexcitée jaillissent les accusations les plus diverses : il a coupé la main d'Epondo, enchaîné des femmes, volé des canards et un chien ! L'attention du Consul ne veut pas s'éveiller en présence du caractère passionné des dépositions ; sans autre garantie de leur sincérité, sans autre contrôle de leur véracité, il considère son enquête comme concluante, et, de même qu'il s'était substitué au Parquet pour l'instruction de l'affaire, de même il préjuge la décision de l'autorité compétente en déclarant à la population assemblée que "Kelengo deserved severe punishment for his illegal and cruel acts." Dramatisant l'incident, il emmène avec lui la prétendue victime, l'exhibe le 10 Septembre devant le Chef de Poste de Coquilhatville, auquel il remet la copie de son enquête, et le 12 Septembre, il adresse au Gouverneur-Général une lettre qu'il qualifie de "personal and private," dans laquelle il prend texte entre autres de l'incident pour accuser "the system of general exploitation of an entire population which can only be rendered successful by the employment of arbitrary and illegal force." Cette enquête terminée, il reprenait aussitôt la route du Bas-Congo.

Les circonstances de fait eussent-elles été exactes, encore serait-on frappé de la disproportion des conclusions que le Consul en déduit, en généralisant avec emphase son système de critiques contre l'État du Congo. Mais le fait même, tel qu'il l'a présenté, est inexact.

En effet, dès la dénonciation du Consul connue du Parquet, celui-ci se rendit sur les lieux en la personne du Substitut du Procureur d'État, M. Gennaro Bosco, et procéda à une enquête judiciaire dans les conditions normales en dehors de toute influence étrangère. Cette enquête démontra que M. le Consul de Sa Majesté Britannique avait été l'objet d'une machination ourdie par les indigènes, qui, dans l'espoir de n'avoir plus à travailler, avaient comploté de représenter Epondo comme la victime de procédés inhumains d'un capita d'une Société commerciale. En réalité, Epondo avait été victime d'un accident de chasse et mordu à la main par un sanglier; la blessure s'était gangrenée et avait occasionné la perte du membre, ce qui avait été habilement exploité par les indigènes vis-à-vis du Consul. Nous joignons (Annexe 3) les extraits de l'enquête faite par le Substitut relatifs à cette affaire Epondo. Les dépositions sont typiques, uniformes et concordantes. Elles ne laissent aucun doute sur la cause de l'accident, attestent que les indigènes ont menti au Consul, et révèlent le mobile auquel ils ont obéi, dans l'espoir que l'intervention du Consul les déchargerait de l'obligation de l'impôt. L'enquête montre Epondo, enfin acculé, rétractant ses premières affirmations au Consul, et avouant avoir été influencé par les gens de son village. Il est interrogé :—

" *D.* Persistez-vous à accuser Kelengo de vous avoir coupé la main gauche ?

" *R.* Non ; j'ai menti.

" *D.* Racontez alors comment et quand vous avez perdu la main.

" *R.* J'étais esclave de Monkekola, à Malele, dans le district des Bangala. Un jour, j'allai avec lui à la chasse au sanglier. Il en blessa un avec une lance, et alors la bête, devenue furieuse, m'attaqua. Je tâchai de me sauver avec la suite, mais je tombai ; le sanglier fut bientôt sur moi, m'arrachant la main gauche, au ventre et à la hanche gauche. Le comparant montre les cicatrices aux endroits désignés, et spontanément se met par terre pour faire voir dans quelle position il se trouvait lorsqu'il fut attaqué et blessé par le sanglier.

" *D.* Depuis combien de temps cet accident vous est-il arrivé ?

" *R.* Je ne me rappelle pas. C'est depuis longtemps.

" *D.* Pourquoi alors aviez-vous accusé Kalengo ?

" *R.* Parce que Momaketa, un des Chefs de Bossunguma, me l'a dit, et après tous les habitants de mon village me l'ont répété.

* * * * * *

" *D.* Les Anglais vous ont-ils photographié ?

" *R.* Oui, à Bonginda et à Lulanga. Ils m'ont dit de mettre bien en évidence le moignon. Il y avait Nenele, Mongongolo, Torongo, et autres blancs, dont je ne connais pas les noms. Ils étaient les blancs de Lulanga. Mongongolo a porté avec lui six photographies."[1]

Epondo a réitéré ses déclarations et rétractations spontanément à un missionnaire Protestant, M. Faris, résidant à Bolengi. Ce Révérend a remis au Commissaire-Général de Coquilhatville la déclaration écrite suivante :—

" Je soussigné E.-E. Faris, missionnaire, résidant à Bolengi, Haut-Congo, déclare que j'ai interrogé l'enfant Epondo, du village de Bosongoma, qui a été chez moi le 10 Septembre, 1903, avec Mr. Casement, le Consul d'Angleterre, et que j'ai mené à la Mission de Bolengi, le 16 Octobre, 1903, selon la requête de M. le Commandant Stevens, de Coquilhatville, et que le dit enfant m'a dit aujourd'hui, le 17 Octobre, 1903, qu'il a perdu sa main par la morsure d'un sanglier.

" Il m'a dit également qu'il a informé Mr. Casement que sa main a été coupé par un soldat, ou bien d'un des travailleurs de blancs, qui ont fait la guerre dans son village pour faire apporter le caoutchouc, mais il affirme que cette dernière histoire qu'il m'a dite aujourd'hui est la vérité.

" E.-E. Faris.

" A Bolengi, le 17 Octobre, 1903."

L'enquête aboutit à une ordonnance de non-lieu ainsi motivée en ce qui concerne le cas Epondo :—

" Nous, Substitut du Procureur d'État près le Tribunal de Coquilhatville ;

" Vu les notes rédigées par le Consul de Sa Majesté Britannique, à l'occasion de sa visite aux villages d'Ikandja et Bossunguma, dans la région des Ngombe, d'où résulte que le nommé Kelengo, garde forestier au service de la Société 'La Lulonga,' aurait—

" (*a.*) Coupé . . . , la main gauche au nommé Epondo.

" (*b.*) . . . .

" (*c.*) . . . .

" Vu l'enquête faite par M. le Lieutenant Braeckman, confirmant en partie l'enquête faite par le Consul de Sa Majesté Britannique, mais le contredisant en partie, et ajoutant aux accusations précédemment faites à Kelengo, celle d'avoir tué un indigène nommé Baluwa ;

Vu les conclusions posées par cet officier de police judiciaire tendant à faire naître des soupçons assez graves sur la vérité de toutes ces accusations ;

" Attendu que tous les indigènes qui ont accusé Kelengo, soit au Consul de Sa Majesté Britannique, soit au Lieutenant Braeckman, convoqués par nous, Substitut, ont pris la fuite, et tout les efforts faits pour les retrouver n'ont abouti à aucun résultat ; que cette fuite discrédite évidemment leurs affirmations ;

" Que tous les témoins interrogés dans notre enquête attestent . . . . qu'Epondo a perdu la main gauche parce qu'un sanglier la lui a arrachée . . . . ;

" Qu'Epondo confirme ces attestations, avouant qu'il a menti par suggestion des indigènes de

[1] Voir Annexe 3.

Bossunguma et Ikondja, qui espéraient de se soustraire à la récolte du caoutchouc moyennant l'intervention du Consul de Sa Majesté Britannique, qu'ils jugeaient très puissant ;

" Que les témoins, presque tous indigènes des villages accusateurs, confirment que tel fut le but de leur mensonge ;

" Que cette version, indépendamment de l'unanimité des affirmations des témoins et des parties lésées, se présente aussi comme la plus plausible, parce que personne n'ignore, soit la répugnance des indigènes pour le travail en général et la récolte du caoutchouc, soit leur facilité à mentir et à porter de fausses accusations ;

" Qu'elle est confirmée par l'opinion, nettement formulée, du missionnaire Anglais Armstrong, qui retient les indigènes 'capables de tout complot pour éviter de travailler, et surtout de faire le caoutchouc' ;

" Que l'innocence de Kelengo étant complètement prouvée, il n'y a pas lieu à le poursuivre ;

" Par ces motifs :

" Nous, Substitut, déclarons non-lieu à poursuivre le nommé Kelengo, garde forestier au service de la Société 'La Lulonga,' pour les crimes prévus par les Articles 2, 5, 11, 19 du Code Pénal.

Le Substitut,
(Signé) Bosco.

" Mampoko, le 9 Octobre, 1903."

Si nous avons insisté sur les détails de cette affaire, c'est qu'elle est considérée par le Consul lui-même comme d'une importance capitale et qu'il se base sur ce seul cas pour conclure à l'exactitude de toutes les autres déclarations d'indigènes qu'il a recueillies.

" Dans le seul cas sur lequel j'ai pu enquêter personnellement, dit-il[1]—celui de l'enfant II—j'ai trouvé cette accusation établie sur les lieux, sans apparemment une ombre de doute quant à la culpabilité de la sentinelle accusée."

Et plus loin :—

" Dans le village de R*, j'ai eu seulement le temps de faire enquête sur l'accusation faite par II.[2]

Et ailleurs :—

" Il était évidemment impossible que je puisse . . . . . vérifier sur place, comme dans le cas de l'enfant, les déclarations que me firent les indigènes. Dans ce seul cas, la vérité des accusations fut amplement démontrée."[3]

C'est aussi à propos de cette affaire que, dans sa lettre du 12 Septembre, 1903, au Gouverneur-Général, il disait :—

" When speaking to M. le Commandant Stevens at Coquilhatville on the 10th instant, *when the mutilated boy Epondo stood before us as evidence of the deplorable state of affairs* I reprobated, I said : 'I do not accuse an individual, I accuse a system.' "

La réflexion s'impose que si les autres informations du Rapport du Consul ont toutes la même valeur que celles qui lui ont été fournies dans cette seule espèce, elles ne peuvent, à aucun degré, être considérées comme probantes. Et il saute aux yeux que dans les autres cas où le Consul, de sa propre déclaration, ne s'est livré à aucune vérification des affirmations des indigènes, ces affirmations ont moins de poids encore, si possible.

Il faut reconnaître, sans doute, que le Consul s'exposait délibérément à d'inévitables mécomptes, de par sa manière d'interroger les indigènes,—ce qu'il faisait, en effet, à l'aide de deux interprètes : " par l'intermédiaire de Vinda, parlant en Bobangi, et de Bateko, répétant ses paroles dans le dialecte local,"[4] de sorte que le Consul était à la merci non seulement de la sincérité de l'indigène interrogé, mais encore de la fidélité de traduction de deux autres indigènes, dont l'un, d'ailleurs, était un de ses serviteurs, et dont l'autre, semble-t-il, était l'interprète des missionnaires.[5] Quiconque s'est trouvé en contact avec l'indigène sait cependant son habitude du mensonge : le Révérend C. H. Harvey constatait :[6]—

" Les natifs du Congo qui nous entouraient étaient méprisables, perfides, et cruels, impudemment menteurs, malhonnêtes et vils."

1 Rapport, p. 58.
2 Idem, p. 58.
3 Idem, p. 56.
4 Voir Annexe No. 2.
5 " Regions Beyond," 1900, p. 198.
6 " Regions Beyond," Janvier-Février 1903, p. 53.

Et le fait n'est pas non plus sans importance,—si l'on veut exactement se rendre compte de la valeur des témoignages,—de la présence aux côtés de Mr. Casement, qui interrogeait les indigènes, de deux missionnaires Protestants Anglais de la région, présence qui, à elle seule, a dû nécessairement orienter les dépositions.[1]

Nous dépasserions nous-mêmes la mesure si, de ce qui précède, nous concluions au rejet en bloc de toutes les informations indigènes enregistrées par le Consul. Mais il en ressort à l'évidence qu'une telle documentation est insuffisante pour asseoir un jugement fondé, et que ces informations obligent à une vérification minutieuse et impartiale.

Que si l'on dégage du volumineux Rapport du Consul, les autres cas qu'il *a vus* et qu'il enregistre comme des cas de mutilation, on constate qu'il en cite deux comme s'étant produits au Lac Matumba[2] "il y a plusieurs années."[3] Il en cite quelques autres—sur le nombre desquels les renseignements du Rapport ne semblent pas être concordants[4]—qu'il renseigne comme ayant été commis dans les environs de Bonginda,[5] précisément en cette région où s'est placée l'enquête Epondo et où, comme on l'a vu, les esprits étaient montés et influencés. Ce sont ces affaires que, dit-il, il n'a pas eu le temps d'approfondir,[6] et qui, au dire des indigènes, étaient imputables aux agents de la Société "La Lulanga." Étaient-ce là des victimes de la pratique de coutumes indigènes, que les natifs se seraient bien gardés d'avouer? Les blessures constatées par le Consul étaient-elles dues à l'une ou l'autre lutte intestine entre villages ou tribus? Ou bien était-ce réellement le fait de sous-ordres noirs de la Société? On ne saurait se prononcer à la lecture du Rapport, les indigènes, ici comme toujours, étant la seule source d'informations du Consul et celui-ci s'étant borné à prendre rapidement note de leurs multiples affirmations en quelques heures de la matinée du 5 Septembre, pressé qu'il était par le temps "to reach K* (Bossunguma) at a reasonable hour.[7]

Nonobstant la considération qu'il attache à "l'air de franchise" et "à l'air de conviction et de sincérité"[8] des indigènes, l'expérience faite par lui-même commande incontestablement la prudence et rend téméraire son appréciation: "qu'il était clair que ces hommes déclaraient soit ce qu'ils avaient réellement vu de leurs yeux, soit ce qu'ils pensaient fermement dans leurs cœurs."[9]

Toutefois, il suffit que soient signalés ces quelques faits, actes de cruauté ou non, auxquels se réduisent en définitive ceux constatés personnellement par le Consul, sans qu'il puisse à suffisance de preuve en établir les causes réelles, pour que l'autorité doive y porter son attention et pour que des enquêtes soient ordonnées à leur sujet. A cet égard, le regret doit être exprimé de ce que l'exemplaire du Rapport, communiqué au Gouvernement de l'État Indépendant du Congo, ait systématiquement omis toute indication de date, de lieu, de noms. Il n'est pas à méconnaître que ces suppressions rendront excessivement malaisée la tâche des Magistrats Instructeurs, et, dans l'intérêt de la manifestation de la vérité, le Gouvernement du Congo formule le vœu d'être mis en possession du texte complet du Rapport du Consul.

On ne s'étonnera pas si le Gouvernement de l'État du Congo s'élève, en cette occasion, contre le procédé de ses détracteurs, mettant dans le domaine public la reproduction de photographies d'indigènes mutilés, et créant cette odieuse légende de mains coupées à la connaissance ou même à l'instigation des Belges en Afrique. C'est ainsi que la photographie d'Epondo, estropié dans les conditions que l'on sait, et qui "a été deux fois photographié," est probablement une de celles circulant dans les pamphlets Anglais comme preuve de l'exécrable administration des Belges en Afrique. On a vu une revue Anglaise reproduisant la photographie d'un "cannibale entouré des crânes de ses victimes," et la légende portait: "In the original photograph, the cannibal was naked. The artist has made him decent by . . . . . covering his breast with the star of the Congo State. It is now a suggestive emblem of the Christian veneered cannibalism on the Congo."[10] A ce compte, il suffirait, pour jeter le discrédit sur l'Administration de l'Uganda, de mettre dans la circulation des clichés reproduisant

[1] Voir Annexe No. 2: "Present, Rev. W. D. Armstrong and Rev. D. J. Danielson, of the Congo Balolo Mission of Bonginda, Vinda Bidiloa (Consul's Headman) and Bateko, as interpreters, and His Britannic Majesty's Consul." Ce passage est omis dans l'Annexe 6 du Rapport du Consul (p. 78).

[2] Rapport, p. 34.

[3] Idem, pp. 76, 77.

[4] Comparez Rapport, pp. 54, 55, et 58.

[5] Rapport, pp. 54, 55.

[6] Idem, p. 56.

[7] Idem, p. 56.

[8] Idem, p. 62.

[9] Idem, p. 57.

[10] "Review of Reviews," February 14, 1903.

les mutilations dont le Dr. Castellani dit, dans une lettre datée d'Uganda, du 16 Décembre, 1902, avoir constaté l'existence aux environs mêmes d'Entebbe : " Il n'est pas difficile d'y rencontrer des indigènes sans nez, sans oreilles, &c."[1]

C'est dire que dans l'Uganda comme au Congo, les indigènes sacrifient encore à leurs instincts sauvages. Mr. Casement a prévu l'objection en affirmant :—

" It was not a native custom prior to the coming of the white man ; it was not the outcome of the primitive instincts of savages in their fights between village and village ; it was the deliberate act of soldiers of a European Administration, and these men themselves never made any concealment that in committing these acts they were but obeying the positive orders of their superiors."[2]

L'articulation d'une aussi grave accusation, sans qu'elle soit en même temps étayée sur des preuves irréfragables, semble donner raison à ceux qui pensent que les emplois antérieurs de Mr. Casement ne l'avaient pas préparé entièrement aux fonctions Consulaires. Mr. Casement est resté dix-sept jours au Lac Mantumba, un lac, dit de 25 à 30 milles de long et de 12 ou 15 milles de large, entouré d'épaisses forêts.[3] Il ne s'est guere éloigné de la rive. On ne voit pas dès lors quelles investigations utiles il a pu faire sur les mœurs d'autrefois et les habitudes anciennes des populations. La constatation que ces tribus sont encore très sauvages et adonnées au cannibalisme[4] permet de croire, au contraire, qu'elles n'étaient pas exemptes de la pratique de ces actes cruels qui, d'une manière générale en Afrique, étaient le cortège habituel de la barbarie des mœurs et de l'anthropophagie. Dans une partie des régions que le Consul a visitées, les témoignages des missionnaires Anglais ne sont à cet égard que trop instructifs. Le Révérend McKittrick, parlant des luttes meurtrières entre indigènes, dit ses efforts d'autrefois auprès des Chefs pour pacifier la contrée : " . . . . Nous leur dîmes qu'à l'avenir nous ne laisserions plus passer par notre station aucun homme armé de lance ou de couteau. Notre Dieu était un Dieu de paix, et nous, ses enfants, nous ne pouvions supporter de voir nos frères noirs se couper et se blesser l'un l'autre (cutting and stabbing each other)."[5] " Lorsque j'allais çà et là dans la rivière, dit un autre missionnaire, on me montrait les endroits de la rive d'où avaient coutume de partir les guerriers pour capturer les canots et les hommes. Il était affligeant d'entendre décrire les terribles massacres qui avaient lieu d'habitude à la mort d'un grand Chef. Un trou profond était creusé en terre, où des vingtaines d'esclaves jetés après que leurs têtes avaient été coupées (after having their heads cut off), et sur cette horrible pile, on plaçait le cadavre du Chef couronnant ce carnage humain indescriptible."[6] Et les missionnaires constatent combien encore en ces jours actuels les indigènes reviennent aisément à leurs anciennes coutumes. Il apparaît aussi que cette autre affirmation du Rapport[7] qu'à la différence d'aujourd'hui, les indigènes autrefois ne s'enfuyaient pas à l'approche d'un steamer, n'est pas d'accord avec les récits des voyageurs et explorateurs.

Il est, en tout cas, à remarquer que le Consul n'a constaté dans le territoire où s'exerce l'activité de la Société A.B.I.R. aucun de ces faits de cruauté qui eût pu être représenté comme imputable aux agents commerciaux. La coïncidence est à relever, puisque la Société A.B.I.R. est précisément une Compagnie à Concession et qu'on ne cesse d'attribuer au régime des Concessions les conséquences les plus désastreuses pour les indigènes.

Ce qui domine les innombrables questions touchées par le Consul et la multiplicité des menus faits qu'il a recueillis, c'est de savoir si vraiment cette sorte de tableau d'une existence misérable, qui serait celle des indigènes, répond à la réalité des choses. Nous prendrons pour exemple la région de la Lulanga et du Lopori, parce que là se trouvent, depuis des années, des centres de Missions de la " Congo Balobo Mission." Ces missionnaires y sont établis en des endroits les plus distants et les plus intérieurs : à Lulonga, Bonginda, Ikau, Bougandanga, et Baringa, tous points situés dans la région où opèrent la Société " La Lulonga " et la Société A.B.I.R. ; Ils sont en contact suivi avec les populations indigènes, et une revue spéciale mensuelle, " Regions Beyond," publie régulièrement leurs lettres, notes, et rapports. Que l'on parcoure la collection de ce recueil ; nulle part, à aucun moment avant Avril 1903—à cette dernière date, la motion de Mr. Herbert Samuel était, il est vrai, annoncée au Parlement—on ne trouve trace d'une appréciation quelconque signalant ou révélant que la situation

1 " La Tribuna " de Rome.
2 Rapport, Annexe 4, p. 77.
3 Rapport, Annexe 4, p. 30.
4 Rapport, p. 30.
5 " Ten Years at Bonginda," D. McKittrick, " Regions Beyond," p. 21.
6 " Congo Contrasts," Mr. Boudot, " Regions Beyond," 1900, p. 197.
7 Rapport, p. 34.

générale des populations indigènes dût être dénoncée au monde civilisé. Les missionnaires s'y félicitent de la sympathie active des agents, officiels, et commerciaux à leur égard,[1] des progrès de leur œuvre d'évangélisation,[2] des facilités que leur apporte la création de routes,[3] de la pacification des mœurs, "dû à la fois aux missionnaires et aux commerçants,"[4] de la disparition de l'esclavage,[5] de la densité de la population,[6] du nombre grandissant de leurs élèves, "grâce à l'État, qui a donné des ordres pour que les enfants fussent menés à l'école,"[7] de la disparition graduelle des pratiques indigènes primitives,[8] du contraste enfin entre le présent et le passé.[9] Admettra-t-on que ces missionnaires Chrétiens et Anglais, qui, au cours de leurs itinéraires, visitaient les postes de factorerie et étaient témoins des marchés de caoutchouc, se seraient rendus complices par leur silence d'un régime inhumain ou tortionnaire? Un des Rapports annuels de la "Congo Bolobo Mission" dit dans ses conclusions: "Dans l'ensemble, le coup d'œil rétrospectif est encourageant. S'il n'y a pas eu une avance considérable, il n'y a pas eu de triste déception, et il n'est aucune opposition définitive à l'œuvre . . . . . Il y a eu de la disette et des maladies parmi les natifs, notamment à Bonginda . . . . . A part cela, il n'y a pas eu de sérieux empêchements au progrès . . . . ."[10] Et, parlant incidemment des effets bienfaisants du travail sur l'état social des indigènes, un missionnaire écrit: "The greatest obstacle to conversion is polygamy. Many evils have been put down, *e.g.*, idleness, thanks to the State having compelled the men to work; and fighting, through their not having time enough to fight."[11] Ces appréciations des missionnaires nous paraissent plus précises que les données d'un Rapport à chaque page duquel, pour ainsi dire, on lit: "I was told;" "it was said;" "I was informed;" "I was assured;" "They said;" "it was alleged;" "I had no means of verifying;" "It was impossible to me to verify;" "I have no means of ascertaining," &c. En dix lignes, par exemple, on rencontre quatre fois l'expression: "appears;" "would seem;" "would seem;" "do not seem."[12]

Le Consul ne semble pas s'être rendu compte que c'est le travail qui constitue l'impôt indigène au Congo, et que cette forme d'impôt se justifie autant par son caractère moralisateur que par l'impossibilité de taxer autrement l'indigène, en raison même du fait, constaté par le Consul, que l'indigène n'a pas de numéraire. Cette dernière considération fait, pour en donner un autre exemple, que sur 56,700 huttes imposées dans la North-Eastern Rhodesia, 19,653 payent la taxe "in labour" et 4,938 la payent "in produce."[13] Que ce travail soit fourni directement à l'État ou à telle ou telle entreprise privée, qu'il soit adapté, selon les possibilités locales, à telles prestations ou à telles autres, sa justification a toujours l'une de ses bases dans ce que le Mémorandum du 11 Février dernier reconnaît être la "necessity of the natives being induced to work." Le Consul s'inquiète surtout de la qualification à donner à la fourniture du travail; il s'étonne, si c'est là un impôt de ce que cet impôt soit payé et recouvrable parfois par des agents commerciaux. Dans la rigueur des principes, il est à reconnaître, en effet, que la rémunération d'un impôt heurte les notions fiscales ordinaires; elle s'explique cependant en fait si l'on songe qu'il s'est agi de faire contracter l'habitude de travail à des indigènes qui y ont été réfractaires de tout temps. Et si cette idée du travail peut être plus aisément inculquée aux natifs sous la forme de transactions commerciales entre eux et des particuliers, faut-il nécessairement condamner ce mode d'action, notamment dans des régions dont l'organisation administrative n'est pas complétée? Mais il s'impose que, dans leurs rapports de cet ordre avec les indigènes, les agents commerciaux, comme d'ailleurs les agents de l'État eux-memes, s'inspirent de pratiques bienveillantes et humaines. A cet égard, les éléments que fournit le Rapport du Consul seront l'objet d'une étude approfondie, et si le résultat de cet examen révélait des abus réels ou commandait des réformes, l'Administration supérieure agirait comme l'exigeraient les circonstances.

Nul n'a jamais pensé, d'ailleurs, que le régime fiscal au Congo eût atteint d'emblée la perfection, notamment au point de vue de l'assiette de l'impôt et des moyens de

1 "Regions Beyond," 1900, p. 150; 1902, p. 209.
2 Idem, *passim*.
3 Idem, 1900, p. 150.
4 Idem, 1901, p. 27.
5 Idem, 1900, p. 199.
6 Idem, 1900, pp. 243, 297, 306.
7 Idem, 1901, p. 40; 1902, p. 315.
8 Idem, 1901, p. 40.
9 Idem, 1900, p. 196.
10 "Regions Beyond," 1901, p. 43.
11 Idem, 1901, p. 60.
12 Rapport, p. 28.
13 "Reports on the Administration of Rhodesia," 1900–1902, p. 408.

recouvrement. Le système des "chefferies," bon en soi en ce qu'il place entre l'autorité et l'indigène l'intermédiaire de son chef naturel, procédait d'une idée mise en pratique ailleurs :—

"The more important Chiefs who helped the Administration have been paid a certain percentage of the taxes collected in their districts, and I think that if this policy is adhered to each year, the results will continue to be satisfactory and will encourage the Chiefs to work in harmony with the Administration."[1]

Le Décret sur les chefferies[2] établissait le principe de l'impôt, et sa perception selon "un tableau des prestations annuelles à fournir, par chaque village, en produits, en corvées, travailleurs ou soldats." L'application de ce Décret a été formulée en des actes d'investiture, des tableaux statistiques et des états de prestation, dont les modèles sont reproduits à l'Annexe IV. Contrairement à ce que pense le Rapport, ce Décret a reçu l'exécution compatible avec l'état d'avancement social des tribus ; de nombreux actes d'investiture ont été dressés et des efforts ont été faits pour établir des états de répartition équitable des prestations. Le Consul eût pu s'en assurer dans les bureaux des Commissariats, notamment des districts du Stanley-Pool et de l'Équateur qu'il a traversés ; mais il a généralement négligé les sources d'informations officielles. Sans doute, l'application fut et devait être limitée dans les débuts, et il a pu en résulter que les demandes d'impôts ont atteint, pendant quelque temps, les seuls villages dans un certain périmètre autour des stations ; mais cette situation s'est améliorée progressivement au fur et à mesure que, les régions plus distantes se trouvant englobées dans la zone d'influence des postes gouvernementaux, le nombre des villages astreints à l'impôt s'est accru successivement et que les taxes ont pu être réparties sur un chiffre plus grand de contribuables. Le Gouvernement vise à ce que le progrès soit constant dans cette voie, c'est-à-dire à ce que l'impôt soit le plus équitablement réparti et soit, autant que possible, personnel ; le Décret du 18 Novembre, 1903, tend à ce but en prescrivant l'etablissement de "rôles des prestations indigènes" de manière que les obligations de chacun des natifs soient nettement précisées.

"Chaque année, dit l'Article 28 de ce Décret, les Commissaires de District dresseront dans les limites de l'Article 2 du présent Règlement (c'est-à-dire dans la limite de quarante heures de travail par mois par indigène), les rôles des prestations à fournir, en espèce et en durée de travail par chacun des indigènes résidant dans les territoires de leur district respectif." Et l'Article 55 punit "quiconque, chargé de la perception des prestations, aura exigé des indigènes, soit comme impôt en nature soit comme heures de travail, des prestations d'une valeur supérieure à celles prévues dans les rôles d'impositions."

Nul n'ignore que le recouvrement de l'impôt se heurte parfois au mauvais vouloir, et même au refus de payer. La démonstration qu'en fait le Rapport du Consul pour le Congo est corroborée par l'expérience faite, par exemple, dans la Rhodésia.

"The Ba-Unga (Awemba district), inhabitants of the swamps in the Chambezi delta, gave some trouble on being summoned to pay taxes."[3]—"Although in many cases whole villages retired into the swamps on being called upon for the hut tax, the general result was satisfactory for the first year (Luapula district)."[4]—"Milala's people have succeeded in evading taxes."[5]—"A few natives bordering on the Portuguese territory, who, owing to the great distance they reside from the Native Commissioners' stations, are not under the direct supervision of the Native Commissioners, have so far evaded paying hut tax, and refused to submit themselves to the authority of the Government. The rebel Chief, Mapondera, has upon three occasions successfully eluded punitive expeditions sent against him. . . . . . Captain Gilson, of the British South Africa Police, was successful in coming upon him and a large following of natives, and inflicting heavy losses upon them. . . . . . His kraal and all his crops were destroyed. He is now reported to be in Portuguese territory. . . . . . Siji M'Kota, another powerful Chief, living in the northern parts of the M'toko district, bordering on Portuguese territory, has also been successful in evading the payment of hut tax, and generally pursuing the adoption of an attitude which is not acceptable to the Government. I am pleased to report that a patrol is at present on its way to these parts to deal with this Chief, and to endeavour to obtain his submission. It will be noted that the above remarks relate solely to those natives who reside along the borders of our territories, and whose defiant attitude is materially assisted by reason of this proximity to the Portuguese border, across which they are well able to proceed whenever they consider that any meeting or contact with the Native Commissioner will interfere in any way with their indolent and lazy life They possess no movable property which might be attached with a view to the recovery of hut tax unpaid for many years, and travel backwards and forwards with considerable freedom, always placing themselves totally beyond the reach of the Native Commissioner."[6]

[1] "Reports on the Administration of Rhodesia," 1900-1902, p. 424.
[2] Décret du 6 Octobre, 1891 ("Bulletin Officiel," 1891, p. 259).
[3] "Reports on the Administration of Rhodesia," 1900-1902, p. 409.
[4] Idem, p. 410.
[5] Idem, p. 410.
[6] Idem, pp. 145, 146.

C'est là un exemple de ces "punitive expeditions" auxquelles l'autorité se voit obligée de recourir parfois, et aussi de ce procédé des natifs, non spécial aux indigènes Congolais, de se déplacer en territoire voisin pour se soustraire à l'exécution de la loi.—Que si, au Congo, dans le recouvrement des prestations indigènes, des cas, parmi ceux cités par le Consul, ont réellement dépassé les limites d'une rigueur juste et pondérée, ce sont là des circonstances de faits que des investigations sur les lieux pourront seules élucider, et des instructions seront, à cet effet, données à l'administration de Boma.

Il ne peut être davantage accepté, jusqu'à plus ample informé, les considérations du Rapport sur l'action des gardes forestiers au service de la Société A.B.I.R. et de "La Lugonga." Ces sous-ordres sont représentés par le Consul comme exclusivement préposés à "obliger par force la récolte du caoutchouc ou les approvisionnements dont chaque factorerie a besoin."[1] Une autre explication a cependant été donnée, mais elle n'émane pas d'un indigène, à savoir que ces gardes forestiers ont pour mission de veiller à ce que la récolte du caoutchouc se fasse rationnellement et d'empêcher notamment que les indigènes ne coupent les lianes.[2] On sait, en effet, que la loi a prescrit des mesures rigoureuses pour assurer la conservation des zones caoutchoutières, a réglementé leur exploitation et a imposé des plantations et replantations, en vue d'éviter l'épuisement complet du caoutchouc, comme on l'a vu par exemple dans la "North-Eastern and Western Rhodesia."[3] Les Sociétés et particuliers exploitants ont de ce chef une lourde responsabilité et ont incontestablement une surveillance minutieuse à exercer sur les modes et procédés de récoltes. La raison d'être de ces gardes forestiers peut donc, en réalité, être tout autre que celle dite par le Consul; en tout cas, les plaintes formulées à ce sujet formeront l'un des points de l'enquête au Congo, de même que cette autre remarque du Rapport que l'armement de ces gardes forestiers serait excessif et abusif. Il faut dès à présent remarquer que dans ses évaluations du nombre des gardes armés, le Consul procède par déductions hypothétiques[4] et qu'il dit lui-même : "I have no means of ascertaining the number of this class of armed men employed by the A.B.I.R. Company."[5] Il donne le détail que le fusil d'un de ces hommes était marqué sur la crosse : "Dépôt 2,210." Or, il est évident qu'une telle indication ne peut avoir la signification que voudrait lui donner le Consul que pour autant qu'il soit établi qu'elle se rapporte à un numérotage des armes utilisées dans la Concession, et tel n'est pas le cas, car cette marque: Dépôt . . . . . n'est employée ni par les Agents de l'État ni par la Société, et il est à supposer qu'elle constitue une ancienne marque, soit de fabrication, soit de magasin. Quant à l'armement des capitas, le Consul ne doit pas ignorer que ce point—qui n'est pas sans difficulté, puisqu'il faut à la fois tenir compte de la nécessité de la défense personnelle du capita et de l'écueil d'un usage abusif de l'arme qui lui est confiée—n'a cessé d'être l'objet de l'attention de l'autorité supérieure. Il n'y a pas que la seule Circulaire du 20 Octobre, 1900, reproduite par le Consul, qui ait traité la question ; il en est tout un ensemble, datant notamment des 12 Mars, 1897, 31 Mai et 28 Novembre, 1900, et 30 Avril, 1901. Nous les reproduisons en Annexes, comme témoignant de l'absolue volonté du pouvoir de faire appliquer strictement les dispositions légales en la matière (Annexe V). Nonobstant les précautions incessantes, le Consul a constaté que plusieurs capitas n'étaient pas porteurs de permis—ces permis ne se trouvait-ils pas au siège de la Direction ?—et que deux d'entre eux étaient armés d'armes de précision.[6] Ces quelques infractions ne suffiraient évidemment pas pour conclure à une sorte de vaste organisation armée, destinée à terroriser les indigènes. Cette autre Circulaire du 7 Septembre, 1903, reproduite à l'Annexe VII du Rapport du Consul, montre, au contraire, le soin que met le Gouvernement à ce que les soldats noirs réguliers eux-mêmes soient en tout temps sous le contrôle des officiers Européens.[7]

Telles sont les premières remarques que suggère le Rapport de M. Casement, et nous nous réservons de le raconter plus en détail, lorsque seront en possession du Gouvernement les résultats de l'enquête à laquelle les autorités locales vont procéder. Il sera remarqué que le Gouvernement, ne voulant pas paraître faire dévier le débat,

[1] Rapport, p. 44.
[2] Annexe 3, p. 26.
[3] "Reports on the Administration of Rhodesia," 1900-1902, pp. 397 et suivantes.
[4] Rapport, p. 57.
[5] Idem, p. 42.
[6] Idem, p. 43.
[7] La Circulaire du 7 Septembre, 1903, concerne "l'interdiction" d'envoyer des soldats armés sous la conduite des gradés noirs, et non, comme le dit la copie erronée produite par le Consul "l'instruction" (Annexe 7 du Rapport, p. 80).

n'a pas soulevé la question préjudicielle au sujet des formes, à coup sûr insolites, en lesquelles le Consul de Sa Majesté Britannique a agi en territoire étranger. Il n'échappera pas combien le rôle que s'est attribué le Consul en instituant des sortes d'enquêtes, en faisant comparaître des indigènes, en les interrogeant comme par voie d'autorité, en émettant même des espèces de jugements sur la culpabilité d'accusés, est en dehors des limites des attributions d'un Consul. Les réserves qu'appelle ce mode de procéder doivent être d'autant plus formelles que le Consul intervenait de la sorte en des affaires où n'étaient intéressés que des ressortissants de l'État du Congo et relevant exclusivement de l'autorité territoriale. M. Casement s'est chargé de se désavouer lui-même lorsque, le 4 Septembre, 1903, il écrivait au Gouverneur-Général: "I have no right of representation to your Excellency save where the persons or interests of British subjects dwelling in this country are affected." Il était donc conscient de ce qu'il outrepassait les devoirs de sa charge, lorsqu'il investiguait sur des faits d'administration purement intérieure et empiétait ainsi sur les attributions des autorités territoriales, à l'encontre des règles du droit Consulaire.

"The grievances of the natives have been made known in this country by . . . . . , who brought over a Petition addressed to the King, praying for relief from the excessive taxation and oppressive legislation of which they complain."

Ces lignes sont extraites du "Report for 1903 de la British and Foreign Anti-Slavery Society," et les natifs dont il est question sont les indigènes des Iles Fiji. Ce Rapport continue :—

"The case has been brought before the House of Commons. The grievances include forced labour on the roads, and restrictions which practically amount to slavery; natives have been flogged without trial by Magistrate's orders and are constantly subject to imprisonment for frivolous causes. Petitions lodged with the local Colonial Secretary have been disregarded. Mr. Chamberlain, in reply to the questions asked in Parliament, threw doubt upon the information received, but stated that the recently appointed Governor is conducting an inquiry into the whole situation in the Fiji Islands, in the course of which the matter will be fully investigated."

Ces conclusions sont les nôtres au sujet du Rapport de M. Casement.

Bruxelles, le 12 *Mars*, 1904.

(Translation.)

DURING the sitting of the House of Commons of the 11th March, 1903, Lord Cranborne observed :—

"We have no reason to think that slavery is recognized by the authorities of the Congo Free State, but reports of acts of cruelty and oppression have reached us. Such reports have been received from our Consular Officers."

The Government of the Congo State addressed a letter on the 14th March, 1903, to Sir C. Phipps, requesting him to be good enough to communicate the facts which had formed the subject of any reports from British Consuls.

No reply was received to this application.

Lord Lansdowne's despatch of the 8th August, 1903, contained the following passage :—

"Representations to this effect (alleged cases of ill-treatment of natives and existence of trade monopolies) are to be found . . . . in despatches from His Majesty's Consuls."

The impression was thus created that at that date His Majesty's Government were in possession of conclusive evidence furnished by their Consuls: but none the less it seemed clearly necessary that Consul Casement should undertake a journey in the Upper Congo. It would appear, therefore, as if the conclusions contained in the note of the 8th August were at least premature; it equally follows that, contrary to what was said in that note, the British Consul was at liberty to undertake any journey in the interior that he thought fit. In any case, it is to be observed that, in spite of the repeated applications of the Congo State, the White Paper ("Africa No. 1 (1904)") recently presented to Parliament does not contain any of these former Consular Reports, which nevertheless would have been the more interesting as dating from a time when the present campaign had not yet been initiated.

The present Report draws attention to the fact that in certain places visited by the Consul the population is decreasing. Mr. Casement does not give the facts on which he bases his comparative figures for 1887 and 1903. The question arises how, during the course of his rapid and hasty visits, he was able to get his figures for this latter year. On what facts, for instance, does he found his assertion that the riverain population of Lake Mantumba *seems* to have diminished from 60 to 70 per cent. in the course of the last ten years. He states that at a certain place designated as F* the population of all the villages together does not at present amount to more than 500 souls; a few lines further on these same villages are spoken of as only containing 240 inhabitants altogether. These are only details, but they show at once what a lack of precision there is in certain of the deductions made by the Consul. It is, no doubt, unfortunately only too true that the population has diminished; but the diminution is due to other causes than to the exercise on the native population of a too exacting or oppressive Administration. It is owing chiefly to the sleeping-sickness, which is decimating the population throughout Equatorial Africa. The Report itself observes that "a prominent place must be assigned to this malady,"[1] and that this malady is "probably one of the principal factors" in the diminution of the population.[2] It is only necessary to read the Rev. John Whitehead's letter, quoted by the Consul (Annex II to the Report) to obtain an idea of the ravages of the malady, to which this missionary attributes half of the deaths which take place in the riverain parts of the district. In a recent interview Mgr. Van Ronslé, Vicar Apostolic of the Belgian Congo, who speaks with the authority of one who has had a large experience of African matters, and has resided for long periods in many different localities in the Congo, explained the development of this scourge and the inevitable decay of the populations it attacks, whatever the conditions of their social existence; mentioning among other cases the terrible loss of life caused by this disease in Uganda. If to this principal cause of the depopulation of the Congo are added small-pox epidemics, the inability of the tribes at the present moment to keep up their numbers by the purchase of slaves, and the ease with which the natives can migrate, it can be explained how the Consul and the missionaries may have been struck with the diminution of the number of inhabitants in certain centres without that diminution necessarily being the result of a system of oppression. Annex I contains the declarations on the subject made by Mgr. Van Ronslé. His remarks as to the effect of the suppression of slavery on the numbers of the population are printed elsewhere:—

"The people (slave) are for the most part originally prisoners of war. Since the Decree of emancipation they have simply returned to their own distant homes, knowing their owners have no power to recapture them. This is one reason why some think the population is decreasing, and another reason is the vast exodus up and down river."[3]

"So long as the Slave Trade flourished the Bobangi flourished, but with its abolition they are tending to disappear, for their towns were replenished by slaves."[4]

The Consul mentions cases, the causes of which, however, are unknown to him, of an exodus of natives of the Congo to the French bank. It is not quite clear on what grounds he attaches blame to the State on their account, to judge at least from the motives by which some of them have been determined—for instance, the examples of such emigration which are given and explained by the Rev. W. H. Bentley, an English missionary. One relates to the station at Lukolela:—

"The main difficulty has been the shifting of the population. It appears that the population, when the station was founded in 1886, was between 5,000 and 6,000 in the riverain Colonies. About two years later the Chief Mpuki did not agree with his neighbours or they with him. When the tension became acute, Mpuki crossed over with his people to the opposite (French) side of the river. This exodus took away a large number of people. In 1890 or 1891 a Chief from one of the lower towns was compelled by the majority of his people to leave the State side, and several went with him. About 1893 the rest of the people at the lower towns either went across to the same place as the deposed Chief or took up their residence inland. Towards the end of 1894 a soldier, who had been sent to cut firewood for the State steamers on an island off the the towns, left his work to make an evil request in one of the towns. He shot the man who refused him. The rascal of a soldier was properly dealt with by the State officer in charge; but this outrage combined with other smaller difficulties to produce a panic, and nearly all the people left for the French side, or hid away inland. So the fine township has broken up."[5]

[1] Report, p. 21.
[2] Idem, p. 26.
[3] M. Boudot, missionary of the Congo Batolo Mission. "Regions Beyond," December 1901, p. 337.
[4] W. H. Bentley. "Pioneering on the Congo," II, p. 229.
[5] Idem, p. 248.

The other refers to the station at Bolobo :—

"It is rare indeed for Bolobo, with its 30,000 or 40,000 people, divided into some dozen clans, to be at peace for any length of time together. The loss of life from these petty wars, the number of those killed for witchcraft, and of those who are buried alive with the dead, involve, even within our narrow limits here at Bolobo, an almost daily drain upon the vitality of the country, and an incalculable amount of sorrow and suffering. . . . . The Government was not indifferent to these murderous ways. . . . . In 1890, the District Commissioner called the people together, and warned them against the burying of slaves alive in the graves of free people, and the reckless killing of slaves which then obtained. The natives did not like the rising power of the State. . . . . Our own settlement among them was not unattended with difficulty. . . . . There was a feeling against white men generally, and especially so against the State. The people became insolent and haughty. . . . . Just at this time . . . . as a force of soldiers steamed past the Moye towns, the steamers were fired upon. The soldiers landed and burnt and looted the towns. The natives ran away into the grass, and great numbers crossed to the French side of the river. They awoke to the fact that Bula Matadi, the State, was not the helpless thing they had so long thought. This happened early in 1891."[1]

It will be seen that these examples do not attribute the emigration of the natives to any such causes as :—

"The methods employed to obtain labour from them by local officials and the exactions levied on them."[2]

The Report dwells at length on the existence of native taxes. It shows how the natives are subject to forced labour of various kinds, in one district having to furnish the Government posts with "chikwangues," or fresh provisions, in another being obliged to assist in works of public utility, such as the construction of a jetty at Bololo, or the up-keep of the telegraph line at F*; elsewhere being obliged to collect the produce of the domain lands. We maintain that such imposts on the natives are legitimate, in agreement on this point with His Majesty's Government, who, in the Memorandum of the 11th February last, declare that the industry and development of the British Colonies and Protectorates in Africa show that His Majesty's Government have always admitted the necessity of making the natives contribute to the public charges and of inducing them to work. We also agree with His Majesty's Government that, if abuses occur in this connection—and undoubtedly some have occurred in all Colonies—such abuses call for reform, and that it is the duty of the authorities to put an end to them, and to reconcile as far as may be the requirements of the Government with the real interests of the natives.

But in this matter the Congo State intends to exercise freely its rights of sovereignty—as, for instance, His Majesty's Government explain in their last Memorandum that they themselves did at Sierra Leone—without regard to external pressure or foreign interference, which would be an encroachment upon its essential rights.

The Consul, in his Report, obviously endeavours to create the impression that taxes in the Congo are collected in a violent, inhuman, and cruel manner, and we are anxious before all to rebut the accusation which has so often been brought against the State that such collection gives rise to odious acts of mutilation. On this point a superficial perusal of the Report is calculated to impress by its easy accumulation not of facts, simple, precise, and verified, but of the declarations and affirmations of natives.

There is a preliminary remark to be made in regard to the conditions in which the Consul made his journey.

Whether such was his intention or not, the British Consul appeared to the inhabitants as the redresser of the wrongs, real or imaginary, of the natives, and his presence at La Lulonga, coinciding with the campaign which was being directed against the Congo State, in a region where the influence of the Protestant missionaries has long been exercised, necessarily had for the natives a significance which did not escape them. The Consul made his investigations quite independently of the Government officials, quite independently of any action and of any co-operation on the part of the regular authorities; he was assisted in his proceedings by English Protestant missionaries; he made his inspection on a steamer belonging to a Protestant Mission; he was entertained for the most part in the Protestant Missions; and, in these circumstances, it was inevitable that he should be considered by the native as the antagonist of the established authorities.

Other proof is not required than the characteristic fact that while the Consul was at Bonginda, the natives crowded down to the bank, as some agents of the La Lulonga

[1] "Pioneering on the Congo," by the Rev. W. Holman Bentley, II, pp. 235–236.
[2] Report, p. 29.

Company were going by in a canoe, and cried out: "Your violence is over, it is passing away; only the English remain; may you others die!" There is also this significant admission on the part of a Protestant missionary, who, in alluding to this incident, remarked:—

"The Consul was here at the time, and the people were much excited and evidently thought themselves on top. . . . . The people have got this idea (that the rubber work was finished) into their heads of themselves, consequent, I suppose, upon the Consul's visit."

In these circumstances, in view of the state of mind which they show to exist among the natives, in view of their impressionable character and of their natural desire to escape taxation, it could not be doubted but that the conclusions at which the Consul would arrive would not be other than those set forth in his Report.

To bring out this point, and to show how little value is to be attached to his investigations, it will be sufficient to examine one case, that on which Mr. Casement principally relies; we allude to the Epondo case. It is that of the child II, mentioned on pp. 56, 58, and 78 of the Report.

It is indispensable to enter somewhat at length into the details of this case, which are significant.

On the 4th September, 1903, the Consul was at the Bonginda station of the Congo Bololo Mission, having returned from a journey on the Lopori, during the course of which he had not come across any of those acts of mutilation which it is the custom to attribute to officials in the Congo.

At Bonginda, the natives of a neighbouring village (Bossunguma) came to him and informed him, amongst other things, that a "sentry" of the La Lulonga Company, named Kelengo,[1] had, at Bossunguma, cut off the hand of a native called Epondo, whose wounds were still scarcely healed. The Consul proceeded to Bossunguma, accompanied by the Rev. W. D. Armstrong and the Rev. D. J. Danielson, and had the mutilated native brought before him, who, "in answer to Consul's question, charges a sentry named 'Kelengo' (placed in the town by the local agent of the La Lulonga Society to see that the people work rubber)" with having done it. Such are the Consul's own words: it was necessary to establish a relation of cause and effect between the collection of india-rubber and this alleged case of cruelty.

The Consul proceeded to question the Chief and some of the natives of the village. They replied by accusing Kelengo; most of them asserted that they were *eye-witnesses* of the deed. The Consul inquired through his interpreters if there were other witnesses who saw the crime committed, and accused Kelengo of it. "Nearly all those present, about forty persons, shouted out with one voice that it was 'Kelengo' who did it."

In order to understand the violence with which the natives accused Kelengo, and the unanimous manner in which the denials of the accused were rejected by his accusers, it is necessary to read the whole of the report of this inquiry, as drawn up by the Consul himself in a kind of *procès-verbaux*, dated the 7th, 8th, and 9th September (Annex II). From all quarters accusers appeared, and the excited crowd gave vent to all sorts of accusations: he had cut off Epondo's hand, chained up women, stolen ducks and a dog! The Consul did not allow his suspicions to be aroused by the passionate character of these accusations; without any further guarantee of their sincerity or further examination into their truth, he looked upon his inquiry as conclusive, and as he had taken upon himself the duties of the Public Prosecutor in making preliminary inquiries into the matter, so he anticipated the decision of the responsible authorities by declaring to the assembled people that "Kelengo deserved severe punishment for his illegal and cruel acts." He proceeded to dramatize the incident by carrying off the pretended victim, and exhibiting him on the 10th September to the official in command of the station at Coquilhatville, to whom he handed a copy of the record of his inquiry, and on the 12th September he addressed a letter to the Governor-General which he marked as "personal and private," and in which he makes the incident in question among others a text for an attack on "the system of general exploitation of an entire population which can only be rendered successful by the employment of arbitrary and illegal force." His inquiry terminated, he immediately started on his return journey to the Lower Congo.

Even if the circumstances had been correctly reported, the disproportion would still

[1] K K in "Africa No. 1 (1904)."

have been striking between them and the conclusions which the Consul draws when emphasizing his general criticisms of the Congo State. But the facts themselves are incorrectly represented.

As a matter of fact, no sooner did the Consul's denunciation reach the Public Prosecutor's Department than M. Gennaro Bosco, Acting Public Prosecutor, proceeded to the spot and held a judicial inquiry under the usual conditions free from all outside influences. This inquiry showed that His Britannic Majesty's Consul had been the object of a plot contrived by the natives, who, in the hope of no longer being obliged to work, had agreed among themselves to represent Epondo as the victim of the inhuman conduct of one of the capitas of a commercial Company. In reality, Epondo had been the victim of an accident while out hunting, and had been bitten in the hand by a wild boar; gangrene had set in and caused the loss of the member, and this fact had been cleverly turned to account by the natives when before the Consul. We annex (Annex No. 3) extracts from the inquiry conducted by the Acting Public Prosecutor into the Epondo case. The evidence is typical, uniform, and without discrepancies. It leaves no doubt as to the cause of the accident, makes it clear that the natives lied to the Consul, and reveals the object which actuated them, namely, the hope that the Consul's intervention would relieve them from the necessity of paying taxes. The inquiry shows how Epondo, at last brought to account, retracted what he had in the first instance said to the Consul, and confessed that he had been influenced by the people of his village. He was questioned as follows:—

Q. Do you persist in accusing Kelengo of having cut off your left hand?

A. No. I told a lie.

Q. State, then, how and when you lost your hand.

A. I was a slave of Monkekola's at Malele, in the Bangala district. One day I went out boar-hunting with him. He wounded one with a spear, and thereupon the animal, enraged, turned on me. I tried to run off with the others, but falling down, the boar was on me in a moment and tore off my left hand and (wounded me) in the stomach and left thigh.

The witness exhibits the scars he carries at the places mentioned, and lying down of his own accord shows the position he was in when the boar attacked and wounded him.

Q. How long ago did this accident happen?

A. I don't remember. It was a long time ago.

Q. Why did you accuse Kelengo?

A. Because Momaketa, one of the Bossunguma Chiefs, told me to, and afterwards all the inhabitants of my village did so too.

* * * * * * *

Q. Did the English photograph you?

A. Yes, at Bonginda and Lulanga. They told me to put the stump well forward. There were Nenele, Mongongolo, Torongo, and other whites whose names I don't know. They were whites from Lulanga. Mongongolo took away six photographs.[1]

Epondo of his own accord repeated his declarations and retractations to a Protestant missionary, Mr. Faris, who lives at Bolengi. This gentleman has sent the Commissary-General at Coquilhatville the following written declaration:—

"I, E. E. Faris, missionary, residing at Bolengi, Upper Congo, declare that I questioned the boy Epondo, of the village of Bosongoma, who was at my house on the 10th September, 1903, with Mr. Casement, the British Consul, and whom, in accordance with the request made to me by Commandant Stevens, of Coquilhatville, I took to the mission station at Bolengi on the 16th October, 1903; and that the said boy has this day, the 17th October, 1903, told me that he lost his hand through the bite of a wild boar.

"He told me at the same time that he informed Mr. Casement that his hand was cut off either by a soldier or, perhaps, by one of those working for the white men ("travailleurs de blanc"), who have been making war in his village with a view to the collection of rubber, but he asserts that the account which he has given me to-day is the truth."

(Signed) "E. E. Faris."

"*Bolengi, October* 17, 1903."

The inquiry resulted in the discharge of the prisoner, which, so far as it concerned the Epondo question, was in the following terms:—

We, Acting Public Prosecutor of the Court of Coquilhatville:

Having regard to the notes made by His Britannic Majesty's Consul, on the occasion of his visit to the villages of Ikandja and Bossunguma in the territory of the Ngombe, from which it would appear that a certain Kelengo, a forest guard in the service of the La Lulonga Company—

(*a.*) Cut off the left hand of a certain Epondo;

(*b.*) . . . . . ;

(*c.*) . . . . . ;

[1] See Annex No. 3.

Having regard to the inquiry instituted by Lieutenant Braeckman, which partly confirms the result of the inquiry instituted by His Britannic Majesty's Consul, but also partly contradicts it, and to the charges already brought against Kelengo adds that of having killed a native of the name of Baluwa;

Having regard to the conclusions arrived at by the police employé in question, which tend to raise grave doubts as to the truth of all these charges;

In view of the fact that all the natives who brought these charges against Kelengo, whether before His Britannic Majesty's Consul or Lieutenant Braeckman, on being summoned by us, the Acting Public Prosecutor, took to flight, and all efforts to find them have been fruitless; that this flight obviously throws doubt on the truth of their allegations;

That all the witnesses whom we have questioned during the course of our inquiry declare . . . . that Epondo lost his left hand from the bite of a wild boar;

That Epondo confirms these statements, and admits that he told a lie at the instigation of the natives of Bossunguma and Ikondja, who hoped to escape collecting rubber through the intervention of His Britannic Majesty's Consul, whom they considered to be very powerful;

That the witnesses, almost all inhabitants of the accusing villages, admit that such was the object of their lie;

That this version, apart from the unanimous declarations of the witnesses and the injured parties, is also the most plausible, seeing that every one knows that the natives dislike work in general and having to collect rubber, and are, moreover, ready to lie and accuse people falsely;

That it is confirmed by the clearly stated opinion of the English missionary Armstrong, who considers the natives to be "capable of any plot to escape work and especially the labour of collecting rubber";

That the innocence of Kelengo having been thoroughly established, there is no reason for proceeding against him;

On the above-mentioned grounds, we, the Acting Public Prosecutor, declare that there are no grounds for proceeding against Kelengo, a forest guard in the service of the La Lulonga Company, for the offences mentioned in Articles 2, 5, 11, and 19 of the Penal Code.

(Signed) BOSCO,
Acting Public Prosecutor.

Mampoko, October 9, 1903

We have dealt at length with the above case because it is considered by the Consul himself as being one of the utmost importance, and because he relies upon this single case for accepting as accurate all the other declarations made to him by natives.

"In the one case I could alone personally investigate," he says,[1] "that of the boy II, I found this accusation proved on the spot without seemingly a shadow of doubt existing as to the guilt of the accused sentry."

And further on:—

"I had not time to do more than visit the one village of R**, and in that village I had only time to investigate the charge brought by II."[2]

And elsewhere:—

"It was obviously impossible that I should . . . . verify on the spot, as in the case of the boy, the statements they made. In that one case the truth of the charges preferred was amply demonstrated."[3]

It is also to this case that he alludes in his letter of the 12th September, 1903, to the Governor-General, where he says:—

"When speaking to M. le Commandant Stevens at Colquilhatville on the 10th instant, when the *mutilated boy Epondo stood before us as evidence of the deplorable state of affairs* I reprobated, I said, 'I do not accuse an individual, I accuse a system.'"

It is only natural to conclude that if the rest of the evidence in the Consul's Report is of the same value as that furnished to him in this particular case, it cannot possibly be regarded as conclusive. And it is obvious that in those cases in which the Consul, as he himself admits, did not attempt to verify the assertions of the natives, these assertions are worth, if possible, still less.

It is doubtless true that the Consul deliberately incurred the certain risk of being misled owing to the manner in which he interrogated the natives, which he did, as a matter of fact, through two interpreters—"through Vinda, speaking in Bobangi, and

[1] Report, p. 58. [2] Idem, p. 58. [3] Idem, p. 56.

Bateko, repeating his utterances . . . . in the local dialect;[1] so that the Consul was at the mercy not only of the truthfulness of the native who was being questioned, but depended also on the correctness of the translations of two other natives, one of whom was a servant of his own, and the other apparently the missionaries' interpreter.[2] But any one who has ever been in contact with the native knows how much he is given to lying; the Rev. C. H. Harvey[3] states that—

"The natives of the Congo who surrounded us were contemptible, perfidious and cruel, impudent liars, dishonest, and vile."

It is also important, if one wishes to get a correct idea of the value of this evidence, to note that while Mr. Casement was questioning the natives, he was accompanied by two local Protestant English missionaries, whose presence must alone have necessarily affected the evidence.[4]

We should ourselves be going too far if from all this we were to conclude that the whole of the native statements reported by the Consul ought to be rejected. But it is clearly shown that his proofs are insufficient as a basis for a deliberate judgment, and that the particulars in question require to be carefully and impartially tested.

On examining the Consul's voluminous Report for other cases which he *has seen*, and which he sets down as cases of mutilation, it will be observed that he mentions two as having occurred on Lake Mantumba[5] "some years ago."[6] He mentions several others, in regard to the number of which the particulars given in the Report do not seem to agree,[7] as having taken place in the neighbourhood of Bonginda,[8] precisely in the country of the Epondo inquiry, where, as has been seen, the general feeling was excited and prejudiced. It is these cases which, he says, he had not time to inquire into fully,[9] and which, according to the natives, were due to agents of the La Lulanga Company. Were these instances of victims of the practice of native customs which the natives would have been careful not to admit? Were the injuries which the Consul saw due to some conflict between neighbouring villages or tribes? Or were they really due to the black subordinates of the Company? This cannot be determined by a perusal of the Report, as the natives in this instance, as in every other, were the sole source of the Consul's information, and he, for his part, confined himself to taking rapid notes of their numerous statements for a few hours in the morning of the 5th September, being pressed for time, in order to reach K* (Bossunguma) at a reasonable hour.[10]

Notwithstanding the weight which he attaches to the "air of frankness" and the "air of conviction and sincerity"[11] on the part of the natives, his own experience shows clearly the necessity for caution, and renders rash his assertion "that it was clear that these men were stating either what they had actually seen with their eyes or firmly believed in their hearts."[12]

Now, however, that the Consul has drawn attention to these few cases—whether cases of cruelty or not, and they are all that, as a matter of fact, he has inquired into personally, and even so without being able to prove sufficiently their real cause—the authorities will of course look into the matter and cause inquiries to be made. It is to be regretted that, this being so, all mention of date, place, and name has been systematically omitted in the copy of the Report communicated to the Government of the Independent State of the Congo. It is impossible not to see that these suppressions will place great difficulties in the way of the Magistrates who will have to inquire into the facts, and the Government of the Congo trust that, in the interests of truth, they may be placed in possession of the complete text of the Consul's Report.

It is not to be wondered at if the Government of the Congo State take this opportunity of protesting against the proceedings of their detractors, who have thought fit to submit to the public reproductions of photographs of mutilated natives, and have started the odious story of hands being cut off with the knowledge and even at the instigation of Belgians in Africa. The photograph of Epondo, for instance, mutilated in

[1] See Annex No. 2 (really Inclosure 6 in No. 3).
[2] "Regions Beyond," 1900, p. 198.
[3] Idem, January-February, 1903, p. 53.
[4] See Annex No. 2. "Present: Rev. W. D. Armstrong and Rev. D. J. Danielson of the Congo Balolo Mission of Bonginda, Vinda Bidilou (Consul's headman) and Bateko as interpreters, and His Britannic Majesty's Consul." This passage is omitted in Annex No. 6 of the Consul's Report (p. 78).
[5] Report, p. 34.
[6] Idem, pp. 76 and 77.
[7] *Cf.* Report, pp. 54 and 55 and p. 58.
[8] Report, pp. 54, 55.
[9] Idem, p. 56.
[10] Idem, p. 56.
[11] Idem, p. 62.
[12] Idem, p. 57.

the manner known, and who has "twice been photographed," is probably one of those which the English pamphlets are circulating as proof of the execrable administration of the Belgians in Africa. One English review reproduced the photograph of a "cannibal surrounded with the skulls of his victims," and underneath was written: "In the original photograph the cannibal was naked. The artist has made him decent by . . . . covering his breast with the star of the Congo State. It is now a suggestive emblem of the Christian-veneered cannibalism on the Congo." [1] At this rate it would suffice to throw discredit on the Uganda Administration if the plates were published illustrating the mutilations which, in a letter dated Uganda, 16th December, 1902, Dr. Castellani says he saw in the neighbourhood of Entebbe itself: "It is not difficult to find there natives without noses or ears, &c." [2]

The truth is, that in Uganda, as in the Congo, the natives still give way to their savage instincts. This objection has been anticipated by Mr. Casement, who remarks:—

> "It was not a native custom prior to the coming of the white man; it was not the outcome of the primitive instincts of savages in their fights between village and village; it was the deliberate act of the soldiers of a European Administration, and these men themselves never made any concealment that in committing these acts they were but obeying the positive orders of their superiors." [3]

That Mr. Casement should formulate so serious a charge without at the same time supporting it by absolute proof would seem to justify those who consider that his previous employment has not altogether been such as to qualify him for the duties of a Consul. Mr. Casement remained seventeen days on Lake Mantumba, a lake said to be 25 to 30 miles long and 12 to 15 broad, surrounded by dense forest.[4] He scarcely left its shores at all. In these circumstances it is difficult to see how he could have made any useful researches into the former habits and customs of the inhabitants. On the contrary, from the fact that the tribes in question are still very savage, and addicted to cannibalism,[5] it would seem that they have not abandoned the practice of those cruelties which throughout Africa were the usual accompaniments of barbarous habits and anthropophagy. In one portion of the districts which the Consul visited, the evidence of the English missionaries on this point is most instructive. The Rev. McKittrick, in describing the sanguinary contests between the natives, mentions the efforts to pacify the country which he formerly made through the Chiefs:—" . . . . We told them that for the future we should not let any man carrying spears or knives pass through our station. Our God was a God of peace, and we, His children, could not bear to see our black brothers cutting and stabbing each other." [6] "While I was going up and down the river," says another missionary, "they pointed out to me the King's beaches, whence they used to dispatch their fighting men to capture canoes and men. It was heartrending to hear them describe the awful massacres that used to take place at a great Chief's death. A deep hole was dug in the ground, into which scores of slaves were thrown after having their heads cut off; and upon that horrible pile they laid the Chief's dead body to crown the indescribable human carnage." [7] And the missionaries speak of the facility with which even nowadays the natives return to their old customs. It would seem, too, that the statement made in the Report,[8] that the natives now fly on the approach of a steamer as they never used to do, is hardly in accordance with the reports of travellers and explorers.

Be this how it may, it is to be observed that nowhere in the territory which is the scene of the operations of the A.B.I.R. Company did the Consul discover any evidence of acts of cruelty for which the commercial agents might have been considered responsible. The coincidence is remarkable, since it so happens that the A.B.I.R. Company is a concessionary Company, and that it is the system of concessions to which are constantly attributed the most disastrous consequences for the natives.

What it is important to discover from the immense number of questions touched on by the Consul, and the multiplicity of minor facts which he has collected, is whether the

[1] "Review of Reviews," February 14, 1903.
[2] The "Tribuna" of Rome.
[3] Report. Annex No. 4, p. 77.
[4] Idem, p. 30.
[5] Idem, p. 30.
[6] "Ten Years at Bonginda." D. McKittrick. "Regions Beyond," 1900, p. 21.
[7] "Congo Contrasts." Mr. Boudot. "Regions Beyond," 1900, p. 197.
[8] Report, p. 34.

sort of picture he has drawn of the wretched existence led by the natives corresponds to the actual state of affairs. We will take, for instance, the district of the Lulanga and the Lopori, as the head-stations of the missions of the "Congo Balolo Mission" have been established there for years past. These missionaries are established in the most distant places in the interior, at Lulonga, Bonginda, Ikau, Bongandanga, and Baringa, all of which are situated in the scene of operations of the La Lulonga and A.B.I.R. Companies. They are in constant communication with the native populations, and a special monthly review, called "Regions Beyond," regularly publishes their letters, notes, and reports. An examination of a set of these publications reveals no trace, at any time previous to April 1903—by that date, it is true, Mr. Herbert Samuel's motion had been brought before Parliament—of anything either to point out or to reveal that the general situation of the native populations was such as ought to be denounced to the civilized world. The missionaries congratulate themselves on the active sympathy shown them by the various official and commercial agents,[1] on the progress of their work of evangelization,[2] on the facilities afforded them by the construction of roads,[3] on the manner in which the natives are becoming civilized, "owing to the mere presence of white men in their midst, both missionaries and traders,"[4] on the disappearance of slavery,[5] on the density of the population,[6] on the growing number of their pupils, "especially since the State has issued orders for all children within reach to attend the mission schools,"[7] on the gradual disappearance of the primitive customs of the natives,[8] and lastly, on the contrast between the present and the past.[9] Will it be admitted that these Christian English missionaries, who, during their journeys, visited the various factories, and witnessed markets of rubber being held, would, by keeping silence, make themselves the accomplices of an inhuman or wrongful system of government? Among the conclusions of one of the Annual Reports of the Congo Balolo Mission is to be found the following: "On the whole, the retrospect is encouraging. If there has been no great advance, there has been no heavy falling off, and no definite opposition to the work. . . . . There has been much famine and sickness among the natives, especially at Bonginda. . . . . Apart from this, there has been no serious hindrance to progress. . . . ."[10] And speaking incidentally of the beneficial effect produced by work on the social condition of the natives, a missionary writes: "The greatest obstacle to conversion is polygamy. Many evils have been put down, *e.g.*, idleness, thanks to the State having compelled the men to work; and fighting, through their not having time enough to fight."[11] These opinions of missionaries appear to us to be more precise than those expressed in a Report on every page of which it may be said one finds such expressions as: "I was told," "it was said," "I was informed," "I was assured," "they said," "it was alleged," "I had no means of verifying," "it was impossible for me to verify," "I have no means of ascertaining," &c. Within a space of ten lines, indeed, occur four times the expressions, "appears," "would seem," "would seem," "do not seem."[12]

The Consul does not appear to have realized that native taxes in the Congo are levied in the shape of labour, and that this form of tax is justified as much by the moral effect which it produces, as by the impossibility of taxing the native in any other way, seeing that, as the Consul admits, the native has no money. It is to this consideration that is due the fact, to give another example, that out of 56,700 huts which are taxed in North-Eastern Rhodesia 19,653 pay that tax "in labour," while 4,938 pay it "in produce."[13] Whether such labour is furnished direct to the State or to some private undertaking, and whether it is given in aid of this or that work as local necessities may dictate, one ground of justification is always to be found in what the Memorandum of the 11th February last recognizes is the "necessity of the natives being induced to work." The Consul shows much anxiety as to how this forced labour should be described; he is surprised that if it be a tax it is sometimes paid and recovered by commercial agents. Strictly speaking, of course, it cannot be denied

[1] "Regions Beyond," 1900, p. 150; 1902, p. 209.
[2] Idem, *passim.*
[3] Idem, 1900, p. 150.
[4] Idem, 1901, p. 27.
[5] Idem, 1900, p. 199.
[6] Idem, 1900, pp. 243, 297, 306.
[7] Idem, 1901, p. 40; 1902, p. 315.
[8] Idem, 1901, p. 40.
[9] Idem, 1900, p. 196.
[10] Idem, 1901, p. 43.
[11] Idem, 1901, p. 60.
[12] Report, p. 78.
[13] Reports on the Administration of Rhodesia, 1900–1902, p. 408.

that the idea of remunerating a person for paying his taxes is contrary to ordinary notions of finance; but the difficulty disappears if it is considered that the object in view has been to get the natives to acquire the habit of labour, from which they have always shown a great aversion. And if this notion of work can more easily be inculcated on the natives under the form of commercial transactions between them and private persons, is it necessary to condemn such a mode of procedure, especially in those parts where the organization of the Administration is not yet complete? But it is essential that in the relations of this nature which they have with the natives, commercial agents, no less than those of the State, should be kind and humane. In so far as it bears on this point the Consul's Report will receive the most careful consideration, and if the result of investigation be to show that there are real abuses and that reforms are called for, the heads of the Administration will act as the circumstances may require.

But no one has ever imagined that the fiscal system in the Congo attained perfection at once, especially in regard to such matters as the assessment of taxes and the means for recovering them. The system of "Chieftaincies," which is recommended by the fact that it enables the authorities and the native to communicate through the latter's natural Chief, was based on an idea carried into practice elsewhere:—

"The more important Chiefs who helped the Administration have been paid a certain percentage of the taxes collected in their districts, and I think that if this policy is adhered to each year, the results will continue to be satisfactory and will encourage the Chiefs to work in harmony with the *Administration*." [1]

The Decree on the subject of these Chieftaincies[2] laid down the principle of a tax, and its levy in accordance with "a table of contributions to be made every year by each village in produce, forced labour, labourers, or soldiers." The application of this Decree has been provided for by deeds of investiture, tables of statistics, and particulars of contributions, forms of which will be found in Annex IV. In spite of what is stated in the Report, this Decree has been carried out so far as has been found compatible with the social condition of the various tribes; numerous deeds of investiture have been drawn up, and efforts have been made to draw up an equitable assessment of the contributions. The Consul might have found this out at the Commissioners' offices, especially in the Stanley Pool and Equator districts, which he passed through; but he neglected as a rule all official sources of information. No doubt the application of the Decree was at first necessarily limited, and it is possible that the result has been that for a certain time only such villages as were within a short distance from stations have been required to pay taxes; but this state of things has little by little altered for the better in proportion as the more distant regions have become included in the areas of influence of the Government posts, the number of villages subject to taxation has gradually increased, and it has been found possible to levy taxes on a greater number of persons. The Government aim at making progress in this direction continuous, that is to say, that taxation should be more equitably distributed, and should as much as possible be personal; it was with this object that the Decree of the 18th November, 1903, provided for drawing up "lists of native contributions" in such a way that the obligations of every native should be strictly defined.

"Article 28 of this Decree lays down that within the limits of Article 2 of the present regulations (that is to say, within the limit of forty hours' work per month per native) the District Commissioners shall draw up annual lists of the taxes to be paid, in kind or duration of labour, by each of the natives resident in the territories of their respective districts. And Article 55 punishes 'whoever, being charged with the levy of taxes, shall have required of the natives, whether in kind or labour, contributions which shall exceed in value those prescribed in the tables of taxes.'"

It is matter of common notoriety that the collection of taxes is occasionally met by opposition, and even refusal to pay. The proofs of this, which are to be found in the Report of the Consul for the Congo, are borne out by what has happened, for instance, in Rhodesia:—

"The Ba-Unga (Awemba district), inhabitants of the swamps in the Zambezi delta, gave some trouble on being summoned to pay taxes." [3]

"Although in many cases whole villages retired into the swamps on being called upon for the hut-tax, the general result was satisfactory for the first year (Luapula district)." [4]

"Milala's people have succeeded in evading taxes." [5]

[1] Reports on the Administration of Rhodesia, 1900-1902, p. 408.
[2] Decree of the 6th October, 1891 ("Bulletin Officiel," 1891, p. 259).
[3] Reports on the Administration of Rhodesia, 1900-1902, p. 409.
[4] Idem, p. 410.
[5] Idem, p. 410.

"A few natives bordering on the Portuguese territory, who, owing to the great distance they reside from the Native Commissioners' Stations, are not under the direct supervision of the Native Commissioners, have so far evaded paying hut tax, and refused to submit themselves to the authority of the Government. The rebel Chief, Mapondera, has upon three occasions successfully eluded punitive expeditions sent against him. Captain Gilson, of the British South Africa Police, was successful in coming upon him and a large following of natives, and inflicting heavy losses upon them. His kraal and all his crops were destroyed. He is now reported to be in Portuguese territory. Siji M'Kota, another powerful Chief, living in the northern parts of the M'toko district, bordering on Portuguese territory, has also been successful in evading the payment of hut tax, and generally pursuing the adoption of an attitude which is not acceptable to the Government. I am pleased to report that a patrol is at present on its way to these parts to deal with this Chief, and to endeavour to obtain his submission. It will be noted that the above remarks relate solely to those natives who reside along the borders of our territories, and whose defiant attitude is materially assisted by reason of this proximity to the Portuguese border, across which they are well able to proceed whenever they consider that any meeting or contact with the Native Commissioner will interfere in any way with their indolent and lazy life. They possess no movable property which might be attached with a view of the recovery of hut tax unpaid for many years, and travel backwards and forwards with considerable freedom, always placing themselves totally beyond the reach of the Native Commissioner." [1]

The above is an instance of those "punitive expeditions" to which the authorities are occasionally obliged to resort, as also of the native custom, which is not peculiar to the natives of the Congo, of moving into a neighbouring territory when they are seeking to evade the operation of the law. Whether in the process of collecting native taxes there have been cases in the Congo, amongst those mentioned by the Consul, in which the limits of a just and reasonable severity have been overstepped is a question of fact which investigation on the spot can alone ascertain, and instructions to this effect will be given to the authorities at Boma.

We are also unable to accept, on the information at present before us, the conclusions of the Report in regard to the conduct of the forest guards in the employ of the A.B.I.R. and La Lulonga Companies. These subordinate officers are represented by the Consul as being exclusively employed in "compelling by force the collection of india-rubber or the supplies which each factory needed." [2] It is true that another explanation has been given—though not, indeed, by a native—according to which the business of these same forest guards is to see that the india-rubber is harvested after a reasonable fashion, and especially to prevent the natives from cutting the plants.[3] It is, indeed, well known that the law has made rigorous provision for preserving the rubber zones, has regulated the manner in which they are to be worked, and has made planting and replanting obligatory, with a view to avoiding the complete exhaustion of the rubber plant which has occurred, for instance, in North-eastern and Western Rhodesia.[4] A heavy responsibility in this direction lies on the Companies and private persons engaged in developing the country, and it is obvious that they are bound to exercise the most careful superintendence over the way in which the harvest is collected. The object for which these forest guards are employed, therefore, may well be quite different from that alleged by the Consul; in any case, the complaints which have been made on this head will form a subject for inquiry in the Congo, as also the other remark of the Report that the manner in which these forest guards are armed is excessive, and liable to abuse. It is to be here observed that in calculating the number of these forest guards the Consul is obliged to rely on hypothesis,[5] and that he himself admits: "I have no means of ascertaining the number of this class of armed men employed by the A.B.I.R. Company." [6] He mentions that the gun of one of these men was marked on the butt "Depôt 2210." But it is evident that such a mark can only have the significance which the Consul would like to see in it, in so far as it can be proved that it refers to the numbering of the arms used in the Concession, and such is not the case, since this particular mark "Depôt" is not used either by the officials of the State or those of the Company, and it would seem that it is an old manufactory or store mark. In regard to the manner of arming the capitas, the Consul can hardly be ignorant that the higher authorities have always given great attention to the matter, which is, indeed, one surrounded with difficulties, seeing that while on the one hand it is necessary to consider the question of the personal protection of the capita, on

[1] Reports on the Administration of Rhodesia, 1900-1902, pp. 145, 146.
[2] Report, p. 44.
[3] Annex III, p. 26.
[4] Reports on the Administration of Rhodesia, 1900-1902, pp. 397, &c.
[5] Report, p. 57.
[6] Idem, p. 42.

the other the possibility of the arms in question being used for improper purposes must not be lost sight of. It is not only in the Circular of the 20th October, 1900, which the Consul has reprinted, that this question is dealt with; there is a whole collection of Circulars on the subject, among which may be mentioned those of the 12th March, 1897, 31st May and 28th November, 1900, and 30th April, 1901. Copies of them are annexed as proof of the fixed determination of the Government to see that the law relating to this question is strictly enforced (Annex V). Yet, in spite of all these precautions, the Consul has ascertained that several capitas were not provided with permits (perhaps they might have been found at the head office), and that two of them were furnished with arms of precision.[1] But these few infractions of the rule are obviously not enough to prove the existence of a sort of vast armed organization destined to strike terror into the natives. On the contrary, the Circular of the 7th September, 1903, printed in Annex VII of the Consul's Report, is a proof of the care taken by the Government that the regular black troops should always be under the control of European officers.[2]

Such are the preliminary remarks suggested by Mr. Casement's Report, and we reserve to ourselves the right of dealing with it more in detail as soon as the Government shall be in possession of the results of the inquiry which the local authorities are about to make. It will be observed that the Government, in its desire not to seem to wish to avoid the discussion, has not raised a question in regard to the manner, surely unusual, in which His Britannic Majesty's Consul has acted in a foreign country. It is obviously altogether outside the duties of a Consul to take upon himself, as Mr. Casement has done, to institute inquiries, to summon natives, to submit them to interrogatories as if duly authorized thereto, and to deliver what may be styled judgments in regard to the guilt of the accused. The reservations called for by this mode of procedure must be all the more formal, as the Consul was thus intervening in matters which only concerned subjects of the Congo State, and which were within the exclusive jurisdiction of the territorial authorities. Mr. Casement, indeed, made it his business himself to point out how little authorized he was to interfere when on the 4th September, 1903, he wrote to the Governor-General: "I have no right of representation to your Excellency save where the persons or interests of British subjects dwelling in this country are affected." It is thus obvious that he was aware that he was exceeding his duties by investigating facts which concerned only the internal administration, and so, contrary to all laws of Consular jurisdiction, encroaching on the province of the territorial authorities.

"The grievances of the natives have been made known in this country by ——, who brought over a petition addressed to the King, praying for relief from the excessive taxation and oppressive legislation of which they complain."

These lines are extracted from the Report for 1903 of the British and Foreign Anti-Slavery Society, and the natives referred to are the natives of the Fiji Isles. The Report goes on:—

"The case has been brought before the House of Commons. The grievances include forced labour on the roads, and restrictions which practically amount to slavery; natives have been flogged without trial by magistrate's orders, and are constantly subject to imprisonment for frivolous causes. Petitions lodged with the local Colonial Secretary have been disregarded. Mr. Chamberlain, in reply to the questions asked in Parliament, threw doubt upon the information received, but stated that the recently appointed Governor is conducting an inquiry into the whole situation in the Fiji Islands, in the course of which the matter will be fully investigated."

Such are also our conclusions in regard to Mr. Casement's Report.

Brussels, March 12, 1904.

---

[1] Report, p. 43.

[2] The Circular of the 7th September, 1903, has reference to the "prohibition" to dispatch armed soldiers in charge of black non-commissioned officers, and not, as would appear from the incorrect copy produced by the Consul, to the "instruction." (Annex VII of the Report, p. 80).

Annexe 1.

Déclaration de Mgr. Van Ronslé, Évêque de Thymbrium, Vicaire Apostolique du Congo Belge.

DANS son numéro du 23 Octobre, le "West African Mail" publie une série de lettres du Révérend J. W. Weeks, missionnaire Anglais, établi à Monsembe, district de Bangala. Ces lettres, émanant d'un auteur qui a habité la contrée de longues années et qui proteste d'ailleurs de sa parfaite sincérité et de sa bonne foi, m'offraient un intérêt particulier, ayant moi-même parcouru et habité la contrée depuis quatorze ans, et en étant revenu récemment.

Mr. Weeks fait preuve de prudence en limitant ses considérations à ce qu'il a vu sur les deux rives du Congo, entre Bokongo et Ikunungu, dans les villages Bangala, avoisinant Nouvelle-Anvers ; mais il se hasarde un peu plus, en étendant ses affirmations à la plus grande partie du Congo navigable, c'est-à-dire, du Stanley-Pool à Bopoto.

Sa thèse est que, sur cet immense espace, les rives se dépeuplent et que les tribus dégénèrent sous l'oppression de l'Etat, au moyen d'un système d'impositions, de déportations, et d'amendes.

Nous le reconnaissons, l'auteur ne formule pas positivement cette thèse ainsi généralisée ; mais après l'avoir formulée spécialement pour Nouvelle-Anvers, il continue à décrire la situation générale de manière à faire croire que les populations riveraines sont toutes décimées parce que toutes sont également opprimées par le Gouvernement. Le lecteur ne peut pas tirer d'autres conclusions de ses lettres, ni interpréter autrement certaines propositions qui les résument.

Le souci de la vérité nous engage à mettre le public en garde contre des conclusions aussi hâtives.

L'auteur sait que parmi les tribus *Bobangi* (citées sous les noms de Bwembe, Bolobo, Lukolela), qui sont un *unfortunate dying people* (un peuple qui dépérit), le Gouvernement n'a jamais fait de recrutement de soldats ni de travailleurs, et que les impositions qui ont été exigées de leurs nombreux villages, établis le long du fleuve sur un parcours de 100 lieues, consistent à ravitailler trois postes, dont celui de Yumbi seul est important, et à entretenir (depuis deux ans) la route de la ligne téléphonique—impositions réellement insignifiantes pour ceux qui y mettent quelque peu de bonne volonté.

C'est un fait, en outre, que ces populations subissaient de grandes pertes dès 1890, époque à laquelle les impositions étaient nulles ; et c'est un autre fait que leurs voisins de la rive Française, qui ne sont pas imposés, se meurent également, notamment ceux qui sont établis dans les environs de la Mission Catholique des Révérends Pères Français : Saint-Louis de Liranga. On pourrait d'ailleurs citer d'autres exemples de populations qui s'éteignent quoique à l'abri d'oppression.

Nous voilà donc en présence de dépeuplements qui ne sont certainement pas causés par l'oppression, et auxquels il faut chercher d'autres causes. Si donc les lettres de Mr. Weeks induisent en erreur pour la généralité des cas, il est dès lors permis de douter qu'elles nous exposent la situation véritable pour Nouvelle-Anvers. N'existe-t-il pas là aussi des causes autres que l'oppression ?

A notre avis, ces causes existent réellement. Il y en a deux qui tendent non seulement au dépeuplement des rives, mais à l'extinction même des tribus de Nouvelle-Anvers. Elles ne sont pas spéciales à cette région, mais communes à tous les villages riverains du fleuve. Elles suffisent à elles seules à expliquer une diminution extraordinaire de la population.

La première et la principale, c'est l'épidémie qu'on nomme communément la maladie du sommeil. Que cette maladie a enlevé beaucoup de monde, Mr. Weeks en convient ; mais il ajoute qu'il pense que le progrès de la maladie a été activé par l'oppression et que sans celle-ci le mal n'aurait pas été si tenace. Mr. Weeks a trop d'expérience de l'Afrique pour ne pas s'apercevoir qu'il avance ici une inexactitude et une erreur.

Il le pense, mais il n'en donne pas la preuve. Il est un fait avéré et reconnu par les médecins et par tous ceux qui ont observé la maladie du sommeil, c'est que ce fléau, une fois introduit dans une région, en abat lentement mais sûrement tous les habitants et reste, quoi qu'on fasse, maître du terrain ; une fois que ce mal a pris pied dans une population, il la détruit sans merci, quelles que soient les conditions de bien-être, de paix, et de tranquillité de cette population.

A l'appui de ceci, nous donnerons deux exemples de dépérissement que l'on ne pourra pas attribuer à l'oppression.

Notre Mission de Berghe-Sainte-Marie, contaminée par le contact des tribus Bobangi parmi lesquelles elle était située, a vu disparaître tous ses habitants jusqu'au dernier. Les 100 familles qui s'y étaient formées vivaient heureuses, dans des conditions presque idéales.

Autre fait : Les journaux ont relaté que dans l'Uganda, des Colonies Anglaises, on perd annuellement 50,000 personnes. Et aujourd'hui, à propos d'une découverte qu'aurait faite le Colonel Bruce, dans la matière en question, un journal écrit un article qui finit comme suit : "La maladie du sommeil continue à faire d'énormes ravages dans l'Uganda. Dans l'Ile de Brevuna, qui comptait 82,000 habitants, il n'y a plus que 22,000 individus, alors que la population de la Province de Basaga est complètement éteinte."

Si le travail et les occupations avaient une influence sur la maladie, ils auraient plutôt un effet tout à fait contraire à celui qu'on leur attribue. Mais nous n'y insistons pas, parce que le travail lui-même n'est pas un remède, mais tout au plus une espèce de réactif temporaire. Jusqu'à présent aucun moyen n'a pu vaincre la ténacité de cette maladie ; mais, à notre avis, ses ravages seraient plus rapides en terrain inerte et endormi qu'en terrain actif.

Et voilà six ans que cette peste, indépendamment de toute autre cause, fait journellement des victimes chez les riverains de Nouvelle-Anvers ; rien d'étonnant donc que la population y diminue

La cause que je place au second rang, en raison de son importance, n'est pas signalée par le Révérend Mr. Weeks. Elle consiste dans la suppression du commerce des esclaves et dans le défaut de la natalité ; même l'hypothèse que les tribus Bangala fussent restées saines, cette cause les aurait rendues incapables de maintenir leur population à niveau, et aurait même eu pour effet de la diminuer considérablement.

Mr. Weeks estime que la population de Nouvelle-Anvers atteignait les 50,000 en 1890. Nous avons observé que parmi cette population, il y avait un nombre très considérable d'esclaves d'origine étrangère, notamment des Mongo. Disons qu'un tiers n'était pas originaire de Nouvelle-Anvers. Les Bangala les avaient acquis, soit par les guerres, soit par les rachats. Cette source d'acquisition leur a été fermée par le Gouvernement.

La natalité leur restait comme seul moyen de remplacer les morts. Or, même avant l'époque de la maladie, la moyenne des naissances était très basse. J'estime qu'elle ne dépassait pas l'unité par femme. Je ne dis pas par famille, parce que les hommes libres y sont tous polygames, au détriment des hommes esclaves, qui le plus souvent, n'ont pas de femme. Avec une telle moyenne de naissances, il ne leur était pas possible de conserver le même nombre d'habitants, et le défaut de la natalité, indépendamment de la maladie, causait nécessairement un recul. Or, depuis que l'épidémie a fait son apparition, ce défaut est doublé, et au moment où, à la suite des nombreux décès, le nombre des naissances aurait dû croître, il a diminué graduellement à mesure que la maladie devenait plus intense.

Le Révérend Mr. Weeks constate avec nous que les enfants sont si peu nombreux que le nombre des décès est de loin en avance sur celui des naissances, mais il attribue ce fait à l'expatriation des jeunes gens.

Qu'il veuille remarquer toutefois, que les jeunes Bangala qui ont été au service de l'État ou des Compagnies Commerciales étaient, à de rares exceptions près, d'anciens esclaves qui, généralement, ne possédaient pas de femme. Cette considération infirme cette dernière manière d'expliquer le petit nombre de naissances, la situation polygame restant à peu près la même après comme avant le départ de ces jeunes gens. Je pourrais corrobérer ma manière de voir en citant l'exemple des tribus Bobangi, où il n'y a pas eu d'expatriations du tout.

Par ce qui a été dit, il est facile de comprendre que les deux causes précitées, de nature, indépendamment l'une de l'autre, au lieu de simplement réduire la population, sont assez puissantes pour l'éteindre complètement dans le cas où elles se combinent, comme à Nouvelle-Anvers et en général dans tous les villages riverains situés en aval de Bohaturaku ; et nous pouvons déjà conclure que les assertions de Mr. Weeks, qui mettent tout le mal sur le compte de l'oppression, ne sont pas soutenables.

Il nous reste à signaler deux autres causes qui ne sont que secondaires. Elles n'ont pas eu d'influence sur le dépérissement constaté chez la race de Bangala : elles ont contribué relativement peu à diminuer le nombre d'individus appartenant à cette race ; mais elles ont hâté le dépeuplement des rives du fleuve.

—L'une de ces causes, c'est l'abandon des emplacements riverains pour d'autres emplacements isolés à l'intérieur des terres, ou retirés dans les îles.—Peut-on légitimement conclure, comme le fait Mr. Weeks, que les populations quittent leurs villages pour échapper à des taxes qui les oppriment ? Aucunement, à notre avis. Il suffit qu'il lui soit demandé un travail régulier quelconque aussi minime qu'il soit, pour que l'indigène mette tout en œuvre pour s'y dérober. S'il juge le déplacement comme un moyen sûr et efficace, il ne manquera pas d'y recourir. Le transport et la reconstruction de ses habitations ne lui demandent d'ailleurs pas grande besogne.

Il est passionné pour la liberté sauvage qu'il goûtait avant l'arrivée des Européens, et par laquelle l'homme libre vivait dans un *dolce farniente*, passant ses journées à se reposer, à fumer, à boire, à " palabrer " et à commander à ses esclaves.

Il y a en outre chez le noir une tendance générale à éviter tout contact avec les Européens, et à reculer devant la civilisation.

Enfin, une mortalité extraordinaire est une cause suffisante pour expliquer les déplacements ; l'indigène, soit par superstition, soit par motif d'hygiène, ne reste pas sur l'emplacement où les décès deviennent nombreux.

L'autre cause enfin consiste dans les expatriations des jeunes Bangala.

Les engagements volontaires, d'abord, ont été nombreux. Se dérober, prendre un terme de service à l'État ou aux Compagnies Commerciales, voyager, voir du pays et gagner de l'argent était à la mode chez les jeunes gens. Mais depuis trois ou quatre ans, le recrutement de travailleurs chez la population riveraine de Nouvelle-Anvers a été interdit par le Gouvernement. Un grand nombre, toutefois, de ceux qui se sont ainsi engagés volontairement ne sont pas rentrés dans leurs foyers, mais restent éparpillés—de plein gré—dans les différentes localités d'Européens, parce qu'ils préfèrent leur état actuel à celui dans lequel ils se trouvaient antérieurement dans leur village. On peut aussi compter qu'il y a eu parmi ces expatriés volontaires un grand nombre de décès, causés principalement par la dysenterie et la pneumonie, surtout parmi ceux qui formaient les équipages des vapeurs.

Viennent ensuite les recrutements de soldats. A ma connaissance, parmi les populations de Nouvelle-Anvers, l'État n'a pas fait des recrutements réguliers pour son armée permanente. Il a jadis recruté des Bangala dans des circonstances exceptionnelles pour les employer comme auxiliaires dans certaines expéditions. Ces auxiliaires ont été rapatriés, ou ont eu l'occasion de l'être.

Les déplacements de villages et les expatriations doivent être considérés comme des causes partielles et secondaires, non pas du dépérissement des tribus, mais simplement de l'abandon des rives, et il n'est pas raisonnable d'en faire un grief au Gouvernement. L'aversion profonde pour tout travail l'attrait pour la sauvage indépendance chez l'homme libre ; le désir de se soustraire à l'esclavage domestique et la passion des voyages, chez la classe inférieure, voilà le fond où il faut chercher les motifs de ces faits.

En examinant en détail les lettres de Mr. Weeks, je n'aurais pas de peine à y trouver d'autres considérations dignes d'être contredites, mais je crois avoir fait un travail suffisant en montrant que la dégénérescence et le dépeuplement constatés à Nouvelle-Anvers sont le résultat de causes et d'influences étrangères à ce que l'auteur des lettres appelle l'oppression.

(Signé) C. VAN RONSLÉ.

Le 14 Novembre, 1903.

Annexe 2.

Notes du Consul Casement sur sa Visite aux Villages d'Ekanza et de Bosunguma dans la Contrée de Ngombe, près de Mompoko, sur la Rive gauche de l'Ileka, Affluent de la Lulongo.

(Traduction.) *Le 17 Septembre*, 1903.

En présence du Révérend W. D. Armstrong et du Révérend D. J. Danielson, de la Congo Balolo Mission de Bonginda, de Vinda Bidiloa ("headman" du Consul) et de Bateko, servant d'interprètes, et du Consul de Sa Majesté Britannique.[1]

Le Chef de cette section de Bosunguma, du nom de Tondebila, avec beaucoup d'hommes du village et quelques femmes et enfants, étant présents.

Un garçon de 14 à 15 ans, du nom d'Epondo, dont la main gauche a été coupée, et dont le moignon est enveloppé dans une pièce de tissu, la blessure étant à peine guérie, apparaît, et en réponse à la question du Consul, accuse de cette mutilation une sentinelle nommée Kelengo (placée dans le village par l'agent local de la Société "La Lulonga" pour veiller à ce que les noirs travaillent le caoutchouc).

Cette sentinelle est appelée, et, après s'être fait quelque peu attendre, se présente armé d'un fusil à capsule.

L'enquête suivante sur les circonstances qui ont entouré la perte de la main d'Epondo est faite alors :—

Le Consul, par l'intermédiaire de Vinda, s'exprimant en Bobangi, et Bateko, répétant ses paroles en Mongo pour Kelengo—et dans le dialecte local pour les autres—demande à Epondo, en présence de l'accusé :

"Qui a coupé votre main ?"

Epondo : "La sentinelle Kelengo que voilà."

Kelengo nie le fait, interrompant, et disant que son nom est Mbilu, et non Kelengo. Le Consul le requiert de garder le silence—qu'il parlera après.

Le Chef du village, Tondebila, est appelé et questionné par le Consul, par l'intermédiaire des interprètes.

Après avoir été prié de dire la vérité sans crainte ni partialité, il déclare :

"La sentinelle Kelengo devant nous a coupé la main d'Epondo."

Le Consul : "Avez-vous été vous-même témoin de l'acte ?"

Réponse : "Oui."

Plusieurs des Chefs du village sont appelés par le Consul pour témoigner.

Au premier d'entre eux, qui déclare se nommer Mololi, le Consul demande, en désignant le poignet mutilé d'Epondo :

"Qui a coupé la main de ce garçon ?"

Mololi, désignant la sentinelle : "Cette homme-là l'a fait."

Le second, qui dit s'appeler Eyileka, est interrogé par le Consul : "Qui a coupé la main de ce garçon ?"

Réponse : "Kelengo."

Le troisième, qui déclare se nommer Alondi, est interrogé par le Consul : "Qui a coupé la main de ce garçon ?"

Réponse : "Cet homme-ci, Kelengo."

Mololi est questionné à nouveau :

"Avez-vous, vous-même, vu cette sentinelle couper la main de ce garçon ?"

"Oui, je l'ai vu."

Eyikela est questionné à nouveau :

"Avez-vous, vous-même, vu cette sentinelle couper la main de ce garçon ?"

Réponse : "Oui, je l'ai vu."

Alondi est questionné à nouveau :

"Avez-vous, vous-même, vu cette sentinelle couper la main de ce garçon ?"

Réponse : "Je le croirais. Si je ne m'étais pas blessé ici—il montre une coupure près du tendon d'Achille, au talon gauche—le même jour en m'enfuyant effrayé. Mon propre couteau m'a blessé . . . je l'ai laissé tomber en m'enfuyant."

Le Consul questionne Epondo :

"Combien de temps y a-t-il que votre main a été coupée ?"

Réponse : Il n'est pas sûr.

[1]. Passage omis dans le texte de ces notes, tel qu'il se trouve reproduit à l'Annexe 6 du Rapport du Consul.

Deux jeunes hommes du même village, nommés Bonjingeni et Maseli, s'avancèrent et dirent qu'ils s'en souvenaient. Cela s'était passé pendant qu'on défrichait la terre sur la rive devant la station à Bonginda, quand on commençait à aménager un point d'accostage (un "slip") pour les steamers.

Mr. Danielson déclare que le travail en question—le défrichement de la rive—en vue de l'établissement du "slip" de la Mission de Bonginda, fut commencé le 21 Janvier de cette année.[1]

Botoko, d'Ekanza, une autre section du village de Bosunguma, est questionné par le Consul:

"Avez-vous vu couper la main de ce garçon?"

Réponse: "Oui. Je ne l'ai *pas* réellement vu couper. Je vins et je vis la main séparée et le sang couler sur le sol. Les gens s'étaient enfuis dans toutes les directions."

Le Consul demande aux interprètes de demander s'il y en avait d'autres qui avaient vu le crime et en accusaient Kelengo.

Presque tous ceux qui étaient présents, à peu près quarante personnes, presque tous des hommes, crièrent d'une seule voix que c'était Kelengo qui l'avait fait.

Le Consul: "Ils sont tous certains que c'était ce Kelengo que voici?"

Réponse unanime: "Oui. Il l'a fait."

Le Consul demande à l'accusé Kelengo: "Avez-vous coupé la main de ce garçon?"

Cette question a été posée dans le langage le plus clair possible, et a été répétée six fois, et il a été demandé qu'une réponse claire, par oui ou par non, soit faite.

L'accusé évite de répondre à la question, commençant à parler d'autres choses n'ayant pas de rapport avec la question—par exemple, que son nom était Mbilu et non Kelengo, et que les gens de Bosungama lui ont fait de méchantes choses.

Il lui a été dit de se confiner dans les limites de la question qui lui a été posée, qu'il pourrait parler d'autres choses après, mais que maintenant il y avait lieu pour lui de répondre aux questions posées, tout aussi simplement et tout aussi clairement que les autres avaient répondu. Il avait entendu ces réponses et l'accusation portée contre lui, et devait répondre aux questions du Consul de la même manière.

L'accusé continua à parler de choses étrangères, et refusa ou évita de donner de réponse à la question qui lui était posée.

Après des tentatives répétées pour obtenir une réponse directe à la question: "Avez-vous, ou n'avez-vous pas, coupé la main de ce garçon Epondo?" le Consul dit: "Vous êtes accusé de ce crime.

"Vous refusez de répondre aux questions que je vous pose clairement et franchement comme vos accusateurs l'ont fait. Vous avez entendu leur accusation.

"Votre refus de répondre comme vous devriez répondre, à savoir par oui ou par non, à une question directe et simple me laisse convaincu que vous ne pouvez nier l'accusation. Vous avez entendu ce dont vous avez été accusé par tout ce monde.

"Puisque vous ne consentez pas à répondre comme ils l'ont fait, vous pouvez raconter votre histoire comme vous voulez.

"Je l'écouterai."

L'accusé commence à parler, mais avant que ses remarques puissent m'être traduites par l'intermédiaire de Bateko d'abord, à qui il parle directement, et de Vinda ensuite, un jeune homme s'avance hors de la foule et interrompt.

Il y eut du bruit, puis cet homme parla.

Il dit qu'il était Cianzo, de Bosunguma. Il avait tué deux antilopes, et il porta deux de leurs jambes à cette sentinelle Kelengo pour lui en faire cadeau. Kelengo refusa son cadeau et lia sa femme. Kelengo dit que ce n'était pas un cadeau suffisant pour lui, et il tint la femme de Cianzo liée jusqu'à ce que lui (Cianzo) eût payé 1,000 baguettes de laiton pour sa rançon.

A ce moment un jeune homme, disant se nommer Ilungo, de Bosunguma, s'avança dans le cercle et accusa Kelengo de lui avoir volé ouvertement deux canards et un chien.

Ils lui furent pris sans aucun motif, sinon que Kelengo en avait besoin, et les prit de force.

Le Consul se tourna de nouveau vers Kelengo, et l'invita à raconter son histoire et à faire une réponse à l'accusation portée contre lui, de la manière qui lui convenait. Le Consul ordonna le silence à tous, et leur enjoignit de ne pas interrompre Kelengo.

Kelengo dit qu'il n'a pas pris les canards d'Ilungo. Le père d'Ilungo lui à donné un canard. (Tous rient.)

Il est vrai que Cianzo a tué deux antilopes et lui en a donné deux jambes en cadeau, mais il n'a pas lié la femme de Cianzo et n'a pas demandé d'argent pour rançon.

Le Consul: "C'est bien. Cela termine les canards et les jambes d'antilope; mais maintenant je veux entendre parler de la main d'Epondo. Racontez-moi ce que vous savez au sujet de la main coupée d'Epondo."

Kelengo élude de nouveau la question.

Le Consul: "Dites-lui ceci. Il est posté par ses maîtres dans ce village, n'est-ce pas? Ceci est son village. Maintenant en vient-il à dire qu'il ne sait pas ce qui se passe ici, où il vit?"

Kelengo dit: "Il est vrai que ceci est son village, mais il ne connaît rien au sujet de la main coupée d'Epondo.

"Peut-être c'était la première sentinelle ici avant qu'il ne vînt qui était un très méchant homme et coupait les mains.

"Cette sentinelle-là est partie; c'était elle qui coupait les mains, pas lui, Mbilu. Il ne sait rien à ce sujet."

Le Consul: Quel était le nom, alors, de cette méchante sentinelle, votre prédécesseur, qui coupait les mains des gens? Le connaissez-vous?"

[1]. Passage omis dans le texte annexé au Rapport.

Kelengo ne donne pas de réponse directe, et la question est répétée. Il commence alors une déclaration au sujet de plusieurs sentinelles. Il en nomme trois: Bobudjo, Ekua et Lokola Longonya, comme ses prédécesseurs ici, à Bosunguma.

Ici, un homme, nommé Makwombondo, bondit et interrompant affirma que ces trois sentinelles ne résidaient pas à Bosunguma, mais avaient été stationnées dans son propre village, le village de Makwonbondo.

Le Consul, à Kelengo: "Depuis combien de temps êtes-vous dans ce village?"

Réponse: "Cinq mois."

Le Consul: "En êtes-vous bien sûr?"

Réponse: "Cinq mois."

Le Consul: "Connaissez-vous alors le garçon Epondo—l'avez-vous déjà vu?"

Réponse: "Je ne le connais pas du tout."

(Ici tout l'auditoire éclate de rire et certains expriment leur admiration pour les aptitudes de Kelengo au mensonge.)

Kelengo, continuant, déclara qu'il était possible qu'Epondo vînt du village de Makwombondo. Quoi qu'il en soit, lui, Kelengo, ne connaît pas Epondo. Il ne le connaît pas du tout.

Ici Cianzo s'avance et dit qu'il est le propre frère d'Epondo; ils ont toujours vécu ici. Leur père était Itengolo, mort maintenant; leur mère est morte également.

Le Consul, à Kelengo: "Alors c'est fini; vous ne connaissez rien de cette affaire?"

Kelengo: "C'est fini. Je vous ai dit tout. Je ne connais rien de cela."

Ici un homme, qui dit se nommer Elenge, d'Ekanza, la section voisine de Bosunguma, s'avança avec sa femme. Il déclara que les autres sentinelles, dans leur village, n'étaient pas aussi méchantes, mais que ce Kelengo était un gredin.

Kelengo a lié sa femme Sondi, la femme avec laquelle il se présenta, et lui a fait payer 500 baguettes avant de la relâcher. Il les a payées.

Ici le Consul demande à Epondo comment sa main a été coupée. Avec Bonjingeni et Maseli, il déclara qu'il avait d'abord reçu un coup de feu dans le bras et que, quand il tomba, Kelengo lui avait coupé la main.

Le Consul: "Avez-vous senti qu'on vous la coupait?"

Réponse: "Oui, je l'ai senti."

Ceci terminait l'enquête.

Le Consul a informé le Chef Tondebila et les indigènes présents qu'il ferait rapport au Gouvernement de ce qu'il avait vu et entendu et qu'il lui demanderait de faire une enquête sur l'accusation portée contre Kelengo, qui méritait une punition sévère pour ses actes illégaux et cruels. Que les faits dont était accusé Kelengo étaient tout à fait illégaux et que si le Gouvernement savait que des choses semblables se commettent, ceux qui se rendent coupables de pareils crimes seraient, dans chaque cas, punis.

(Signé) ROGER CASEMENT,
Consul de Sa Majesté Britannique.[1]

La déclaration qui précède a été lue par nous et nous déclarons par la présente qu'elle est un compte rendu juste et fidèle de ce qui a été dit en notre présence hier au village de Bosunguma, en témoignage de quoi nous avons apposé nos signatures ci-dessous.

(Signé) WILLIAM DOUGLAS ARMSTRONG.
D.-J. DANIELSON.

Signé par les prénommés William Douglas Armstrong et D.-J. Danielson, missionnaires à Bonginda, ce 8 Septembre, 1903.

(Signé) ROGER CASEMENT,
Consul de Sa Majesté Britannique.

Je déclare par la présente que j'ai entendu lire par le Consul de Sa Majesté Britannique la déclaration ci-dessus et qu'elle est un compte rendu juste et fidèle des déclarations faites par les témoins questionnés hier à Bosunguma par le Consul de Sa Majesté Britannique par mon intermédiaire agissant comme interprète.

(Signé) VINDA BIDILOA.

Signé par Vinda Bidiloa, à Bonginda, ce 8 Septembre, 1903, par devant moi,

(Signé) ROGER CASEMENT,
Consul de Sa Majesté Britannique.

Je certifie que ce qui précède est une copie véritable et fidèle des notes originales, en ma possession, sur ce qui s'est passé le 7 Septembre, 1903, au village de Bosunguma, dans la contrée de Ngombe, sur la Rivière Lulanga, où je me suis rendu le 7 Septembre, 1903, sur la demande d'indigènes de ce village.

En foi de quoi j'ai apposé ci-dessous ma signature et le sceau de mon office, à Lulanga, ce 9 Septembre, 1903.

(Signé) ROGER CASEMENT,
Consul de Sa Majesté Britannique.

---

[1]. Les déclarations suivantes sont omises dans le texte annexé au Rapport.

Annexe 3.

Enquête du Substitut du Procureur d'État, Gennaro Bosco, à charge de Kelengo.

(Extraits relatifs à l'affaire Epondo.)

L'an 1903, le 28 Septembre, à Coquilhatville, devant nous, Substitut, comparaît Efundu, Chef du village Bosunguma, qui après serment, répond comme d'après aux questions que nous lui posons :

* * * * *

D. Parlez de la main d'Epondo ?

R. Je ne puis que répéter ce qu'Epondo même m'a raconté. Il m'a dit que dans les Bangala, il était allé à la chasse au sanglier avec un camarade, dont il ne me dit pas le nom. Celui-ci blessa un sanglier et il voulut l'attraper par les oreilles, mais le sanglier le mordit si fortement qu'une main tomba, après gangrène.

D. Pourquoi les indigènes d'Ekanza et Bosunguma accusent-ils Kelengo ?

R. Pour ne pas faire de caoutchouc. Kelengo est sentinelle de caoutchouc. Les indigènes n'aiment pas de faire du caoutchouc et ont décidé, sachant que les Anglais étaient là, de leur dire un mensonge dans l'espoir de ne plus faire de caoutchouc.

D. Étiez-vous présent lorsque le Consul Anglais interrogeait les indigènes ?

R. Non, j'étais dans la forêt.

D. Lorsque le Consul Anglais fut parti, qu'est-ce que disaient entre eux les indigènes ?

R. "Maintenant, c'est bien. Maintenant qu'il croit qu'on m'a coupé la main, nous ne ferons plus de caoutchouc ; nous ne ferons que la kwanga."

D. Avez-vous entendu dire que Kelengo avait tué un homme et coupé la main à deux autres parce qu'on refusait de lui donner une antilope qu'on avait tuée ?

R. C'est ce qu'on est allé raconter aux Anglais, mais c'est un mensonge.

D. Savez-vous que Kelengo a amarré pour la même raison la femme de Ciango et qu'il ne l'a laissée qu'après un paiement de 1,000 mitakos ?

R. C'est encore un mensonge. Je ne connais pas ce Ciango. C'est un nom qui n'est pas même usité parmi les indigènes.

D. Savez-vous que Kelengo a volé un canard et un chien d'Ilungo ?

R. Mensonge. Cet Ilungo n'existe pas.

Dont procès-verbal lu et signé, hors le témoin illettré.

Le Substitut,
(Signé) BOSCO.

Après comparaît Mongombe, d'Ikandja, qui, interrogé, après serment, déclare :

Epondo a perdu la main à la chasse du sanglier dans les Bangala. Lui-même l'a raconté en disant que son camarade, dont il ignore le nom, avait blessé le sanglier, et il avait voulu l'attraper par les oreilles. Le sanglier alors lui avait arraché la main.

* * * * *

D. Pourquoi les indigènes accusent-ils Kelengo ?

R. Ils ne veulent pas faire le caoutchouc et sont allés dire des mensonges aux Anglais dans l'espoir de ne pas faire de caoutchouc, et quand les Anglais sont partis, ils disaient : "Maintenant, c'est bien. Maintenant plus de caoutchouc. Seulement la kwanga." J'ai entendu ces expressions plusieurs fois. Kelengo n'a pas amarré la femme de Sandjo, ni tué personne. L'histoire de l'antilope est un mensonge. Je ne connais pas Ilungo.

D. Êtes-vous au courant du complot des indigènes pour aller dire des mensonges aux missionnaires ?

R. Oui ; j'ai entendu les indigènes se plaindre qu'ils travaillaient beaucoup pour rien, que les Chefs s'emparaient des mitakos que les blancs payaient pour la récolte du caoutchouc ; enfin, qu'ils mouraient de faim. Ils ajoutaient qu'ils avaient réclamé plusieurs fois inutilement et qu'ils allaient essayer si, par l'intermédiaire des Anglais, qui étaient très puissants, ils pouvaient obtenir de changer leur sort. Et ils disaient : "Allons, allons vite, vite chez les Anglais ; allons dire que Kelengo coupe les mains."

D. Avez-vous entendu ces mots ?

R. Oui ; je les ai entendus parfaitement.

Dont procès-verbal lu et signé, hors le témoin illettré.

Le Substitut,
(Signé) BOSCO.

Après comparaît Bangwala, d'Ikandja, qui, interrogé, après serment, déclare :—

* * * * * *

D. Parlez maintenant de la main d'Epondo.

R. Il l'a perdue à cause d'une morsure de sanglier, dans les Bangala. C'est Epondo lui-même qui le disait.

D. Pourquoi les indigènes accusent-ils Kelengo ?

R. Ils ne veulent plus faire de caoutchouc et ont cru, en accusant Kelengo, de se soustraire à ce travail. J'ai entendu de mes oreilles lorsqu'ils disaient : "Allons vite, vite dire des mensonges aux Anglais." Ils allèrent donc appeler les Anglais pour leur faire voir l'homme sans mains et les Anglais vinrent. Et quand ils furent partis, ils disaient : " Bien, bien, nous allons faire la kwanga seulement. Maintenant le caoutchouc est fini."

Dont procès-verbal lu et signé, hors le témoin illettré.

(Signé) BOSCO.

Après comparaît Momobo, de Bossunguma, qui, interrogé, après serment, déclare :—

* * * * * *

Epondo a perdu la main à cause de la morsure d'un sanglier ; Kelengo n'a tué personne.

Dont procès-vérbal lu et signé, hors le témoin illettré.

(Signé) BOSCO.

Après comparaît Ekumeloko, de Boselembe, travailleur à la Société Lulonga, qui, interrogé, après serment, déclare :—

* * * * * *

D. Et qui a coupé la main d'Epondo ?

R. Epondo arriva dans notre village sans une main et nous montra qu'un sanglier la lui avait coupée.

D. Pourquoi les indigènes accusent-ils Kelengo ?

R. Pour se soustraire au travail du caoutchouc ; ils racontèrent des mensonges aux Anglais et bornent leur travail à la kwanga pour les Anglais.

D. Kelengo a-t-il tué quelqu'un ?

R. Personne.

Dont procès-verbal lu et signé, hors le témoin illettré.

(Signé) BOSCO.

Après, nous interrogeons l'un après l'autre Bundja, de Bosibendama, et Bawsa, de Bossundjulu, travailleurs de la Société Lulonga, qui font une déclaration identique à la précédente.

Dont procès-verbal lu et signé, hors les comparants illettrés.

(Signé) BOSCO.

L'an 1903, le 19 Septembre, devant nous, Substitut, comparaît Kelengo, de Bokakata, qui, renseigné sur l'accusation qu'on lui fait, déclare :—

Mon nom officiel (kombo na mukanda) est Mbilu, mais les indigènes m'appellent Kelengo. Je n'ai pas coupé les mains d'Epondo . . . . Je ne connais pas même Epondo. Je sais seulement qu'un sanglier lui a mordu la main . . . . Du reste, je ne suis dans le village de Bosunguma que depuis cinq mois. J'ai été surpris lorsque les indigènes m'ont accusé près des Anglais, mais je dois vous dire que quelques jours après, ils m'ont donné 100 mitakos pour que je n'aille pas réclamer chez le blanc et m'ont avoué qu'ils avaient dit des mensonges aux Anglais pour se soustraire au travail du caoutchouc. Je portai ces 100 mitakos à Bumba (M. Dutrieux), qui dit : " Les indigènes sont des menteurs."

D. Le Chef Tondebila dit qu'il vous a vu lorsque vous coupiez la main d'Epondo.

R. Il est un menteur. D'ailleurs pourquoi s'est-il sauvé ? Il a été arrêté deux fois pour venir ici rendre son témoignage La première fois par Bumba, la seconde par le Commandant de la Compagnie (Braeckman), et il a pris toujours la fuite. Moi aussi, j'aurais pu m'enfuir et je n'ai pas voulu parce que je suis innocent.

D. Mololi, Botoko, Eykela, et Alondi vous accusent comme auteur de la mutilation d'Epondo.

R. Ils mentent. Je ne connais ni Botoko, ni Eykela, ni Alandi. Je connais seulement Momoli.

D. On vous accuse aussi d'avoir amarré la femme de Ciango parce que celui-ci, ayant tué deux antilopes, ne vous en avait donné que les cuisses et de n'avoir laissé cette femme qu'après avoir reçu un cadeau de 1,000 mitakos. On vous accuse en outre d'avoir volé ou de vous être emparé par force de deux canards et d'un chien appartenant à Ilungo. Que répondez-vous ?

R. Mensonge. Je ne connais pas Ciango. Je connais Ilungo, mais je n'ai rien pris. Quand on m'apporte des cadeaux, je les accepte, mais je ne prends pas les objets des indigènes, parce que Bumba nous l'a défendu sous menace de nous mettre en prison.

D. Vous êtes accusé par Ilengi d'avoir amarré la femme de Sundi et de l'avoir libérée seulement après paiement de 500 mitakos.

R. Mensonge. Ilundji et Sundi appartiennent à une autre section. Ils dépendent d'une autre sentinelle, un nommé Ikangola. C'est un complot des indigènes pour se soustraire au travail du caoutchouc. Ils me disaient toujours qu'ils ne voulaient pas le faire, qu'ils préféraient faire la kwanga pour les Anglais et prétendaient d'y parvenir avec leur aide.

Dont procès-verbal lu et signé, hors le témoin illettré.

(Signé) BOSCO.

Après, nous interrogeons successivement tous les témoins : Bandja, Bansu, Ekumaleko, Mambo, Bangula, Monsumbu, Ffundu, pour leur demander depuis combien de temps Kelengo se trouve à Bosunguma, et tous disent qu'il s'y trouve depuis quatre mois.

(Signé) BOSCO.

L'an 1903, le 4 Octobre, à Mampoko, devant nous, Substitut, à Coquilhatville, comparaît Dutrieux, Charles-Alexandre, né à Namur, Directeur de la Société Lulonga, qui, interrogé, après serment, déclare :—

Je connais Kelengo sous le nom de M'Bilo. Il est au service de le Société Lulonga en qualité de garde forestier, depuis le mois de Mars dernier. Sa tâche est uniquement celle d'accompagner les indigènes à la récolte du caoutchouc et de leur empêcher de couper les lianes. Je ne sais rien au sujet de l'atrocité dont on l'accuse. . . . . Je ne sais pas maintenant pourquoi on accuse Kelengo ou Mbilu d'avoir coupé une main à un garçon. Je sais seulement que le nommé Kelengo ou Mbilu est venu chez moi le jour d'arrivée du Lieutenant Braeckman, c'est-à-dire, sauf erreur, le 12 Septembre, m'apporter 100 mitakos en me disant que les indigènes les lui avaient donnés pour qu'il ne me dise pas qu'ils avaient menti près des Anglais, dans le but de ne pas faire de caoutchouc. Le Lieutenant Braeckman a fait rendre ces mitakos au Chef du village de Bossunguma.

Dont procès-verbal lu et signé.

(Signé) BOSCO.

(Signé) DUTRIEUX.

Après, Pingo, de Bokakata, qui, interrogé, après serment, déclare :—

Je suis boy de M. Dutrieux. Un jour, le nommé Mbilu est venu chez mon maître lui apporter 100 mitakos, disant que le Chef de Bossunguma, nommé, si je ne me troupe, Mateka ou Lofundu, les lui avait donnés comme cadeau pour qu'il n'aille pas dire que les indigènes avaient menti près des Anglais en l'accusant d'avoir coupé une main à un gamin, mensonge qu'ils avaient dit pour se soustraire au travail du caoutchouc.

Dont procès-verbal lu et signé, hors le témoin illettré.

(Signé) BOSCO.

L'an 1903, le 6 Octobre, à Mampoko, devant nous, Substitut, à Coquilhatville, comparait le nommé Eponga, *alias* Mondondo, de Bossunguma, qui, interrogé, après serment, déclare :—

Epondo a une main coupée parce que, dans les Bangala, un sanglier la lui a arrachée. . . . .

D. Pourquoi alors les habitants de votre village ont-ils accusé Kelengo ?

R. Pour se soustraire au travail du caoutchouc ; ils ont dit des mensonges aux Anglais, qui ont répondu : "Nous ferons une lettre au Juge."

D. Est-ce qu'ils ont ajouté quelque autre chose ?

R. Non.

D. Combien de temps sont-ils restés dans votre village ?

Le témoin indique où se trouvait le soleil lorsqu'ils sont arrivés et lorsqu'ils sont partis. Nous calculons qu'ils sont restés au moins quatre heures.

D. Est-ce que les Anglais ont écrit quand ils étaient au village ?

R. Oui ; ils ont écrit sur un grand papier.

Dont procès-verbal lu et signé, hors le témoin illettré.

(Signé) BOSCO.

Après comparaît Liboso, fils de Lekela, de Bossunguma, qui, interrogé, après serment, déclare —

Epondo a une main coupée parce qu'un sanglier l'a mordue. . . . . .

D. Pourquoi les indigènes ont-ils accusé Kelengo ?

R. Parce qu'ils étaient fatigués de faire du caoutchouc, qui n'était plus dans leur forêt. Ils ont cru qu'avec l'intercession des Anglais ils pourraient se soustraire à un travail très dur, et pour interposer les Anglais, ils sont allés leur dire que la sentinelle de Bumba (Dutrieux) avait coupé une main.

D. Qui est allé parler avec les Anglais ?

R. Bodjengene et un autre, dont je ne me rappelle pas le nom. Les Anglais dirent : "Vous mentez. Où est cet homme avec la main coupée ? Allez le prendre." Alors ils sont allés chercher . . Epondo et l'ont présenté aux Anglais.

D. Lorsque les Anglais sont venus à votre village, qu'est-ce qu'ils ont fait ?

R. Ils ont parlé avec les habitants qui se plaignaient de ce qu'ils devaient travailler beaucoup. Ils disaient que le caoutchouc n'était plus dans leur forêt, qu'ils voulaient faire un travail moins dur, comme la kwanga et la pêche. Les Anglais répondirent : "C'est bien ; vous êtes des hommes de Bula Matari. Nous écrirons à Bula Matari." Et dans leur village ils firent une grande moukande, comme vous maintenant.

(Signé) BOSCO.

Après comparaît Etoko, fils d'Ilembe, décédé, de Bossunguma, qui, interrogé, après serment, déclare :—

Un sanglier coupa la main d'Epondo . . . . .

D. Pourquoi les indigènes ont-ils accusé Kelengo ?

R. Pour rien. Pour se soustraire au travail du caoutchouc ; ils ont dit des mensonges aux Anglais.

D. Qui est allé parler aux Anglais ?

R. Bodjengene.

D. Bodjengene seul

R. Oui ; lui seul. Après, Epondo est allé travailler chez les Anglais, où il se trouve maintenant. . . . . .

Dont procès-verbal lu et signé, hors le témoin illettré.

(Signé) BOSCO.

Après comparaît Akindola, de Bossunguma, qui, interrogé, après serment, déclare :—

Un sanglier a coupé la main d'Epondo.

D. Pourquoi les indigènes accusent-ils Kelengo ?

R. Non ; ils n'accusent pas Kelengo.

D. N'étiez-vous pas présent lorsque le Consul Anglais est venu dans votre village ?

R. Non ; j'étais dans la forêt et je ne sais rien de ce qui s'est passé.

Dont procès-verbal lu et signé, hors le témoin illettré.

(Signé) BOSCO.

Après comparaît Mafambi, de Bossunguma, qui, interrogé, après serment, déclare :—

Un sanglier a mordu la main d'Epondo, et c'est pour cela qu'il l'a perdue . . . . . Kelengo est innocent. Les habitants des Bossunguma l'ont accusé espérant d'éviter la récolte du caoutchouc.

D. Êtes-vous allé à la Mission de Bonginda pour vous plaindre ?

R. Moi, non, Bodjengene ; et les Anglais lui ont répondu de s'adresser au Juge.

D. Ikabo n'est-il pas allé chez les Anglais ?

R. Non. Epondo alla chez les Anglais. Ikabo resta au village. Les Anglais vinrent après chez nous et nous dirent que la question du caoutchouc n'était pas de leur compétence.

D. Ont-ils recherché Ikabo ?

R. Non ; ils ont recherché Epondo seulement.

D. Les avez-vous vus ?

R. Oui.

D. A quelle heure sont-ils venus et à quelle heure sont-ils partis ?

Le témoin, indiquant où se trouvait le soleil, fait supposer qu'ils sont arrivés vers midi et sont repartis vers deux heures.

Dont procès-verbal lu et signé, hors le témoin illettré.

(Signé) BOSCO.

Après comparaît Ekombo, de Bossunguma, qui, interrogé, après serment, déclare :—

Epondo a perdu la main à la chasse du sanglier. . . . . . Les indigènes ont accusé Kelengo, espérant se soustraire au travail du caoutchouc.

D. Qui alla à Bonginda chez les Anglais pour leur parler ?

R. Ikabo, Bodjengene, et Epondo. Les Anglais leur dirent de s'adresser au Juge.

D. Ikabo, Bodjengene, et Epondo sont-ils restés à Boginda ou sont-ils rentrés à Bossunguma ?

R. Ils sont rentrés, hors Epondo, qui est resté à Bonginda, et lorsque les Anglais sont venus à Bossunguma Epondo les a accompagnés et est retourné avec eux à Bonginda.

D. Est-ce que les Anglais vous ont dit : Le caoutchouc est fini ?

R. Non. C'est nous qui l'avons dit.

Dont procès-verbal lu et signé, hors le témoin illettré.

(Signé) BOSCO.

Après comparaît Mondonga, de Bossunguma, qui, interrogé, après serment, déclare :—

D. Qui est allé à Bonginda pour appeler les Anglais ?

R, Bodjengene.

D. Seulement lui ?

R. Oui.

D. Ekabo et Epondo ne sont-ils pas allés à Bonginda ?

R. Oui, mais après, parce que les Anglais ont dit de vouloir les voir. Alors Ikabo est retourné au village et Epondo est resté à Bonginda. Lorsque les Anglais sont venus à Bossunguma, Epondo les a accompagnés et est rentré avec eux à Bonginda. Ikabo est resté à Bossunguma.

D. Quelle heure était-il lorsque les Anglais sont venus à Bossunguma ?

R. D'après les indications du témoin, on dirait qu'ils sont arrivés vers 1 heure de l'après-midi et sont rentrés vers 5 heures.

D. Est-ce qu'ils ont écrit à Bossunguma ?

R. Non.

D. Le comparant fait une déclaration conforme à celle des autres témoins en ce qui concerne la mutilation d'Epondo et les raisons pour lesquelles les indigènes ont accusé Kelengo.

Dont procès-verbal lu et signé, hors le témoin illettré.

(Signé) BOSCO.

Après comparaît Makurua, de Bossunguma, qui, après serment, déclare :—

J'étais à la chasse et je ne sais rien du tout. Je sais seulement que Kelengo n'a coupé aucune main.

Dont procès-verbal lu et signé, hors le témoin illettré.

(Signé) BOSCO.

Après comparaît Lopembe, de Bossunguma, qui, interrogé, après serment, déclare :—

D. Qui est allé à Bonginda parler aux Anglais ?

R. Personne. Nous n'avons pas appelé les Anglais.

D. Pourquoi les Anglais sont-ils alors venus à Bossunguma ?

R. Parce que Bodjengene les a appelés pour la question du caoutchouc, mais Kelengo n'a coupé la main à personne ; il n'a tué personne ; il n'a amarré aucune femme. . . . . .

D. Lorsque les Anglais sont arrivés à Bossunguma, Epondo où était-il ?

R. Dans leur pirogue. Il les a accompagnés à Bossunguma, et quand ils sont partis pour rentrer à Bonginda, il les a suivis et est resté avec eux.

D. Lorsque les Anglais sont venus à Bossunguma, ont-ils écrit ?

R. Oui. Ils ont écrit sur un petit papier, beaucoup plus petit que celui sur lequel vous écrivez.

Dont procès-verbal lu et signé, hors le comparant illettré.

(Signé) BOSCO.

L'an 1903, le 7 Octobre, à Bonginda, devant nous, Bosco Gennaro, Substitut à Coquilhatville, comparaît Mr. Armstrong, William Douglas, missionnaire, qui, interrogé, après serment, déclare :—

Un Dimanche soir le nommé Ikabo, accompagné par deux ou trois indigènes, vint à la Mission et demanda de parler au Consul Anglais. Je le vis, mais je ne sais pas ce qu'il dit au Consul Anglais. Les indigènes voulaient que le Consul les voyât.

D. Le Consul a-t-il interrogé lui-même Ikabo ?

R. Je pense qu'il l'interrogea avec l'aide de son interprète et d'un autre encore. Moi aussi je suis intervenu. Nous étions assis autour de la même table, et moi-même j'ai posé des questions en m'adressant à un noir, qui les répétait à Ikabo. Moi, je parlais le dialecte local de Bonginda et le noir répétait mes demandes en langue Ngombe.

D. Quelles sont les questions que vous avez posées à Ikabo ?

R. Je ne m'en rappelle pas exactement ; mais elles se référaient à la mutilation qu'on lui a faite subir.

D. Qui a dit qu'à Bossunguma il y avait un autre garçon avec la main coupée ?

R. Les indigènes qui accompagnaient Ikabo. Après, le lendemain, nous sommes allés, avec M. le Consul, à Bossunguma, avons vu Epondo, et tout le village nous dit que Kelengo l'avait mutilé. On dit aussi qu'il avait tué un homme et lui avait coupé les deux mains. Le Consul dressa procès-verbal à Bossunguma, où nous sommes restés deux ou trois heures. Nous arrivâmes vers 7 heures du matin.

D. Les indigènes se sont-ils plaints que le travail du caoutchouc était excessif et qu'ils voulaient un autre travail moins dur ?

R. Ils se plaignaient toujours du travail du caoutchouc, et dans cette occasion, ils répétèrent leurs plaintes. Nous les exhortâmes à continuer à travailler pour leurs maîtres.

D. Comment alors expliquez-vous que les gens mêmes de votre Mission ont crié deux fois, la première fois à la pirogue et la seconde au bateau où se trouvait M. Spelier, agent de La Lulonga, que le caoutchouc était fini et que les Sociétés devaient partir ?

R. La première fois j'étais dans ma maison et j'ai entendu des cris sans comprendre ce qu'ils disaient. La seconde fois j'étais dans l'église ; j'ai entendu encore des cris, sans pourtant comprendre ce qu'on disait ; mais, ayant vu les boys qui criaient, je les ai réprimandés. Ils m'ont répondu qu'ils saluaient leurs amis qui étaient sur le bateau, et en ce qui concerne la première fois, ayant fait une enquête, on m'a dit que c'étaient des gens qui n'appartenaient pas à la Mission qui avaient crié, des Ngombe et des indigènes de Bokemjola (près de Boieka).

D. Pourtant, croyez-vous que ces cris aient été réellement poussés ?

R. Il est très possible que le caoutchouc est la bête noire des indigènes. Je ne crois pas que les hommes de la Mission aient poussé ces cris, puisqu'ils ne s'occupent pas de caoutchouc, et nous sommes très prudents à ce sujet, ayant soin de ne pas en parler.

D. Comment expliquez-vous le bruit que maintenant on ne doit plus faire de caoutchouc et que le Consul Anglais allait supprimer ce travail dans toute la rivière ?

R. Le désir est père de la pensée. Les noirs sont paresseux, et ils seraient capables de tout complot pour éviter de travailler, partant de faire du caoutchouc. Du reste, lorsque le Consul Anglais est allé à Bossunguma, il a dit qu'il aurait porté à la connaissance de la justice le crime, dont on accusait Kelengo, mais il n'a pas dit un mot qui pût être interprété, soit comme instigation à ne pas travailler, soit comme promesse de son intercession près des autorités de l'État, pour la suppression ou la diminution du travail.

D. D'après votre opinion, depuis combien de temps la mutilation a eu lieu ?

R. Je ne saurais pas, mais on dit depuis six mois.

Dont procès-verbal lu et signé.

(Signé) BOSCO.

(Signé) W.-D. ARMSTRONG.

Après comparaît Epondo, de Bossunguma. Le comparant a la main gauche coupée. Il prête serment et déclare :—

Il ne comprend que le Ngombe, et comme à la Mission Anglaise il n'y a personne qui connaisse cette langue, nous l'interrogeons, par l'entremise de son frère Nnele, boy de la Mission Anglaise, qui prête serment de remplir fidèlement la mission qui lui est confiée, et nous procédons à l'interrogatoire d'Epondo.

D. Qui vous a coupé la main ?

R. Kelengo.

D. Pourquoi ?

R. Pour le caoutchouc. Il est venu faire la guerre dans notre village et a tué Elua et m'a coupé une main. Je suis tombé presque mort. Je me suis réveillé après un certain temps et je me suis trouvé sans main.

D. Connaissez-vous Bossole ?

R. Non ; je connais Kelengo.

D. Etes-vous sûr que c'est Kelengo qui vous a coupé la main ? Ce n'est pas Bossole ?

R. Non ; c'est Kelengo.

*   *   *   *   *

D. Dans le temps, n'êtes-vous pas allé chez les Bangala ?

R. Non ; je suis resté toujours dans mon village.

D. Votre main ne vous a-t-elle pas été enlevée par un sanglier ?

R. Non. Kelengo me l'a coupée.

Dont procès-verbal lu et signé, hors le témoin illettré.

(Signé) BOSCO

Après nous interrogeons Nnele, qui, après serment, déclare :—

Je ne savais pas que mon frère avait la main coupée. Je le vis revenir avec les Anglais avec la main coupée, et c'est alors qu'il m'apprit que c'était Kelengo qui la lui avait coupée.

Dont procès-verbal lu et signé.

(Signé) BOSCO.

(Signé) NNELE.

Après comparaît nouvellement Mr. Armstrong, qui, après serment, déclare :—

D. Depuis combien Nnele est au service de la Mission ?

R. Depuis environ cinq ans.

D. Vous a-t-il jamais dit d'avoir un frère sans une main ?

R. Non ; jamais.

Dont procès-verbal lu et signé.

(Signé) BOSCO.

(Signé) W.-D. ARMSTRONG.

Nous, Substitut, donnons ordre à Epondo de nous suivre à Mampoko.

Après, le même jour, à Mampoko, comparaît nouvellement Epondo, que nous interrogeons nouvellement avec l'aide de Korony, qui prête entre nos mains le serment d'accomplir fidèlement la mission d'interprète qui lui est confiée. Epondo prête nouvellement serment et déclare :—

D. Êtes-vous esclave de Bandebonja ? Vous a-t-il conduit dans la Ngiri ?

R. Je ne connais ni Bandebonja ni la Ngiri.

D. N'avez-vous jamais été blessé à la chasse du sanglier ? Ne vous a-t-il pas mordu à la main ?

R. Non ; jamais. Kelengo m'a coupé la main.

D. Les habitants de votre village ne vous ont-ils pas suggéré d'accuser Kelengo près des Anglais pour se soustraire au travail du caoutchouc ?

R. Il y a presque un mois, deux Anglais sont venus à notre village et nous ont dit : Beaucoup de monde meurt pour le caoutchouc. Dorénavant vous ne ferez plus de caoutchouc, vous ferez seulement la kwanga pour nous.

Nous, Substitut, appelons, comme second interprète, Munenge Gabriel, qui, après serment, traduit la réponse d'Epondo identiquement à Korony. La réponse est rappelée deux fois.

D. Qui étaient ces Anglais ?

R. Torongo et Mongougolo. Ils m'ont vu, m'ont questionné et m'ont fait aller avec eux à Bonginda. Les habitants de mon village ne m'ont jamais suggéré de dire que Kelengo m'avait coupé la main. Les Anglais m'ont fait monter dans leur bateau et m'ont conduit à Coquilhatville pour me montrer au Juge, mais le Juge était dans l'Ubangi. Alors nous sommes allés à Bolengi, et après Mongongolo est allé en Europe et moi je suis retourné en pirogue à Bonginda.

D. Les Anglais vous ont-ils photographié ?

R. Oui, à Bonginda et à Lulanga. Ils m'ont dit de mettre bien en évidence le moignon. Il y avait Nnele, Mongongolo, Torongo et autres blancs dont je ne connais pas les noms. Ils étaient les blancs de Lulanga. Mongongolo a porté avec six photographies.

Dont procès-verbal lu et signé, hors le témoin illettré.

(Signé) BOSCO.

L'an 1903, le 8 Octobre, devant nous, Substitut, comparaît Bofoko, Chef du village Ikandja. Comparaît aussi, comme interprète, le nommé Korony, qui prête entre nos mains le serment de remplir fidèlement la mission qui lui est confiée. Le comparant Bofoko prête serment et déclare :—

D. Savez-vous qui a coupé la main d'Epondo . . . . . ?

R. Personne n'a coupé la main d'Epondo. Il est allé avec son maître Makekele à la chasse au sanglier à Malela, dans le district des Bangala, et le sanglier lui a arraché la main. C'est lui-même qui, à son retour dans son village, nous a raconté d'avoir été victime de cet accident de chasse . . . . .

D. Lorsque d'après les coutumes indigènes, on coupe une main pour punir quelqu'un, quelle est la main que l'on coupe ?

R. Toujours la main droite.

D. Pourquoi alors les habitants de Bossunguma ont-ils accusé Kelengo d'avoir commis ces atrocités ?

R. Parce qu'ils trouvent que le travail du caoutchouc est trop dur et ont cru de pouvoir s'en libérer, et pour les induire à s'en occuper, ils sont allés leur conter des mensonges.

D. Pourquoi vous-même avez-vous déclaré au Consul Anglais avoir vu la main coupée par terre ; le sang coulait et les habitants du village qui couraient dans toutes les directions ?

R. Je n'ai pas parlé avec les Anglais. Je ne les ai pas même vus. Quand ils sont arrivés à Bossunguma, je n'étais pas là.

D. Vous mentez, parce que le Consul Anglais déclare avoir parlé avec vous.

R. Oui, c'est vrai. J'y étais. J'ai dit comme les autres. Tout le monde se plaignait que le travail du caoutchouc était trop dur.

D. Et le Consul Anglais qu'est-ce qu'il a dit ?

R. Il a dit qu'il aurait parlé au Juge et il a écrit un grand papier pour vous.

D. Donc, vous n'avez pas vu la main coupée, le sang qui coulait, les gens qui se sauvaient dans toutes les directions ?

R. Non ; je n'ai rien vu.

D. Est-ce que Kelengo aurait tué ou blessé quelqu'un ? A-t-il amarré des femmes ?

R. Non ; il n'a tué personne. Il n'a amarré aucune femme. On a dit comme ça pour interposer les Anglais, pour faire voir que le blanc était violent.

D. Où sont Tonbebola, Mileli, Eykela, Alondi, Boningeni, Mopili ? Pourquoi ne sont-ils pas venus ?

R. Ils sont dans la forêt ; ils ont peur.

Dont procès-verbal lu et signé, hors le témoin illettré.

(Signé) BOSCO.

Après comparaît Mongombe, d'Ikondju, qui, après serment, déclare :

J'atteste qu'Epondo, d'après ce que lui-même a raconté, a perdu la main gauche à la chasse au sanglier. La bête blessée l'aurait attaqué et lui aurait arraché la main. Ce ne serait pas arrivé dans le village, mais dans le pays des Bangala, où il était avec un homme dont j'ignore le nom . . . . .

D. Lorsque les indigènes coupent les mains pour punir ou pour se venger, coupent-ils la main droite ou la main gauche ?

R. Toujours la main droite.

D. Pourquoi a-t-on accusé Kelengo ?

R. Nous sommes fatigués du caoutchouc et avons voulu obtenir une diminution de travail avec l'aide du Chef des Anglais, en lui montrant la violence du blanc. En effet les Anglais sont arrivés et ont fait un grand papier pour le Juge. Leur Chef disait : "Nous verrons, nous verrons."

D. Savez-vous si Kelengo a tué quelqu'un, s'ils ont amarré des femmes ?

R. Non. Il n'a tué personne et il n'a amarré aucune femme.

D. Où sont Tondebola, Molili, Eykela, Alondi, Bonsigeni, Mopili ?

R. En fuite ; ils ont peur.

Dont procès-verbal lu et signé, hors le témoin illettré.

(Signé) BOSCO.

Après nous interrogeons successivement Lopimbe, de Bassombwene, Boloko, de Bossonguma Alekois, de Bassombwene, Itoke et Itobe, de Bossunguma, et leur posons les mêmes questions que nous avons posées aux deux précédents témoins. Les comparants prêtent serment et répondent identiquement concordément à Botoko et Monjombeki, affirmant l'innocence absolue de Kelengo.

(Signé) BOSCO.

Après comparaît nouvellement Epondo, qui prête serment et déclare :

D. Persistez-vous à accuser Kelengo de vous avoir coupé la main gauche ?

R. Non ; j'ai menti.

D. Racontez alors comment et quand vous avez perdu la main.

R. J'étais esclave de Monkekola, à Malele, dans le district des Bangala. Un jour, j'allai avec lui à la chasse au sanglier. Il en blessa un avec une lance, et alors la bête, devenue furieuse, m'attaqua. Je tâchai de me sauver avec la suite, mais je tombai, le sanglier fut bientôt sur moi, m'arrachant la main gauche, au ventre et à la hanche gauche. Le comparant montre les cicatrices aux endroits désignés et spontanément se met par terre pour faire voir dans quelle position il se trouvait lorsqu'il fut attaqué et blessé par le sanglier.

D. Depuis combien de temps cet accident vous est-il arrivé ?

R. Je ne me rappelle pas. C'est depuis longtemps.

D. Pourquoi alors aviez-vous accusé Kelengo ?

R. Parce que Momaketa, un des Chefs de Bossunguma, me l'a dit et après tous les habitants de mon village me l'ont répété.

Dont procès-verbal lu et signé, hors le comparant illettré.

(Signé) BOSCO.

Annexe 4.

(A.)

État Indépendant du Congo.

(Département de l'Intérieur.)

District de , No. .[1]

Chefferies Indigènes.

(Arrêté du 2 Janvier, 1892.—Formule No. 1.)

Procès-verbal d'Investiture.

L'an 1880 le jour du mois d Nous, Commissaire de District d , avons confirmé[2] chef de[3]

et de la région de [4]

relevant du Chef de [5] dans l'autorité qui lui est attribuée par les us et coutumes locaux en tant qu'ils n'ont rien de contraire à l'ordre public ni aux lois de l'État et lui avons fait remise de l'insigne décrit à l'Article 3 de l'Arrêté du 2 Janvier, 1892.

Le Chef prédésigné s'est engagé à fournir les prestations annuelles indiquées au tableau ci-annexé et à exécuter ou faire exécuter les travaux y mentionnés.

De tout quoi nous avons dressé le présent procès-verbal en double original aux jour, mois et an que dessus.

Le Commissaire de District,

Le Chef reconnu,

N.B.—Ce Chef est le successeur du Chef confirmé suivant le procès-verbal No. .

(B.)

Chefferies indigènes reconnues. District de .

Tableau Statistique Chefferie de .

(Arrêté du 2 Janvier, 1892.—Formule No. 2.)

Villages soumis à l'Autorité du Chef.	Leur Situation et leurs Limites.	Noms des Sous-Chefs et des Notables.	Nombre des Cases.	Population.			Observations.
				Hommes.	Femmes.	Enfants.	

[1]. Numéro d'ordre du procès-verbal.
[2]. Nom du Chef reconnu.
[3]. Nom du village ou des villages sous la dépendance du Chef.
[4]. Région sur laquelle il exerce son autorité.—Mentionner si l'investiture lui a été donnée pour toute la région.
[5]. Nom du Chef auquel il peut être soumis.

(C)

Chefferies indigènes reconnues. District de .

TABLEAU des prestations annuelles à fournir par le Chef de .

(Arrêté du 2 Janvier, 1892.—Formule No. 3.)

Villages soumis à l'Autorité du Chef.	Produits à fournir par chaque Village.	Corvées.	Travailleurs.	Soldats.	Travaux à Exécuter.	Observations.

Le Chef indigène reconnu,

Le Commissaire de District,

Annexe 5.

(A.)

Circulaire Interprétative des Prescriptions concernant les Formalités du Permis de Port d'Armes.

Boma, le 12 *Mars*, 1897.

J'ai constaté, au sujet des prescriptions concernant les formalités du permis de port d'armes, des divergences d'interprétation qu'il convient de dissiper.

Certaines personnes pensent, à tort, qu'il suffit de se munir *d'un seul* permis de port d'armes, sans avoir à tenir compte ni de l'usage qui sera fait des armes importées, ni de leur lieu de destination.

Ainsi que le dit le dernier paragraphe de ma Circulaire A, VI, 58, du 8 Juillet, 1893, la taxe de 20 fr., exigée pour la délivrance des permis de port d'armes, ne doit être perçue *qu'une seule fois par permis, quelle que soit la quantité d'armes y figurant;* mais il doit être bien entendu qu'il faut un permis *distinct par destination des armes*, c'est-à-dire, qu'autre le permis individuel, il y a le permis par établissement et par bateau.

Les capitas qui, dans le Haut-Congo, parcourent le pays pour compte de commerçants et qui sont pourvus d'un fusil, doivent également être munis d'un permis de port d'armes.

Je rappelle à ce propos que les capitas ne peuvent avoir en leur possession aucune arme perfectionnée autre que le fusil à piston *non rayé;* des permis de port d'armes ne pourront, en conséquence, leur être délivrés que pour des fusils de l'espèce, et ceux concernant des fusils, " Albini " ou " Chassepot " qui se trouveraient entre leurs mains devraient être retirés.

Les commerçants peuvent seuls disposer, pour la défense éventuelle de leurs factoreries et bateaux de fusils " Albini," " Chassepot " ou autres armes rayées.

Jusqu'ici on s'était servi d'un imprimé, uniforme pour la délivrance de permis de port d'armes.

Afin que des erreurs ne puissent plus se produire à l'avenir, il sera fait usage, selon le cas, des imprimés dont les modèles sont ci-contre.

Celui portant la lettre (A) est l'imprimé ancien dont l'emploi sera exclusivement réservé à la délivrance de permis individuels.

Celui portant la lettre (B) est l'imprimé qui servira aux permis à délivrer pour des armes destinées à la défense d'un établissement ou d'un bateau.

Celui portant la lettre (C) est l'imprimé à utiliser pour les permis se rapportant aux fusils à piston confiés aux capitas.

Ces permis ne doivent pas indiquer les noms des capitas qui en sont porteurs; ils peuvent être établis au nom d'un établissement et chaque permis a une durée de validité de cinq années pour une *même* arme.

Les Commissaires de District, Chefs de Zone, et Chefs de Poste ou leurs délégués ont à exercer une surveillance très sérieuse pour empêcher que les armes perfectionnées dont disposent les commerçants ne passent aux mains des indigènes.

Ils ont à vérifier minutieusement les permis de port d'armes et à faire procéder à des poursuites lorsque ceux-ci ne sont pas strictement en règle. Ils ont notamment à examiner si le nombre d'armes existant correspond bien à celui renseigné sur les permis, et à faire saisir les armes pour lesquelles les formalités prescrites n'auraient pas été accomplies.

Je crois utile de rappeler, au sujet des permis de port d'armes, le § 2 de l'Article VI du Décret du 10 Mars, 1892 (" Bulletin Officiel " de 1892, p. 14), sur les armes à feu:

"Le porteur d'un permis de port d'armes peut être requis, en tout temps, par le Commissaire de District compétent de justifier de la possession de l'arme ou des armes renseignées sur ce permis ; à défaut de cette justification, il encourra les pénalités prévues par l'Article IX du Décret."[1]

Le Gouverneur-Général,
(Signé) WAHIS.

(B.)

Circulaire rappelant les Prescriptions sur l'Importation et la Détention des Armes à Feu perfectionnées.

Boma, le 31 *Mai*, 1900.

J'ai acquis la certitude que les commerçants établis sur le territoire de l'État ne font aucun effort, malgré les pressantes recommandations qui leur ont été adressées, pour remplir les obligations imposées par la législation sur les armes à feu.

Quantité d'armes qu'ils ont été autorisés à importer pour la défense des établissements de négoce, des bateaux et la protection des capitas de négoce ne sont pas inscrites sur les permis réglementaires ou figurent sur des permis périmés, ou encore ont disparu sans qu'ils en aient été donné connaissance aux autorités.

J'ai l'honneur d'attirer encore l'attention des intéressés sur les dispositions législatives en vigueur en cette matière, en les prévenant que je donne les ordres les plus sévères pour la recherche des infractions et l'application rigoureuse des pénalités édictées par l'Article 9 du Décret du 10 Mars, 1892, reproduit ci-après :

"Quiconque commettra ou laissera commettre par ses subordonnés des infractions au présent Décret, ainsi qu'aux Arrêtés et Règlements d'exécution, sera puni de 100 fr. à 1,000 fr. d'amende et de servitude pénale n'excédant pas une année, ou de l'une de ces peines seulement. . . . ."

L'importation de toute arme perfectionnée, y compris le fusil à *piston non rayé*, est subordonnée à la délivrance d'un permis de port d'armes.

Celui-ci se subdivise, suivant la destination des armes, en trois catégories :

1. Le permis individuel ou particulier ;
2. Le permis collectif applicable aux armes destinées à la défense des établissements de commerce ou des bateaux ; il peut comprendre, suivant le cas, vingt-cinq ou quinze fusils, maximum d'armes autorisées par le Gouvernement, pour un établissement ou un bateau ;
3. Le permis de capita. Celui-ci ne peut comprendre qu'une seule arme, le fusil à piston *non rayé*. Il ne doit pas indiquer le nom du capita qui en est porteur, mais le nom de l'établissement auquel ce dernier est attaché.

Ce sont là les trois cas bien déterminés, où l'importation et l'usage des armes perfectionnées sont autorisés.

Les armes ne peuvent, en aucune circonstance, être distraites, sans autorisation préalable, de leur première destination.

Elles ne peuvent, sous aucun prétexte, être employées à des incursions à l'intérieur des terres. La répression de séditions ou d'actes de brigandage est *inclusivement* réservée aux autorités de l'État.

Tout permis de port d'armes est valable pour cinq ans.

Le porteur d'un permis peut être requis en tout temps par les Commissaires de District, leurs délégués ou les agents du service des finances, de justifier de la possession de l'arme ou des armes renseignées sur ce permis ; à défaut de cette justification, il encourra les pénalités prévues par l'Article 9 du Décret du 10 Mars, 1892. (Article 6 du Décret du 10 Mars, 1892, et Arrêté du 26 Mars, 1900.)

Si, dans certaines circonstances, des chefs de factoreries avaient à diriger des convois de négoce, soit par voie d'eau, soit par terre, à travers des régions qu'ils jugeraient peu sûres, ils auraient, dans chaque cas, à demander l'escorte nécessaire au Commissaire du District dans lequel ils se trouvent, ou au Chef du Poste de l'État le plus rapproché.

Cette escorte ne peut, en aucune circonstance, être constituée par des agents à leur service, à moins qu'ils n'aient obtenu, à ce sujet, un permis qui ne pourra être délivré que par le Commissaire de District, et qui devra se trouver entre les mains du chef de l'escorte et pouvoir être exhibé à tout agent de l'État chargé du contrôle des armes.

Les contraventions aux différentes prescriptions ci-dessus édictées, pourront amener, outre les pénalités, la fermeture des établissements qui auront contrevenu à la loi.

Le Gouverneur-Général,
(Signé) WAHIS.

---

[1]. Article 9 du Décret du 10 Mars, 1892 ("Bulletin Officiel" de 1892, p. 14) :—

"Quiconque commettra ou laissera commettre par des subordonnés, des infractions au présent Décret, ainsi qu'aux Arrêtés et Règlements d'exécution, sera puni de 100 à 1,000 fr. d'amende et de servitude pénale n'excédant pas une année, ou de l'une de ces peines seulement. La peine de servitude pénale sera toujours prononcée, et elle pourra être portée à cinq ans lorsque le délinquant se sera livré au trafic des armes à feu ou de leurs munitions dans les régions où sévit la Traite.

"Dans les cas prévus ci-dessus, les armes, la poudre, les balles, et cartouches sont confisquées."

(C.)

Circulaire relative aux Prescriptions sur la Détention des Armes à Feu perfectionnées à l'Usage des Maisons de Commerce.

Boma, le 28 Novembre, 1900.

Je constate par des rapports qui me sont adressés des diverses parties du territoire, que les prescriptions en matière d'armes à feu perfectionnées à l'usage des Sociétés commerciales ne reçoivent pas leur exécution.

Depuis la publication, en Juin dernier, de ma Circulaire No. 30/g du 31 Mai, 1900, qui a été adressée à tous les chefs des firmes commerciales établies dans l'État, ces derniers auraient pu se mettre en règle vis-à-vis de la loi, soit en demandant des permis de port d'armes, soit en requérant les modifications nécessaires aux permis qu'ils possèdent déjà, mais qui ne correspondent plus à l'armement de leurs factoreries, ou au nombre maximum fixé par la loi, pour un établissement.

Ils auraient pu donner des instructions formelles à leurs agents, à l'effet de leur défendre de faire servir les armes à tir rapide à d'autres usages qu'à celui de la défense des établissements de négoce, et les fusils à piston à couvrir des convois de négoce, sans autorisation préalable.

Il m'a été signalé que ces dernières armes étaient parfois confiées à des indigènes non munis de licences.

L'inobservation des dispositions législatives et réglementaires régissant l'importation et la détention des armes à feu, doit amener des désordres qu'il faut empêcher.

Ce n'est qu'en sévissant avec rigueur contre les personnes en faute qu'on parviendra à faire respecter la loi.

Je prescris donc à tous les fonctionnaires chargés des fonctions d'officier de police judiciaire et notamment les Commissaires de District, les Chefs de Zone, et leurs Chefs de Poste, de vérifier, chacun dans son ressort, les permis de port d'armes et l'armement des factoreries qui y sont établies. Toutes les infractions seront constatées par procès-verbaux dont une expédition me sera transmise concurremment avec celle qui doit être remise au Parquet.

Les armes, objet du délit, devront être saisies.

Ces vérifications doivent commencer dès la réception de la présente Circulaire.

Les autorités territoriales me feront rapport, à bref délai, sur les prescriptions qui y sont contenues.

Le Gouverneur-Général,
(Signé) WAHIS.

(D.)

Circulaire faisant suite à l'Arrêté du 30 *Avril*, 1901, *sur les Permis de Port d'Armes édictant des Règles en ce qui concerne le système qui sera dorénavant suivi en cette matière, ainsi que concernant certaines mesures précautionnelles que les Commissaires de District et les Chefs de Zone pourront prescrire et la sanction administrative qui y sera attachée.*

Boma, le 30 *Avril*, 1901.

De récents événements ont encore démontré que les prescriptions en matière d'armes à feu étaient à chaque instant violées par les chefs ou gérants des établissements de commerce en dépit des nombreux avis de l'autorité.

Il a aussi été établi que le dépôt d'un certain nombre de fusils perfectionnés dans ces établissements pouvait, à d'autres égards, compromettre la sécurité publique, en ce que les armes pouvaient à un moment donné être utilisées par le personnel indigène de l'établissement pour former des bandes armées dont les premiers méfaits portaient sur la vie des Européens qui les employaient et sur leur propriété.

Le danger est d'autant plus grand que le personnel indigène des établissements de commerce est constitué souvent par d'anciens militaires, qui connaissent bien le maniement des armes perfectionnées.

Il y a donc lieu de prendre de nouvelles mesures non seulement pour renforcer les moyens que la loi met à la disposition de l'autorité pour faire respecter par les gérants d'établissements de commerce les prohibitions édictées notamment par ma Circulaire No. 30/g du 31 Mai, 1900, mais également pour empêcher que les dépôts d'armes perfectionnées autorisées par le Gouvernement dans les établissements de commerce ou à bord des bateaux, et pour la défense de ces établissements ou de ces bateaux, ne donnent point à des rebelles à la loi la possibilité de commettre les pires méfaits.

En ce qui concerne le premier point, mon Arrêté en date de ce jour a pour but d'assurer l'action répressive contre ceux qui, contrairement aux règles qui avaient été déterminées, notamment par ma Circulaire 30/g du 31 Mai, 1900, déplaceraient les armes dont l'introduction et la détention ont été permises pour la défense des établissements de commerce ou des bateaux.

D'après le système qui sera dorénavant suivi, les permis de port d'armes (B) de la Circulaire du 12 Mars, 1897, seront délivré au nom du Directeur ou Chef en Afrique de la Société ou de l'entreprise qui a sollicité l'introduction et la détention de ces armes; le permis devra stipuler, en vertu de l'Article 1er de l'Arrêté en date de ce jour, à quel établissement les armes, ainsi que les munitions y afférentes, sont destinées, et prescrire l'obligation de justifier l'emploi de celles-ci.

Les anciens permis délivrés en conformité avec la Circulaire du 12 Mars, 1897, seront modifiés endéans le délai de six mois ; les Directeurs ou Chefs des Sociétés ou entreprises seront invités par le Receveur des Impôts compétent à représenter les permis actuellement existants, et à former des demandes en conformité avec l'Article 2 de mon Arrêté en date de ce jour. L'Administration en délivrant de nouveaux permis stipulera que les armes et les munitions y afférentes ne pourront sortir des établissements auxquels elles sont destinées.

La délivrance de permis pour les armes destinées à de nouveaux établissements se fera dans les mêmes conditions.

La sanction pénale pourra s'exercer ainsi, en conformité avec l'Article 9 du Décret du 12 Mars, 1892, contre le gérant de l'établissement qui se servirait des armes et des munitions dans un but autre que celui pour lequel le permis a été délivré, et le cas échéant, contre le Directeur de la Société ou entreprise.

Les permis devront être renouvelés, ou tout au moins modifiés, lorsque la direction de la Société ou de l'entreprise sera donnée à une autre personne que celle au nom de laquelle le permis a été délivré.

Les permis pour capita, permis (C) de la Circulaire du 12 Mars, 1897, seront également délivrés à titre individuel soit par le Commissaire de District ou Chef de Zone, soit par un agent désigné par eux.

La même sanction prévue par l'Article 9 du Décret du 12 Mars, 1892, atteindra l'individu qui serait porteur d'un fusil à piston sans avoir de permis régulier délivré en son nom, et, le cas échéant, le Directeur ou Gérant de la Société, de l'établissement, ou de l'entreprise.

De plus, sans préjudice aux poursuites répressives éventuelles, les infractions aux règles prescrites, notamment par mon Arrêté en date de ce jour, en ce qui concerne les armes pour lesquelles un permis est délivré, pourront avoir pour suite le retrait du permis, quelles que soient les conséquences qui en résulteraient pour l'établissement.

Pour satisfaire à l'autre intérêt que je signale au début de cette Circulaire, je soumets de plus la délivrance du permis (B) et (C) à l'engagement pour les chefs d'établissements d'admettre et de respecter les mesures précautionnelles que le Commissaire de District ou Chef de Zone croira devoir prescrire pour prévenir tout danger, et qui pourront être différentes selon les circonstances ; ainsi ces fonctionnaires pourront, et devront dans la majorité des cas, prescrire :—

(*a.*) Que les armes perfectionnées, et les munitions destinées à l'établissement ou au bateau (ou même les fusils à piston du moment que leur nombre est supérieur à cinq), soient remises dans un local spécial, présentant des garanties suffisantes de solidité pour empêcher l'effraction, fermé soigneusement, et de telle sorte que l'accès ne puisse en être possible qu'au blanc qui en détient les clefs ;

(*b.*) Que la garde en soit confiée à un homme sûr ;

(*c.*) Que l'établissement lui soumette mensuellement la liste du personnel indigène qu'il emploie en renseignant, pour chacun des membres de celui-ci, la tribu à laquelle il appartient, ses services antérieurs, et tous autres renseignements utiles, notamment quant à son esprit, et sans préjudice aux prescriptions de l'Article 14 du Décret du 8 Novembre, 1888, de l'Article 11 de l'Arrêté du 1er Janvier, 1890, celles de l'Article 46 du Décret du 4 Mai, 1895, et celles de l'Arrêté du 4 Avril, 1899.

Les Commissaires de District et Chefs de Zone veilleront à la stricte observation des mesures qu'ils auront édictées à ce sujet ; ils visiteront, soit par eux-mêmes, soit par délégués, le plus souvent possible, les établissements auxquels des permis (B) et (C) ont été accordés, s'assureront que les prescriptions légales ou administratives à ce sujet sont rigoureusement respectés et contrôleront le personnel.

Dans les cas où des infractions à la loi ou aux mesures précautionnelles qu'ils auraient édictées seront relevées, ou que d'une façon quelconque et par suite de circonstances spéciales, le dépôt d'armes perfectionnées auxquelles s'appliquent les permis collectifs (B) et (C) serait une cause de danger pour la sécurité générale, ils m'en référeront en me faisant connaître d'une façon détaillée les infractions ou la situation, de façon à me mettre à même de juger en connaissance de cause s'il y a lieu ou non de retirer le permis.

Ils veilleront, dans tous les cas où il y aura eu révocation ou retrait du permis, à ce que les armes et munitions qui y sont portées soient déposées dans un entrepôt public pour telle suite qu'il conviendra.

Le Gouverneur-Général,
(Signé) WAHIS.

No. 2.

The Marquess of Lansdowne to Sir C. Phipps.

Sir, *Foreign Office, April* 19, 1904.

THE "Notes" prepared by the Congo Government, and handed to you on the 13th ultimo as a preliminary reply to Mr. Casement's report, contain statements, to the careful consideration of which some time must be devoted.

His Majesty's Government desire, however, to express at once their great satisfaction at learning that the Congo Government concur in their view of the general principles which should prevail in dealing with the native African races, and at the announcement that a searching and impartial inquiry will be made into the allegations against the administration of the Free State, and that if real abuses or the necessity for reform should be thereby disclosed, the central Government will act as the necessities of the case may demand.

His Majesty's Government have every confidence that an investigation of this character will be followed by the redress of any grievances or actual wrongs which may be proved to exist, and that if the present administrative system should be found to provide no adequate security against the abuse of power by those who are employed by the State, or by the Companies over which the State has control, the necessary steps will be taken to remedy these grave defects. His Majesty's Government have been actuated in this matter by no other motive than a desire to arrive at the truth, and to fulfil the obligation which is incumbent upon all the Powers who were parties to the Berlin Act, "to watch, so far as each may be able, over the preservation of the native tribes, and to care for the improvement of the conditions of their moral and material well-being." They are, therefore, glad to observe that the notes do not indorse the regrettable and unfounded insinuation contained in M. de Cuvelier's communication of the 17th September, 1903, that the interests of humanity have been used in this country as a pretext to conceal designs for the abolition and partition of the Congo State.

The request made in the notes for the full text of Mr. Casement's report raises a question of considerable difficulty.

Personal names and indications of place and date were suppressed, not from any want of confidence in the central Government at Brussels, but from the knowledge that if these particulars were published they would of course be accessible to the very officials in the Congo to whom abuses are attributed. The knowledge of these particulars would have given these persons opportunities for exercising pressure upon those who gave evidence, or for concealing the evidence of their own malpractices, so as to render impossible that effective inquiry which it is the object of the Congo Government to secure. These apprehensions appear, in some degree at least, to be borne out by the fact, mentioned in the "Notes" when quoting M. Bosco's report, that those who gave evidence in the Epondo Case had taken flight, and that all efforts to find them had been fruitless. His Majesty's Government are naturally desirous to further, so far as lies in their power, the inquiry which they are now assured will take place. They feel bound, however, to proceed on this point with the utmost caution, and, before considering whether they can hand over the complete text of the report, they must ask whether the Congo Government will accept full responsibility for the manner in which the information thus furnished is used, and whether they will communicate to His Majesty's Government the measures which they are prepared to adopt and enforce in order to protect the witnesses, both European and native, from any violence or acts of retaliation on the part of those against whom they have given evidence.

With regard to the application, renewed in the "Notes," for previous reports from British Consular officers, it is necessary to explain that these reports, though forwarding testimony upon which reliance could apparently be placed, were founded on hearsay, and lacked the authority of personal observation, without which His Majesty's Government were unwilling to come to any definite conclusion unfavourable to the administration of the Congo State. Moreover, some of the reports are of old date; the Congo State have admittedly been very active in pushing forward occupation of the country, and it would be unjust to bring forward statements regarding a condition of affairs which may have entirely passed away. In the despatch of the 8th August, 1903, His Majesty's Government explicitly declared that they were unaware to what extent the allegations made against the Congo State might be true, and it was in order to obtain direct and personal information as to the state of things actually existing that Mr. Casement undertook the journey of which the results are recorded in his report.

I request you to read this despatch to M. de Cuvelier, and to hand a copy of it to his Excellency. Copies will be transmitted to the Powers with which, as Parties to the Berlin Act, His Majesty's Government have been in communication.

I am, &c.

(Signed) LANSDOWNE.

No. 3.

Acting Consul Nightingale to the Marquess of Lansdowne.—(*Received May* 3.)

(Extract.) *Boma, April* 7, 1904.

I HAVE the honour to transmit herewith, for your Lordship's information, a copy of the Judgment in Appeal in the cases of M. Caudron and Silvanus Jones.

I am informed that the Procureur d'État demanded the severest punishment for Caudron, accusing him of being the direct cause of the murder in cold blood of over 122 natives (this is the number verified, but many more are supposed to have been murdered of which there is no record) during his expeditions and raids in the Mongalla district for the obtainment of rubber, in order to reap a handsome commission on his extortions from the natives.

The lawyer for the defence sought, on the other hand, to prove by documents and other evidence that Caudron committed no individual act save the accidental shooting of the women at Muibembetti; that the whole of the responsibility of the régime in vogue in Mongalla lay at the door of the State, who employed the Société Commerciale Anversoise as its tax collector, the State itself being half shareholder and taking three-fourths of all the profits of the Company; that the Company operated on the Domaine Privé of the State, having no lands of its own; that all the attacks on the natives were ordered by the Commissaire-General of the district, who gave written orders to his deputies, and that Caudron was only requisitioned to accompany those expeditions as being the only person who knew every nook and corner of the Mongalla River.

As your Lordship will observe, Caudron's sentence was reduced from twenty years' penal servitude to fifteen years', whilst that of Silvanus Jones, of ten years, was upheld, but with a strong recommendation for a speedy reduction of the sentence, which was the least the Court could impose.

After the Judgment in Appeal, I obtained permission from the Vice-Governor-General to go and visit Jones in prison, and inclosed I send a note of my interview with him.

On speaking to the Director of Justice, after my interview with Jones, I mentioned the fact that the man had not been defended by counsel, to which the Director replied that his case ran concurrently with that of Caudron's, and that there was no necessity for him to employ counsel.

As a matter of fact, Jones was not asked whether he wished to employ counsel to defend him, neither was he (according to his statement) aware of the nature of the charges made against him. He had money, and would have engaged some one to defend him had he known what those charges were. He was, he said, under the impression that he had been brought to Boma as a witness against Caudron.

I inclose a further note, given me by the Director of Justice, which gives the different Decrees dealing with arms and showing the infractions committed by Jones.

"Out of evil comes good" is an old saying, and it is my opinion that, if the Upper Congo were thrown open to free trade and the concessionnaire Companies done away with, when once confidence were restored amongst the natives and they were given to understand that they could bring in and sell their produce to whomsoever they pleased, the Congo State would in a short while become the biggest export market for rubber in the world.

The African native is a born trader, and now it is so well known the value the white men set upon rubber they would naturally commence to bring it in when once confidence were fully restored. The State would reap its reward in the trading licences and export duties. And that is all it is fairly entitled to.

Before closing I would call your Lordship's attention to the fact that, in the "Bulletin Officiel" (No. 12) for last December there is a Decree published giving powers to the agents of the Katanga Company to collect the State taxes. This means that the same abuses may go on in the Katanga country as have hitherto gone on in the Mongalla district, unless most stringent measures are adopted to prevent them.

Inclosure 1 in No. 3.

Judgment in Appeal respecting the Cases of M. Caudron and S. Jones.

Le Tribunal d'Appel de Bome, siégeant en Matière Pénale, a rendu l'Arrêt suivant :—

Audience Publique du 15 Mars, 1904.

(No. du role 395.)
En cause : Ministère Public contre—

(1) CAUDRON, PHILLIP CHARLES FRANÇOIS, né à Auderlecht, Belgique, Chef de Zone commercial de la Melo, au service de la Société Anversoise du Commerce au Congo ; et

(2) Jones, Silvanus, originaire de Lagos, clerc au service de la même Société :

Prévenus—le premier à la fin de l'année 1902, et au commencement de l'année 1903, alors qu'il était Chef de Zone commercial de la Melo, au service de la Société Anversoise du Commerce au Congo :

1. D'avoir fait attaquer pendant la nuit le village de Liboké par les hommes à fusil de la Société armés d'Albini, provoquant ainsi directement la mort d'un certain nombre d'indigènes du dit village de Liboké ;

2. D'avoir circulé avec une troupe composée de soixante soldats de l'État et de vingt hommes à fusil de la Société Anversoise du Commerce au Congo, armés d'Albini, et avoir fait attaquer par cette troupe, divisée en petits détachements, les indigènes des villages Magugu, Tariba, Mandingia, Muibembetti, et Kakoré, provoquant ainsi directement la mort d'un grand nombre d'indigènes des dits villages ;

3. D'avoir à Muibembetti volontairement fait des blessures à la femme Menniegbiré, en lui tirant un coup de fusil de chasse dans les seins ;

4. D'avoir fait détenir arbitrairement à Mimbo, pendant près d'un mois, une vingtaine de prisonniers fait au cours des expéditions dans les villages Magugu, Teriba, Mandingia, Muibembetti, et Kakoré ;

5. D'avoir à Mimbo été la cause directe de la mort d'un prisonnier, ayant antérieurement donné aux sentinelles armées sous ses ordres la consigne de tuer tout prisonnier qui tenterait de s'enfuir ;

6. D'avoir au poste de Binga-État donné l'ordre aux sentinelles de tuer un Chef Mogwande, ordre qui a été exécuté par le soldat Kamassi ;

7. D'avoir établi ou laissé établir à Bussu-Baya, et à Dengeseke, des factoreries de commerce où se trouvaient installés des travailleurs armés d'Albini et de cartouches faisant partie de l'armement des factoreries de Mimbo et de Binga, ces armes et munitions ayant été déplacées sans autorisation, et ayant servi à commettre les infractions pour lesquelles sont poursuivis Jones, Silvanus, chef de la factorerie de Bussu-Baya, et Bangi, le domestique du précédent ;

8. D'avoir, au poste de Mimbo, remis à son Capita Kassango, 100 cartouches d'Albini, appartenant à l'État, et au poste de Binga, en avoir remis 200 à Houart, chef de cette factorerie ; ces faits constituant une soustraction frauduleente de cartouches au préjudice de l'État, ou subsidiairement une infraction aux dispositions sur les armes à feu—infractions prévues par les Articles 1er, 2, 3, 4, 11, 18, 19 du Code Pénal, 101 *bis*, 101 (4), du Code Pénal, Décret du 27 Mars, 1900 ; 2 et 9 du Décret du 10 Mars, 1892 ; et l'Arrêté du 30 Avril, 1901, sur les armes à feu.

Le second d'avoir, à la fin de l'année 1902, envoyé des travailleurs de la Société Anversoise du Commerce au Congo, armés de fusils Albini, dans les environs de la factorerie de Bussa-Baya, en leur donnant l'ordre de tuer les indigènes, et avoir ainsi été la cause directe de la mort d'une femme de Bassango, tuée d'un coup d'Albini par son domestique Bangi—infractions prévues par les Articles 1er et 9 du Décret du 10 Mars, 1892, et l'Arrêté du 30 Avril, 1901, sur les armes à feu, et 1 et 2 du Code Pénal ;

Vu la procédure à charge des prénommés ; vu le Jugement du Tribunal de Première Instance du Bas-Congo, en date du 12 Janvier, 1904, condamnant le premier à une servitude pénale de vingt ans et aux sept huitièmes des frais du procès ; le second à une servitude pénale de dix ans, et à un huitième des frais du procès ;

Vu les appels interjetés contre le dit Jugement par le Ministère Public et le prévenu Caudron, suivant déclarations reçues au Greffier du Tribunal d'Appel le 12 Février, 1904 ;

Vu les notifications des dits appels au Ministère Public, et aux prévenus en date du même jour ;

Vu l'assignation donnée aux prévenus par acte du 22 Février, 1904 ;

Ouï le Juge Albert Sweerts en son rapport ;

Vu l'instruction faite devant le Tribunal d'Appel ;

Ouï M. le Procureur d'État en ses réquisitions ;

Ouï les prévenus en leurs dires et moyens de défense présentés pour Caudron par M. de Neutor, défenseur agréé par le Tribunal ;

Attendu que le Tribunal d'Appel est saisi par l'appel du prévenu Caudron, et en même temps par l'appel du Ministère Public relatif à ce dernier et à l'autre prévenu, Jones, Silvanus ;

Que l'appel du prévenu Caudron n'est pas recevable, l'appelant n'ayant pas consigné préalablement les frais conformément à l'Article 78 du Décret du 27 Avril, 1889 ;

Que, cependant, l'appel du Ministère Public remet tout en question même dans l'intérêt des intimés ;

En ce qui concerne le prévenu Caudron :

Sur les première et deuxième préventions :—

Attendu qu'il est établi par les dépositions des témoins et par les pièces versées au dossier :

1. Que, dans la nuit du 15 au 16 Octobre, 1902, au poste d'Akula dans la région de la Melo, le prévenu Caudron, Chef de Zone de la Société Anversoise du Commerce au Congo dans cette région, pour punir les indigènes du village de Liboké de ne pas avoir fourni les corvées qu'il exigeait d'eux, a donné ordre à cinq de ses travailleurs, armés d'Albini, de se rendre au dit village et de tirer sur les indigènes, ordre que les travailleurs ont exécuté, en tuant le Chef et plusieurs indigènes de ce village ;

2. Que, dans le courant des mois de Janvier, Février, et Mars 1903, dans le but de forcer les indigènes de la région des Banga à augmenter la récolte du caoutchouc, il a fait une expédition dans la dite région avec vingt de ses travailleurs, armés d'Albinis, et accompagné d'un sous-officier et de cinquante soldats de l'État ; que, au cours de cette expédition, il a envoyé les travailleurs armés d'Albini, et les soldats divisés en petits détachements, dans les localités de Mogugu, Teriba, Bongu, Muibembetti, et Kakoré, avec ordre de tirer sur les indigènes qu'ils auraient rencontrés, ordre que les travailleurs et les soldats ont exécuté, causant ainsi la mort d'un grand nombre d'indigènes ;

Que le prévenu reconnaît ces faits dans leur ensemble, mais qu'il allègue pour sa défense d'avoir agi d'accord avec l'autorisation, et même par ordre de l'autorité, représentée lors du fait de Liboké par M. Nagant, et lors de l'expédition chez les Banga par M. Jamart—tous les deux Chefs du Poste de Police de Binga ;

Attendu, en ce qui concerne le fait de Liboké, que tous les témoins interrogés à ce sujet à l'audience de Première Instance et d'Appel ont nié de la manière la plus formelle que M. Nagant aurait été à Akula lors de l'attaque du dit village, et qu'il ait pu par conséquent ratifier par sa présence l'ordre donné par le prévenu Caudron, ainsi que celui-ci le soutient;

Que, cependant, existent au dossier les copies certifiées conformes de deux lettres qui auraient été adressées par M. Collet, gérant du poste d'Akula, à M. Nagant, la première en date du 12 Octobre, 1902, demandant son intervention contre le village de Liboké, et la deuxième en date du 16 Octobre, c'est-à-dire, au lendemain de l'attaque, le remerciant de son intervention et l'informant que les indigènes s'étaient présentés le matin au poste et s'étaient engagés à fournir régulièrement les impositions ; que l'accusation conteste l'authenticité de ces lettres, et soutient qu'elles ont été forgées après pour les besoins de la cause ;

Que, cependant, le fait qu'elles ont été versées au dossier par le Magistrat-Instructeur, qu'elles ont été trouvées dans les bureaux du poste de police, et le fait qu'elles ont été confirmées par M. Collet à l'instruction préparatoire ne permettent pas de les considérer comme fausses et de les écarter ;

Que puisqu'un doute subsiste il faut admettre la version la plus favorable au prévenu, c'est-à-dire, que le Chef du Poste de Police Nagant se trouvait à Akula lors de l'attaque de Liboké, et qu'il a connu et autorisé cette attaque ;

Que, par conséquent, tout supplément d'instruction relativement aux dites circonstances serait, dans l'intérêt de la défense, absolument inutile ;

Attendu, en ce qui concerne l'expédition chez les Banga, que la présence dans cette expédition du Chef du Poste de Police Jamart avec cinquante soldats de l'État n'est pas contestée, et qu'il est aussi prouvé que le prévenu a agi dans cette occasion toujours de parfait accord avec lui ; qu'il reste donc à examiner si la présence et l'autorisation de ces représentants de l'autorité pourraient justifier le fait du prévenu ;

Attendu que c'est un principe de droit consacré même expressément dans les Codes dont notre législation s'est inspirée que, pour qu'il n'y ait pas d'infraction, il ne suffit pas que le fait ait été commandé par l'autorité, mais qu'il faut en même temps qu'il soit ordonné par la loi ; qu'il est hors de doute qu'il s'agit dans l'espèce uniquement de délits de droit commun, c'est-à-dire, d'homicides commis pour un intérêt privé dans le but de forcer les indigènes à fournir leur travail ou leur produits;

Que, quoiqu'on ait parlé parfois vaguement de rétablissement de l'ordre, il résulte bien formellement des déclarations de tous les témoins et même des rapports adressés par le prévenu au Directeur de la Société, et de ses lettres aux gérants de sa zone, qu'il ne visait dans les actes d'hostilité posés contre ces indigènes que l'intérêt de son commerce, et notamment l'augmentation de la récolte du caoutchouc ;

Que si un doute pouvait être soulevé en ce qui concerne l'expédition précédemment faite chez les Gwakas, aucun doute ne peut exister à cet égard pour les faits objet de la prévention ;

Que, en tout cas, il est bien établi qu'au moment où ces faits se sont passés, l'ordre n'avait été nullement troublé ni à Liboké ni chez les Banga ; qu'il ne résulte pas que les victimes de ces faits aient commis d'autre faute que de ne pas avoir fourni à la Société la quantité de travail qu'elle exigeait ;

Attendu, d'autre part, que le seul fait de ne pas avoir payé les impôts, même s'ils étaient légalement dus (ce qui n'était pas dans l'espèce, puisqu'aucune loi ne les avait encore autorisés), ne pourrait jamais justifier des répressions sanglantes ;

Qu'on pourrait encore moins parler dans l'espèce de faits de guerre, car ce n'est certainement pas faire la guerre que d'attaquer des populations tranquilles et de tirer des coups de feu sur des individus isolés et inoffensifs ;

Qu'il est prouvé par les dépositions des témoins, et par les déclarations du prévenu lui-même, que jamais au cours de ces faits les indigènes n'ont attaqué ou posé un acte d'hostilité quelconque ;

Que ni parmi les soldats, ni parmi les hommes de la Société, il y a eu un seul tué ou un seul blessé ;

Qu'il serait donc absurde de parler de guerre ; que tuer dans ces conditions ne peut que constituer un crime qu'aucune loi, aucune nécessité n'autorise, et qui tombe sous l'application de la Loi Pénale, qu'il soit commis par un particulier ou par un agent de l'autorité ;

Attendu, d'autre part, que le prévenu ne peut non plus invoquer en sa faveur l'excuse de l'obéissance hiérarchique, car cette excuse n'existe que pour les agents de l'autorité qui exécutent l'ordre d'un supérieur hiérarchique et dans les limites du ressort de celui-ci ;

Que le prévenu n'était pas agent de l'autorité ; qu'il ne devait obéissance hiérarchique à personne ; qu'il ne rentrait aucunement dans ses attributions d'agent de Société de coopérer à des actes de répression ; qu'il avait donc tout le droit de refuser d'exécuter les ordres qu'on pouvait lui donner à ce sujet, et que s'il les exécutait, c'était à ses risques et périls ;

Qu'il est du reste de principe que même l'obéissance hiérarchique ne constitue plus une excuse lorsque l'illégalité de l'ordre est évidente ;

Attendu, d'ailleurs, qu'il est tout à fait contraire à la vérité que le prévenu n'aurait fait, ainsi qu'il l'affirme, qu'exécuter les ordres des Chefs du Poste de Police ;

Que la vérité, au contraire, est que ces derniers étaient en fait sous ses ordres ;

Qu'un simple sous-officier comme Nagant, un simple adjoint militaire (caporal) comme Jamart, ne pouvait certainement avoir aucune autorité sur le prévenu qui occupait la haute position de Chef de Zone de la Société Anversoise du Commerce au Congo, et qui avait sous ses ordres un nombreux personnel blanc et noir ;

Que tous les témoins ont été d'accord pour déclarer que dans toutes les expéditions qu'il a faites avec les Chefs du Poste de Police, c'était lui qui commandait, qui donnait des ordres, et qui punissait, non seulement ses hommes, mais même les soldats de l'État; que notamment, en ce qui concerne l'expédition contre les Banga, il est bien évident que le Caporal Jamart, tout jeune homme, à peine arrivé en Afrique, ne connaissant ni la langue, ni le pays, et pour surplus malade au point de devoir se faire presque toujours porter et rester en arrière même de plusieurs jours, n'était qu'un simple comparse dont le prévenu se servait dans la croyance de pouvoir, par sa présence, couvrir les illégalités qu'il commettait, et enchaîner à la sienne la responsabilité de l'État;

Que c'est en vain donc que le prévenu invoque sa bonne foi pour avoir agi d'accord avec les représentants de l'autorité;

Qu'il savait bien qu'on ne pouvait pas tuer et d'autant moins dans un intérêt commercial;

Il savait que les lois de l'État ne le tolère pas;

Il savait aussi que plusieurs de ses prédécesseurs et de ses collègues dans la même région, et dans la même Société, avaient été très sévèrement condamnés par les Tribunaux pour des faits semblables;

Il a cru être plus adroit que les autres en tachant de couvrir sa responsabilité en se servant des agents de l'État;

Mais si cette précaution se montre à la preuve impuissante, s'il s'aperçoit trop tard que la responsabilité pénale ne peut pas s'éluder si facilement, il n'a pas le droit de se dire la victime d'une erreur;

Que s'il s'est trompé, c'est non pas sur la moralité des actes qu'il posait, mais sur la valeur de la ruse qu'il a employée pour les couvrir;

Attendu, cependant, que le prévenu insiste sur la demande qu'il avait déjà présentée en Première Instance; que le Tribunal ordonne un supplément d'instruction pour faire verser au dossier les rapports politiques envoyés par les autorités supérieures administratives de la région au Gouvernement local, d'où il résulterait que les dites autorités avaient connu et approuvé les faits qui lui sont reprochés, et même d'autres expéditions antérieures et postérieures qu'il aurait faites avec les troupes de l'État, que le Gouvernement local, interpellé par le Magistrat-Instructeur, a déclaré qu'en principe il ne croyait pas pouvoir donner communication de ces pièces, que, du reste, elles ne renfermaient rien pouvant se référer aux faits indiqués par le prévenu;

Que la défense conteste ces déclarations en droit et en fait;

Attendu qu'en principe on ne pourrait certainement pas contester le droit de l'autorité judiciaire de demander et même de rechercher en tout lieu public ou privé toute pièce pouvant servir à conviction ou à décharge;

Que ce droit, qui est donné à l'autorité par la loi, ne pourrait être limitée que par la loi elle-même; que ni la législation Congolaise, ni la législation dont elle s'est inspirée ne fixent aucune limitation en faveur des Administrations publiques;

Que si on reconnaît une exception en faveur des agents diplomatiques, c'est à cause de la fiction d'exterritorialité de leur résidence; qu'il n'existe pas de lieu d'asile;

Attendu, toutefois, qu'il est du devoir de l'autorité judiciaire de procéder en cette matière avec la plus grande réserve et dans le seul cas où les pièces requises pourraient être d'une utilité évidente pour l'accusation ou la défense;

Que dans l'espèce la défense croit pouvoir déduire de ces pièces l'approbation et en tous cas la tolérance de l'autorité relativement à ces agissements;

Qu'ainsi qu'on l'a ci-dessus exposé même l'ordre formel et à plus forte raison la tolérance des autorités ne pourrait justifier des faits contraires à la loi; que ce principe a été déjà depuis longtemps et à plusieurs reprises affirmé par les Tribunaux de l'État;

Que par conséquent dans aucun cas le prévenu ne pourrait trouver dans les pièces dont il demande la production la justification des faits mis à sa charge;

Que, tout au plus, il pourrait invoquer la tolérance des autorités comme circonstance atténuante;

Qu'à cet égard, il y a lieu d'observer que la preuve d'une certaine tolérance de la part des autorités résulte des pièces même du dossier et des dépositions des témoins;

Qu'en effet, la présence et la coopération des Chefs du Poste de Police de Binga lors des affaires de Qiboko et de l'expédition chez les Banga ont été admises par le Tribunal; qu'il résulte aussi des dépositions des témoins que précédemment et postérieurement le prévenu avait fait d'autres expéditions de répression contre les indigènes accompagné d'agents et de soldats de l'État;

Que cela suffit pour faire tout au moins supposer la tolérance des autorités supérieures de la région, et pour faire admettre cette tolérance comme circonstance atténuante en faveur du prévenu ;

Que par conséquent tout supplément d'instruction à ce sujet, s'il pourrait servir à prouver la responsabilité d'autres personnes, ne pourrait avoir aucune utilité pour le prévenu ;

Sur la *troisième prévention* :

Attendu qu'il est prouvé par les dépositions des témoins et qu'il est reconnu par les prévenus qu'à Muibembetti au cours d'une expédition contre les Banga s'étant mis en colère pour un retard des porteurs, il a déchargé sur eux son fusil de chasse chargé à petit plomb ; qu'un des deux coups a blessé une femme indigène au dos ; que la blessure a été légère et n'a entraîné aucune incapacité de travail ;

Sur la quatrième prévention :

Attendu que le prévenu reconnaît avoir fait détenir à la factorerie de Mimbo une vingtaine d'indigènes faits prisonniers au cours de l'expédition contre les Banga et que leur détention n'avait d'autre but que de forcer leurs villages à la récolte de caoutchouc ; qu'il allègue pour sa défense que ces gens avaient été arrêtés avec l'autorisation et le concours du Chef du Poste de Police Judiciaire Jamart ; qu'ils attendaient à Mimbo les instructions du Commandant des troupes de police ; qu'il soutient que ce fait était parfaitement légal, puisque le Gouvernement avait, depuis le mois d'Avril 1901, autorisé la Société Anversoise du Commerce au Congo à exiger le caoutchouc à titre d'impôt de la population indigène, et avait édicté en cas de refus la peine de la contrainte par corps ;

Attendu qu'en effet le Ministère Public a déclaré à l'audience de Première Instance avoir été autorisé à déclarer qu'il existe une lettre du Gouverneur-Général au Commissaire de District de Nouvelle-Anvers, donnant le droit à la Société Anversoise du Commerce au Congo d'exiger le caoutchouc à titre d'impôt ; que cette lettre ajoute que le commandant du corps de police pourra, en cas de refus, exercer la contrainte par corps ; qu'il pourra déléguer ce droit même à un agent de la Société Anversoise du Commerce au Congo, mais qu'il appartiendra toujours à lui de décider s'il faut ou non maintenir la détention ;

Attendu qu'il est trop évident qu'on ne pouvait pas, par simple lettre, établir des impôts, et édicter la contrainte par corps en cas de non-paiement ;

Que le droit d'établir des impôts sur les populations et fixer des peines, ne peut appartenir qu'au Roi-souverain, ou à l'autorité par lui légalement déléguée à cet effet ;

Que le pouvoir judiciaire manquerait à son devoir et à sa mission s'il reconnaissait à d'autre autorité les pouvoirs qui sont réservés à l'autorité souveraine ;

Qu'il aurait fallu donc une loi dûment édictée et publiée ;

Qu'une pareille loi n'a paru que tout dernièrement très longtemps après les faits objet de la prévention, et qu'elle exige d'ailleurs pour l'application de la contrainte par corps des conditions qui n'existent pas dans l'espèce ;

Que par conséquent la lettre du Gouverneur-Général, ne pouvant pas déroger à la loi pénale, ne pourrait pas justifier l'atteinte portée à la liberté individuelle ;

Qu'on conçoit bien que le prévenu ait pu se tromper sur ce point, mais que la bonne foi, pour erreur de droit, ne peut pas être admise ; qu'il est juste toutefois d'en tenir compte pour appliquer sur ce chef au prévenu des circonstances atténuantes dans la mesure la plus large possible;

Sur la cinquième prévention :

Attendu qu'il est établi et reconnu par les prévenus qu'un des prisonniers détenus à Mimbo, ayant tenté de s'évader pendant la nuit, fût tué d'un coup d'Albini par la sentinelle de garde ;

Que le prévenu soutient être absolument étranger à ce fait ;

Attendu que, quoiqu'il soit établi par les dépositions des témoins que le prévenu avait toujours donné à ses hommes la consigne de tirer sur les prisonniers qui tentaient de s'évader, il n'est pas prouvé, cependant, que la sentinelle qui a tiré était un des hommes placés directement sous ses ordres ;

Qu'il paraît, au contraire, résulter des débats que c'était un travailleur du poste de Mimbo et qu'il avait été placé de sentinelle par le gérant de cette factorerie ;

Que ce meurtre, par conséquent, ne pourrait pas être imputé au prévenu ;

Sur la sixième prévention :

Attendu que le prévenu reconnaît qu'au retour de son expédition chez les Banga un Chef indigène a été tué dans la prison du poste de police de Banga par les soldats de ce poste ;

Qu'il reconnaît qu'à deux reprises les soldats, alors qu'il se trouvait avec Jamart, étaient venus demander des instructions relativement à ce prisonnier, qui causait du désordre ; qu'il reconnaît aussi qu'il se trouvait présent dans la prison lorsque le prisonnier a été tué ; qu'il affirme cependant que ni lui, ni Jamart, n'avait donné aucun ordre aux soldats, et qu'il s'était rendu à la prison uniquement pour induire le prisonnier à rester tranquille ;

Attendu que tous les témoins entendus sur ce fait à l'instruction préparatoire, et à l'audience, ont, de la manière la plus précise et concordante dans les moindres détails, affirmé que le prévenu a donné deux fois l'ordre de tuer : une première fois au Sergent Tangua, qui était allé demander des instructions, et une deuxième fois au même sergent, et au soldat Rixassi, lorsqu'ils étaient revenus pour se faire confirmer l'ordre, et que c'est le prévenu même, qui, dans la prison, après que le sergent eut tiré sur le prisonnier, en lui manquant, a passé le fusil au soldat Rixassi, qui l'a tué ;

Que ce dernier détail a été donné aussi par le témoin Houart, détenu à la prison de Boma alors que les autres témoins se trouvaient encore dans la haute rivière ; qu'il est impossible donc qu'il ait été inventé ;

Que ces deux circonstances, absolument établies même par des dépositions autres que celles des témoins noirs, que le prévenu se trouvait dans la prison, et qu'il a passé le fusil à l'homme qui a tiré, confirment de la manière la plus certaine que c'est bien lui qui a donné l'ordre de tuer, ordre que les soldats, qui revenaient de l'expédition, où ils avaient considéré toujours le prévenu comme Commandant, ne pouvaient pas hésiter à exécuter ;

Qu'il est du reste très évident qu'ils n'auraient certainement pas tué sans ordre, même en la présence du prévenu ;

Sur la septième prévention :

Attendu que les faits indiqués à l'assignation sont établis et reconnus par le prévenu qu'ils constituent des contraventions aux dispositions sur les armes à feu ;

Sur la huitième prévention :

Attendu qu'ainsi que l'a déclaré le premier Juge, il ne s'agit dans l'espèce que d'un simple échange de la munition entre les troupes de l'État et les hommes armés de la Compagnie ; qu'un simple échange ne peut constituer ni une soustraction frauduleente, ni (lorqu'il s'agit de cartouches, et non pas de l'arme elle-même) une contravention aux dispositions sur les armes à feu ;

Attendu que, pour les motifs repris ci-dessus, le prévenu doit être déclaré coupable de meurtres avec préméditation, comme auteur moral, pour abus d'autorité, des faits mis à sa charge par les première, deuxième, et sixième préventions ; de coups et blessures pour la troisième prévention ; de détention arbitraire pour la quatrième ; de contravention aux dispositions sur les armes à feu pour la septième prévention ; et qu'il doit être renvoyé des fins de la poursuite pour le surplus de la prévention ;

Attendu qu'il y a lieu d'accorder au prévenu des circonstances atténuantes, non seulement à raison des considérations exposées aux numéros un, deux, et quatre de la prévention, mais à raison aussi de ses bons antécédents pendant son long séjour en Afrique, et des graves difficultés dans lesquelles il a dû se trouver devant accomplir sa mission au milieu d'une population absolument réfractaire à toute idée de travail, et qui ne respecte d'autre loi que la force, ne connaît d'autre persuasion que la terreur ;

Qu'il faut reconnaître qu'il doit être bien difficile de se tenir dans la légalité dans un pays encore absolument barbare et sauvage, et notamment lorsque les lois à suivre dans ce pays sont les mêmes qui régissent les peuples les plus civilisés ;

Qu'il est en fin équitable de tenir compte que, quoique les faits soient en eux-mêmes très graves, ils perdent cependant une partie de leur gravité lorsqu'ils sont mis en rapport avec le milieu, où, d'après la coutume séculaire, la vie humaine n'a pas de valeur, et où le pillage, le meurtre, et le cannabalisme ont constitué jusqu'à hier la vie habituelle ;

En ce qui concerne le prévenu Jones, Silvanus :

Attendu qu'il est demeuré établi par les dépositions concordantes des témoins et par les contradictions même du prévenu, que dans le courant du mois d'Octobre 1902, alors qu'il était Chef du Poste de la Société Anversoise de Commerce au Congo à Bussa-Baya, il a ordonné aux hommes placés sous ses ordres de se rendre dans les environs de la factorerie et de tuer les indigènes qu'ils avaient rencontrés, pour les punir de ne pas avoir fourni une quantité suffisante de caoutchouc, ordre que son domestique Bongi a exécuté en tuant une femme;

Attendu que le prévenu soutient subsidiairement qu'en tout cas il aurait agi, ainsi qu'en d'autres circonstances, d'après les ordres de ses supérieurs, et notamment du Chef de Zone M. Caudron;

Attendu que, quoique ces ordres ne soient pas bien établis, les procédés employés par le Chef de Zone Caudron pour obtenir du caoutchouc des indigènes, et le fait que le prévenu avait été placé à Bussa-Baya clandestinement, et qu'on avait armé ce poste de huit fusils Albini sans permission, permet tout ou moins de supposer, dans l'intérêt du prévenu, que réellement il n'a fait que suivre les instructions de ses Chefs;

Que cependant, pour les raisons déjà exposées, ces ordres ne pourraient en aucun cas justifier ou excuser le prévenu;

Qu'on ne pourrait pas même le considérer comme un instrument passif et inconscient entre les mains de ses Chefs, puisque, quoique noir, il a une certaine culture d'esprit et appartient à un pays déjà en partie civilisé;

Qu'il devait bien savoir que tuer est un crime;

Qu'il a agit d'ailleurs aussi, dans son intérêt particulier, puisqu'il était payé en proportion du caoutchouc qu'il percevait;

Que cependant il est juste de lui faire application des circonstances atténuantes dans la mesure la plus large possible, en tenant compte du milieu où il se trouvait et des exemples qu'il recevait de ces Chefs; qu'il faut reconnaître que bien difficilement un noir aurait pu se soustraire à l'influence des exemples;

Que le Tribunal d'Appel, par conséquent, exprime le vœu que la libération conditionnelle vienne, aussitôt qu'il sera possible, tempérer pour ce prévenu la rigueur de la peine que, par application de la loi, il est forcé de confirmer;

Par ces motifs et ceux non contraires du premier juge;

Le Tribunal d'Appel:

Vu les Articles 78 du Décret du 27 Avril, 1889; 3, 4, 11, 98, 101 *bis*, et 101 (4) du Code Pénal, 2 et 9 du Décret du 10 Mars, 1892, et l'Arrêté du 30 Avril, 1901, déclare l'appel du prévenu Caudron non recevable;

Et statuant sur l'appel du Ministère Public;

Émendant le Jugement dont appel relativement au prévenu Caudron, en ce qui concerne la peine prononcée, le condamne, du chef de meurtres avec préméditation; de coups et blessures, de détentions arbitraires, et de contraventions aux dispositions sur les armes à feu, avec circonstances atténuantes, à cinq ans de servitude pénale;

Confirme pour le surplus le Jugement dont appel même en ce qui concerne l'autre prévenu, Jones, Silvanus;

Dit que les frais d'appel resteront à charge de l'État.

Ainsi jugé et prononcé en audience publique, où siégeaient—M. Giacomo Nisco, Président; MM. Albert Sweerts et Michel Cuciniello, Juges; M. Fernand Waleffe, Ministre Public; M. Paul Hodüm, Greffier.

Le Président,
(Signé) G. NISCO.

Les Juges,
(Signé) SWEERTS.
M. CUCINIELLO.
Le Greffier,
P. HODÜM.

(Translation.)

Judgment in Appeal respecting the Cases of M. Caudron and S. Jones.

The Court of Appeal at Boma, sitting for the consideration of Criminal Cases, has pronounced the following Judgment:—

Public Hearing of March 15, 1904.

(No. on the list 395.)
The Public Prosecutor *versus*—

(1.) CAUDRON, PHILLIP CHARLES FRANÇOIS, born at Auderlecht, Belgium, Superintendent of the Melo Commercial Zone, in the service of the Société Anversoise du Commerce au Congo; and

(2.) Jones, Silvanus, a native of Lagos, clerk in the service of the said Company:

The charges against the first-named were that, at the end of 1902, and at the beginning of 1903, when he was Superintendent of the Melo Commercial Zone, in the service of the Société Anversoise du Commerce au Congo:

1. He caused the village of Liboké to be attacked at night by the servants of the Society, armed with Albini rifles, thus directly bringing about the death of a certain number of natives of the said village of Liboké;

2. That he went about the country with a force composed of sixty State soldiers and of twenty servants of the Société Anversoise du Commerce au Congo, armed with Albinis, and caused the natives of the villages of Magugu, Teriba, Mandingia, Muibembetti and Kakoré to be attacked by this force, divided into small detachments, thus directly bringing about the death of a great number of natives of the said villages;

3. That he, at Muibembetti, deliberately wounded the woman Menniegbiré by discharging a shot-gun into her breast;

4. That he arbitrarily detained at Mimbo for nearly a month about twenty prisoners taken during his expeditions in the villages of Magugu, Teriba, Mandingia, Muibembetti, and Kakoré;

5. That at Mimbo he directly caused the death of a prisoner, having previously given instructions to the armed sentries under his orders to kill any prisoner who might attempt to escape;

6. That at the station of Binga-État, he gave an order to the sentries to kill a Mogwande Chief, an order which was executed by the soldier Kamassi;

7. That he established, or allowed to be established, at Bussu-Baya, and at Dengeseke, commercial factories where workmen were installed, armed with Albinis and cartridges, forming part of the armament of the factories of Mimbo and Binga, these arms and ammunition having been moved without authority, and having been used in committing the breaches of law, for which Silvanus Jones, chief of the factory of Bussu-Baya, and Bangi, his servant, are being prosecuted;

8. That, at the post of Mimbo, he handed over to his Headman ("Capita") Kassango 100 Albini cartridges belonging to the State, and, at the post of Binga, handed over 200 cartridges to Houart, head of that factory; which proceedings constituted a fraudulent abstraction of cartridges, the property of the State; and, in the second place, a breach of the Regulations in regard to fire-arms, offences covered by Articles 1, 2, 3, 4, 11, 18, 19 of the Penal Code, 101 *bis*, 101 (4) of the Penal Code, Decree of 27th March, 1900; 2 and 9 of the Decree of 10th March, 1892, and the Order of 30th August, 1901, respecting fire-arms.

The charges against the second were that, at the end of 1902, he sent workmen of the Société Anversoise du Commerce au Congo, armed with Albinis, into the neighbourhood of the factory of Bussu-Baya, with instructions to kill the natives, and thus directly caused the death of a woman of Bassango, who was killed by a rifle-shot by his servant Bangi—offences covered by Articles 1 and 9 of the Decree of 10th March, 1892, and by the Order of 30th April, 1901, respecting fire-arms, and 1 and 2 of the Penal Code;

In view of the terms of the indictment against the above-named persons, and the verdict of the Court of First Instance of the Lower Congo, dated the 12th January, 1904, condemning the first-named to twenty years' penal servitude and to seven-eighths of the costs of the action, and the second to ten years' penal servitude and to one-eighth of the costs of the action;

Whereas appeals against the said verdict were made by the Public Prosecutor and by the accused Caudron, according to declarations received at the office of the Registrar of Court of Appeal on the 12th February, 1904;

Whereas the said appeals were notified to the Public Prosecutor and to the accused on the same day;

Whereas a summons was served on the accused on the 22nd February, 1904;

Whereas Judge Albert Sweerts has reported on the case;

Whereas the case has been heard before the Court of Appeal;

Whereas the Procureur d'État has addressed the Court for the prosecution;

Whereas the statements and defence of the accused have been heard, being presented on behalf of Caudron by M. de Neutor, the defending Counsel accepted by the Court;

Whereas the Court of Appeal has received the appeal of the accused Caudron, and the appeal of the Public Prosecutor relating to the latter, and to the other accused, Silvanus Jones;

Whereas the appeal of the accused Caudron is inadmissible, the appellant not having deposited the costs in advance, in conformity with Article 78 of the Decree of the 27th April, 1889;

Whereas, nevertheless, the appeal of the Public Prosecutor reopens the whole case even in the interest of those served with the notice of appeal.

With regard to the accused Caudron;

On the first and second counts:

Whereas it is proved by the evidence of the witnesses and by the documents included in the "dossier": (1) that, on the night of the 15th to 16th October, 1902, at the station of Akula in the district of the Melo, the accused Caudron, District Superintendent of the Société Anversoise du Commerce au Congo, with a view to punish the inhabitants of the village of Liboké for not furnishing the forced labour required of them, gave orders to five of his workmen, armed with Albinis, to go to the said village and fire on the inhabitants, orders which the workmen executed, killing the Chief and several inhabitants of the village;

(2) That in the course of the months of January, February, and March 1903, in order to force the natives of the region of the Banga to furnish a greater supply of rubber, he conducted an expedition into the said region with twenty of his workmen, armed with Albinis, and accompanied by a non-commissioned officer and fifty soldiers of the State; that in the course of this expedition he dispatched the workmen, armed with Albinis, and the soldiers, in small detachments, into the localities of Magugu, Teriba, Bongu, Muibembetti and Kakoré, with instructions to fire upon any natives they might meet—instructions which the workmen and soldiers carried out, thereby causing the death of a large number of natives;

Whereas the accused acknowledges the general truth of these facts, but pleads in extenuation that he acted in accordance with the authorization, and even by the order, of the authorities, represented, in the case of the Liboké incident, by M. Nagant, and, in the case of the expedition against the Banga, by M. Jamart, both Heads of the police-station at Binga;

Whereas, in the case of the Liboké incident, all the witnesses questioned on this point before the Court of First Instance and before the Court of Appeal denied categorically that M. Nagant was at Akula when the attack against that village took place, and that consequently he could not have authorized by his presence the order given by the accused Caudron, as the latter maintains;

Whereas the "dossier" contains, however, certified copies of two letters addressed by M. Collet, Manager of the station of Akula, to M. Nagant, the first dated the 12th October, 1902, asking him to take action against the village of Liboké, and the second dated the 16th October—that is, the day after the attack—thanking him for his action, and informing him that the natives had come in in the morning to the station and had undertaken to accomplish their allotted tasks with regularity; and the authenticity of these letters is denied by the prosecution, who maintain that they were forged subsequently in the interest of the accused;

Whereas, however, the three facts: that they have been included in the "dossier" by the Magistrate in charge of the case; that they were found in the office of the police-station, and that they were admitted by M. Collet in the course of the preliminary inquiry, do not allow of their being considered as forgeries and consequently rejected;

Whereas, since a doubt exists, the version most favourable to the accused must be accepted—that is to say, that the Chief of the police station, Nagant, was at Akula when the attack on the village of Liboké took place, and that he was aware of, and authorized that attack;

Whereas, consequently, any supplementary examination relative to the said circumstances would be absolutely useless in the interest of the defence;

Whereas, in the case of the expedition against the Banga, the presence in that expedition of the Chief of Police, Jamart, with fifty soldiers of the State is not denied, and it is, moreover, proved that the accused acted throughout on that occasion in perfect accord with the former; whereas it remains, therefore, to be determined whether the presence and the authorization of these representatives of authority may be taken as justifying the action of the accused;

Whereas it is a principle, expressly recognized by the codes on which our legislation is based, that, in order to exclude the idea of an offence, it is not enough that the action may have been ordered by the Executive authorities, but it is necessary also that it should be prescribed by the law;

Whereas there is no doubt in the present instance that it is a case of offences against common law, that is to say, of manslaughter committed for a private purpose with the object of forcing the natives to supply labour or produce;

Whereas although the restoring of order has been occasionally vaguely mentioned it is clearly shown by the evidence of all the witnesses, and even by the reports addressed by the accused to the Director of the Company, and by his letters to the officers of the district, that, in committing these acts of hostility against the natives, he only had in view the interest of his Company's trade, and more especially the increase in the amount of rubber collected;

Whereas, even if there could be any doubt as to the nature of the previous expedition against the Gwakas, no doubt can exist in this respect in connection with the facts which are the subject of the prosecution;

Whereas, in any case, it is a well-established fact that at the time these acts took place order had in no way been disturbed, either at Liboké or among the Banga; that it does not appear that the victims of these actions had committed any other fault than that of failing to furnish the Company with the amount of labour required by it;

On the other hand, seeing that the sole fact of not having paid the taxes, even if they had been legally due (which they were not in this case, because no law had yet authorized their collection), could not justify such sanguinary measures;

In the present instance it is still less possible to speak of war-like acts, because to attack peaceable people and to fire upon single and inoffensive individuals is certainly not making war;

Whereas it is proved by the evidence of the witnesses, and by the statements of the accused himself, that on no occasion during these events did the natives attack or commit any sort of hostile act;

Whereas there was not one killed or wounded among the soldiers or among the Company employés;

Whereas, therefore, it would be absurd to call it war; and killing under such circumstances constitutes a crime which no law or necessity authorizes, and which is punishable by the Penal Code, whether it be committed by a private person or by a representative of authority;

Whereas, on the other hand, the accused cannot plead in extenuation the principle of official subordination, in view of the fact that such a plea is only valid in the case of representatives of authority who carry out the orders of an official superior, and then only so far as the authority of that superior extends;

Whereas the accused was not a representative of authority and he did not owe official obedience to any one; it was in no way part of his duty as an agent of a Company to co-operate in measures of repression; he was, therefore, fully entitled to refuse to execute the orders which might be given him to this effect, and, if he executed them, it was at his own risk;

Whereas, moreover, it is a principle of law that even obedience to one's official superior does not constitute a valid plea, when the illegality of the order is obvious;

Further, whereas there is no truth in the statement that the accused, as he affirms, only obeyed the orders of the Chiefs of the police station;

Whereas the truth, on the contrary, is that the latter were, in point of fact, under his orders;

Whereas a mere non-commissioned officer like Nagant; a mere military assistant (corporal) like Jamart, could not have any authority over the accused, who occupied the high position of a District Superintendent of the Société Anversoise du Commerce au Congo, and had under his orders a large staff of white men and natives;

Whereas all the witnesses were unanimous in stating that in all the expeditions which he made with the Chiefs of the police station, it was he who commanded, gave orders to, and punished, not only his own men, but even the soldiers of the State; whereas, especially in the case of the expedition against the Banga, it is evident that corporal Jamart, quite young and but recently arrived in Africa, knowing neither the language nor the country, and, besides, so ill that he nearly always had to be carried, and remained several days' journey to the rear, was simply a lay figure made use of by the accused in the belief that by Jamart's presence he would be able to cover his own illegal actions and to involve the State in his own responsibility;

Whereas it is therefore useless for the accused to plead good faith in having acted in accord with the representatives of authority;

Whereas he knew that he ought not to kill, and that he was even less justified in so doing in the interests of trade;

He knew that it is not tolerated by the laws of the State;

He knew, also, that several of his predecessors and colleagues in the same region and belonging to the same Company had received very severe sentences from the Court for similar offences;

He thought he would be cleverer than the others in trying to cover his responsibility by making use of State employés;

But if this precaution turns out to be ineffectual—if he realizes too late that criminal responsibility cannot be so easily eluded—he has no right to describe himself as the victim of an error;

Whereas, if he was mistaken, it was not with regard to the morality of the actions which he committed, but with regard to the value of the ruse which he made use of to cover them;

Whereas, however, the accused insists upon the request which he had already made in First Instance—to wit, that the Tribunal should order a supplementary inquiry, in order to have incorporated in the "dossier" the political Reports sent by the higher administrative authorities of the region to the Local Government—which would show that the said authorities had known and approved of the actions of which he is accused, and even of previous and subsequent expeditions which he had made with the troops of the State; whereas the local Government, questioned by the examining Magistrate, declared that, as a matter of principle, it did not think it possible to produce these documents, and, moreover, the said documents contained nothing that could refer to the facts mentioned by the accused;

Whereas the defence contests these declarations in law and in fact;

Whereas the right of the judicial authority to demand, and even to search for in any public or private place, any document which might lead to a conviction or an acquittal, cannot be denied in principle;

Whereas this right, which is given to the judicial authority by law, can only be curtailed also by law; whereas neither the Congo legislation, nor the legislation on which it is founded, fixes any limitation in favour of the Public Departments;

Whereas if an exception be made in the case of diplomatic representatives, that is on account of the fiction of the extra-territoriality of their residence; whereas there is no place of asylum;

Whereas, however, it is the duty of the judicial authority to proceed in such matters with the greatest circumspection, and only if the documents demanded are of obvious use to the prosecution or the defence;

Whereas, in the present instance, the defence thinks that it can deduce from these documents the approval, and, in any case, the toleration of the authorities in connection with these actions;

Whereas, as has been set forth above, even the definite order, and, therefore, still less the toleration of the authorities, could not be held to justify acts contrary to the law;

Whereas this principle has already, for a long time past, and on several occasions, been affirmed by the Tribunals of the State;

Whereas, consequently, in no case could the accused find in the documents, the production of which he demands, justification for the actions with which he is charged;

Whereas the utmost he could do would be to adduce the toleration of the authorities as an extenuating circumstance;

Whereas, in this connection, it may be fittingly observed that the documents of the "dossier" itself, and the evidence of witnesses, go to prove the existence of a certain toleration on the part of the authorities;

Whereas, indeed, the presence and the co-operation of the heads of the police station of Binga, at the time of the Qiboke affair, and of the expedition against the Banga, have been admitted by the Tribunal. Whereas the evidence of the witnesses also goes to prove that the accused, accompanied by agents and soldiers of the State, had, previously and subsequently, conducted other punitive expeditions against the natives;

Whereas this is sufficient ground at least for presuming the toleration of the higher authorities of the district, and for admitting this toleration as an extenuating circumstance in favour of the accused;

Whereas, consequently, all supplementary inquiry on this subject, even if it might serve to prove the responsibility of other persons, could be of no service to the accused;

On the third count:

Whereas it is proved by the evidence of witnesses, and admitted by the men accused, that at Muibembetti, in the course of an expedition against the Banga, the accused in question, having lost his temper owing to a delay on the part of the carriers, fired upon them with his shot-gun loaded with small shot; one of the two discharges wounded a native woman in the back; and the wound was slight and did not cause her to be incapacitated from work;

On the fourth count:

Whereas the accused admits having caused to be detained at the factory of Mimbo some twenty natives who had been taken prisoners in the course of the expedition against the Banga, and that their detention had no other object than to force their villages to collect rubber; whereas he alleges in his defence that these people had been arrested with the authorization and assistance of Jamart, the Chief of the police station; whereas they were awaiting at Mimbo the instructions of the Commander of the police forces; whereas he maintains that this act was perfectly legal because the Government had, since the month of April 1901, authorized the Société Anversoise du Commerce au Congo to exact rubber as a tax from the people, and had decreed the penalty of detention in the case of refusal;

Whereas, in fact, the Public Prosecutor declared in the course of a trial before the Court of First Instance that he was authorized to state that a letter was in existence from the Governor-General to the Commissioner of the district of Nouvelle-Anvers, granting to the Société Anversoise du Commerce au Congo the right to exact rubber as a tax; whereas this letter adds that the Commander of the police force may, in case of refusal, put in force the penalty of detention; that he may delegate that right to an agent of the Société Anversoise du Commerce au Congo, but that it will always rest with him to decide if the detention is to be confirmed or not;

Whereas it is quite evident that taxes could not be established, or detention in case of non-payment decreed, by a mere letter;

And whereas the right of imposing taxes on the people, and of fixing penalties can only belong to the King Sovereign, or to those to whom he has legally delegated his authority for that purpose;

And whereas the Judicature would fail in its duty and its mission if it recognized in any other authority those powers which are reserved to the sovereign authority;

And whereas a law duly decreed and published would therefore have been necessary;

And whereas such a law has only appeared quite recently, a very long time after the acts which form the subject of the prosecution, and it requires, moreover, in order to render the penalty of detention applicable, conditions which do not exist in this case;

Whereas, consequently, the letter of the Governor-General being unable to run counter to the Penal Code could not justify the violation of individual liberty;

And whereas it is quite possible that the accused may have been mistaken on this point, but the fact of acting in good faith cannot be taken as a justification for a breach of the law;

Whereas it is just, however, to take this into consideration in order to give the accused, on this head, the benefit of extenuating circumstances to the greatest extent possible;

On the fifth count:

Whereas it is established and admitted by the men accused that one of the prisoners detained at Mimbo, having attempted to escape during the night, was killed with an Albini rifle by the sentry on guard;

And whereas the accused maintains that he had absolutely nothing to do with this act;

Whereas, although it is established by the evidence of the witnesses that the accused had always given his men orders to fire on prisoners who tried to escape, it is not, however, proved that the sentry who fired was one of the men placed directly under his orders;

Whereas, on the contrary the proceedings seem to show that the man in question was a workman of the post of Mimbo, and that he had been placed as a sentry by the Manager of that factory;

And whereas the murder, therefore, could not be imputed to the accused;

On the sixth count:

Whereas the accused admits that upon his return from the expedition against the Banga, a native Chief was killed in the prison of the police station of Banga by the soldiers of that station;

Whereas he admits that on two occasions, when he was in the company of Jamart, the soldiers came to ask for instructions relating to this prisoner, who was making a disturbance; and he also admits that he was actually present in the prison when the prisoner was killed; whereas, however, he affirms that neither he, nor Jamart, gave any order to the soldiers, and that he went to the prison solely to induce the prisoner to remain quiet;

Whereas all the witnesses interrogated on this point in the course of the preliminary inquiry, and at the hearing of the case, did, in a manner the most precise, and consistent in the most minute details, affirm that the accused twice gave the order to kill; first to Sergeant Tangua, who had come for instructions; and on the second occasion to the same sergeant and to the soldier Rixassi when they returned to get the order confirmed; and that it was the accused himself, who, in the prison, after the sergeant had fired upon the prisoner and missed him, handed the gun to the soldier Rixassi, who killed him;

Whereas the latter detail was also given by the witness Houart, confined in the prison at Boma, when the other witnesses were still in the Upper Congo; and it is, therefore, impossible that it was invented;

Whereas these two circumstances, absolutely established by other evidence as well as that of native witnesses, that the accused was in the prison and that he handed the gun to the man who fired, confirm in the most positive manner the fact that it was he who gave the order to fire, an order which the soldiers who were returning from the expedition, on which they had always looked upon the accused as their Commandant, could not hesitate to execute;

Whereas it is, moreover, amply evident that they certainly would not have killed without instructions, even in the presence of the accused;

On the seventh count:

Whereas the facts cited in the prosecution are established, and admitted by the accused, and constitute breaches of the Regulations as to fire-arms;

On the eighth count:

Whereas, as the first Judge declared, it is merely a question in this case of a simple exchange of ammunition between the troops of the State, and the Company's armed men; and whereas a simple exchange cannot constitute a fraudulent abstraction, or (when it is only a question of cartridges, and not of the weapon itself) a contravention of the Regulations as to fire-arms;

Whereas, for the reasons given above, the accused must be declared guilty of murders with premeditation, as the moral author, through abuse of authority, of the deeds he is charged with on the first, second, and sixth counts; of blows and wounds on the third count; of arbitrary detention on the fourth count; of contraventions of the Regulations as to fire-arms on the seventh count; and he should be acquitted on the remainder of the counts;

Whereas there are reasons for granting extenuating circumstances to the accused, not only on account of the considerations submitted on the first, second, and fourth counts, but also on account of his good previous character during his long stay in Africa, and the great difficulties under which he must have laboured, as he had to do his duty in the midst of a population entirely hostile to all idea of work, and which only respects the law of force, and knows no other argument than terror;

Whereas it must be recognized that it must be very difficult to act within the law in a country still absolutely barbarous and savage, more especially when the laws to be obeyed in that country are the same as those which govern the most civilized peoples;

Whereas, to conclude, it is just to bear in mind that, although the acts are in themselves very grave, they lose a part of their gravity when they are considered in connection with the surroundings, in which, according to immemorial custom, human life has no value, and pillage, murder, and cannibalism were, until the other day, of ordinary occurrence.

As regards the accused Silvanus Jones:

Whereas it is duly established by the consistent testimony of the witnesses, and even by the contradictory evidence of the accused himself, that, during the month of October 1902, when he was Chief of the post of the Société Anversoise du Commerce au Congo at Bussa-Baya, he ordered the men placed under his orders to proceed to the neighbourhood of the factory, and to kill the natives that they met, to punish them for not having furnished a sufficient quantity of rubber, an order which his servant Bongi executed by killing a woman;

Whereas the accused maintains, as a subsidiary plea, that in any case he acted, as in other circumstances, in accordance with the orders of his superiors, especially with those of the District Chief M. Caudron;

Whereas—although these orders are not well established—the methods adopted by the District Chief Caudron to obtain rubber from the natives, and the fact that the accused had been placed at Bussa-Baya secretly, and that that post had been armed with eight Albini rifles without permission, give colour to the supposition, in favour of the accused, that in point of fact, he did but follow the instructions of his Chiefs;

And whereas, however, for the reasons already given, these orders could in no way justify or exculpate the accused;

And whereas he could not even be regarded as a passive and unconscious instrument in the hands of his Chiefs, because, although a black, he possesses some mental culture and belongs to a country already partly civilized;

And whereas he must have known perfectly well that to kill is a crime;

And whereas he, moreover, acted in his personal interest because he was paid in proportion to the rubber he collected;

Whereas, however, it is just to concede to him extenuating circumstances to the greatest possible extent, taking into account his surroundings and the example set by his Chief; and whereas it must be admitted that it would have been very difficult for a black man to withstand the influence of example;

And whereas, therefore, the Court of Appeal expresses the hope that the rigour of the penalty, which, according to law, it is compelled to confirm, may, in the case of this prisoner, be modified as soon as possible, by his conditional release;

For these reasons and those, cited by the First Judge, which do not conflict with them;

The Court of Appeal:

Taking into consideration Articles 78 of the Decree of the 27th April, 1889; 3, 4, 11, 98, 101 (*bis*) and 101 (4) of the Penal Code; 2 and 9 of the Decree of the 10th March, 1892, and the Order of the 30th April, 1901;

Declares the appeal of the accused Caudron to be inadmissible;

And, on the appeal of the Public Prosecutor—

Amends the Judgment appealed against with respect to the accused Caudron, in regard to the penalty pronounced, and condemns him on the count of murders with premeditation, of blows and wounds, of arbitrary detention, and contraventions of the Regulations as to fire-arms, with extenuating circumstances, to five years' penal servitude;

Confirms in other respects the Judgment which was the subject of appeal, also as regards the accused Silvanus Jones;

Ordains that the costs of the appeal shall be borne by the State.

Thus judged and pronounced in public sitting by the Tribunal, composed of M. Giacomo Nisco, President; MM. Albert Sweerts and Michel Cuciniello, Judges; M. Fernand Waleffe, Public Prosecutor; M. Paul Hodüm, Clerk.

The President,
(Signed) G. NISCO.

The Judges,
(Signed) SWEERTS.
M. CUCINIELLO.

The Clerk,
P. HODÜM.

Inclosure 2 in No. 3.

Acting Consul Nightingale's Interview with Silvanus Jones, a Native of Lagos, under Sentence of Ten Years' Penal Servitude, in the Prison at Boma, for certain Atrocities committed whilst in the Employ of the S.C.A. (Société Congolaise Anversoise).

Q. HOW long have you been in the employ of the S.C.A.?—*A.* I served five years, and then went home to Lagos, and after staying at home some time I returned to the Congo, and was re-engaged by the same Company. I am now completing the second year of my new contract.

Q. In what capacity were you engaged by the S.C.A.?—*A.* As a carpenter.

Q. How is it that, being engaged as a carpenter, you were buying rubber?—*A.* There was no more carpentering to be done, and as I had not completed my contract, I was ordered to buy rubber. Formerly I used to buy rubber at the same time as I was doing the carpentering.

Q. Have you ever killed, ill-treated the natives, or burnt down their houses?—*A.* On my oath, I never have.

Q. Do you understand the nature of an oath?—*A.* Yes; and if there were a Bible here I would swear on it.

Q. Can you read and write?—*A.* Only a very little—just my name.

Q. Were you aware that people were being shot or otherwise ill-treated, and that their villages were burnt?—*A.* Yes; I heard of such things going on, but I never witnessed anything of the sort except on one occasion at my own station. It was one day (the 9th December, 1902) when I was lying down, and suddenly I heard firing from outside, and a shot came through my house and nearly hit me. When I went outside I found a white agent of the Company, who had ordered his men (soldiers) to fire on a man and woman from about 120 yards' distance. They were both killed. The woman was pregnant. When I asked the white agent (whose name I cannot remember) why he came and upset the people of my station, he replied, "How dare you speak to me, you black man; don't you see that I am a white man, and can give what orders I like!"

Q. Were you ever ordered to go and punish the natives?—*A.* Yes. On one occasion, especially, I was ordered to send and punish some people who had fled into the bush. So I thought for a time as to what I should do, and at last resolved to send four soldiers into the bush to try and catch the people and bring them to me to see if I could make friends with them. I ordered the soldiers not to shoot any one, and sent my boy (a Bangala) with them to see that no shooting was done. They caught a man and a woman in the bush and took them to Little Basango (about three hours from my station), instead of coming back to me. It was my Bangala boy who shot the woman whilst she was stooping down at the side of the river, and she fell into the water and was carried away. I never saw the woman or her corpse, as it was carried away by the stream. I went down the river (about two and a-half hours' journey in a canoe going there, and about six hours to come back) to report the affair to the white agent at the post there. It is for this affair, I am given to understand, that I am punished. But really I am not to blame, as I gave strict orders to the soldiers not to shoot any one.

Q. Did you know when you were sent for to come to Boma that you were going to be tried for committing certain outrages on the natives?—*A.* No.

Q. Were you brought down to Boma under a military escort?—*A.* No; I came down alone; but when I arrived at Boma I was met by a guard of soldiers, and was taken to the prison, where I remained five days, and was then let out.

Q. Did you know that you were going to be tried for various outrages committed on the natives?—*A.* No; I was under the impression that I had been called as a witness against that man.

[Jones pointed to a man who was writing at a desk in the gaoler's office, who, I was told, was M. Caudron.]

Q. You knew absolutely nothing about your being kept in Boma to be tried for serious offences you were accused of having committed?—*A.* I knew absolutely nothing.

Q. Would you have employed an advocate to defend you had you known that you were going to be tried for such serious offences against the laws of the country?—*A.* Most certainly I would. I brought down with me 3,500 fr., and the Judge has got 3,000 fr. of that sum, which I wish you to mind for me. I think you have the receipt.

[*Note.*—The receipt was handed to Mr. Nightingale by a Lagos man named Shanu a few days ago.]

Q. You know, I suppose, that you have been sentenced to ten years' penal servitude?—*A.* Yes; I was sentenced to ten years by the first Judge, but the second Judge reduced it to two and a-half years; and they say that if I behave properly that I may get my liberty in six months.

[*Note.*—Jones has misunderstood his sentence. The sentence of ten years passed in the Court of First Instance was upheld in the Appeal Court.]

Q. What work have they given you to do here?—*A.* I am employed on the carpentering work of this building (pointing to a stone house that is in course of construction).

Q. You declare you are perfectly innocent of the charges brought against you, and for which you have been condemned to ten years' penal servitude?—*A.* Yes, Sir; I am innocent.

Q. You wish me to hold the 3,000 fr. for you.—*A.* Yes; if you please, Sir.

(Signed) A. NIGHTINGALE.

Boma, March 21, 1904.

Inclosure 3 in No. 3.

Note.

JONES, SILVANUS, originaire de Lagos, clerc au service de la Société Commerciale Anversoise, prévenu d'avoir, à la fin de l'année 1902, envoyé des travailleurs de la Société Anversoise du Commerce au Congo, armés de fusils Albini, dans les environs de la factorerie de Bussu-Baya et avoir ainsi été la cause directe de la mort d'une femme de Bassanga, tuée d'un coup d'Albini, par son domestique Bangi—infractions prévues par les Articles 1 et 9 du Décret de 10 Mars, 1892, et l'Arrêté du 30 Avril, 1901, sur les armes à feu et 1 et 2 du Code Pénal.

L'Article 1 du Décret du 10 Mars, 1892 (B.O., 1892, p. 14), interdit l'importation, le trafic, le transport, et la détention d'armes à feu quelconques, ainsi que la poudre, de balles et de cartouches. L'Article 9 du même Décret punit toute infraction à cette disposition d'une amende de 100 fr. à 1,000 fr., et d'une servitude pénale n'excédant pas une année, ou de l'une de ces peines seulement. L'Arrêté du 30 Avril, 1901 (R.M., p. 86), subordonne à certaines formalités les demandes pour la délivrance de permis de port d'armes. L'Article 1 du Code Pénal (L. 11) définit l'homicide et les lésions corporelles volontaires. L'Article 2 définit le meurtre et le punit de la servitude pénale à perpétuité.

(Translation.)

SILVANUS JONES, native of Lagos, clerk in the Service of the Société Commerciale Anversoise, accused of having, at the end of the year 1902, sent some workmen in the employ of the Société Anversoise du Commerce au Congo, armed with Albini rifles, to the neighbourhood of the Bussu-Baya factory and thus been the direct cause of the death of a woman of Bassanga, who was killed by a shot from an Albini fired by his servant Bangi—which offences are covered by Articles 1 and 9 of the Decree of the 10th March, 1892, and the Order of the 30th April, 1901, respecting fire-arms and 1 and 2 of the Penal Code.

Article 1 of the Decree of the 10th March, 1892 (B.O., 1892, p. 14), forbids the importation, trade in, transport and keeping of, any fire-arms whatever, or of powder, bullets, or cartridges. Article 9 of the same Decree punishes every infraction of this provision by a fine of 100 fr. to 1,000 fr. and by a term of penal servitude not exceeding one year, or by one only of those penalties. The Order of the 30th April, 1901 (R.M., p. 86), attaches certain formalities to requests for the delivery of permits to carry arms. Article 1 of the Penal Code (L. 11) defines homicide and wilful bodily injury. Article 2 defines murder and punishes it by penal servitude for life.

No. 4.

Sir C. Phipps to the Marquess of Lansdowne.—(*Received May* 16.)

My Lord, *Brussels, May* 14, 1904.

M. DE CUVELIER handed to me this evening a Memorandum, of which I have the honour to inclose copy, which has been drawn up at the Congo Ministry in rejoinder to the points raised in your Lordship's despatch of the 19th ultimo, on the subject of the administration of the Congo.

I have, &c.
(Signed) CONSTANTINE PHIPPS.

Inclosure in No. 4.

Memorandum.

LA dépêche de Lord Lansdowne du 19 Avril, 1904, dont copie a été remise par Son Excellence Sir Constantine Phipps au Gouvernement du Congo le 27 Avril suivant, appelle quelque considérations.

Relativement à l'appréciation contre laquelle s'élève cette dépêche "that the interests of humanity have been used in this country as a pretext to conceal designs for the abolition of the Congo State," l'on voudra bien se souvenir qu'un membre de la Chambre des Communes déclarait qu'il préfèrerait "voir la vallée du Congo passer une Puissance étrangère," et que des pamphlets indiquaient comme "absolute and immediate necessities," "Disruption of the Congo Free State," "Partition of the Congo Free State among the Powers," et suggéraient même les bases d'un tel partage, tandis que des organes de la presse Anglaise envisageaient soit l'alternative "advocated by the more thorough-going critics of the present Administration, namely, the disruption of the Congo Free State," soit l'alternative de "the partition of the Congo territory among the Great Powers whose possessions in Africa border those of the Congo State," ou déclaraient "what Europe ought to do, under the leadership of Great Britain, is summarily to sweep the Congo Free State out of existence." La Note de l'État du Congo du 17 Septembre a relevé ces suggestions, dont nous n'indiquons ici que la tendance et qui toutes avaient pour objet de spolier le Roi-Souverain, de le déposséder de l'État qui était sa création personnelle—suggestions qui se concilient bien mal avec le respect du droit et des Traités, et avec les motifs d'ordre purement humanitaire et philanthropique dont se disent exclusivement animés les adversaires de l'État dans la campagne passionnée qu'ils mènent contre lui.

En réponse aux objections que le Gouvernement de Sa Majesté élève contre la communication du texte intégral du Rapport de Mr. Casement, le Gouvernement de l'État du Congo fait remarquer qu'il a demandé la communication de ce Rapport complet en vue précisément de le transmettre aux autorités judiciaires et administratives compétentes, sans quoi cette communication serait sans objet. Le souci d'une enquête impartiale et les droits de la défense exigent impérieusement que les accusés connaissent, d'une manière précise et dans leurs détails, les faits mis à leur charge, et l'appréhension que les personnes accusées pourraient, de par la connaissance qu'elles auraient de ces détails, influencer ou supprimer des témoignages ne semble pas justifiée par ce seul fait que des indigènes, qui, dans l'affaire Epondo, avaient fourni au Consul des informations mensongères, ont évité par la suite de se représenter devant le Magistrat enquêteur; la fuite de ces témoins s'explique plus naturellement par le sentiment de la faute grave qu'ils avaient commise en trompant sciemment le Consul Anglais. Si le Gouvernement du Congo peut donner, et donne volontiers, l'assurance que tout acte ou toute tentative de subornation de témoins serait poursuivi, il n'est évidemment pas en son pouvoir de préjuger ou d'enrayer les mesures légales que croiraient devoir prendre, dans l'intérêt de leur honneur ou de leur considération, des personnes qui se trouveraient avoir été faussement accusées.

Le Gouvernement de l'État du Congo regrette que le Gouvernement de Sa Majesté Britannique n'estime pas devoir lui communiquer les autres Rapports Consulaires antérieurs auxquels faisait allusion la dépêche de Lord Lansdowne du 8 Août, 1903. Ainsi que le disaient les notes du 12 Mars dernier, ces rapports présentaient l'intérêt d'avoir été écrits à une date à laquelle de débat actuel n'était pas né.

Une copie de ce Mémorandum sera adressée aux Puissances auxquelles a été transmise la copie de la dépêche de Lord Lansdowne du 19 Avril dernier.

État Indépendant du Congo, Bruxelles,
le 14 *Mai*, 1904.

(Translation.)

LORD LANSDOWNE'S despatch of the 19th April, 1904, a copy of which was handed to the Congo Government on the 27th April by his Excellency Sir Constantine Phipps, calls for certain remarks.

With regard to the opinion to which this despatch takes exception, "that the interests of humanity have been used in this country as a pretext to conceal designs for the abolition of the Congo State," it will be well to remember that a Member of the House of Commons declared that he would prefer "to see the Valley of the Congo pass into the hands of a foreign Power," and that some pamphlets described the "Disruption of the Congo Free State," the "Partition of the Congo Free State among the Powers," as absolute and immediate necessities, and even went so far as to suggest the bases of such a partition, while the organs of the English press contemplated one of two alternatives, either that "advocated by the more thorough-going critics of the present Administration, namely, the disruption of the Congo Free State," or "the partition of the Congo territory among the Great Powers whose possessions in Africa border those of the Congo Free State," or declared that "what Europe ought to do, under the leadership of Great Britain, is summarily to sweep the Congo Free State out of existence." The Congo State Note of the 17th September has called attention to these suggestions, of which we merely point out the tenour in this instance, and which all aimed at despoiling the Sovereign King, and at dispossessing him of the State which was his own creation—suggestions which are entirely incompatible with respect for rights and Treaties, and with the motives of a purely humanitarian and philanthropic nature by which the enemies of the State allege themselves to be exclusively animated in the passionate campaign which they are conducting against it.

In reply to the objections raised by His Majesty's Government against the communication of the entire text of Mr. Casement's Report, the Government of the Congo State points out that it has asked for the complete Report precisely with a view to transmitting it to the competent judicial and administrative authorities, without which this communication would be purportless. The anxiety to obtain an impartial inquiry and the rights of the defence render it an imperative necessity that the men accused should be informed, in a precise and fully-detailed manner, of the acts laid to their charge; the fear that the persons accused might be able, by means of the knowledge they would have of the details, to influence or suppress evidence, does not appear to be justified by the mere fact that the natives, who, in the Epondo case, had given mendacious information to the Consul, subsequently avoided presenting themselves before the Magistrate presiding over the inquiry; the flight of these witnesses is explained more naturally by the fact that they were conscious of the grave fault they had committed in wittingly deceiving the English Consul. If the Congo Government be permitted to give an assurance, which it does willingly, that any case of suborning witnesses, or any attempt to do so, would form the subject of a prosecution, it is evidently not within its power to prejudice or quash such legal measures as persons who might find themselves wrongfully accused might consider it necessary to take, either in the interests of their honour or their dignity.

The Government of the Congo State regrets that His Majesty's Government does not deem it necessary to communicate to it the other previous Consular Reports to which Lord Lansdowne's despatch of the 8th August, 1903, alluded. As was stated in the notes of the 12th March last, these reports possessed the interest of having been written at a date anterior to the inception of the present discussion.

A copy of this Memorandum will be addressed to the Powers to whom copies of Lord Lansdowne's despatch of the 19th April last was transmitted.

Congo Free State, Brussels,
May 14, 1904.

No. 5.

The Marquess of Lansdowne to Sir C. Phipps.

Sir, *Foreign Office, June* 6, 1904.

WITH reference to my despatch of the 19th April, I transmit to you, for communication to the Congo Government, a Memorandum on the remaining points in the "Notes" handed to you on the 13th March which would appear to His Majesty's Government to call for observation.

I request you, in presenting this Memorandum, to take the opportunity of stating that His Majesty's Government much regret that, in M. de Cuvelier's Memorandum of the 14th May, a more definite reply is not returned to the inquiries which they deemed it necessary to make before considering whether they could furnish the full text of Mr. Casement's Report. My despatch explained that the names in the Report had been suppressed, not from any want of confidence in the Central Government of the Congo State, but from apprehension that the information, if made generally public, would place it in the power of persons charged with abuses to procure the suppression or repudiation of evidence, or to punish those who had given it. His Majesty's Government asked, therefore, whether the Congo Government would accept full responsibility for the use which would be made of the information, and would communicate the measures they were prepared to adopt and enforce in order to protect the witnesses who gave evidence to Mr. Casement from the possibility of exposure to acts of intimidation or retaliation. It was clearly incumbent upon His Majesty's Government to provide as far as possible for the safety of those at any rate whose statements to a British officer were made with no knowledge that they would be cited by name as responsible for charges upon which public proceedings would be based. They entertained therefore no doubt that the Congo Government would appreciate their motives, and would willingly undertake, in furtherance of the object which both Governments have in view, to meet, so far as lay in their power, the requirements of the case. The Memorandum handed to you by M. de Cuvelier, after dwelling upon the necessity of full information for the purpose of investigation, merely declares that the Government of the Congo are ready to give an assurance that proceedings will be taken against all who attempt to suborn witnesses, but that they cannot prejudice or prevent legal measures instituted in defence of their honour or reputation by those who may have been falsely accused.

His Majesty's Government cannot accept as adequate or satisfactory an answer which implies that the information which they are asked to supply will be accessible to the very persons whose conduct has been impugned, before any measures have been taken to shield the witnesses from the exercise of improper pressure. They have, of course, never entertained the idea that the Congo Government would connive at any such malpractice as the subornation of witnesses. They have not asked, and have never intended to suggest, that legal remedies should be denied to those against whom unfounded accusations have been publicly brought, nor do they desire that those, if any, who have given such false evidence should be shielded from the proper legal penalty for their offence. What they require is that the Congo Government, in accordance with the recognized principles of civilized administration, will take every means to secure that the witnesses, if their names should be divulged, will suffer no harm in their property or persons from the unlawful violence of those to whose desire for revenge they may be exposed. No argument can be entertained to the effect that acts of violence are improbable or impossible under a system such as that revealed by the Judgment pronounced by the Court of Appeal at Boma in the Caudron Case, and His Majesty's Government earnestly trust that the Congo Government will recognize the immense service that will be rendered both to the cause of humanity and to the credit of their own officers by promoting unreservedly a full and public investigation by a Tribunal of recognized competence and impartiality into the charges made against their agents and against their system of administration.

There is another point to which His Majesty's Government must call attention. The inquiry promised in the "Notes" is, no doubt, intended to be of a searching and impartial character, and His Majesty's Government hoped that they would before now have received some indication of the measures designed to carry out this intention. In the peculiar circumstances which have arisen, strict impartiality will hardly be attributed to an investigation conducted as in the Epondo case solely by the officers of the State or by the agents of the Concessionary Companies, nor will the result carry conviction to the degree which seems essential. The matter is one which must be left to the decision of the Congo Government, and it is only because, in the judgment of His Majesty's Government, the whole question at issue turns in a great measure upon the position and character of those charged with the inquiry that they feel justified in mentioning the point, and in suggesting that a Special Commission should be appointed, composed of Members of well-established reputation, and in part, at least, of persons unconnected with the Congo State, to whom the fullest powers should be intrusted both as regards the collection of evidence and the measures for the protection of witnesses. Were a Commission of this character appointed His Majesty's Government would be prepared to place at the disposal of the Members, for their own use and guidance, all the information they possess respecting the position of affairs in the Congo, and would give them every assistance, in the confident belief that an independent Commission such as they have suggested would elicit the truth, and effect in a manner commanding general acceptance a settlement of the existing controversy.

You will read this despatch to M. de Cuvelier and give a copy of it to his Excellency. Copies of the despatch and of the inclosed Memorandum will also be forwarded to the Powers who were Parties to the Berlin Act.

I am, &c.

(Signed) LANSDOWNE.

Inclosure in No. 5.

Memorandum.

THE first portion of the "Notes" refers to the desire expressed by the Congo Government for the production of the previous Reports of His Majesty's Consuls alluded to in the Circular of His Majesty's Government of the 8th August last. This matter has already been dealt with in the despatch addressed to Sir C. Phipps on the 19th of April.

The next point in the "Notes" is the statement made by Mr. Casement that the population has decreased in certain districts; doubt is expressed as to how, in the course of his rapid visits, he was able to arrive at the figures which he gives, and attention is drawn to alleged discrepancies in those figures. With regard to Mr. Casement's ability to form an opinion on the subject, it is to be observed that the means at his disposal for doing so were neither greater nor less than those of Mgr. van Ronslé, viz., personal knowledge of what the population had been in former years and what it appeared to him to be at the date of his last visit. The alleged discrepancy in his figures consists in the fact that, having estimated the population of the entire community of the F line of villages at 500, a few lines further on he estimates that of "the several villages whose task it is to keep the wood post victualled" at 240. The explanation is to be found in the fact that in the first instance Mr. Casement alluded to all the villages comprising the Settlement, whereas in the second he referred only to the inhabitants of that portion of the Settlement whose business it was to supply food for the neighbouring wood-cutting post.

The Congo Government admit that Mr. Casement attributes, equally with Mgr. van Ronslé, a large share of the diminution of the population to the sleeping sickness, but attach to another cause, viz., the facility with which the natives are able to migrate, greater weight than appears to His Majesty's Government to be justifiable, since more than one reference in the Consul's Report shows that the natives are not allowed to leave their own districts.

On p. 4 of the "Notes" (p. 3, *supra*) the complaint is made that Mr. Casement's Report contains, not exact, precise, and proved facts, but statements and declarations by natives. It is difficult, however, to see how the facts dealt with can be proved without hearing the statements and declarations of natives: the grounds of their complaints at all events can be learnt exactly and precisely from them alone.

In the last paragraph of p. 4 (p. 3, *supra*) an attempt is made to show that because during his journey into the interior of the Congo State, Mr. Casement was not the guest of the authorities, and because during that journey he visited his countrymen, therefore his presence must "inevitably" have been considered by the natives as antagonistic to "established authority." Mr. Casement was, however, obviously at liberty to move about his Consular district without previous consultation with the authorities, and he was at special pains to impress on the people that he had no authority to set things right. It is clear from his Report, as indeed is borne out by the "Notes," that he was careful to refer the natives to the Government of the State. As a matter of fact, in many parts of the country the natives did not know who he was, while it is equally certain that the rumour of the "campagne menée contre l'État du Congo" to which allusion is made as having influenced the inhabitants could not possibly have reached them, since it is difficult to imagine that a population who are represented as among the most savage and backward of mankind, and dwelling in the heart of Africa, could be aware of debates in a European assembly, or of the press comments made thereon.

Mr. Casement could not, as asserted, have appeared to all the natives of the Lulongo River in the character attributed to him, and this is shown in a letter the agent of the Lulanga Company at Bokakata addressed to Mr. Ellery, of the Congo Balolo Mission at Ikau, on the 28th August.

Mr. Casement had found women hostages tied up and guarded by two sentries of that Company who told him how it was these women came to be captured and detained, in order to compel their husbands to bring in rubber.

This letter begins by stating that—

> "Avant-hier, disent les indigènes, des missionnaires de la Congo Balolo Mission se sont rendus à Yvumi *(Ifomi), où ils ont été recueillir certaines réclamations après au préalable avoir* fait instiguer les habitants de ce village par le personnel du steamer."

The letter then seeks to show that the scene Mr. Casement had witnessed had no foundation in fact, and ends with the request that Mr. Ellery should communicate its contents "au *monsieur qui s'est rendu à Yvumi. Je regrette, ne le connaissant pas, de* ne pouvoir m'adresser à lui."

It is evident from this letter that neither the natives of the village referred to, the sentries placed there, nor the European agent responsible for placing them there had any knowledge of the rôle of "redresseur des griefs" which is now attributed to Mr. Casement.

This is the more significant, since Mr. Casement had passed Bokakata the day before this letter was written, on his way to Ikau, whither the Lulanga Company's steamer, with the Director on board, followed on the 28th August in search of an unknown traveller who the natives said was a missionary.

That Mr. Casement travelled independently of Government assistance was a perfectly legitimate action on his part, and one calling for neither comment nor explanation. The necessity for this, moreover, is made clear by that passage in his Report (p. 24) wherein he points out the difficulty of getting suitable accommodation on the Government steamer "Flandre," by which he had at first thought of quitting Leopoldville.

It may also be observed that it was only when he failed to find a French steamer available at Brazzaville (which he visited in that hope on the 25th and 26th June) that he decided to seek the loan of a steamer belonging to an American Mission.

A visit to his countrymen was a correct proceeding on his part, and it was but natural that he should be assisted by them. As their Consul, it was right he should visit his compatriots dwelling in isolated stations amid savage surroundings; and since he was desirous of coming to an independent judgment on the conditions of native life, it was much more natural that he should choose his own means of separate, independent conveyance than restrict himself to the not always convenient itinerary of Government steamers or place himself under the guidance or conduct of local authorities, who, if abuses did exist, were hardly likely to disclose them. His Majesty's Government can in no way accept the view that Mr. Casement necessarily fell under the influence of the missionaries, neither can they think that the English Protestant missionaries are opposed, still less necessarily antagonistic, to the Government of a friendly State in which they reside. Mr. Casement moreover visited several American mission stations, and it is not the case, as asserted in the "Notes," that it was only by English missionaries that he was assisted. The steamer he travelled on was the property of the American Baptist Missionary Union, lent to him by their Board; the Mission station at which he spent the longest time is an American station, and he had on several occasions Americans with him as his guests on board and during his visits to the natives.

The Congo Government endeavour to support their assertion that Mr. Casement's attitude was one of antagonism to established authority by alleging as "characteristic" the fact that while he was at Bonginda the natives collected on the banks of the river, and as the agents of the Lulanga Company went by shouted out, "Votre violence est finie; elle s'en va; les Anglais seuls restent! Mourez vous autres!"

Had the incident referred to occurred as recorded, it would indicate not so much that the natives of the locality named were excited against "established authority," as against the agents of a trading Company.

But the above is hardly a correct description of the occurrence, as the Congo Government must admit, seeing that they have themselves placed on record a totally different version of the incident.

On the 2nd December, 1903, the Secretary-General of the Congo State, in drawing the attention of Dr. H. Grattan Guinness to the subject of this pretended "disorder." of the natives, described it in the following terms:—

> "On a vu dernièrement, après le voyage du Consul Britannique dans la Lulanga, des indigènes en rapport avec la mission de la Congo Balolo Mission, établie à Bonginda, s'attrouper au passage d'un agent de l'État, en s'écriant dans leur dialecte—
>
> "'Votre violence est finie; elle s'en va; les Anglais seuls restent! Mourez vous autres!'
>
> "Ces propos séditieux étaient proférés en présence de missionnaires de Bonginda."

Without further enlargement upon so trivial an altercation as that which actually occurred between the canoe boys of a passing trader and some natives of the neighbourhood, it is only necessary to call attention to the discrepancy which exists between M. de Cuvelier's complaint of the 2nd December and the terms in which it is now formulated.

In the former communication the Secretary of the Congo Government addressed the Congo Balolo Mission in terms of reproof upon a subject upon which he was obviously but imperfectly informed, since he asserted the incident to have occurred after Mr. Casement's departure from Bonginda, and the offensive words to have been addressed to a Government official. Dr Guinness, however, explained to M. de Cuvelier that the incident occurred when Mr. Casement was present, that it had no significance, and that the canoe jeered at by the natives contained, not a State Agent, but an agent of the Lulanga Company; further, that the words used were, in reality, not those imputed, but: "The rubber is finished; the people refuse to work rubber." Yet in spite of this explanation, which seems amply sufficient, the "Notes" still maintain that the incident shows that Mr. Casement's attitude was incorrect.

The next subject discussed in the "Notes" is what has come to be known as the Epondo Case.

This is dealt with at great length, and the explanation for so doing is afforded by a statement that His Majesty's Consul himself attributed a capital importance to it. The inference that it is intended to draw would seem to be that since the result of the investigations made by the local authorities, subsequent to Mr. Casement's departure, is said to have demonstrated quite other facts than those he had too hastily assumed, the rest of his Report need not be taken seriously.

From a consideration of the Consul's Report, it will be seen that the case of this boy Epondo is dealt with in one single paragraph of thirty-seven lines of print on p. 56, and is referred to again in some few lines of p. 58, in all less than one page of a document of thirty-nine pages; while in the Appendix of nearly twenty-three pages of print a copy of the notes taken by Mr. Casement in the case at Bosunguma extends to less than two pages.

On the other hand, the Congo Government, in their reply, devote some six or seven pages of a document of eighteen pages in all to endeavouring to show that in the case of this one mutilated individual, the boy's hand had not been cut off by a sentry, but had been bitten off by a wild boar; and in the Appendix to the "Notes," which comprises nineteen pages of small print, more than ten pages are devoted to extracts from the proceedings in this one case.

Thus, of a document running to thirty-seven pages in all, almost one-half is assigned to a single incident which, in Mr. Casement's Report, had given occasion for some two and a quarter pages of remark and notes out of nearly sixty pages of printed matter.

Far from having attributed capital importance to this incident, it is evident from the Report itself that it was but one of many cases calling for explanation brought to Mr. Casement's notice during his journey, and that he himself by no means attributed to it undue weight.

To show how far he was from generalizing from this one incident, it is only necessary to cite a letter he addressed to the Governor-General on the 4th September when in the Lopori River, 150 miles away from Bosunguma (of the existence of which he did not then know), written some days before the cases of mutilation on the Lower Lulongo were brought to his notice. In that letter, which dealt mainly with certain illegalities he had observed in the Abir territory at Bongandanga, he said:—

> "I am sure your Excellency would share my feelings of indignation had the unhappy spectacles I have witnessed of late come before your Excellency's own eyes.
>
> "I cannot believe that the full extent of the illegality of the system of arbitrary impositions, followed by dire and illegal punishments, which is in force over so wide an area of the country I have recently visited, is known to, or properly appreciated by, your Excellency or the Central Administration of the Congo State Government."

Also after recording some of the outrages practised upon women and children he had witnessed in order to obtain food supplies, or compel the production of india-rubber, he said, in referring to one of these so-called trading factories:—

> "I must confess with pain and astonishment that, instead of visiting a trading or commercial establishment, I felt I was visiting a penal settlement."

A study of the case will show the successive steps by which the statement made on p. 7 of the "Notes" (p. 5, *supra*) is reached:—

> "L'enquête montre Epondo, enfin acculé, retractant ses premières affirmations au Consul, et avouant avoir été influencé par les gens de son village."

The facts throw a light on the motives which inspired, or the influences which compelled, this retractation by the mutilated boy other than the "Notes" afford, and show that a not unimportant part of the inquiry was conducted under conditions which scarcely merit the description of an "enquête judiciaire dans les conditions normales en dehors de toute influence étrangère," as, on p. 6 of the "Notes" (p. 4, *supra*), it is said to have been.

A noteworthy illustration of the method adopted to arrive at an impartial finding in this case will be found to consist in the fact that an inquiry into grave charges preferred against an agent of the Lulanga Company was conducted in part through agents of that Society—itself primarily involved; that the Substitut du Procureur d'État visited the district as the guest of that Company, putting up at its stations and travelling on its steamer in company with its agents, and that the "retractation" of Epondo only took place when the boy had been removed to the head-quarters of that Company, on the steamer of that Company, surrounded, not by friends, but by the agents of the very Company which had an obvious interest in securing a withdrawal of the charge.

Had the "retractation" of Epondo, first made at Mampoko, the head-quarters of the Lulanga Company, on the 8th October (see p. 31, "Notes") (p. 35, *supra*) been sincere and quite uninfluenced by the environment to which he found himself removed at Bonginda, its sincerity would best have been demonstrated by its being repeated before Mr. Armstrong at Bonginda, whence the boy had just been removed.

Mr. Armstrong had cognizance of the case from the first. Bonginda lies only some 8 miles from Mampoko, and it would have been but just to Mr. Armstrong, as well as much more convincing, if, when the boy altered his statement, he had been taken back to where only the day before (see p. 29, "Notes") (p. 33, *supra*) he had reiterated in the presence of Mr. Armstrong the original charge against Kelengo.

Instead of adopting this simple course, however, the boy, having been brought to "retract," was carried off to Coquilhatville—fully 80 miles away—and a week later a declaration is required from Mr. Faris, a missionary, whose residence was situated far from the scene of the occurrences, who had no knowledge of the boy's antecedents, or any means of testing his statement by cross-examination or otherwise.

A retractation by a lad of some 15 years of age brought about at Mampoko under influences not unfavourable to the accused sentry cannot be held as satisfactory. That the authorities at Coquilhatville did not themselves consider it convincing is clear from their action in calling upon Mr. Faris to furnish an extraneous support to the decision arrived at by their own magisterial inquiry at Mampoko.

Epondo's "retractation" was made on the 8th October at Mampoko, and one statement in it, as given on p. 31 of the "Notes," (p. 35, *supra*) throws doubt on much of the rest.

Question (by the Substitut): "Depuis combien de temps cet accident vous est-il arrivé?"
Answer (Epondo): "Je ne me rappelle pas: c'est depuis longtemps."

When Mr. Casement visited Bosunguma on the 7th September the boy's mutilated stump had evident signs of not being then completely healed: blood showed still in two places, over which the skin had not entirely formed, and it was wrapped up in a cloth.

The "Notes" (p. 9) (p. 7, *supra*) allude to the attitude of the missionaries in the following words:—

"Et le fait n'est pas non plus sans importance, si l'on veut exactement se rendre compte de la valeur des témoignages, de la présence aux côtés de Mr. Casement, qui interrogeait les indigènes de deux missionnaires Protestants Anglais de la région, présence qui, à elle seule, a dû nécessairement orienter les dépositions."

If it is permissible to cast this reflection upon the attitude towards the Government of the missionaries of the district, it is certainly relevant to point out that the presence beside Lieutenant Braeckman (who conducted the preliminary inquiry) and the Substitut du Procureur d'État of the agents of the Company having a deep interest in the charge against its employé, and the part those agents were permitted to take in the inquiry, must have vitally affected the testimony of the witnesses who deposed at Mampoko that the charge against the Lulanga sentry was inspired solely by a desire on the part of the natives to escape their rubber dealings with that firm.

It appears that there were two inquiries: the first conducted by Lieutenant Braeckman, at which the original witnesses against the sentry and others reaffirmed their accusation that it was he who had mutilated Epondo. At the second inquiry, conducted by the Substitut, which took place some fortnight later, none of the original witnesses against Kelengo appeared (see "Ordonnance de Non-Lieu," p. 8, "Notes") (p. 6, *supra*); but a number of persons—some of them servants of the Lulanga Company—made statements, contradictory in many respects, but agreeing with much unanimity that a wild boar, which no one of them had seen, at a date no one could assign, in an indeterminate locality, had eaten off the hand of this lad of 14 or 15 years of age, who, according to the first deposition cited (that of Efundu, on the 28th September, at Coquilhatville, p. 24, Annexe III) (p. 29, *supra*), had attempted to catch the wounded and infuriated creature by the ears!

It is obvious that the "conclusions posées" as the result of his inquiry by Lieutenant Braeckman (see "Ordonnance de Non-Lieu" of the 9th October, p. 8 of "Notes") must, in part, have rested on evidence of natives he had interrogated at Bosunguma, in Mr. Armstrong's presence, on the 14th September.

In this "Ordonnance" we find, however, that while the "conclusions" of Lieutenant Braeckman are accepted, the evidence on which those "conclusions," in some part, must have rested is rejected on the ground that the witnesses took flight, and did not reappear at the second inquiry.

If the "conclusions" are accepted, the evidence on which they are founded should be also admissible.

There is, moreover, open contradiction if one turns to the evidence of the "Chief Bofoko, of Ikundja," cited on p. 30 of Annexe III in the "Notes" (p. 34, *supra*).

This deponent appeared before the Substitut at Mampoko on the 8th October, and in the course of his interrogatory it is asserted that he was one of those who had originally testified against Kelengo before the British Consul.

Question (by Substitut): "Pourquoi vous-même avez-vous déclaré au Consul Anglais avoir vu la main coupée par terre, le sang coulait, et les habitants du village qui couraient dans toutes les directions?"

Answer (Bofoko): "Je n'ai pas parlé avec les Anglais. Je ne les ai pas même vus. Quand ils sont arrivés à Bosunguma, je n'étais pas là."

Substitut: "Vous mentez, parce que le Consul Anglais déclare avoir parlé avec vous."

Answer (Bofoko): "Oui, c'est vrai. J'y étais. J'ai dit comme les autres," &c.

Despite this record by himself on the 8th October of the *procès-verbal* of the evidence of Bofoko, the Substitut, on the following day, draws up his "Ordonnance de Non-Lieu," wherein, in the third paragraph, he states that—

"Attendu que tous les indigènes qui ont accusé Kelengo, soit au Consul de Sa Majesté Britannique, soit au Lieutenant Braeckman, convoqués par nous, Substitut, ont pris la fuite, et tous les efforts faits pour les retrouver n'ont abouti à aucun résultat: que cette fuite discrédite évidemment leurs affirmations"—(p. 8 of "Notes").

In view of a discrepancy of this kind, it is, perhaps, needless further to investigate the character of the evidence upon which a sustained effort is made to discredit Mr. Casement's testimony.

It may be observed that the natives cited by the Congo Government concurred in describing the accusation against the Lulanga Company's sentry as prompted by the wish of the natives to escape from their rubber dealings with that Company.

If these dealings are but those of commerce, as has been repeatedly asserted (*e.g.*, "Bulletin Officiel," June 1903), there would not appear to be any sufficient pretext for the accusation these natives are said to have brought against that Company's sentry.

We find it stated that the "liberté du commerce" the men of Bosunguma enjoyed presented itself to them in the following guise:—

"Pour ne pas faire de caoutchouc: Kelengo est sentinelle du caoutchouc. (Efundu, the 28th September, 1903, p. 24.)

"Oui; j'ai entendu les indigènes se plaindre qu'ils travaillent beaucoup pour rien; que les Chefs s'emparaient des mitakos que les blancs payaient pour la récolte du caoutchouc; enfin, qu'ils mouraient de faim. Ils ajoutaient qu'ils avaient réclamé plusieurs fois inutilement," &c. (Mongombe, the 28th September, 1903, p. 25.)

"Parce qu'ils étaient fatigués de faire du caoutchouc, qui n'était plus dans leur forêt. Ils ont cru qu'avec l'intervention des Anglais ils pourraient se soustraire à un travail très dur, &c. . . . . Ils ont parlé avec les habitants, qui se plaignaient de ce qu'ils devaient travailler beaucoup. Ils disaient que le caoutchouc n'était plus dans leur forêt, qu'ils voulaient faire un travail moins dur," &c. (Liboso, the 6th October, 1903, p. 27, "Notes.")

"Parce qu'ils trouvent que le travail du caoutchouc est trop dur, et ont cru de pouvoir s'en libérer, et pour les induire à s'en occuper ils sont allés leur conter des mensonges." (Bofoko, the 8th October, 1903, p. 30, "Notes.")

If, as the Congo "Notes" assert on p. 6 (p. 5, *supra*), these "dépositions sont typiques, uniformes, et concordantes, elles ne laissent aucun doute sur la cause de l'accident, attestent que les indigènes ont menti au Consul, et révèlent le mobile auquel ils ont obéi"—

they unquestionably leave no doubt that the relations of the Lulanga Company to the natives of the surrounding country were not those of a trading Company engaged in exclusively commercial dealings, but of an organization compelling, with the approval and support of the Executive, a widespread system for which no legal authority exists.

Whatever may have been the truth of the charge against the sentry, the very evidence cited to disprove it attests that the natives spoke truly as to their abject condition, and shows that in a region repeatedly visited by Government officials, traversed weekly by Government steamers, lying close to the head-quarters of the Executive of the district, the trading operations of a private Company depended for their profits upon the "obligation de l'impôt."

The appended Table of exports and imports of the Congo State, taken from the "Bulletin Officiel" for April 1903 (No. 4), will suffice to indicate the larger aspect of the situation of the native producer :—

	Exports from Congo State.	Imports to Congo State.
	Fr.	Fr
1895	10,943,019	10,685,847
1896	12,389,599	15,227,776
1897	15,146,976	21,181,462
1898	22,163,481	23,084,446
1899	36,067,959	22,325,846
1900	47,377,401	24,724,108
1901	50,488,394	23,102,064
1902	50,069,514	18,080,909

The exports of native produce ("le négoce des autres produits indigènes"—"Bulletin Officiel," April 1903, p. 65), it is seen, have enormously increased. They have considerably more than trebled in the six years from 1897 to 1902.

During the same period the imports into the Congo State—a small portion of which are trade goods for the purchase of produce or the remuneration of the producers—remained not merely stationary, but even decreased by 4,000,000 fr. during the last year.

These figures, as they stand, are remarkable. Their significance is increased when it is borne in mind that the population of the regions exporting this great increase of native produce has enormously decreased during the same period. That decrease is admitted by the authorities. ("Du reste, il n'est malheureusement que trop exact que la diminution de la population a été constatée"—"Notes," p. 2) (p. 2, *supra*). We thus find that a diminishing population,* a diminishing market-value of the article produced and a diminishing means of purchase have been accompanied during a period of only six years by a more than trebled production.

It may be permitted to doubt whether this state of affairs is adequately explained anywhere in the Congo Government "Notes."

It is not met by the statement on p. 14 (p. 9, *supra*) of this document :—

> "Qu'il s'est agi de faire contracter l'habitude de travail à des indigènes qui y ont été réfractaires de tout temps.
>
> "Et si cette idée du travail peut être plus aisément inculquée aux natifs sous la forme de transactions commerciales entre eux et des particuliers, faut-il nécessairement condamner ce mode d'action ?" &c.

On the same page of the "Notes" (14) it is sought to institute a comparison between the system of taxation in force on the Congo and that in operation in North and Eastern Rhodesia, and the conclusion is drawn that, since the latter is justified in a British Colonial administration, no exception can be taken to the former.

It is only necessary to point out that in North and Eastern Rhodesia, or in any other British Colony where direct taxation of the natives exists by law, the tax collector is a Government officer responsible for the sums levied to a central authority, not a trading agent having a direct personal interest in the amount of the "obligation de l'impôt."

The native under the British system knows the fixed amount of his obligation, and, once discharged from it, he is free to seek, where he will, labour or leisure. The

* See Circular of Governor-General of 29th March, 1901, printed as an Appendix to Mr. Casement's Report in "Africa No. 1 (1904)," p. 81.

Congo taxpayer with an ever-present, perpetually-recurring, weekly or fortnightly imposition to make good, may not even leave his village, save as a fugitive, and is a close bondsman to these endless tasks.

With regard to the arming of the sentries or "forest guards" in the employ of the trading Companies on the Upper Congo, the "Notes" throw doubt on the estimate Mr. Casement formed of the number of these guns, and the use to which they are put, and it cites Circulars of the Governor-General of the Congo State, dating from the 12th March, 1897, to the 30th April, 1901, as evidence that the Executive authority had been careful to guard against a possible misuse of the arms.

But the issue of successive Circulars, which, by their own terms, show clearly that the law had been ignored or evaded, cannot be claimed as an effective fulfilment of a weighty obligation of the Executive.

It must further be borne in mind that the Congo Executive were themselves the direct agency for placing all the arms these Circulars refer to in the hands of those who are there shown to have ignored the law.

Every gun misused on the Upper Congo, with its accompanying ammunition, was carried to its destination by the vessels of the Government flotilla, which charged a considerable sum for their transport. They were housed in Government stores *en route*, for which a charge of "magasinage" is levied, and were distributed to the "factories" from Government steamers by Government Agents, who, having made a profit from their agency in the matter, subsequently issued circular instructions to those into whose hands they knowingly gave the weapons.

"Les capitas qui, dans le Haut-Congo, parcourent le pays pour compte de commerçants, et qui sont pourvus d'un fusil, doivent également être munis d'un permis de port d'armes."
(Circular of the 12th March, 1897. Annexe V. "Notes," p. 34.)

"On a voulu y voir l'attribution aux Directeurs de ces Sociétés, et même à des agents subalternes, du droit de diriger des opérations militaires offensives, 'de faire la guerre' aux populations indigènes; d'autres, sans même s'inquiéter d'examiner quelles pourraient être les limites de ce droit de police, se sont servis de moyens que cette délégation avait mis entre leurs mains, pour commettre les abus les plus graves.

"Les armes perfectionnées que les Sociétés posséderaient dans leurs diverses factoreries ou établissements, et qui doivent faire l'objet comme les armes d'autres Sociétés n'ayant pas le droit de police, d'un permis Modèle B, ne peuvent en aucun cas sortir des établissements pour lesquels elles ont été délivrées. Quant aux fusils à piston, ils ne peuvent être mis en dehors des factoreries qu'entre les mains des capitas et à condition que ceux-ci aient un permis suivant Modèle C."
(Circular of the 20th October, 1900; see p. 78, Mr. Casement's Report.)

If the native sentries or capitas of these factories ranged the country with unlicensed arms, if these "Commercial" Companies made war on the natives, it was the Congo Government which carried those arms to their destinations and placed them in the hands of those who used them illegally.

"Nonobstant les précautions incessantes, le Consul a constaté que plusieurs capitas n'étaient pas porteurs de permis."
("Notes" of the Congo Government, the 12th March, 1904.)

The law prescribes clearly that no weapon can be issued for individual use save on the authority and personal licence of the Government.

That this law can be effectively observed was evidenced in Mr. Casement's own case. A Winchester rifle for his use arrived on the Congo while he was in the interior. It could not be dispatched to him from Boma to Stanley Pool (where he found it on coming down river) until a licence had been granted. This rifle was branded and numbered according to law and the tax of 20 fr. levied.

A law thus rightly obligatory in the case of a foreign official, who could not be suspected of misuse of the weapon he had imported, should have had at least as stringent application to the capitas, and forest guards and sentries of the numerous Companies, which are shown by the Government Circulars quoted to have been recognized for years as seeking to evade the law.

That the Congo Government have intimate cognizance of the exact number of guns in use by the commercial Companies on the Upper Congo is evident, since every case of rifles and "ballot de fusils" imported into the Congo State has to enter the custom-house of Boma or Matadi, where it can only be withdrawn by authority.

Its subsequent transport to the interior is effected often by direct Government carriage, and always under Government control and supervision.

The Government of the Congo State, in concluding these preliminary "Notes" on Mr. Casement's Report, formulate a complaint as to the manner in which he proceeded in investigating native statements brought to his notice.

This complaint has application to the one case of the boy Epondo, and to that case alone.

In no other instance did he attempt to interrogate, "comme par voie d'autorité," any of the many natives whose homes he visited during his journey. In that one case it may be urged that, however unusual were the proceedings, it was clearly his duty not to turn a deaf ear to the appeal the people of Bosunguma addressed to him.

Whether they spoke truly or falsely in accusing the sentry of the act of mutilation, he had no option but to seek to arrive at the truth if he wished his intervention with the local authorities to have any effect.

Had he contented himself with merely listening to and reporting the accusation the natives of Bosunguma brought to him at Bonginda, the officials at Coquilhatville would have said he had formulated a grave charge against an individual on mere native report, without having taken the trouble to satisfy himself of its truth.

He could not, clearly, leave the mutilated boy in the town, where his assailant was represented as terrorizing the inhabitants.

It was his obvious duty to go to the spot, to see with his own eyes what truth lay in the report brought to him at Bonginda.

Once in Bosunguma, the only way to arrive at anything like the truth was to see the accusers and the accused face to face and to hear what each said.

He distinctly disclaimed any right of intervention or power to help; but if he was going to report the charge made against the sentry, and to ask for investigation, it was clearly necessary that he should first find out whether there was good ground for addressing the local authorities.

With regard to the question of mutilation, His Majesty's Government note with interest that the Congo Government are aware that Mr. Casement is not alone in his opinion that such atrocities occur (§ 5, p. 5, of "Notes") (§ 5, p. 4, *supra*).

The accusation as to "forced labour on the roads and restrictions which practically amount to slavery in Fiji" are due to an imperfect understanding of the communal system under which land is held there.

Individual land ownership does not exist, and the members of each commune have to perform their share of the necessary work, whatever it may be.

There is also the custom of "lala," under which the local Chiefs are entitled to exact a certain number of days' work from their commoners for the purpose of planting their gardens, building their houses, &c.

The Chiefs are bound to feed the workers so employed, and it is nothing more than a contribution towards their maintenance, paid by the commoners in work instead of taxes.

Instances have, no doubt, occurred in which these rights have been abused, but every effort is made to prevent them.

The whole system has been in force for centuries, and when His Majesty's Government took over the islands it was thought expedient to continue it. It is understood by the natives, and is eminently suited to the needs of a primitive and half savage race.

The allegation as to the flogging of natives is, doubtless, an allusion to a case which occurred in 1902, of which the facts are briefly as follows:—

A native was arrested for two cases of indecent assault upon European women. He was tried according to native custom by the Commissioner and Chiefs of the island to which he belonged, having first been given his choice of being tried in this way or being referred to the Supreme Court. He pleaded guilty to one assault, and there was strong evidence against him in the other case. He was, accordingly, sentenced to be flogged.

Although for various reasons this summary procedure was advantageous, the case should properly have been referred to the Supreme Court. The Commissioner was, therefore, severely censured for his action.

The statement that the natives are constantly subject to imprisonment for frivolous causes is not borne out by any evidence in the possession of His Majesty's Government.

---

tration of the Independent State of the Congo.

[In continuation of "Africa No. 1 (1904)."]

Presented to both Houses of Parliament by Command of His Majesty. June 1904.

LONDON
PRINTED BY HARRISON AND SONS.

LONDON
PRINTED BY HARRISON AND SONS.

AFRICA. No. 14 (1903).

DESPATCH

TO CERTAIN OF

HIS MAJESTY'S REPRESENTATIVES ABROAD

IN REGARD TO

ALLEGED CASES OF ILL-TREATMENT OF NATIVES

AND TO THE EXISTENCE OF

TRADE MONOPOLIES IN THE INDEPENDENT STATE OF THE CONGO.

Presented to both Houses of Parliament by Command of His Majesty.
October 1903.

LONDON:
PRINTED FOR HIS MAJESTY'S STATIONERY OFFICE,
BY HARRISON AND SONS, ST. MARTIN'S LANE,
PRINTERS IN ORDINARY TO HIS MAJESTY.

And to be purchased, either directly or through any Bookseller, from
EYRE AND SPOTTISWOODE, EAST HARDING STREET, FLEET STREET, E.C.,
AND 32, ABINGDON STREET, WESTMINSTER, S.W.;
OR OLIVER AND BOYD, EDINBURGH;
OR E. PONSONBY, 116, GRAFTON STREET, DUBLIN.

[Cd. 1809.] *Price* 1*d*.

AFRICA. No. 7 (1904).

Despatch to certain of His Majesty's Representatives abroad in regard to alleged Cases of Ill-treatment of Natives and to the Existence of Trade Monopolies in the Independent State of the Congo.

The Marquess of Lansdowne to His Majesty's Representatives at Paris, Berlin, Rome, St. Petersburgh, Vienna, Madrid, Constantinople, Brussels, Lisbon, the Hague, Copenhagen, and Stockholm.

Sir, *Foreign Office, August* 8, 1903.

THE attention of His Majesty's Government has during recent years been repeatedly called to alleged cases of ill-treatment of natives and to the existence of trade monopolies in the Independent State of the Congo. Representations to this effect are to be found in Memorials from philanthropic Societies, in communications from commercial bodies, in the public press, and in despatches from His Majesty's Consuls.

The same matters formed the subject of a debate in the House of Commons on the 20th ultimo, when the House passed the Resolution, a copy of which is inclosed.

In the course of the debate, the official record of which is also inclosed, it was alleged that the object of the Administration was not so much the care and government of the natives as the collection of revenue; that this object was pursued by means of a system of forced labour, differing only in name from slavery; that the demands upon each village were exacted with a strictness which constantly degenerated into great cruelty, and that the men composing the armed force of the State were in many cases recruited from the most warlike and savage tribes, who not infrequently terrorized over their own officers and maltreated the natives without regard to discipline or fear of punishment.

As regards the ill-treatment of natives, a distinction may be drawn between isolated acts of cruelty committed by individuals, whether in the service of the State or not, and a system of administration involving and accompanied by systematic cruelty or oppression.

The fact that many individual instances of cruelty have taken place in the Congo State is proved beyond possibility of contradiction by the occurrence of cases in which white officials have been convicted of outrages on natives. These white officials must, however, in view of the vast extent of the territory under their administration, in most cases be of necessity isolated the one from the other, with the result that detection becomes additionally difficult. It is therefore not unfair to assume that the number of convictions falls considerably short of the number of actual offences committed.

It is, however, with regard to the system of administration that the most serious allegations are brought against the Independent State.

It is reported that no efforts are made to fit the native by training for industrial pursuits; that the method of obtaining men for labour or for military service is often but little different from that formerly employed to obtain slaves; and that force is now as much required to take the native to the place of service as it used to be to convey the captured slave. It is also reported that constant compulsion has to be exercised in order to exact the collection of the amount of forest produce allotted to each village as the equivalent of the number of days' labour due from the inhabitants, and that this compulsion is often exercised by irresponsible native soldiers uncontrolled by any European officer.

His Majesty's Government do not know precisely to what extent these accusations may be true; but they have been so repeatedly made, and have received such wide credence, that it is no longer possible to ignore them, and the question has now arisen whether the Congo State can be considered to have fulfilled the special pledges, given under the Berlin Act, to watch over the preservation of the native tribes, and to care for their moral and material advancement.

The graver charges against the State relate almost exclusively to the upper valleys of the Congo and of its affluents. The lands forming these vast territories are held either by the State itself or by Companies closely connected with the State, under a system which, whatever its object, has effectually kept out the independent trader, as opposed to the owner or to the occupier of the soil, and has consequently made it difficult to obtain independent testimony.

His Majesty's Government have further laboured under the disadvantage that British interests have not justified the maintenance of a large Consular staff in the Congo territories. It is true that in 1901 His Majesty's Government decided to appoint a Consul of wide African experience to reside permanently in the State, but his time has been principally occupied in the investigation of complaints preferred by British subjects, and he has as yet been unable to travel into the interior and to acquire, by personal inspection, knowledge of the condition of the enormous territory forming his district.

His reports on the cases of British subjects, which have formed the basis of representations to the Government of the Independent State, afford, however, examples of grave maladministration and ill-treatment. These cases do not concern natives of the Congo State, and are therefore in themselves alien to the subject of this despatch; but as they occurred in the immediate vicinity of Boma, the seat of the central staff, and in regard to British subjects, most of whom were under formal engagements, they undoubtedly lead to the belief that the natives, who have no one in the position of a Consul to whom they can appeal and have no formal engagements, receive even less consideration at the hands of the officers of the Government.

Moreover, information which has reached His Majesty's Government from British officers in territory adjacent to that of the State tends to show that, notwithstanding the obligations accepted under Article VI of the Berlin Act, no attempt at any administration of the natives is made, and that the officers of the Government do not apparently concern themselves with such work, but devote all their energy to the collection of revenue. The natives are left entirely to themselves, so far as any assistance in their government or in their affairs is concerned. The Congo stations are shunned, the only natives seen being soldiers, prisoners, and men who are brought in to work. The neighbourhood of stations which are known to have been populous a few years ago is now uninhabited, and emigration on a large scale takes place to the territory of neighbouring States, the natives usually averring that they are driven away from their homes by the tyranny and exaction of the soldiers.

The sentiments which undoubtedly animated the founders of the Congo State and the Representatives of the Powers at Berlin were such as to deserve the cordial sympathy of the British Government, who have been loath to believe either that the beneficent intentions with which the Congo State was constituted, and of which it gave so solemn a pledge at Berlin, have in any way been abandoned, or that every effort has not been made to realize them.

But the fact remains that there is a feeling of grave suspicion, widely prevalent among the people of this country, in regard to the condition of affairs in the Congo State, and there is a deep conviction that the many charges brought against the State's administration must be founded on a basis of truth.

In these circumstances, His Majesty's Government are of opinion that it is incumbent upon the Powers parties to the Berlin Act to confer together and to consider whether the obligations undertaken by the Congo State in regard to the natives have been fulfilled; and, if not, whether the Signatory Powers are not bound to make such representations as may secure the due observance of the provisions contained in the Act.

As indicated at the beginning of this despatch, His Majesty's Government also wish to bring to the notice of the Powers the question which has arisen in regard to rights of trade in the basin of the Congo.

Article I of the Berlin Act provides that the trade of all nations shall enjoy complete freedom in the basin of the Congo; and Article V provides that no Power which exercises sovereign rights in the basin shall be allowed to grant therein a monopoly or favour of any kind in matters of trade.

In the opinion of His Majesty's Government, the system of trade now existing in the Independent State of the Congo is not in harmony with these provisions.

With the exception of a relatively small area on the lower Congo, and with the further exception of the small plots actually occupied by the huts and cultivation patches of the natives, the whole territory is claimed as the private property either of the State or of holders of land concessions. Within these regions the State or, as the case may be, the concession-holder alone may trade in the natural produce of the soil. The fruits gathered by the natives are accounted the property of the State, or of the concession-holder, and may not be acquired by others. In such circumstances, His Majesty's Government are unable to see that there exists the complete freedom of trade or absence of monopoly in trade which is required by the Berlin Act. On the contrary, no one other than the agents of the State or of the concession-holder has the opportunity to enter into trade relations with the natives; or if he does succeed in reaching the natives, he finds that the only material which the natives can give in exchange for his trade goods or his money are claimed as having been the property of the State or of the concession-holder from the moment it was gathered by the native.

His Majesty's Government in no way deny either that the State has the right to partition the State lands among *boná fide* occupants, or that the natives will, as the land is so divided out among *boná fide* occupiers, lose their right of roaming over it and collecting the natural fruits which it produces. But His Majesty's Government maintain that until unoccupied land is reduced into individual occupation, and so long as the produce can only be collected by the native, the native should be free to dispose of that produce as he pleases.

In these circumstances, His Majesty's Government consider that the time has come when the Powers parties to the Berlin Act should consider whether the system of trade now prevailing in the Independent State is in harmony with the provisions of the Act; and, in particular, whether the system of making grants of vast areas of territory is permissible under the Act if the effect of such grants is in practice to create a monopoly of trade by excluding all persons other than the concession-holder from trading with the natives in that area. Such a result is inevitable if the grants are made in favour of persons or Companies who cannot themselves use the land or collect its produce, but must depend for obtaining it upon the natives, who are allowed to deal only with the grantees.

His Majesty's Government will be glad to receive any suggestions which the Governments of the Signatory Powers may be disposed to make in reference to this important question, which might perhaps constitute, wholly or in part, the subject of a reference to the Tribunal at the Hague.

I request that you will read this despatch to the Minister for Foreign Affairs, and leave a copy of it with his Excellency.

I am, &c.
(Signed) LANSDOWNE.

THE CASEMENT REPORT

by Roger Casement (1864–1916), and others.

Three Command Papers on the treatment of natives in the Congo. This report includes Cd. 1933. Correspondence and Report from His Majesty's Consul at Boma respecting the Administration of the Independent State of the Congo. Africa. No. 1 (1904); Cd. 2097. Further Correspondence respecting the Administration of the Independent State of the Congo. Africa. No. 7 (1904); Cd. 1809. Despatch to certain of His Majesty's Representatives abroad in regard to Alleged Cases of Ill-treatment of Natives and to the Existence of Trade Monopolies in the Independent State of the Congo. Africa. No. 14 (1903). Source: House of Commons. Accounts and Papers. Volume 62. 1904. This work is in the public domain.

This edition is a facsimile of the original printed, adapted and published by HYPERHOUSE / Ahmad Makia in 2023 as a print-on-demand publication.
ISBN: 978-1-956938-05-0
PO BOX 60904, United Arab Emirates
Designed by Moylin Yuan
Typeset in Nihilist and Times New Roman

www.ingramcontent.com/pod-product-compliance
Lightning Source LLC
Chambersburg PA
CBHW060901270326
41935CB00004B/56
* 9 7 8 1 9 5 6 9 3 8 0 5 0 *